Language Hub

INTERMEDIATE
Teacher's Book

BOBBY DUNNETT

B1+

Macmillan Education
4 Crinan Street
London N1 9XW
A division of Springer Nature Limited

Companies and representatives throughout the world

Language Hub Intermediate Teacher's Book
ISBN 978-1-380-01718-5
Language Hub Intermediate Teacher's Book with Teacher's App
ISBN 978-1-380-01712-3

Written by Bobby Dunnett

The author has asserted their right to be identified as the author of this work in accordance with the Copyright, Designs and Patents Act 1988.

First published 2019

Teacher's Edition credits:
Design by SPi Technologies India Private LTD
Based on original design by EMC Design LTD
Illustrated by Pablo Gallego (Beehive Illustration)
Cover design by The Restless
Cover image by Getty Images/Peathegee Inc.

Author's acknowledgements

The author would like to thank Tabbie, Dulcie and Felix.

The author and publishers would like to thank the following for permission to reproduce their photographs:

Bananastock W20; **Brand X** W39(m); **Corbis** W39(tl); **Getty Images** W38(b), Getty Images/Thinkstock Images/altrendo images W5(tr), Getty Images/Eric Audras Onoky W31, Getty Images/Levi Bianco W10(ml), Getty Images/iStockphoto/Thinkstock/Joggie Botma W5(m), Getty Images/Caiaimage/Paul Bradbury W17, Getty Images/Caiaimage W28, Getty Images/Nancy R. Cohen W37, Getty Images/E+/bo1982 W2, Getty Images/iStockphoto/Daniel Ernst W3(t), Getty Images/FatCamera W27, Getty Images/Food Collection W1(b), Getty Images/Fotosearch W16(tl), Getty Images/funstock W36, Getty Images/Fuse W21(tl), W34; Getty Images/Thinkstock Images/GOTO_TOKYO W26, Getty Images/Michael Haegele W8(tl), Getty Images/Hero Images Inc W22(tr), W31(r), Getty Images/kali9 W39(mr), Getty Images/Darren Muir/EyeEm W38(t), Getty Images/iStockphoto W30(tl), Blend Images/Jetta Productions/Blend Images W4(m), Getty Images/Blend Images/KidStock W5(tl), Getty Images/Brian A Jackson/iStockphoto W8(tr), Getty Images/jaroszpilewski W40, Jupiterimages W10(tr), Getty Images/Maskot W1(t), Getty Images/Emir Memedovski W23(tl), Getty Images/Photodisc W10(b), W16(mr), W29(tr), Getty Images/Compassionate Eye Foundation/Justin Pumfrey W24, Getty Images/EyeEm Ronik Rawat W16(ml), Getty Images/iStockphoto/Thinkstock/Luiz Rocha W11, Getty Images/Caiaimage/David Schaffer W6, W39(tm), Getty Images/Elisabeth Schmitt/Flickr W3(b), Getty Images/skynesher W30(tr), Getty Images/iStockphoto/STEEX W4(t), Getty Images/visualspace W22(tl), vm W18; Getty Images/Westend61 W31(l), Getty Images/iStockphoto Thinkstock Images/XiXinXing W21(tr); **Guardian News and Media** XV(tr); **Image Source** W4(b), Jasper White CM W13, W23(tr); **Springer Nature Limited** Paul Bricknell W19; W39(ml); Creative Listening XV(mr); **Stockbyte** W39(tr); **Superstock** W29(tl).

The author and publisher are grateful for permission to reprint the following copyright material:

Extracts from: '700 Classroom Activities New Edition' © David Seymour and Maria Popova 2005, Published by Springer Nature Limited. Used with permission. All rights reserved.

Extracts from: 'Learning Teaching 3rd Edition Student's Book' © Jim Scrivener 2011, Published by Springer Nature Limited. Used with permission. All rights reserved.

Extracts from: 'Teaching English Grammar' © Jim Scrivener 2010, Published by Springer Nature Limited. Used with permission. All rights reserved.

Student's Book credits:
Text, Design and Illustration © Springer Nature Limited 2019
Written by Jeremy Day and Gareth Rees
With thanks to Edward Price for additional authoring and to Signature Manuscripts for the Grammar Hub pages.

The authors have asserted their right to be identified as the authors of this work in accordance with the Copyright, Designs and Patents Act 1988.

The right of Sue Kay and Vaughan Jones to be identified as authors of the Speaking Pages in this work has been asserted by them in accordance with the Copyright, Designs and Patents Act 1988.

Designed by emc design ltd
Illustrated by Rasmus Juul (Lemonade Illustration Agency) Daniel Limon (Beehive Illustration)
Cover design by Restless
Cover image by Peathegee Inc/Getty Images
Picture research by Emily Taylor and Victoria Gaunt
Café Hub videos produced by Creative Listening
Café Hub video scripts written by James and Luke Vyner

The authors and publishers are grateful for permission to reprint the following copyright material:

p8 Extract from 'Why being bilingual helps keep your brain fit' by Gaia Vince. Originally published in Mosaic Science, 06 August 2016. © The Wellcome Trust Limited 2018. Republished under a Creative Commons licence. https://mosaicscience.com/bilingual-brains/

p18 Extract from 'War veteran, 89, posts ad for job to stop him 'dying of boredom'' by Alexandra Topping. Originally published in The Guardian, 29 November 2016. Copyright © Guardian News & Media Ltd 2018. Reprinted with permission of The Guardian.

p18 Extract from 'Eager 89-year-old seeks job: café snaps him up' by Alexandra Topping. Originally published in The Guardian, 01 December 2016. Copyright © Guardian News & Media Ltd 2018. Reprinted with permission of The Guardian.

p28 Epley, N., & Schroeder, J. (2014). Mistakenly seeking solitude. Journal of Experimental Psychology: General, 143(5), 1980–1999.

Full acknowledgements for photographs in facsimile pages can be found in the Student's Book ISBN 978-1-380-01715-4.

These materials may contain links for third party websites. We have no control over, and are not responsible for, the contents of such third party websites. Please use care when accessing them.

The inclusion of any specific companies, commercial products, trade names or otherwise, does not constitute or imply its endorsement or recommendation by Springer Nature Limited.

Printed and bound in Lebanon

2023 2022 2021 2020 2019
10 9 8 7 6 5 4 3 2

Contents

Language Hub for Teachers

Student's Book Introduction

Language Hub is a new six-level general English course for adult learners, which takes the complexity out of teaching English. It is designed to promote effective communication and helps to build learners' confidence with regular opportunities for meaningful practice. With its firm pedagogic foundation and syllabus aligned to the revised CEFR, Language Hub has clear learning outcomes which make it easy to use in a variety of teaching situations.

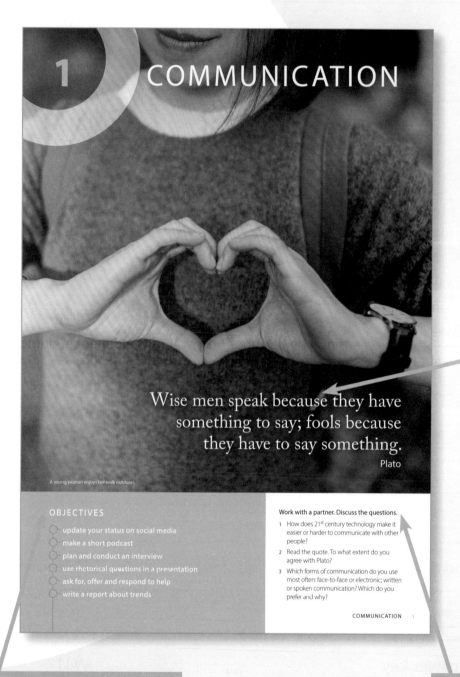

The engaging photograph and famous quotation help teachers to focus students and familiarise themselves with the ideas in the unit. Teachers can also encourage students to label the picture.

Student's Book unit opener

The first page of every Language Hub unit is the unit opener. It is an exciting visual opportunity for students to engage with the theme of the unit and see at a glance the CEFR learning objectives for each lesson.

There is a quick warm up speaking activity. Teachers can use this time to prepare the class for their lesson and delay the main start for five minutes until all the students arrive.

Student's Book lessons 1 and 2 first spread

Reading and Listening
Reading and listening sections allow students to practise their receptive skills. All sections have tasks that move from global to detailed understanding so students can achieve a good overall comprehension. The key skills focus is clearly marked in the activity titles. The texts and scripts also present target vocabulary, grammar or pronunciation.

Grammar
The Language Hub approach to grammar is inductive. Students are exposed to new language in context. Each grammar section prompts the student to notice the feature in context and to discover its form and use. Students then have further opportunities for controlled practice before using their new language in more authentic spoken or written output.

1.1 Communication today
● Update your status on social media
● Make a short podcast

G present simple and present continuous   V seeing and hearing   P schwa /ə/   listening to check predictions

READING

A SPEAK Work in groups and discuss the questions.
1 Do you ever use social media sites? Which ones?
2 What sort of information do people usually post on social media?

B PREDICT Match the pictures (1–3) with the social media status updates (a–c). How do you think the people in the pictures are feeling? What can you guess about their lives?
a On my way to the top! Looking forward to an amazing view!
b Can't believe we're on holiday again! We're having a wonderful time!
c Our lovely new kitchen! Looks good, doesn't it?

C READ FOR GIST Read the social media posts quickly to check your predictions from Exercise B. Make notes about the true stories behind the pictures.

My *perfect* online life

@Katia … is feeling confused
8 hours ago

Had a very strange experience today. I met my old school friend @Elisa for the first time in eight years. "You're so lucky!" she said. "You have such a perfect life! I'm so jealous!"

A perfect life? Me? I have a very normal life: I get up early every day, take the bus to work, watch / ... and that's all. In fact, Elisa seems to have a perfect life: her pictures always show her wonderful family relaxing in the sunshine on a beautiful beach. But now I'm writing this post, I think I understand what happened: on social media, our lives look perfect, but the reality is very different.

For example, last week I posted a selfie from the top of a mountain. In the picture, you can see I'm smiling. But in fact, I felt absolutely exhausted and just wanted to go home as quickly as possible! But you can't see that in the picture!

And did you see the picture of our new kitchen a few weeks ago? Well, yes, it's lovely, but I didn't mention that it took six months to finish. Six months without a kitchen! And it cost us twice as much as we expected, so now we're getting worried about money. But no one ever talks about money problems on social media, do they?

I'm not complaining, though. I'm very happy with my life! I love being normal … and I don't mind that my life is becoming a bit boring! In fact, I'm thinking of staying at home this evening – just me, my husband and a takeaway pizza! Perfect!

Reply from @Elisa
4 hours ago

Hey, @Katia! Great to see you this morning. I know what you mean about our 'perfect lives'. I guess I need to explain about all those beach pictures. You see, I work really hard all year, and the only time I use social media is when I'm on holiday. That's why I'm sitting on the beach in all my pictures! It usually rains for most of the week we're on holiday, but of course we only take pictures when the sun's shining!

Glossary
jealous (adj) : unhappy because someone has something that you would like or can do something that you would like to do

D READ FOR DETAIL Read again and answer the questions.
1 How do Katia and Elisa know each other?
2 Why was Katia confused?
3 When did Katia go to the top of the mountain?
4 How does Katia feel about her new kitchen?
5 How does Katia feel about her 'boring' life?
6 Why doesn't Elisa post pictures when she isn't on holiday?

E SPEAK Work in pairs and discuss the questions.
1 Does your life look perfect on social media? What about your friends' lives?
2 Do you ever feel jealous when you see other people's status updates?

GRAMMAR
Present simple and present continuous

A Look at the underlined verbs in the social media posts. Which verbs are in the present simple? Which are in the present continuous?

B WORK IT OUT Match the sentences (a–f) with the rules (2–5).
a In the picture, you can see I'm smiling.
b I know what you mean about our 'perfect lives'.
c But now I'm writing this post, …
d You have such a perfect life!
e I get up early every day.
f So now we're getting worried about money.

Present simple and present continuous
1 Dynamic verbs (talk, go) usually describe actions.
2 We use the present simple with dynamic verbs to talk about actions that always, usually or never happen.
3 We use the present continuous with dynamic verbs:
   a to talk about actions that are in progress at the moment of speaking or writing.
   b to describe actions in a picture, video, etc.
   c to describe trends (e.g. something is happening more and more these days).
4 Stative verbs (want, seem) often describe feelings and ideas. We use the present simple with stative verbs.
5 A few verbs (have, look, speak, think) have two or more meanings. They are sometimes dynamic verbs and sometimes stative verbs.

C Find at least one more example of each rule (2–5) in the posts.

D Go to the Grammar Hub on page 122.

E Are the verbs stative verbs (S) or dynamic verbs (D)?
1 contain __S__   7 include ___
2 cost ___   8 mean ___
3 depend ___   9 own ___
4 deserve ___   10 relax ___
5 enjoy ___   11 seem ___
6 happen ___   12 shine ___

F SPEAK Work in groups and discuss the questions.
1 Why are you studying English? Why do you need English?
2 How is this week different from your normal weekly routine? What are you doing differently this week? What do you normally do?
3 What are people doing more and more these days? What are some trends in your own life?

SPEAKING

A Work in groups. If you have some pictures on your phone, choose two or three to discuss with your group. If you do not, think about some of your favourite pictures of you and your friends or family.

B Tell your group:
• What's happening in the pictures?
• Does your life seem perfect or exciting in the pictures? What's the real story behind the pictures?
• Do you have any pictures of you doing normal things, e.g. watching TV? Why/Why not?

C Write a short social media status update for one or two of your pictures. Decide whether to make your life seem perfect or normal.

Writing a status
We often leave out the subject and be from the beginning of status updates when it's easy for the reader to guess the missing words.
• (It) Looks good, doesn't it?
• (I) Had a very strange experience today.
• (It was) Great to see you this morning.

D Read some of your classmates' social media status updates. Do their lives look perfect or normal?

2 COMMUNICATION   COMMUNICATION 3

Skill labels
By focusing students' attention on the skills labels next to each exercise number, teachers can highlight which skills are being practised and recycled.

Topics
Language Hub topics contextualise the language input for the lesson. They have been selected to allow opportunities for personalisation.

Speaking
Each lesson starts with a CEFR unit objective which the lesson is designed to address. Students will often use the grammar, vocabulary and pronunciation from the lesson to complete a Speaking activity linked to the unit objective. Language Hub allows students to safely practise speaking in pairs after most sections. This ensures that they feel confident to take an active role in the final speaking task.

Language Hub for Teachers

Student's Book lessons 1 and 2 second spread

Reading and Listening Skill
Every unit includes a task designed to practise a key reading or listening skill. This ensures students are given the tools they need to effectively process a wide variety of texts and scripts. By the end of each book, students will have been exposed to 20 different skills for reading or listening.

Pronunciation
In Language Hub, lessons focus on both word-level and sentence-level pronunciation. This not only allows students to improve their accuracy, but also fluency through sentence-level intonation, which helps students understand how to add meaning through their pronunciation.

1.1

LISTENING

A SPEAK Work in pairs and discuss the questions.
1 What do you use your mobile phone for?
2 How did people do those things before they had mobile phones? What problems did they have?

B PREDICT Work in pairs. You are going to listen to *A week without phones!* Look at the pictures and discuss the questions. Use the strategies in the box to help you.

Listening to check predictions
Before you listen to something in English, it's always a good idea to predict what you will hear.
If there's a title and pictures, you can try to predict the connection between them. Then you can listen to check your predictions.

1 Who are the people in picture a? What are they doing?
2 What is the device in picture b?
3 What does the title mean? What's the connection with the people and the device?

C LISTEN FOR GIST Listen to Part 1 of the podcast and check your answers to Exercise B.
1.1

D PREDICT Work in pairs and discuss the questions. Then listen to Part 2 and check your answers.
1.2
1 What went wrong when Olivia and Jackson tried to meet up on Monday?
2 How did they solve the problem?

E PREDICT Work in pairs and discuss what you think Olivia and Jackson did differently on Tuesday when they met. Then listen to Part 3 and check your answer.
1.3

F PREDICT Work in pairs and discuss the questions. Then listen to Part 4 and check your answers.
1.4
1 Do you think Olivia and Jackson are enjoying the experiment?
2 What do you think they're doing more or less of than usual?

COMMUNICATION

G LISTEN FOR DETAIL Listen again. Choose the correct answers, a, b or c.
1.5
1 When is the last day of the experiment?
  a Tuesday
  b Thursday
  c Sunday
2 Why does Olivia decide to stop waiting outside on Monday?
  a She doesn't want to get wet.
  b She thinks Jackson isn't coming.
  c She knows the university closes at four o'clock.
3 How does Sebastian know Jackson and Olivia?
  a They study together at university.
  b Olivia met Sebastian outside the cake shop.
  c Sebastian has seen them before in pictures and videos.
4 Why is Olivia enjoying the concert more than usual on Tuesday?
  a She isn't recording it on her phone.
  b The audience isn't having as much fun.
  c Jackson isn't there with her.
5 On Thursday, why is Olivia surprised at the end of the podcast?
  a The university buildings are amazing.
  b Jackson doesn't usually talk so much.
  c She can't believe Jackson forgot his camera.

H SPEAK Work in groups and discuss the questions.
1 What problems did Olivia and Jackson have during the experiment?
2 What good things happened as a result?
3 Do you think Olivia and Jackson's experiment was a good idea?
4 Would you like to try a similar experiment? Why/Why not?

VOCABULARY
Seeing and hearing

A Choose the correct verbs to complete the sentences from *A week without phones!* Then listen again and check your answers.
1 In this week's podcast, we're *looking at / seeing / watching* phones.
2 It *looks / sees / watches* like he isn't coming, and I'm not sure what to do.
3 I'm *looking / seeing / watching* for Olivia, but I can't *look at / see / watch* her.
4 I *hear / listen to / sound* your podcast every week, and I *look at / see / watch* all your videos.
5 Yeah, that *hears / listens / sounds* like a great idea. Thanks a lot.
6 Maybe you can *hear / listen to / sound* the music in the background.
7 He plays the guitar in the band, and he *hears / listens / sounds* really good.
8 It doesn't *look / see / watch* great, but it's good for telling the time!

B WORK IT OUT Complete the rules with the correct form of *hear, listen, look, see, sound* and *watch*.

hear, listen, look, see, sound and watch
1 When you ●_____ / _see_ or ●_____ something, it just happens, not because you're trying to do it.
2 When you ●_____ / ●_____ to something, you do it because you decide to do it.
3 When you ●_____ something, you look at it for a period of time, perhaps because it's moving.
4 When something ●_____ good or ●_____ good, it probably is good, but you aren't sure.
5 When it ●_____ like or ●_____ like something is happening, it probably is happening, but you aren't sure.

C Go to the Vocabulary Hub on page 142.

D Complete the questions with the verbs in the box. There are two extra verbs.

notice   observe   recognise   spot   stare

1 Do you ever sit in a café and _____ the people through the window? Why do people enjoy doing this?
2 Are you good at remembering people's faces? Do you always _____ people when you meet them the second time?
3 When you're travelling around (e.g. by bus), do you usually _____ the buildings around you?

E SPEAK Work in groups. Ask and answer the questions in Exercise D.

PRONUNCIATION
Schwa /ə/

Schwa /ə/
Schwa is the most common sound in English. We use it for most unstressed vowel sounds, especially in words like *a, the, of, to, and* and *but*.

A Listen to the sentences from *A week without phones!* Underline all schwas. The numbers in brackets tell you how
1.7 many schwas to find. The first one has been done for you.
1 We're not looking at our phones for a whole week! (3)
2 We arranged to meet here, outside the university, at four o'clock. (5)
3 It's Monday afternoon and I'm late meeting Olivia. (3)
4 I'll buy you a cake to say thank you, and you can tell us what you think of our podcasts. (6)
5 Yes, I'm wearing a watch today – an old one from when I was a teenager. (7)

B SPEAK Work in pairs. Practise saying the sentences. Listen and check your partner's pronunciation.

SPEAKING HUB

A Work in groups. You are going to make a short podcast about an experiment. Choose one of the ideas in the box or use your own ideas.

a week of doing something completely new every day
a week speaking only English
a week without complaining
a week without the internet/TV, etc
a week without spending any money
a week of helping as many people as possible

B PLAN Plan a short podcast (about two minutes). Imagine you are in the middle of your experiment. Make notes on:
• what you can see and hear during your podcast.
• what's going well and/or badly with your experiment.
• what you're doing more or less as a result of your experiment.

C SPEAK Record your podcast and present it to the class.

D SHARE After listening to the podcasts, discuss the questions.
• Which group's experiment worked well?
• Which podcast did you enjoy most?

E REFLECT Work in new groups and discuss the questions.
• Will you try any of the experiments in real life? Why/Why not?
• Would you like to make a real podcast? What would your podcast be about? Do you think other people would want to listen to it?

○– Update your status on social media
○– Make a short podcast

COMMUNICATION

Vocabulary
Language Hub teaches vocabulary in topic-related sets to help students categorise the new words they learn. Key vocabulary sets are built on and revised in the back of the book.

Speaking Hub
At the end of each lesson, students perform a longer speaking turn which is staged to allow planning and idea creation. Students should apply their learning from the whole unit in the performance of their long speaking turn.

Student's Book Lesson 3

Functional Language
Each video provides a model for functional language so that students are able to access an ever-expanding bank of phrases. This language helps students to communicate effectively in a range of real-world situations.

Café Hub
The final lesson in each unit has a focus on video. Café Hub videos are a series of amusing 'situation comedy' short films. Meet Milly, Sam, Neena, Zac and Gaby as they take you through their adventures in London. Find out how they start their journey as complete strangers but become the best of friends.

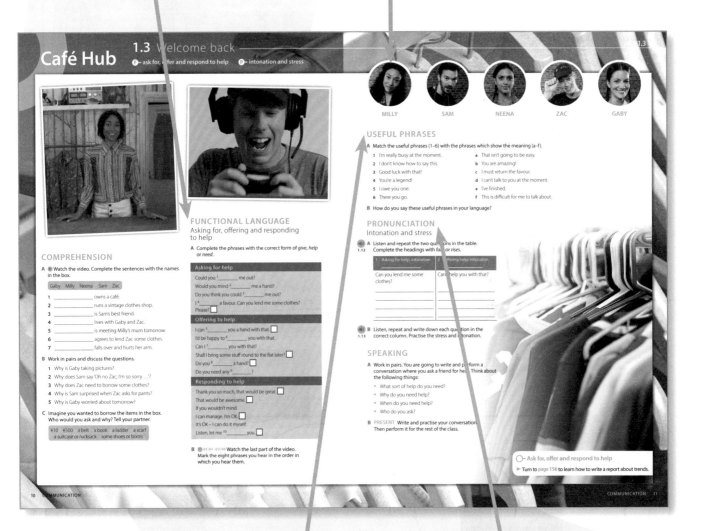

Useful Phrases
The video also provides an opportunity to learn a variety of useful phrases that students can use to bring authenticity to their language output.

Pronunciation
Lesson 3 has a focus on stress and intonation. Students notice the stress and rhythm of British and American English pronunciation in the video before preparing to speak themselves.

Language Hub for Teachers

Student's Book Hubs

Writing Hub

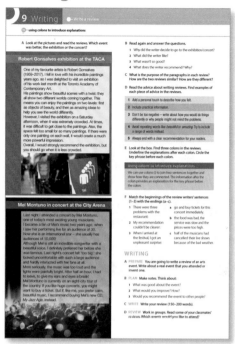

The Student's Book has an individual writing page at the back of the book for each unit. Each writing lesson is aligned to the unit topic and teaches a different writing genre and writing skill. Students can see completed writing models to analyse before they begin to write their own work.

Grammar Hub

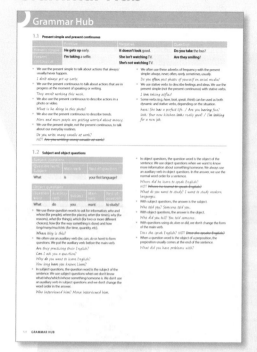

Clear explanations and further practice activities for each grammar point in the syllabus are provided at the back of the book. These can be used in class or set for homework to free up classroom time for communication.

Vocabulary Hub

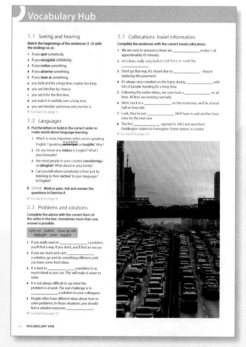

The Vocabulary Hub provides extra practice of key vocabulary presented in each unit. As with the Grammar Hub sections, these can either consolidate work done in class or be used for further self-study.

Communication Hub

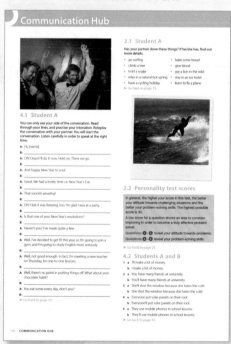

The Communication Hub is used to set up longer communicative activities, such as information exchanges, quizzes and roleplays.

Workbook

A Workbook is sold separately for Language Hub. This includes 360 print activities practising the language from the Student's Book. For each lesson there are corresponding practice exercises of grammar, vocabulary and pronunciation. There is further practice of the reading and listening skills from Lessons 1 and 2 and extension practice of the functional language from Lesson 3. There is also a page dedicated to the unit's writing genre and skill. All of these pages develop learning from the main lessons of the Student's Book.

Vocabulary and Grammar
The Workbook practises vocabulary and grammar that students have attended to in the Student's Book. By reminding themselves of the words and skills they have recently seen, students are better able to imbed learning and have it ready for recall during speaking practice.

Listening and Reading
The Workbook provides additional listening and reading texts that explore the topics in the Student's Book. These give students the opportunity to develop the key receptive skills from the unit.

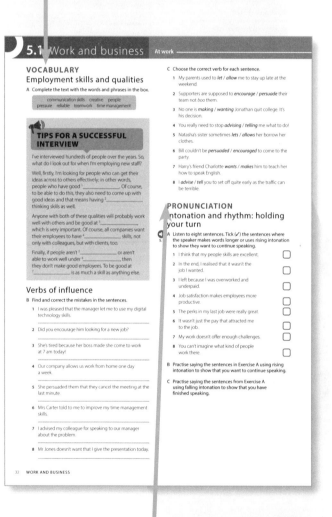

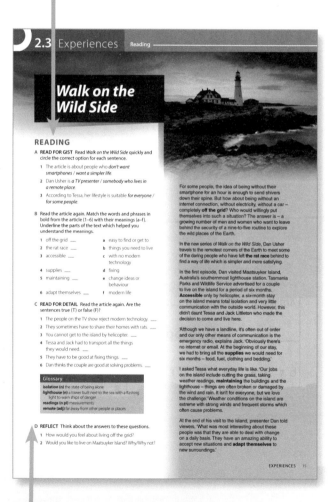

Pronunciation
The Workbook also consolidates the pronunciation topics from the Student's Book through further controlled practice.

Reflect
Each reading and listening page has a Reflect section so that students can use their Workbooks in class if they wish to reflect on their learning with their peers.

Language Hub for Teachers

Teacher's Book

Worksheets
The bank of communicative worksheets at the back of the Teacher's Book provide additional controlled and freer practice of every vocabulary and grammar section.

Extra activities
The Extra activity boxes help teachers extend the content of the lesson, both in and out of the classroom.

Interleaved pages
Every level of Language Hub has a Teacher's Book interleaved with pages of the Student's Book. The answers to all of the Student's Book activities are annotated on the page so there is no need for teachers to flick backwards and forwards to find information.

2.1 Important decisions

D Tell students to read the text again more slowly and carefully and then answer the questions.

E Put students into pairs to share their opinions about the text. Monitor and draw out any different views students have and encourage them to expand on them.

GRAMMAR

A Tell students the sentences are all from the blog they've just read. To check students are familiar with the terminology, ask them to underline the past simple verbs and circle the present perfect simple verbs. Explain that identifying the structures is, of course, not as important as understanding why they're used. Tell students to match the sentences to the timelines in feedback, check students understand that the different parts of the timelines represent. A lot of students find timelines very helpful, but some can find them confusing. The key thing is to make sure the connection between the events in the sentences and the way they're represented on the timelines is explicit.

B Tell students to look back at the blog and find the adverbs of time from the box. Tell students to look at the way the adverbs are used in context to help them match them with the definitions.

C Tell students to look back at the example sentences, timelines and definitions from Exercises A and to help them complete the rules. In feedback, elicit which sentences from Exercises A and B are examples of each rule.

D Direct students to the Grammar Hub on pages 124 and 125 (see TB14 and below). Use the Grammar Worksheet on W5 for extra practice.

PRONUNCIATION
Tell students to listen carefully to the pairs of sentences to identify which one is in the present perfect simple. If students find this difficult, ask why. Elicit that the contracted auxiliaries 's and 've are unstressed and hard to hear. Play the audio again if necessary to give students more practice at picking up the sounds. Drill pronunciation with the students.

SPEAKING

A Put students into pairs and tell student A to turn to the Communication Hub on page 148 and student B to turn to page 153. Tell students to find out if their partner has done any of the things on their list, and if so, to find out more details. Model the task and elicit the questions students will need to ask such as *Have you ever …?* for the initial question followed by *Where / When / How did you …?* to find out more information.

B Tell students they're now going to write their own achievable bucket list. Tell students to choose eight things, either from the lists they've just read or using their own ideas. Remind students that they must be achievable but also positive and life-enhancing. You could give examples of absurd or mundane ideas and elicit if these would be appropriate, so students are clear what not to include. Monitor to check students are on task and to help with language if necessary.

C Put students into bigger groups to compare their ideas. Tell them they must agree on ten things for their group bucket list. If students have very different ideas, encourage them to argue the case for the inclusion of theirs, but also make sure students realise that they are aiming to reach a consensus so compromise may be necessary. Monitor as they do this, noting errors and good language use to highlight in feedback.

D Put students into new groups containing one representative of each previous group. Tell them to explain their lists to each other and justify their choices.

Extra activity
You can keep the bucket lists in the classroom and use these as a spring board for further activities. Writing tasks can involve students recording their experiences of completing a task on the bucket list, or even recording them on a blog.

Students can also report back on their experiences at the start of a class. You can ask them how they felt before, during and after doing something from the list.

GRAMMAR HUB

2.1 Present perfect simple and past simple
A Choose the correct option.

1 I *have swum* / swam with dolphins before.
2 Martin *dreamt* / has dreamt about the pyramids last night.
3 We *haven't climbed* / didn't climb Mt Everest yet.
4 Did you hear / *Have you heard* Leon's good news already?
5 *Did Zac learn* / Has Zac learnt how to make a fire at camp last summer?
6 *Have you ever taken* / Did you ever take a trip abroad?

B Correct the mistakes in each sentence. Use contractions where possible.

1 She ~~has seen~~ a beautiful sunset last week. saw
2 They ~~made~~ a short film already. 've
3 Molly ~~didn't prepare~~ a list yet. hasn't prepared
4 Mohammed ~~travelled never~~ around Asia before. 's never travelled
5 ~~Did you deal~~ with a serious problem before? Have you dealt
6 He ~~has come~~ up with a smart plan yesterday. came

C Complete each sentence with the correct form of the verb in brackets.

1 Giralt _has never been_ (never / be) to America.
2 Dan _has just finished_ (just / finish) a charity walk.
3 Katerina worked hard but she _didn't achieve_/did not achieve (not / achieve) her goal.
4 When the time was right, the chess champion _put_ (put) his plan into action.
5 _Have you read_ (you / read) other people's bucket lists before?
6 I _'ve already done_ (already / do) two parachute jumps this year.
➤ Go back to page 15.

EXPERIENCES

D READ FOR DETAIL Read again. Answer the questions.

1 How many things on her first bucket list has the writer not done? 49
2 Why is it not possible to do all the things on a typical bucket list? You need a lot of time and money.
3 How is her new list similar to her original list? It has positive activities.
4 How many outdoor activities are there on her new list? Four

E SPEAK Work in pairs. Read again and discuss the questions.

1 Are the writer's choices good ideas for an achievable bucket list?
2 Which choices do you like most and why?

GRAMMAR
Present perfect simple and past simple

A WORK IT OUT Look at the sentences (1–4) from *Not yet? No more!* Underline the verbs in the past simple and circle the verbs in the present perfect simple. Then match each sentence with a diagram (a–d).

1 I <u>wrote</u> mine on New Year's Day five years ago. b
2 I've only done one thing on that list. a
3 This year, I've seen lions in the wild. d
4 Last year, I <u>watched</u> the sun rise and set on the same day. c

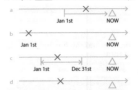

a
 ———————×————△———————
      Jan 1st   NOW

b
 ——×——————————△———————
 Jan 1st   NOW

c
 ——————×—————————△———
  Jan 1st   Dec 31st   NOW

d
 ——————————————△———————
                  NOW

B Look at the adverbs of time in the box. Can you find them in the blog? Match the adverbs with the definitions (1–5).

already	just	never	not yet	still

1 at no time in the past — never
2 a short time ago — just
3 a situation has not changed or not completely ended — still
4 not happened before now, but will probably happen — not yet
5 happened before a point in time, perhaps sooner than expected — already

C Complete the rules with *present perfect simple* or *past simple*.

Present perfect simple and past simple
For actions that we completed:
during a finished period of time, we use the 1 _past simple_
during a period of time that continues to now, we use the 2 _present perfect simple_
at a specific time in the past, we use the 3 _past simple_
before now, but we do not say exactly when, we use the 4 _present perfect simple_
We often use adverbs of time with these tenses, but we do not use yet and already with actions in the 5 _past simple_.

D Go to the Grammar Hub on page 124.

PRONUNCIATION
's and 've
Listen to the pairs of sentences (1–6). Which sentence (a or b) is in the present perfect simple?

1 b   3 b   5 a
2 a   4 b   6 a

SPEAKING

A Work in pairs. You are going to write an achievable bucket list. Student A – read the bucket list on page 148, Student B – read the list on page 153. Has your partner done any of the things on your list? If they have, find out more details.

B Work in pairs. Choose eight things to put on your achievable bucket list. Use the ideas on the lists and your own ideas. They should be positive, life-enhancing and achievable.

C Work in groups. Compare your lists and choose ten things for a group bucket list.

D Compare your list with another group. Are their ideas the same or different?

EXPERIENCES 15

Grammar explanations
Where the Student's Book asks the students to look at the Grammar Hub, the teacher can find this already annotated on the Teacher's Book page. In this way the teacher has everything they need at the correct point in the lesson, with the Grammar Hub reference activities from the Student's Book positioned close to the grammar sections they correspond to. This makes it easier for teachers to mark homework in class or refer to succinct grammar explanations.

Annotated answers
The answers to reading and listening exercises are annotated on the interleaved pages of the Student's Book. These provide a quick reference tool for teachers.

Teacher's Book: Macmillan Books for Teachers

Lead-in
Suggested lead-ins can be used to activate prior knowledge, generate interest in the lesson topic or focus on useful lexis.

Procedural notes
The lessons include procedural notes for teachers. These offer support to teachers on how to deliver the lesson rather than telling them how to teach. The notes are designed to be brief and easy to read.

Teaching Idea
Tips and ideas from *The Macmillan's Books for Teachers series* are included in the teacher's notes to give some new ideas for instant communicative activities in the lesson. These can usually be used without paper preparation as warmers to get the class moving or as a flexible stage where there is time to fill.

Methodology Hub
Ideas for professional development from Jim Scrivener's *Learning Teaching Third Edition* are presented in every unit to help new teachers pick up helpful tips to add to their repertoire or just reflect on a new way to use Language Hub with their class.

4.1

READING

A Choose the correct sentence endings.

1 Self-help books …
 a contain instructions for doing something, especially operating a machine.
 b are designed to help you solve your own problems or improve your life.

2 Self-help books are usually written in …
 a a formal style that is for experts only.
 b an informal style for anyone.

B SCAN Read *Life Cycle* quickly. Match the phrases (1–5) with the topics (a–e).

1 Helena Schneiderlin — a a journey
2 *Life Cycle* — b the author's next book
3 Paris to Moscow — c the author's passion
4 cycling — d the author
5 *Inner Pedal Power* — e the author's first book

Life Cycle: *How to find what you love and love what you find*

About this book
Ten years ago, Helena Schneiderlin was a hard-working mum with no time for herself. Like many people, she didn't know what she really wanted to do with her life. Today, Schneiderlin is a cyclist who is well known for going on long and difficult journeys. She has ridden from Paris to Moscow by herself. She has also ridden across Australia, and last year she rode from the bottom of South America to the top.

Thanks to her cycling experiences, and the effect they have had on her life, Schneiderlin has also become a leading lifestyle expert. Her talks have been watched millions of times online, and she is often asked to speak at international lifestyle events and conferences.

In *Life Cycle*, which is her first book, she describes how finding her true passion changed her life, and explains how you can find yours.

'This isn't a book about cycling,' says Schneiderlin. 'It's a book about finding the thing that you enjoy doing most, and helping to make that thing benefit all other areas of your life.'

In *Life Cycle*, Schneiderlin uses her own story as an example for others to follow. She describes how she found her passion for cycling while on holiday with her family, and what it has taught her about commitment, sacrifice and success. She provides valuable advice and life lessons that apply to all of us, including chapters on getting rid of the things in life that aren't helping, and how to identify the things that make you feel better about yourself.

> I believe that everyone has a passion, but they may not know what it is. I also believe that when you find that passion, you should use it to improve every area of your life. In my case, it was cycling – but it could have been anything. What's important is finding the thing that you love, and then using it in the right way.

40 CHANGE

4.1 Personal change

READING

A With books closed, write the word *self-help book* on the board with some of the letters missing and replaced by a dash, e.g. s__-h__b__. Explain the concept of a self-help book and try to elicit. To check the understanding of the concept, ask students what type of problems you might buy a self-help book to help with. Tell students to open their books and answer the questions.

B Tell students they're going to read about a self-help book. Tell them to look at the images and to predict what they think the book will be about. Elicit some predictions, then tell students to scan the text to match the phrases with the topics. Explain that scanning means reading quickly to find specific information, so students don't need to worry about unknown vocabulary to do this.

C Point out the strategies for summarising in the box and make sure they understand the purpose of a summary. Tell students to read the two summaries and choose which is best and why, thinking about the summarising strategies as they do this. Let students compare answers in pairs before checking answers as a whole class. Ask students to justify their choice with reference to the strategies.

1 repeats too many details, and some phrases are copied word for word. It doesn't give a clear overview of all of the information in the description.

2 is the best summary. It mentions all of the most important pieces of information from the book description but it doesn't copy the description word for word.

D Tell students to discuss with a partner whether or not they would like to read *Life Cycle* and why. Discuss as a whole class and ask if students have ever read any similar books to this. If they have, what did they think of them and would they recommend them.

TEACHING IDEA by David Seymour and Maria Popova

Topic: Hobbies

Use this activity to extend the topic.

(Arrange the students so that they are standing/sitting in a circle. Stand in the middle. Ask each of these questions to individual students at random. After they answer it, tell them to repeat the question to the next student and make a note of the student's answer. Indicate that they should continue the chain so the question progresses around the class. Meanwhile, introduce the other questions so that in the end there are lots of questions moving around the class.)

What sports do you play, if any? How much time do you spend watching TV? Have you got a hobby? What hobby would you like to take up? What do you do on Sunday afternoons? How much free time do you have? What do you read for enjoyment? What hobbies did you use to have as a child? When and where did you last go to the seaside? What are the main leisure activities in your family?

Turn your notes into full sentences, e.g. *Maria wants to take up hang gliding.*

In small groups, discuss these questions.

What are the main leisure activities in the UK/USA and in your country? What about other countries? What do you understand by the expressions quality time, the work ethic and the leisure society? How much quality time do you get? What do you think is the right balance between work and play?

TEACHING IDEA by David Seymour and Maria Popova

Topic: Leisure survey

Use this activity to extend the topic.

In small groups, find out who:
• watches TV the most
• has the most interesting hobby
• has had the most hobbies
• has been a collector of something

METHODOLOGY HUB by Jim Scrivener

The importance of skills work

Don't underestimate the importance of skills work. Not every lesson needs to teach new words or new grammar. Lessons also need to be planned to give students opportunities to practise and improve their language skills. Skills work is not something

to add in at the end of a five-year course in English. There is no need to wait for extensive knowledge before daring to embark on listening, reading and speaking work. On the contrary, it is something so essential that it needs to be at the heart of a course from the start. Even a beginner with one day's English will be able to practise speaking and listening usefully.

CHANGE TBXI

Language Hub for Teachers

Teacher's App

The Language Hub Teacher's Book comes with a Teacher's App, which gives access to the Resource Centre, Test Generator and Tap and Teach.

Tap and Teach is Macmillan's new presentation kit. Designed to be displayed on an interactive whiteboard (IWB) or using a projector, it enables teachers to play video and audio or show interactive activities in class. Tap and Teach is user-friendly for the teacher but also for the student, with activities being clearly visible for the whole class. Answer-by-answer reveal enables teachers to elicit student responses and check answers one by one.

Tools
Embedded tools make it possible to highlight and annotate texts to prompt noticing or self-correction. Teachers have the option to turn on an audioscript, which is timed to sync with the dialogue, when listening to audio or watching video.

Teachers can zoom into each activity with one click. Then they can either move smoothly through the activities or zoom out to see the whole page. They can also create a whiteboard area for additional notes.

Video
Teachers can also access the video and audio for the course, including the authentic video from The Guardian.

Homework
The app allows teachers to assign homework directly to their students' devices and alert them when they have activities to complete.

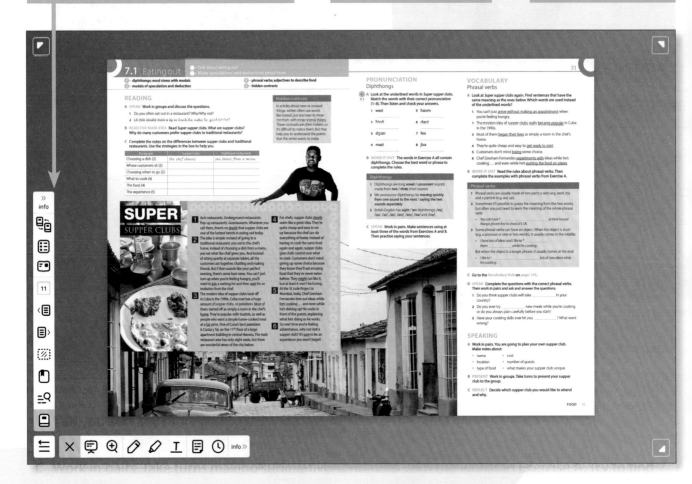

Online Preparation and Practice
Teachers can also configure student preparation and practice using the Teacher's App. Using the practice activities available, teachers can select and publish content to their students which they will receive through a push notification when they access their app. This enables teachers to personalise the amount and type of practice students do every week and to track their progress. Students can practise the grammar or vocabulary for the week before they go to class, allowing more time in the class for communication.

Test Generator
The Teacher's App also gives access to the Test Generator. In the Test Generator, teachers can create tests or use the pre-built tests for each level of the course and print these to assign to students. There are unit tests, mid- and end-of-course tests for each level, testing vocabulary, grammar and the four skills.

Student's App

Each Student's Book includes a code for the Student's App, to engage and encourage your students to practise their English on the move. Students can access grammar, vocabulary and pronunciation activities to prepare them for the lesson. Students are able to complete activities with varying levels of challenge and earn points.

Preparation
Allows more time for communicative activities in the class by providing pre-lesson exposure to the language covered in the Student's Book.

Practice
Provides additional practice to consolidate, revise and extend areas covered in the Student's Book.

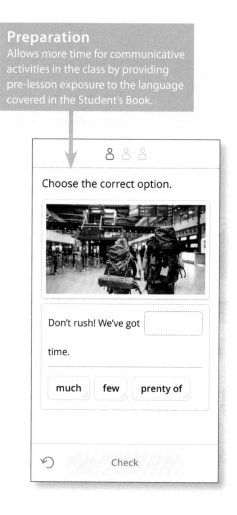

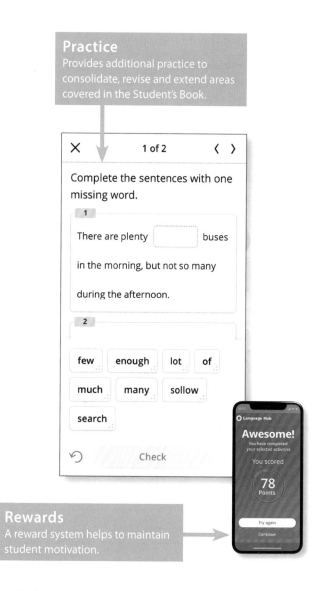

Rewards
A reward system helps to maintain student motivation.

Video

Two types of video are available with the course. Café Hub is a situation comedy which models functional language. Video Hub uses content from The Guardian as a resource for authentic English. All the videos from the course relate to the unit topics, and offer listening practice and scaffolding for speaking output.

Video Hub

Café Hub

Student's Book Contents

READING · LISTENING	SPEAKING · WRITING
read a text about 'My perfect online life' listen to a homemade podcast **KEY SKILL** Listening to check predictions	discuss pictures on your phone write a social media update SPEAKING HUB make a podcast about an experiment
listen to a discussion about English language **KEY SKILL** Rhetorical questions	interview a classmate about their experience of English SPEAKING HUB give a presentation about language learning
▶ watch a video about someone asking for help	ask a friend for help
read a blog about achievable bucket lists listen to a radio interview about a life-changing decision **KEY SKILL** Listening for the main idea	write and discuss your achievable bucket list SPEAKING HUB interview a classmate about a life-changing decision
read a news article about an older man looking for employment **KEY SKILL** Deducing the meaning of unknown words from context listen to four people taking about a time they overcame a problem	give a presentation about an inspirational person SPEAKING HUB ask and answer interview questions about problem-solving skills
▶ watch a video about a photoshoot	ask for and give permission for something
listen to a radio phone-in programme about bad travel experiences read a social science article on talking to people on public transport **KEY SKILL** Skim-reading to build a map of a text	tell a story for a radio show SPEAKING HUB discuss annoying behaviour on public transport
read an article about Helsinki's *Kutsuplus* transport scheme listen to a town council meeting discussing 'car-free days' **KEY SKILL** Listening for signposting language	discuss Helsinki's *Kutsuplus* transport scheme SPEAKING HUB evaluate proposals to reduce the traffic problems and pollution in a city
▶ watch a video about someone telling a story	tell a story about someone you used to spend time with
listen to two friends talking about resolutions on a Skype call read about the book *Life Cycle* **KEY SKILL** Summarising listen to four people talking about books or films that changed their lives	make and compare resolutions SPEAKING HUB discuss how a book or film changed your life
read a text about super-forecasters listen to a radio programme about the future of the countryside in Japan **KEY SKILL** Paraphrasing	discuss predictions for life in the future SPEAKING HUB discuss solutions to predicted problems
▶ watch a video about complaints	act out a restaurant scene
listen to a conversation between a careers advisor and client read a text about modern offices **KEY SKILL** Following reference links in a text	SPEAKING HUB interview a classmate to give careers advice SPEAKING HUB discuss and agree a plan to redesign an office
read a text about a business that is selling bottled air listen to a business podcast about marketing **KEY SKILL** Listening for examples	SPEAKING HUB present a company for an award SPEAKING HUB talk about an environmental business idea on a podcast
▶ watch a video about a presentation	give a presentation about a personal possession

READING · LISTENING	SPEAKING · WRITING
read an article about the sport of snowball fighting in Scotland listen to a talk about eSports **KEY SKILL** Listening for main and supporting points	describe a sport or a game and discuss sports SPEAKING HUB give a persuasive talk about a sport or a game
listen to a radio programme about hobbies and free time activities read about a person who tries something new every month for six months **KEY SKILL** Identifying tone	SPEAKING HUB interview your classmates about their free time activities SPEAKING HUB talk and ask about new activities
watch a video about different types of food	give an opinion about doing exercise
read an article about supper clubs **KEY SKILL** Hidden contrasts listen to a conversation at a dinner party	plan and present a supper club SPEAKING HUB describe a dish you would like to bring to a dinner party
read a food fad blog listen to a radio show about household food waste **KEY SKILL** Identifying people's opinions	ask and answer questions using superlatives SPEAKING HUB give a presentation about how to reduce food waste in the home
watch a video about a problem and a suggestion	talk about possible solutions to problems
read a text about a Canadian inventor read a short text on 'thinking outside the box' listen to friends discussing what you can do to be more creative **KEY SKILL** Listening for problems and solutions	talk about a person, a place and an object SPEAKING HUB talk about ideas for creating a website
listen to a podcast about new gadgets read a magazine article about gadgets **KEY SKILL** Topic sentences	invent a new gadget and promote it SPEAKING HUB give advice to a friend who wants to buy a gadget
watch a video about people assembling furniture	follow and give practical instructions
listen to finalists from a public arts competition read an article about immersive theatre **KEY SKILL** Using linking words to understand the writer's opinion	discuss proposals for an arts venue and suggest improvements SPEAKING HUB discuss ideas for an immersive theatre performance
listen to two friends talking about *The Great Gatsby* read an extract from *The Great Gatsby* listen to two friends talking about storytelling **KEY SKILL** Listening for definitions of new words	talk about books and stories and report a conversation SPEAKING HUB create and tell a collaborative story
watch a video about a film	describe a favourite film
read an article about thinking rationally and decision making listen to a conversation between two friends about a failed shopping trip **KEY SKILL** Listening for phrases that support an argument	discuss different outcomes of past events SPEAKING HUB discuss past mistakes
listen to a conversation on the power of habit read about the psychology of the to-do list **KEY SKILL** Bridge sentences	talk about wishes, hopes, regrets and dreams SPEAKING HUB make a wish list into a to-do list
watch a video about an apology	act out conversations to make and accept apologies

Welcome

GRAMMAR
Verb tenses and structures

A Choose the correct verb forms to complete the conversation.

A: Excuse me. I [1]*look* / **'m looking** for room 14. I have an English lesson today, but I [2]**don't know** / *'m not knowing* where to go.

B: Room 14? It's right here. It looks like we're [3]*being* / **going to be** in the same group. My name's Diego, by the way.

A: Hi, Diego. I'm Yulia. So [4]*did* / **have** you studied at this school before?

B: Yes. I [5]*was* / **'ve been** in the same group last year. The teacher, Helena, is really nice. [6]*You* / **You'll** like her, I'm sure. So … why [7]**did you decide** / *were you deciding* to join this school, Yulia?

A: Well, about two weeks ago, I [8]**'ve tried** / *was trying* to help my son with his English homework, but I couldn't remember anything! So I decided to come back to school, after all these years!

B Find and correct the mistakes in four of the sentences or questions.

1 How ~~many~~ *much* time do you spend doing homework every day?

2 In my English class, we speak a lot of English every lesson, but we don't have to speak English all the time.

3 It's an online course, so all the answers are check*ed* by a computer.

4 What kind of things do you want to talk about in your English lessons?

5 Everybody make*s* mistakes when they speak English – even English speakers!

6 Is it better to speak quickly with a lot of mistakes or slowly with no mistakes?

7 It's important to learn a lot of new words, but I don't really enjoy ~~to~~ study*ing* vocabulary.

C SPEAK Work in pairs and discuss the questions.

1 Why did you decide to join this class? Use the ideas from the conversation in Exercise A to help you.

2 What is the best way to learn English? Use the ideas in Exercise B to help you.

VOCABULARY
Describing places, illnesses and transport

A Complete the table with the words in the box.

attractive   coach   ~~cold~~   ~~dirty~~   headache   helicopter
modern   noisy   ~~plane~~   temperature   toothache   tram

Describing places	Illnesses	Transport
dirty	a *cold*	a *plane*
attractive	a headache	a coach
modern	a toothache	a helicopter
noisy	a temperature	a tram

Collocations

B Choose the correct words to complete the collocations.

1 Is it better if somebody helps you *by* / *for* / *to* / **with** your homework, or should you always work alone?

2 When was the last time you *did* / *made* / **took** / *went* a day off school or work?

3 Are you good **at** / *in* / *from* / *on* cooking?

4 Is it better to **borrow** / *earn* / *lend* / *pay* money from your friends or from the bank?

5 Is it possible to *have* / **keep** / *make* / *play* fit without spending a lot of time or money?

6 Do you prefer to pay *by* / *on* / *for* / *with* your shopping by card or in cash?

7 What is the best way to *fall* / **get** / *meet* / *win* a good job in your country?

C SPEAK Work in pairs. Ask and answer the questions in Exercise B. Ask your partner to explain his/her answers.

A: I think it's better to do your homework with someone.
B: Really? Why do you think so?

PRONUNCIATION

🔊 Listen and choose the words you hear.

0.1

1 *where* / **were**   5 **have** / *of*
2 **can** / *can't*   6 *this* / **these**
3 *work* / **walk**   7 **cap** / *cup*
4 **mouth** / *mouse*

FUNCTIONAL LANGUAGE

Match the sentences (1–9) with the responses (a–i).

1 My name's Adam, by the way.

2 What a nice surprise. Long time, no see!

3 What do you think I should do?

4 Would you like me to check it for you?

5 Are you doing anything this evening?

6 Do you fancy watching a film this weekend?

7 I feel really ill today … and I've got an exam later.

8 In my opinion, young people these days are incredibly rude.

9 It was really nice to see you again.

a Why don't you try to find a new job?

b Sounds great. I'll just check that I'm free.

c You, too. See you later. Take care.

d Nice to meet you.

e Some are, but then some adults are, too.

f No. Why? Shall we go out?

g Oh, no! Poor you! That sounds terrible.

h Yeah, I know! What are you doing these days?

i Yes, please. That would be really helpful.

1 COMMUNICATION

Communication (n) the process of giving information or of making emotions or ideas known to someone.
Synonyms: interaction (n), contact (n)

> Wise men speak because they have something to say; fools because they have to say something.
>
> Plato

Plato means that people should more carefully consider what they choose to say and when they say it.

Plato (428–348 BCE) was a classical Greek philosopher. He was the founder of the Academy in Athens, which was the first higher-learning institution in the Western world.

A young woman enjoys her walk outdoors.

OBJECTIVES

- update your status on social media
- make a short podcast
- plan and conduct an interview
- use rhetorical questions in a presentation
- ask for, offer and respond to help
- write a report about trends

Work with a partner. Discuss the questions.

1 How does 21st century technology make it easier or harder to communicate with other people?

2 Read the quote. To what extent do you agree with Plato?

3 Which forms of communication do you use most often: face-to-face or electronic; written or spoken communication? Which do you prefer and why?

COMMUNICATION 1

OBJECTIVES

Read the unit objectives to the class.

UNIT OPENER QUESTIONS

1 Focus students' attention on the picture to engage them in the topic and help generate ideas. Elicit one way in which 21st-century technology makes it easier to communicate with other people and one way in which it makes 'real' communication harder. Put students into pairs to think of more ways before whole-class feedback.

2 Put students into pairs and encourage them to explain the meaning of the quote and to discuss if they agree with it. Ask one or two pairs to share their ideas with the class. Encourage the students to listen to each other and respond with their own ideas and opinions.

3 Elicit examples of the four types of communication mentioned in the question, e.g. instant messaging. Then ask students to discuss the question with their partner. Monitor and record any interesting vocabulary on the board. Give feedback at the end of the activity.

WORKSHEETS

Lesson 1.1 Communication today

Grammar: Present simple and present continuous (W1)

Vocabulary: Seeing and hearing (W2)

Lesson 1.2 Who owns English?

Grammar: Subject and object questions (W3)

Vocabulary: Languages (W4)

G— present simple and present continuous V— seeing and hearing P— schwa /ə/ S— listening to check predictions

READING

A SPEAK Work in groups and discuss the questions.

1 Do you ever use social media sites? Which ones?

2 What sort of information do people usually post on social media?

B PREDICT Match the pictures (1–3) with the social media status updates (a–c). How do you think the people in the pictures are feeling? What can you guess about their lives?

a On my way to the top! Looking forward to an amazing view! 2

b Can't believe we're on holiday again! We're having a wonderful time! 3

c Our lovely new kitchen! Looks good, doesn't it? 1

C READ FOR GIST Read the social media posts quickly to check your predictions from Exercise B. Make notes about the true stories behind the pictures.

D READ FOR DETAIL Read again and answer the questions.

1 How do Katia and Elisa know each other?

2 Why was Katia confused?

3 When did Katia go to the top of the mountain?

4 How does Katia feel about her new kitchen?

5 How does Katia feel about her 'boring' life?

6 Why doesn't Elisa post pictures when she isn't on holiday?

My **perfect** online life

@Katia … is feeling confused
6 hours ago

Had a very strange experience today. I met <u>my old school friend **@Elisa**</u> for the first time in eight years. 'You're so lucky!' she said. 'You <u>have</u> such a perfect life! I'm so jealous!'
<u>A perfect life? Me? I have a very normal life: I get up early every day, take the bus to work, watch TV … and that's all. In fact, Elisa seems to have a perfect life: her pictures always show her wonderful family relaxing in the sunshine on a beautiful beach.</u>
But now I<u>'m writing</u> this post, I <u>think</u> I <u>understand</u> what happened: on social media, our lives <u>look</u> perfect, but the reality is very different.
For example, <u>last week</u> I posted a selfie from the top of a mountain. In the picture, you can see I<u>'m smiling</u>. But in fact, I felt absolutely exhausted and just wanted to go home as quickly as possible! But you can't see that in the picture!
And did you see the picture of our new kitchen a few weeks ago? Well, yes, <u>it's lovely, but I didn't mention that it took six months to finish. Six months without a kitchen! And it cost us twice as much as we expected</u>, so now we<u>'re getting</u> worried about money. But no one ever <u>talks</u> about money problems on social media, do they?
<u>I'm not complaining</u>, though. I'm very happy with my life! I <u>love</u> being normal … and <u>I don't mind that my life is becoming a bit boring!</u> In fact, I<u>'m thinking</u> of staying at home this evening – just me, my husband and a takeaway pizza! Perfect!

Ex D Q1
Ex D Q2
Ex D Q3
Ex D Q4
Ex D Q5

⟲ Reply from @Elisa
4 hours ago

Hey, **@Katia**! Great to see you this morning. I <u>know</u> what you <u>mean</u> about our 'perfect lives'. I <u>guess</u> I <u>need</u> to explain about all those beach pictures. You <u>see</u>, I <u>work really hard all year, and the only time I use social media is when I'm on holiday</u>. That's why I<u>'m sitting</u> on the beach in all my pictures! It usually <u>rains</u> for most of the week we're on holiday, but of course we only take pictures when the sun<u>'s shining</u>!

Ex E Q6

Glossary

jealous (adj) unhappy because someone has something that you would like or can do something that you would like to do

1.1 Communication today

LEAD-IN

With books closed, put students into pairs and give them one minute to list as many means of communication as they can. The pair with the most wins.

READING

A If you ever use social media sites, tell the students which ones and what sort of information you post. If you don't, give an example about someone you know. Ask students to do the same in pairs, telling each other about their social media habits and what people generally use social media for. As you monitor, encourage students to expand on their answers to generate plenty of interest in the topic.

B Ask students to look at picture 1 and call out ideas about the man's feeling and life in general. Then ask students to work with a partner to discuss the other pictures and match them to social media updates. As a whole class, confirm the correct answers to the matching task but don't accept or reject any other predictions at this stage.

C Tell students they can now check their predictions as they read some social media posts by the two women shown in the pictures. Ask students to read and make notes about the stories behind the pictures. Check with the class which predictions were closest to the truth.

Picture 1: It took six months to finish and cost twice as much money as she expected.
Picture 2: Katia felt cold, wet and tired and wanted to go home.
Picture 3: Elisa only goes on holiday for one week per year, and it usually rains for most of the time.

D Tell students to work alone to read the text again to answer questions 1–6. Point out the glossary, with a definition of *jealous*, an important word to understand the text. Allow students to check their answers with a partner before checking as a whole class.

1 They were friends at school, but they last saw each other eight years ago.
2 Because she and Elisa both thought the other one had a perfect life.
3 Last week.
4 It's lovely, but it caused a lot of problems.
5 She loves it.
6 She's too busy.

E You could tell students about the acronym FOMO (fear of missing out), which is common when discussing this topic. Ask if students have heard of this and if they ever have this feeling. Ask one or two pairs to share what they discussed, then encourage the rest of the class to say whether they have similar or different feelings.

> **Extra activity**
> The discussion questions could be used to introduce a short class debate on the theme of social media: for example, does social media make us more or less happy? Break your class into groups. Ensure that students argue both for and against the motion, even if they aren't adopting their real position. Allow the class time to organise their arguments. Set a time limit on speeches. After the debate students can vote on the motion.

METHODOLOGY HUB by Jim Scrivener

Activity route map

Here is a basic route map plan for running a simple activity. In some bigger activities, there may be a number of clearly separate 'sections' within the task, in which case you would go through steps 3, 4 and 5 a few times.

1 Before the lesson: Familiarise yourself with the material and activity; prepare any materials or texts you need.
2 In class: Prepare for the activity.
3 Set up the activity (or section of activity), i.e. give instructions, make groupings, etc.
4 Run the activity (or section): Students do the activity, maybe in pairs or small groups while you monitor and help.
5 Close the activity (or section) and invite feedback from the students.
6 Post-activity: Do any appropriate follow-on work.

Here is some advice for step 1 in more detail:

1 Before the lesson:
- Familiarise yourself with the material and the activity.
- Read through the material and any teacher's notes.
- Try the activity yourself.
- Imagine how it will look in class.

- Decide how many organisational steps are involved.
- What seating arrangements/rearrangements are needed?
- How long will it probably take?
- Do the learners know enough language to be able to make a useful attempt at the activity?
- What help might they need?
- What questions might they have?
- What errors (using the language) are they likely to make?
- What errors (misunderstanding the task) are they likely to make?
- What will your role be at each stage?
- What instructions are needed?
- How will they be given (explained, read, demonstrated)?
- Prepare any aids or additional material.
- Arrange seating, visual aids, etc.
- Most importantly, you need to think through any potential problems or hiccups in the procedures. For example, what will happen if you plan student work in pairs, but there is an uneven number of students? Will this student work alone, or will you join in, or will you make one of the pairs into a group of three?

GRAMMAR

A Do the first verb together as a class, before students work alone.

Present simple: have, get up, take, watch, seems, show, think, understand, look, talks, love, don't mind, know, mean, guess, need, see, work, use, rains

Present continuous: is feeling, 'm writing, 'm smiling, 're getting, 'm not complaining, is becoming, 'm thinking, 'm sitting, 's shining

B–C Put students into pairs to complete the exercises.

Possible answers:

Rule 2: Her pictures always <u>show</u> her wonderful family… / But no one ever <u>talks</u> about money problems…

Rule 3a: Katia…<u>is feeling</u> confused / <u>I'm not complaining</u>, though

Rule 3b: That's why <u>I'm sitting</u> on the beach in all my pictures! /…we only take pictures when the sun<u>'s shining</u>!

Rule 3c: My life <u>is becoming</u> a bit boring

Rule 4: I <u>love</u> being normal…and I <u>don't mind</u> that… / I <u>guess</u> I <u>need</u> to explain …

Rule 5: I <u>think</u> I <u>understand</u> what happened / <u>I'm thinking</u> of staying at home this evening …

D Direct students to the **Grammar Hub** on page 122 (see below).

E–F Put students into pairs then groups to complete the exercises. Use the **Grammar Worksheet** on W1 for extra practice.

SPEAKING

A Tell students to look on their phones for two or three pictures that might be posted on social media.

B Put students into groups to show their pictures to each other and discuss the questions.

C Monitor as the students are writing, helping if they need vocabulary.

D Either display the students' updates on the walls for students to walk around and read or pass them around so everyone gets a chance to read as many as possible. Tell students to think about whether the updates make their classmates' lives seem perfect or normal. In feedback, ask a few students to tell you which updates they found particularly interesting and why.

GRAMMAR HUB

1.1 Present simple and present continuous

	Positive	Negative	Question
Present simple	**He gets up** early.	**It doesn't look** good.	**Do you take** the bus?
Present continuous	**I'm taking** a selfie.	**She isn't watching** TV. **She's not watching** TV.	**Are they smiling**?

- We use the present simple to talk about actions that always/usually/never happen.

  I don't always get up early.
- We use the present continuous to talk about actions that are in progress at the moment of speaking or writing.

  They aren't working this week.
- We also use the present continuous to describe actions in a photo or video.

  What is he doing in this photo?
- We also use the present continuous to describe trends.

  More and more people are getting worried about money.
- We use the present simple, not the present continuous, to talk about our everyday routines.

  Do you write many emails at work?
  NOT ~~Are you writing many emails at work?~~

- We often use these adverbs of frequency with the present simple: _always, never, often, rarely, sometimes, usually._

  Do you **often** post photos of yourself on social media?
- We use stative verbs to describe feelings and ideas. We use the present simple (not the present continuous) with stative verbs.

  I love taking selfies!
- Some verbs (e.g. have, look, speak, think) can be used as both dynamic and stative verbs, depending on the situation.

  have: She **has** a perfect life. / Are you **having** fun?
  look: Your new kitchen **looks** really good! / I'm **looking** for a new job.

1.1 Present simple and present continuous

A Choose the correct option.

1 Sarah (is showing)/ _shows_ me her holiday photos. They're lovely!

2 (Are they working)/ _Do they work_ today?

3 _Are you always getting up_ /(Do you always get up) early on weekdays?

4 They (are relaxing)/ _relax_ on the beach in this picture.

5 We _are not usually_ /(don't usually) watch TV but this programme is really good!

6 I (am becoming)/ _become_ more worried about my social media posts.

B Complete the email with the correct form of the verb in brackets. Use contractions where possible.

Hi Sarah!

We [1] <u>'re having</u> (_have_) a great time here in Spain! The sun [2] <u>'s shining</u> (_shine_) and the country is beautiful. We [3] <u>have</u> (_have_) a lovely room in a little hotel with a view of the beach. I [4] <u>'m sitting</u> (_sit_) on the balcony to write this email and I can see Paul down on the beach. He [5] <u>'s playing</u> (_play_) football with the boys on the sand. The children [6] <u>like</u> (_like_) it here – they say they [7] <u>don't want</u> (_not want_) to go home! Hope you [8] <u>aren't working</u> (_not work_) too hard!

See you next week!

Love, Mary

➤ Go back to page 3.

E SPEAK Work in pairs and discuss the questions.

1 Does your life look perfect on social media? What about your friends' lives?

2 Do you ever feel jealous when you see other people's status updates?

GRAMMAR
Present simple and present continuous

A Look at the underlined verbs in the social media posts. Which verbs are in the present simple? Which are in the present continuous?

B WORK IT OUT Match the sentences (a–f) with the rules (2–5).

a In the picture, you can see I'm smiling. rule 3 b

b I know what you mean about our 'perfect lives'. rule 4

c But now I'm writing this post, … rule 3 a

d You have such a perfect life! rule 5

e I get up early every day. rule 2

f So now we're getting worried about money. rule 3 c

Present simple and present continuous

1 Dynamic verbs (*talk*, *go*) usually describe actions.

2 We use the present simple with dynamic verbs to talk about actions that always, usually or never happen.

3 We use the present continuous with dynamic verbs:

  a to talk about actions that are in progress at the moment of speaking or writing.

  b to describe actions in a picture, video, etc.

  c to describe trends (e.g. something is happening more and more these days).

4 Stative verbs (*want*, *seem*) often describe feelings and ideas. We use the present simple with stative verbs.

5 A few verbs (*have*, *look*, *speak*, *think*) have two or more meanings. They are sometimes dynamic verbs and sometimes stative verbs.

C Find at least one more example of each rule (2–5) in the posts.

D Go to the Grammar Hub on page 122.

E Are the verbs stative verbs (S) or dynamic verbs (D)?

1	contain	*S*	7 include	*S*
2	cost	*S*	8 mean	*S*
3	depend	*S*	9 own	*S*
4	deserve	*S*	10 relax	*D*
5	enjoy	*D*	11 seem	*S*
6	happen	*D*	12 shine	*D*

F SPEAK Work in groups and discuss the questions.

1 Why are you studying English? Why do you need English?

2 How is this week different from your normal weekly routine? What are you doing differently this week? What do you normally do?

3 What are people doing more and more these days? What are some trends in your own life?

SPEAKING

A Work in groups. If you have some pictures on your phone, choose two or three to discuss with your group. If you do not, think about some of your favourite pictures of you and your friends or family.

B Tell your group:

- What's happening in the pictures?

- Does your life seem perfect or exciting in the pictures? What's the real story behind the pictures?

- Do you have any pictures of you doing normal things, e.g. watching TV? Why/Why not?

C Write a short social media status update for one or two of your pictures. Decide whether to make your life seem perfect or normal.

Writing a status

We often leave out the subject and *be* from the beginning of status updates when it's easy for the reader to guess the missing words.

- (*It*) *Looks good, doesn't it?*

- (*I*) *Had a very strange experience today.*

- (*It was*) *Great to see you this morning.*

D Read some of your classmates' social media status updates. Do their lives look perfect or normal?

LISTENING

A SPEAK Work in pairs and discuss the questions.

1 What do you use your mobile phone for?

2 How did people do those things before they had mobile phones? What problems did they have?

B PREDICT Work in pairs. You are going to listen to *A week without phones!* Look at the pictures and discuss the questions. Use the strategies in the box to help you.

> **Listening to check predictions**
>
> Before you listen to something in English, it's always a good idea to predict what you will hear.
>
> If there's a title and pictures, you can try to predict the connection between them. Then you can listen to check your predictions.

1 Who are the people in picture a? What are they doing? brother and sister

2 What is the device in picture b? a voice recorder

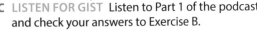

3 What does the title mean? What's the connection with the people and the device? a week without using their mobile phones, making a podcast about it

C LISTEN FOR GIST Listen to Part 1 of the podcast 1.1 and check your answers to Exercise B.

D PREDICT Work in pairs and discuss the questions. 1.2 Then listen to Part 2 and check your answers.

1 What went wrong when Olivia and Jackson tried to meet up on Monday?

2 How did they solve the problem?

E PREDICT Work in pairs and discuss what you 1.3 think Olivia and Jackson did differently on Tuesday when they met. Then listen to Part 3 and check your answer.

F PREDICT Work in pairs and discuss the questions. 1.4 Then listen to Part 4 and check your answers.

1 Do you think Olivia and Jackson are enjoying the experiment?

2 What do you think they're doing more or less of than usual?

G LISTEN FOR DETAIL Listen again. Choose the correct answers, 1.5 a, b or c.

1 When is the last day of the experiment?

  a Tuesday

  b Thursday

  (c) Sunday

2 Why does Olivia decide to stop waiting outside on Monday?

  (a) She doesn't want to get wet.

  b She thinks Jackson isn't coming.

  c She knows the university closes at four o'clock.

3 How does Sebastian know Jackson and Olivia?

  a They study together at university.

  b Olivia met Sebastian outside the cake shop.

  (c) Sebastian has seen them before in pictures and videos.

4 Why is Olivia enjoying the concert more than usual on Tuesday?

  (a) She isn't recording it on her phone.

  b The audience isn't having as much fun.

  c Jackson isn't there with her.

5 On Thursday, why is Olivia surprised at the end of the podcast?

  a The university buildings are amazing.

  (b) Jackson doesn't usually talk so much.

  c She can't believe Jackson forgot his camera.

H SPEAK Work in groups and discuss the questions.

1 What problems did Olivia and Jackson have during the experiment?

2 What good things happened as a result?

3 Do you think Olivia and Jackson's experiment was a good idea?

4 Would you like to try a similar experiment? Why/Why not?

1.1 Communication today

LISTENING

A Put students into pairs to discuss the questions.

B Ask them to look at the strategies in the *Listening to check predictions* box. Put students into pairs to discuss the questions. Get feedback but don't confirm or deny anything yet.

🔊 **C–H** Put students into pairs to make predictions and
1.1–1.5 discuss questions. Allow them enough time to make predictions before playing tracks. Also for the last stage, ensure they have shared some ideas in pairs before opening out to a wider class discussion.

AUDIOSCRIPT

🔊 **1.1**

Listening, Exercise C
J = Jackson   O = Olivia

J: Hello. Welcome to the Tec-cast. I'm Jackson, and this is my big sister, Olivia.

O: Hello. In this week's podcast, we're looking at phones. Or rather, we're not looking at our phones for a whole week!

Ex G Q1 J: Yes, that's right. Our experiment runs for seven days. We started on Monday and today's Thursday, so we're halfway through it.

O: Exactly. And instead of our phones, we're both carrying around one of these voice recorders all week, so we can record our experiences. And it's been quite a week! I arranged to meet Jackson outside the university on Monday afternoon, but it didn't really work, did it, Jackson?

J: Er, no. Sorry. Let's listen to our recordings from earlier in the week.

🔊 **1.2**

Listening, Exercise D
J = Jackson   O = Olivia   S = Sebastian

O: Hi. Olivia here. It's 4.20 on Monday afternoon and I'm waiting for Jackson. We arranged to meet here, outside the university, at four o'clock, but I can't see him and it's starting to rain. So it looks like he isn't coming and I'm not sure what to do. Hmm, I can't call him because I haven't got my phone. OK, I know.
Ex G Q2 I'll go and wait in that cake shop over there – at least I'll stay dry, and I'll be able to see Jackson through the window when he arrives.

Ex D Q1 J: Hi. This is Jackson. It's Monday afternoon and I'm late meeting Olivia. I think. I don't actually know the time because I never wear a watch; I always use the clock on my phone. Anyway, I missed my bus and I couldn't check the time of the next one – the timetables are all online now. So I decided to walk. But then I got lost because I didn't have a map – I usually use the map on my phone! And I couldn't call Olivia to tell her I'd be late. And now it's raining! OK, so I'm just arriving at the university now and I'm looking for Olivia, but I can't see her. Hmm, now I don't know what to do.

S: Excuse me. Are you looking for Olivia?

J: Er, yes. Why?

S: Hi. I'm Sebastian. I'm a student at the university here.
Ex G Q3 I listen to your podcast every week, and I watch all your videos. I love them!

J: Really? Wow! Thanks. Er … but how do you know I'm looking for Olivia?

Ex D Q2 S: I spotted her here a few minutes ago. I recognised her from your videos. She went into that cake shop over there.

J: Oh, excellent. Thank you so much. Look, do you want to come and join us? I'll buy you a cake to say thank you, and you can tell us what you think of our podcasts.

S: Yeah, that sounds like a great idea. Thanks a lot.

🔊 **1.3**

Listening, Exercise E
J = Jackson   O = Olivia

O: Hi. Me again. It's quarter past 11 on Tuesday morning, and yes, I'm waiting for Jackson, again.
Ex E He's 15 minutes late, again, but it's OK because we arranged a plan B: what to do if something goes wrong. So I'm enjoying a nice open-air concert in the park right now, by a really cool band. Maybe you can hear the music in the background. Our new friend Sebastian told us about the concert yesterday – he plays the guitar in the band, and he sounds really good. It's strange because all the other people in the audience are filming the concert on their mobile
Ex F Q1 phones, but I think they're missing half the fun! I'm
Ex G Q4 just listening and enjoying it – and it's much better. In fact, I think I'll stop recording now so I can listen!

J: Hi. It's Tuesday morning, and I'm late for a meeting with Olivia, again, but it's OK because we discussed where she'll be at 11, 11.30, 12.00 and 12.30. And yes,
Ex E I'm wearing a watch today – an old one from when I was a teenager. It doesn't look great, but it's good
Ex E for telling the time! Anyway, today, I decided to walk the same way I came yesterday – so I checked a map before I left home! I wanted to come back to this part of town because I noticed that the buildings are really beautiful and interesting. I don't normally look at the buildings around me – I usually just stare
Ex F Q2 at my phone. But it's really nice to look around and think about where I am and … how to get to the park from here. So I'm not exactly lost again; I'm just exploring the city a bit more than usual.

🔊 **1.4**

Listening, Exercise F
J = Jackson   O = Olivia

O: Hello again. So, as I said, it's now Thursday, and we're halfway through our experiment. How's it going for you, Jackson?

J: Surprisingly well! I mean, I think I'm seeing a lot more than usual – now I'm looking at the real world, not my phone all the time.

O: Yeah, me too. I really enjoyed observing all the people outside the university on Monday! So what about those amazing buildings? Did you take any pictures?

J: Er, no. Because I didn't have my phone! But I can tell you about them, if you want.

Ex G Q5 O: Wow! You usually just show me your pictures. You see! We're talking more than before, too! Our experiment is working! So tell me about those buildings!

VOCABULARY

1.6

A Tell students that all the sentences come from the podcasts they listened to earlier. Students first try to choose the correct verb before listening to check. Get feedback, but don't explain why any of the answers are correct or incorrect yet.

B Ask the class whether the eyes or the ears are used for each of the words, e.g. *hear = ears*. Students then use the symbols to work out the rules. As you monitor, direct them to the sentences in Exercise A to help them if necessary. Check answers with the class.

C Direct students to the **Vocabulary Hub** on page 142 for further practice of verbs of seeing and hearing. Allow time for students to compare answers in pairs before checking each exercise.

D Tell students to complete the questions with the verbs in the box. In feedback, check students fully understand the meaning of the verbs and the differences between them.

E Put students into groups to discuss the questions. Get feedback from one or two students about the most interesting things they talked about. Use the **Vocabulary Worksheet** on W2 for extra practice.

PRONUNCIATION

1.7

A Focus students' attention on the information about the schwa, the most common sound in English (especially British English). Model the sound so students know what it is, then tell them to listen and underline the schwas they hear in the sentences from the podcast.

B Tell students to practise saying the sentences in pairs. Encourage them to check and correct each other's use of the schwa. Join in yourself and make this light-hearted and fun. Point out how using the schwa is a very effective way to sound more natural, and therefore be more easily understood.

SPEAKING HUB

A Tell students that they're going to make a short podcast. Put students into small groups of three or four and tell them to choose one of the ideas in the box or to think of one of their own.

B Give groups time to plan their podcasts. Encourage students to make notes, but not to write out the whole podcast word for word. Monitor and help with vocabulary and pronunciation as they do this.

C Students can either record their podcast and play it to the class or present it live. Encourage students to listen carefully to the other podcasts and think about whether they would like to try any of the experiments.

D Put students into groups to discuss the questions. Call on each group to say what they discussed and encourage other students to comment on what the group says.

E Put students into new groups to discuss what experiments they would like to try and whether they would want to make a real podcast.

Extra activity

You could encourage students to complete their experiment outside class. Before they start, students can make predictions about the outcomes of their experiments. Help students plan how they will carry the experiments out. Will they use a smartphone or voice recorder to record their impressions? Or will they keep a diary of their experiment?

After their experiment, students can reflect on whether their predictions came true and what they have learnt from doing it. Finally, students can report back to the rest of their class about their experiment.

TEACHING IDEA by David Seymour and Maria Popova

Topic: Bare necessities

Use this activity to revise the topic.

In pairs, brainstorm a list of the 20 most important things that you need on a day-to-day basis and put them in order from most to least important. See how your list and order compare with another pair.

What is the bare minimum that a person needs to survive? List a few other things that people say they need but might not in fact be necessary.

TEACHING IDEA by David Seymour and Maria Popova

Topic: World needs

Use this activity to revise the topic.

Work in small groups and write five ideas under each of these headings:

- what the world needs now
- what things need doing to improve this town/country
- what people need in order to live in harmony

Discuss how the needs of different countries compare.

METHODOLOGY HUB by Jim Scrivener

Language skills

As well as working with the language systems (which we can think of as what we know, i.e. 'up-in-the-head' knowledge), we also need to pay attention to what we do with language. These are the language skills. Teachers normally think of there being four important macro language skills: listening, speaking, reading, writing. Listening and reading are called receptive skills (the reader or listener receives information but does not produce it); speaking and writing, on the other hand, are the **productive skills**. Skills are commonly used interactively and in combination rather than in isolation, especially speaking and listening. It's arguable that other things (e.g. thinking, using memory and mediating) are also language skills.

VOCABULARY
Seeing and hearing

A Choose the correct verbs to complete the sentences from *A week without phones!* Then listen again and check your answers.

1 In this week's podcast, we're *looking at* / *seeing* / *watching* phones.

2 It *looks* / *sees* / *watches* like he isn't coming, and I'm not sure what to do.

3 I'm *looking* / *seeing* / *watching* for Olivia, but I can't *look at* / *see* / *watch* her.

4 I *hear* / *listen to* / *sound* your podcast every week, and I *look at* / *see* / *watch* all your videos.

5 Yeah, that *hears* / *listens* / *sounds* like a great idea. Thanks a lot.

6 Maybe you can *hear* / *listen to* / *sound* the music in the background.

7 He plays the guitar in the band, and he *hears* / *listens* / *sounds* really good.

8 It doesn't *look* / *see* / *watch* great, but it's good for telling the time!

B WORK IT OUT Complete the rules with the correct form of *hear*, *listen*, *look*, *see*, *sound* or *watch*.

---

hear, listen, look, see, sound and watch

1 When you 👁 ____see____ or 👂 ____hear____ something, it just happens, not because you're trying to do it.

2 When you 👁 ____look____ *at* or 👂 ____listen____ *to* something, you do it because you decide to do it.

3 When you 👁 ____watch____ something, you look at it for a period of time, perhaps because it's moving.

4 When something 👁 ____looks____ good or 👂 ____sounds____ good, it probably is good, but you aren't sure.

5 When it 👁 ____looks____ like or 👂 ____sounds____ like something is happening, it probably is happening, but you aren't sure.

C Go to the Vocabulary Hub on page 142.

D Complete the questions with the verbs in the box. There are two extra verbs.

notice   observe   recognise   spot   stare

1 Do you ever sit in a café and ____observe____ the people through the window? Why do people enjoy doing this?

2 Are you good at remembering people's faces? Do you always ____recognise____ people when you meet them the second time?

3 When you're travelling around (e.g. by bus), do you usually ____notice____ the buildings around you?

E SPEAK Work in groups. Ask and answer the questions in Exercise D.

PRONUNCIATION
Schwa /ə/

Schwa /ə/

Schwa is the most common sound in English. We use it for most unstressed vowel sounds, especially in words like *a*, *the*, *of*, *to*, *and* and *but*.

A Listen to the sentences from *A week without phones!* Underline all schwas. The numbers in brackets tell you how many schwas to find. The first one has been done for you.

1.7

1 We're not looking at our phones for a whole week! (3)

2 We arranged to meet here, outside the university, at four o'clock. (5)

3 It's Monday afternoon and I'm late meeting Olivia. (3)

4 I'll buy you a cake to say thank you, and you can tell us what you think of our podcasts. (6)

5 Yes, I'm wearing a watch today – an old one from when I was a teenager. (7)

B SPEAK Work in pairs. Practise saying the sentences. Listen and check your partner's pronunciation.

⭕ SPEAKING HUB

A Work in groups. You are going to make a short podcast about an experiment. Choose one of the ideas in the box or use your own ideas.

---

a week of doing something completely new every day
a week speaking only English
a week without complaining
a week without the internet/TV, etc
a week without spending any money
a week of helping as many people as possible

B PLAN Plan a short podcast (about two minutes). Imagine you are in the middle of your experiment. Make notes on:

- what you can see and hear during your podcast.
- what's going well and/or badly with your experiment.
- what you're doing more or less as a result of your experiment.

C SPEAK Record your podcast and present it to the class.

D SHARE After listening to the podcasts, discuss the questions.

- Which group's experiment worked well?
- Which podcast did you enjoy most?

E REFLECT Work in new groups and discuss the questions.

- Will you try any of the experiments in real life? Why/Why not?
- Would you like to make a real podcast? What would your podcast be about? Do you think other people would want to listen to it?

◯– Update your status on social media
◯– Make a short podcast

TOP 10

ENGLISH SPEAKING COUNTRIES

1. USA 251,388,301
95.81% of population

2. India 125,226,449
11.38% of population

3. Philippines 89,800,000
92.58% of population

4. Nigeria 79,000,000
53.34% of population

5. UK 59,600,000
97.74% of population

6. Germany 46,272,000
56% of population

7. Canada 25,246,220
85.18% of population

8. France 23,000,000
36% of population

9. Australia 17,357,800
97.03% of population

10. Italy 17,000,000
29% of population

*The most amazing fact is that **only 11.38% of India's population** speaks English and yet it is the second largest English speaking nation in the world.*

USVisaTalk.com

LISTENING

A SPEAK Work in groups and discuss the questions.

1 Look at the infographic. What does it show? What do you know about the countries and the languages that people in those countries speak? Are you surprised by any of the numbers?

2 Who owns English? Who has the power to decide what's good and bad English?

B LISTEN FOR MAIN IDEA Listen to an interview about different types of English and answer the questions.
1.8

1 Why does Mona want to interview Juan?

2 Why did Juan enjoy his journey?

3 Where did Juan have problems with English?

4 How is Multicultural London English (MLE) different from the English we learn at school?

5 What's the connection between 'Standard English' and 'standard class' on a train?

6 Why is Standard English useful?

C LISTEN FOR DETAIL Listen again. Which person (Juan, Mona or Both) thinks …
1.8

1 travelling is a good way to practise your English?   Both

2 it's difficult to understand people in England?   Juan

3 MLE grammar contains mistakes?   Mona

4 Standard English is boring but useful?   Juan

5 it's sometimes better when you don't sound like a native speaker?   Both

D SPEAK Work in groups. Look at the sentences from the interview. For each one, discuss what Juan and Mona were talking about. Do you agree with their opinions?

1 'Millions of people speak like that, so how can it be wrong?'

2 'There are hundreds of other forms of English all over the world … They're all different, but I think that's really cool!'

3 'Surely Standard English is better, isn't it?'

4 'We don't need to speak like native speakers. In fact … it's often better when we don't speak like native speakers.'

1.2 Who owns English?

LEAD-IN

Ask students what they think the top ten English-speaking countries are. Students then open their books to check.

LISTENING

A Tell students to discuss the questions in small groups.

1 For a blog post. She wants to interview him about his experiences of using English during his trip across Europe.
2 He met a lot of great people and had amazing conversations
3 In England
4 Mostly pronunciation but also some grammar differences.
5 On a train, first class is better than standard class. Juan thinks non-standard English is better (for some purposes) than Standard English.
6 Juan thinks it is useful for international communication.

 B–D Students can check in pairs before whole-class feedback.

Possible answers:

1 They are discussing MLE. Juan doesn't think the grammar can be wrong as so many people use it.
2 They are discussing other non-standard forms of English, such as Jamaican English and Indian English.
3 Mona thinks it's better to use Standard English because it's good English.
4 Standard English is easier for non-native speakers to understand, so it's better to use this.

AUDIOSCRIPT

 1.8

Listening, Exercise B
M = Mona   J = Juan

Ex B Q1 M: Hey, Juan. I'm writing a blog post for our website. I thought it might be nice to interview you. Can I ask you a few questions?

J: Yes, of course. Go ahead. But why do you want to talk to me? What do you want to talk about?

Ex B Q1 M: Well, I hear you've just got back from a trip across Europe. It'd be nice to hear about your experiences of using English during your trip.

J: Oh, right. Yes, no problem.

M: Great. I'll just turn on my microphone … OK, so thanks, Juan, for agreeing to talk to me today about your recent trip to Europe. Which countries did you visit?

J: Well, I started in Russia, and then I travelled through Belarus, Poland, Germany, the Netherlands and England. It was a long journey, but I met a lot of great people and I had some amazing conversations. It was a good way to practise my English.

Ex B Q2

M: Yes, I'm sure it was! It sounds like a great way of practising. Was it hard to communicate in English?

J: No, actually I found it really easy to communicate all the way from Russia to the Netherlands. But when I got to England … well, it was terrible!

Ex B Q3

M: Really? What happened in England?

J: Everybody spoke so fast! And they used really strange words and phrases – lots of idioms that I'd never heard before. Plus, the people had very strong accents, so I couldn't understand very much at all!

M: Oh, no! So what did you do?

J: I just asked people to slow down. 'Can you say that again, please?'; 'Could you speak slowly, please?', and so on!

M: And did that help?

J: Yes. I mean, the people were very nice, and they were happy to talk to me. But they speak very strange English! I guess it's because English is changing all the time.

M: Really? How is English changing? Can you give me an example?

J: Yes, of course. When I was in London, I heard many people speaking a new variety of English called MLE – Multicultural London English. It's becoming extremely popular.

M: Really? I've never heard of it. Who uses MLE?

J: Mostly young people in London.

M: So how is MLE different from normal English?

Ex B Q4 J: Well, it's mostly a question of pronunciation. But there are also grammar differences. For example, in MLE, they don't say 'you were'; they say 'you was'. 'I was', 'you was', 'he was', 'she was', 'we was', 'they was'. And then in negative sentences, it's 'I weren't', 'you weren't', 'he weren't', 'she weren't', and so on.

M: What? That's terrible! But isn't that a mistake?

J: Well, it isn't Standard English, of course. But millions of people speak like that, so how can it be wrong?

M: Hmm … what do you mean by 'Standard English'?

J: Well, Standard English is the form they use in books and newspapers. It's a kind of cleaned-up version of English. But it isn't the only form of English, and most native speakers don't speak Standard English – at least, not all the time. There are hundreds of other forms of English all over the world – like Jamaican English, Nigerian English, Indian English and so on. They're all different, but I think that's really cool!

M: OK, but isn't it just a question of good English and bad English? Surely Standard English is better, isn't it?

Ex B Q5 J: No. I don't think so. 'Standard' doesn't always mean 'the best'. When I travelled by train across Europe, I went by 'standard class', not 'first class'. And I think Standard English is like 'standard class' in a train: simple and basic, but a bit boring. I think non-standard English is much more interesting.

M: So are you saying we need to learn non-standard English?

Ex B Q6 J: No, not at all. Standard English is perfect for international communication. As I say, Standard English worked well for me all the way from Russia to the Netherlands. I only had a problem when I got to England. So it depends what you need English for. I think for most learners of English around the world, it's better to learn Standard English. We don't need to speak like native speakers. In fact, as I learned on my trip, it's often better when we don't speak like native speakers.

M: Wow! Yes, I see what you mean, and I certainly agree with you on that last point. OK, so thanks a lot for that interview, Juan. You've given me lots to think about … and to write about on the blog.

1.2 Who owns English?

🔊 GRAMMAR

1.9 **A–E** Go to the **Grammar Hub** on pages 122 and 123 (see below).

PRONUNCIATION

You can see the *Pronunciation* and *Speaking* activities on TB8.

GRAMMAR HUB

1.2 Subject and object questions

Subject questions		
Question word/ Subject	Main verb	Rest of question
What	is	your first language?

Object questions				
Question word	Auxiliary verb	Subject	Main verb	Rest of question
What	do	you	want	to study?

- We use these question words to ask for information: *who* and *whose* (for people), *where* (for places), *when* (for times), *why* (for reasons), *what* (for things), *which* (for two or more different choices), *how* (for the way something is done) and *how long/many/much*/etc (for time, quantity, etc).

  Whose blog is this?

- We often use an auxiliary verb (*be, can, do* or *have*) to form questions. We put the auxiliary verb before the main verb.

  Are they practising their English?
  Can I ask you a question?
  Why do you want to learn English?
  How long have you known Liam?

- In subject questions, the question word is the subject of the sentence. We use subject questions when we don't know what/who/which/whose something/someone is. We don't use an auxiliary verb in subject questions and we don't change the word order in the answer.

  Who interviewed him? Mona interviewed him.

- In object questions, the question word is the object of the sentence. We use object questions when we want to know more information about something/someone. We always use an auxiliary verb in object questions. In the answer, we use the normal word order for a sentence.

  Where did he learn to speak English?
  NOT ~~Where he learnt to speak English?~~
  What do you want to study? I want to study modern languages.

- With subject questions, the answer is the subject.

  Who told you? Someone told you.

- With object questions, the answer is the object.

  Who did you tell? You told someone.

- With questions using *do, does* or *did*, we don't change the form of the main verb.

  Does she speak English? NOT ~~Does she speaks English?~~

- When a question word is the object of a preposition, the preposition usually comes at the end of the sentence.

  What did you have problems with?

A Read the answers and write questions. Use the question words in the box.

> how   what   where   which   who   why

1 *Why are you taking an umbrella?* — Because it's raining!
2 Where is your house? — My house is near the school.
3 What are you watching/doing? — I'm watching the news.
4 How do you get to work? — I get to work by bus.
5 Where do you want to visit? — I want to visit Poland.
6 Who is helping you? / What is David doing? — David is helping me.

B Put the words in order to make questions.

1 you / want / about / to talk / do / what / ?
  What do you want to talk about?
2 I / am / pronouncing / right / this word / ?
  Am I pronouncing this word right?
3 please / say / you / that again, / can / ?
  Can you say that again, please?
4 often / do / at work / use English / you / ?
  Do you often use English at work?
5 this / phone / whose / is / ?
  Whose phone is this? / Whose is this phone?
6 the graph / what / does / show / ?
  What does the graph show?
7 you / me / help / this / article / with / can / ?
  Can you help me with this article?
8 hours / how / you / English / study / week / do / many / each / ?
  How many hours of English do you study each week?

C Correct the mistakes in each question.

1 How long you have your phone?
  How long have you had your phone?
2 Where you are working at the moment?
  Where are you working at the moment?
3 You understand these words?
  Do you understand these words?
4 Who laptop is this?
  Whose laptop is this?
5 Where you keep your English books?
  Where do you keep your English books?
6 How many people do they speak English in the world?
  How many people speak English in the world?
7 How long it takes you to get to work?
  How long does it take you to get to work?
8 Who you met yesterday?
  Who did you meet yesterday?
9 Where they are learning English?
  Where are they learning English?
10 Does he uses the app to practise his pronunciation?
  Does he use the app to practise his pronunciation?

➤ Go back to page 7.

GRAMMAR
Subject and object questions

A Put the words in the correct order to make questions. Then listen to the interview again and check your answers.

1 you / I / a / questions / ask / can / few / ?

   <u>Can I ask you a few questions?</u>

2 countries / did / which / visit / you / ?

   <u>Which countries did you visit?</u>

3 England / happened / what / in / ?

   <u>What happened in England?</u>

4 changing / English / is / how / ?

   <u>How is English changing?</u>

5 MLE / uses / who / ?

   <u>Who uses MLE?</u>

6 mean / do / 'Standard English' / by / you / what / ?

   <u>What do you mean by 'Standard English'?</u>

7 to / you / need / non-standard English / saying / are / learn / we / so / ?

   <u>So are you saying we need to learn non-standard English?</u>

B WORK IT OUT Match the questions (1–7) in Exercise A with the rules (a–c).

Subject and object questions

a When we make questions in English, we usually put the auxiliary verb (*be*, *have*, *can*) before the subject.　　　　<u>1</u> , <u>4</u> , <u>7</u>

b In sentences with no auxiliary verb, we add *do*, *does*, or *did* when we make a question.　　<u>2</u> , <u>6</u>

c When the question is about the subject, we use the same word order as in sentences. We don't add *do*, *does* or *did*.　　<u>3</u> , <u>5</u>

C PRACTISE Make questions about the missing information.

1 (Somebody) writes a blog for a website.

   Who <u>writes a blog for a website</u> ?

2 Juan visited (a number of countries).

   How many <u>countries did Juan visit</u> ?

3 You (can/can't) give me an example.

   <u>Can you give me an example</u> ?

4 (A form of English) is becoming popular in London.

   Which <u>form of English is becoming popular in London</u> ?

5 (A number of people) speak non-standard English.

   How many <u>people speak non-standard English</u> ?

6 Most native speakers (speak/don't speak) Standard English.

   <u>Do most native speakers speak Standard English</u> ?

D Go to the Grammar Hub on page 122.

E SPEAK Work in pairs. Student A – go to the Communication Hub on page 149. Student B – go to the Communication Hub on page 150.

PRONUNCIATION
Pronouncing questions

 A Listen to two people asking questions from the interview. What differences do you notice in the way they speak? Who is easier to understand?
1.10

1 *Why do you want to talk to me?*

2 *What do you want to talk about?*

a Which speaker joined the words together?　Speaker 2

b Which speaker is easier to understand?　Speaker 1

B SPEAK Work in pairs. Read the information in the box. Then practise saying the questions. First, try to say them by joining the words together. Then try to say them as clearly as possible.

- What do you think?
- Where did you go?
- Do you want to talk about it?
- Why did you say that?

Pronouncing questions

Many English speakers join words together when they speak quickly. In questions with *do/did* + *you*, it can be difficult to hear whether the speaker is saying *do* or *did*.

- *What do you want to do?* /wɒdʒə wɒnə duː/
- *How did you travel?* /haʊdʒə trævəl/

 C SPEAK Work in pairs. Listen to two people asking the questions in Exercise B. Which version is better for you to use, the first or the second speaker? Why? Tell your partner.
1.11

SPEAKING

A Work in pairs. You are going to interview another student about their experiences of using English and communicating with English speakers. Write five questions. Use the prompts to help you. You can also use your own ideas.

- often communicate / English speakers?
- using English in the classroom / in real life?
- for work / while travelling?
- problems: speaking/understanding?
- Standard/non-standard English?
- advice for others?

B Work in new pairs. Use your questions to interview your partner. Listen carefully and ask follow-up questions.

Follow-up questions

Really? Why?

What happened? What went wrong?

Can you give me an example?

C Work in groups and discuss the questions.

1 What was the most interesting thing you learnt from your interview?

2 What advice can you give to other people about using English in real life?

READING

A SPEAK Work in pairs and discuss the questions.

1 Look at the title of the magazine article. What do you think it means?

2 Think of some examples where you can lose something if you stop using it. Have you ever lost a skill or an ability because you didn't use it?

B READ FOR GIST Read *Use it or lose it?* quickly and answer the questions.

1 Is the writer generally positive or negative about learning languages?

2 What's the connection between the pictures, the word cloud and language learning?

Use it or lose it?

1 What's the worst thing about learning a language? Is it the hundreds of hours you need to spend studying and practising? No, although that's bad enough. In fact, the worst thing is how easy it is to forget everything!
Ex C
Ex C

2 How do I know? From bitter experience! Many years ago, I lived in Spain for a year and studied Spanish for hours every day. By the end of that year, I spoke Spanish fluently (but not very accurately). But now, 20 years later, it's all gone. My only evidence that I ever spoke Spanish is an old certificate.
Ex C

3 So is there any hope for me and my Spanish? Recent research suggests that there is. Imagine your brain is like a big library. As you keep adding new information to that library, the old information doesn't disappear; it just gets harder to find.
Ex C
Ex B Q2

4 How does this work in practice? When I see a dog, my English-speaking brain thinks of the word *dog*. But when I lived in Spain, my brain had two words to choose from, *dog* and *perro* (and yes, that's *dog* in Spanish!). My brain learnt to block the wrong word: it blocked *dog* when I was speaking Spanish and *perro* when I was speaking English. Over time, my brain got very good at blocking words.
Ex C

5 And what happened when I left Spain? The word *perro* stayed blocked. And, like a door that's been closed for years is harder to open, it became harder to unblock the word! Now, 20 years later, all those Spanish words are still in my brain. But they're blocked behind heavy old doors.
Ex C
Ex B Q2

6 How can I open those doors? Two things: I need to make an effort to push the doors open again; and I need to keep the doors open by practising regularly.
Ex C

7 Is there anything good to say about this 'blocking' process? In fact, there's lots of evidence that it makes your brain work better. For example, look at the words in the box. As quickly as possible, say what colour they're written in. Try it now. Did you notice how hard it was to say the colour when the
Ex C

word itself was a colour? That's because 'bad information' (the word on the page) blocked the 'good information' (the colour of the word).

8 What's the connection with language learning? It turns out that bilingual people are much better at activities like this than monolingual people, because their brains are trained to block 'bad information' quickly and accurately. And in the modern world, where we have to deal with too much information all the time, the ability to block 'bad information' is the key to success.
Ex C
Ex B Q2

9 What's the best thing about learning a language? Is it the ability to communicate with different people around the world? No, although that's amazing enough. In fact, the best thing is that it makes our brains more powerful.
Ex C
Ex C

PRONUNCIATION

A Tell students they're going to listen to two questions from the interview. Tell them to listen carefully and think about questions 1 and 2.

B Ask students to read the information in the *Pronouncing questions* box. Model the pronunciation of the questions or play the audio again to ensure students understand. Tell students to work in pairs to practise saying the questions in two different ways and to discuss the questions.

C Tell students to listen to the different pronunciations of the questions from Exercise B and then to discuss the questions in Exercise C. Elicit answers and stress that there is no right or wrong answer here!

SPEAKING

A Tell students they are going to interview another student about their experience of using English. However, first, they need to work with a different student to prepare questions. Monitor to help with language.

B Give students a new partner and tell them they're going to ask each other the questions they have prepared. Before they do this, point out the *Useful language* for asking follow-up questions. Model the pronunciation of these and get students to repeat, focusing on sounding genuinely interested. Encourage students to use these follow-up questions in their interviews.

C Put students into groups to discuss the questions. Check answers and encourage students to expand on their answers.

READING

A Write *Use it or lose it* on the board and elicit what it means (that you may lose an ability to do something if you don't practise it regularly). Put students into pairs to think of examples and then elicit ideas from the class.

B Tell students that *Use it or lose it* is the title of an article about learning languages. Focus students' attention on the pictures and elicit what they show. Set a time limit and tell students to skim the text to answer the two questions. Point out the glossary, with the definitions of *block* and *evidence* which are important to understand the text. Explain that students shouldn't worry about any other unknown vocabulary or anything else that they don't understand at this stage, as they're going to read the text again more closely later. Stress that it wouldn't be possible to read the whole text carefully in the time limit, but it is possible to answer the two questions, which is all students need to do. Stick to the time limit. Allow students to check their answers with a partner before checking as a whole class.

Possible answers:
1 *Positive (especially in the second half).*
2 *Library picture: Our brains are like a library. When we add more and more information, the old information is still there, but it gets harder to find it. That's why we feel like we forget languages that we once spoke.*
Door picture: When we don't use a foreign word for a long time, it becomes blocked by the word from our own language. After some time, it becomes hard to unblock that word, just like it's hard to open a door that's been closed for a long time.
Colourful words: This is an example of bad information (the words themselves) blocking the good information (the colour they're written in), just like words in our first language block foreign words that we're trying to remember.

METHODOLOGY HUB by Jim Scrivener

Skimming and scanning

Many activities designed to increase reading speeds are variations on the following two ideas:

• Skimming = Read quickly to get the gist of a passage (e.g. to discover key topics, main ideas, overall theme, basic structure, etc). A typical skimming task would be a general question from the teacher, such as *Is this passage about Jill's memories of summer or winter?* or *Is this story set in a school or a restaurant?* The learners would attempt to find the answer quickly, without reading every word of the passage.

• Scanning = Move eyes quickly over the text to locate a specific piece of information (e.g. a name, address, fact, price, number, date, etc) without reading the whole text or unpacking any subtleties of meaning. A common scanning activity is searching for information in a leaflet or directory, and a typical scanning task would be *What time does the Birmingham train leave?*

Skimming and scanning are both 'top-down' skills. Although scanning is involved with finding individual points from the text without reading carefully through every word of the text, the way that a reader finds that information involves some degree of processing of the overall shape and structure of the text, moving his/her eyes quickly over the whole page, searching for keywords or clues from the textual layout and the content that will enable her to focus in on smaller sections of text that she is likely to get answers from.

METHODOLOGY HUB by Jim Scrivener

How do people learn languages?

If we want to plan lessons that are more than simply random entertainment, we need a clear idea of how we think people learn language. The activities we plan can then closely reflect those things that we believe are an important part of the learning process.

The following list charts one possible explanation of a student's progress when learning a new item of language:

1 The learner doesn't know anything about the item.

2 The learner hears or reads examples of the item (maybe a number of times), but doesn't particularly notice it.

3 The learner begins to realise that there is a feature he/she doesn't fully understand.

4 The learner starts to look more closely at the item and tries to work out the formation rules and the meaning, possibly with the help of reference information, explanations or other help.

5 The learner tries to use the item in his/her own speech or writing (maybe hesitantly, probably with many errors).

6 The learner integrates the item fully into his/her own language and uses it (without thinking) relatively easily with minor errors.

C Focus students' attention on the information about rhetorical questions in the box. Check students understand what a rhetorical question is and elicit the first one in the text as an example. Tell students to find as many more in the text as they can. For weaker classes, you could tell students there are 12 and ask them to find them.

D Point out that each paragraph starts with a rhetorical question. Ask students to work in pairs to look again at the rhetorical questions in the text and discuss the answer. Check the answers as a class. Turn to TB8 where the answers are underlined.

E Give a personal example and elicit a few from the class. Put students into pairs to discuss the question. In feedback, encourage students to give their own ideas and examples.

VOCABULARY

A Focus students' attention on the sentences. Explain that the sentences come from the interview between Mona and Juan from earlier in the unit and from *Use it or lose it?*. Tell students to match the underlined words to the definitions. Check answers and check students fully understand the meaning of the words and the difference between *phrases* and *idioms*. Model and drill pronunciation.

B Direct students to the Vocabulary Hub on page 142 for further practice of vocabulary related to languages. Allow time for students to compare answers in pairs before checking each exercise. Use the Vocabulary Worksheet on W4 for extra practice.

SPEAKING HUB

A Put students into groups of three or four and tell them that they're going to give a presentation about learning and using languages. Tell each group to agree on a topic from the box or an idea of their own.

B Tell students to write three or four rhetorical questions about their topic. Give your own examples about a topic of your choice as a model. Tell students to think about how they could go on to answer the questions they write. Tell them to make notes, but stress that they shouldn't write out what they want to say word for word.

C Tell each group to give their presentation. Tell the groups who are listening to note down questions to ask the speakers after each presentation. During the presentations, note down a few instances in which students successfully used language and errors you could focus on in feedback.

D Put students into new groups to discuss the questions. Finish with whole-class feedback. You could ask whether rhetorical questions are as commonly used in the students' own language, and what students think about them as a rhetorical device.

TEACHING IDEA by David Seymour and Maria Popova

Vocabulary: Study skills

Use this activity to revise the vocabulary.

In pairs, compare the way you study, including these categories:

notes, filing, dictionaries, other reference books, speaking in class, asking questions, handouts, vocabulary learning techniques

In small groups, discuss the advice you would give to a student who wants to learn a new language. Agree on your top ten suggestions for effective study, e.g. *Keep a vocabulary notebook using different colours for different parts of speech.* Ask the teacher if you do not understand something.

TEACHING IDEA by David Seymour and Maria Popova

Vocabulary: Class contract

Use this activity to revise the vocabulary.

In small groups, make two lists of duties to help make a class effective: 1 students' duties and 2 the teacher's duties, e.g. *The students must arrive on time. The teacher must correct written work within a week.* Compare your lists with the other groups.

Which duties should go in a class contract? (Elicit ideas and write them on the board.)

TEACHING IDEA by David Seymour and Maria Popova

Speaking Hub: Languages

Listen to the countries and write the nationality and the language of each one. In small groups, compare your lists and write down any words that are new to you.

Germany (German – German)	Senegal (Senegalese – French, Pulaar, Wolof)
Peru (Peruvian – Spanish, Quechua)	Wales (Welsh – English, Welsh)
France (French – French)	Canada (Canadian – English, French, Indian)
Iran (Iranian – Farsi, Azerbaijani)	Kenya (Kenyan – English, Gikuyu, Swahili)
Holland (Dutch – Dutch)	Israel (Israeli – Hebrew, Arabic)
Japan (Japanese – Japanese)	Sweden (Swedish – Swedish)
Brazil (Brazilian – Portuguese)	Ethiopia (Ethiopian – Amharic, Tigrigna)
Turkey (Turkish – Turkish, Kurdish)	Ireland (Irish – English, Gaelic)
Switzerland (Swiss – German, French, Italian, Romance)	

C SCAN Read again. How many rhetorical questions are there? Use the information in the box to help you.

> **Rhetorical questions**
>
> A rhetorical question is a question that you ask when you don't expect other people to answer it. You often answer the question yourself. It's a useful way of presenting information because it makes the reader or listener think about the answer.
>
> When you read a rhetorical question at the beginning of a paragraph, always pause to predict the answer first. Then read the rest of the paragraph to check.

D Work in pairs. Look at the rhetorical questions at the start of each paragraph. Discuss the answers. Then read the paragraph again to check.

E SPEAK Work in pairs and discuss the questions.

What does the writer mean by 'we have to deal with too much information all the time'? Can you think of any examples from your own life?

> **Glossary**
>
> **block (v)** to stop something from moving through something else
> **evidence (n)** facts or physical signs that help to prove something

VOCABULARY
Languages

A WORK IT OUT Look at the sentences from the interview between Mona and Juan and from *Use it or lose it?* Then use the correct form of the underlined words to complete the definitions (1–5).

They used really strange words and <u>phrases</u> – lots of <u>idioms</u> that I've never heard before.

Plus, the people had very strong <u>accents</u>, so I couldn't understand very much at all!

By the end of that year, I spoke Spanish <u>fluently</u> (but not very <u>accurately</u>).

It turns out that <u>bilingual</u> people are much better at activities like this than <u>monolingual</u> people.

1 If you're ___monolingual___, you only speak one language; if you're ___bilingual___, you speak two languages.

2 A(n) ___phrase___ is a group of two or more words that go together as a unit (e.g. heavy old doors).

3 Your ___accent___ is the way you pronounce words. It sometimes shows which part of a country you are from.

4 A(n) ___idiom___ has its own meaning (e.g. 'Use it or lose it'). It's often hard to work out the meaning just by looking at the words.

5 If you speak ___fluently___, you don't pause to think in the middle of sentences. If you speak ___accurately___, you don't make mistakes.

B Go to the Vocabulary Hub on page 142.

◯ SPEAKING HUB

A Work in groups. You are going to give a short presentation about learning and using languages. Choose a topic from the list or use your own ideas. You can talk about English, your own language or both.

- accents
- standard and non-standard varieties
- advice on fluency and accuracy
- advice on how to practise
- how the language is changing
- why it's good to be bilingual

B PLAN Write three or four rhetorical questions about your topic. Then plan how you can answer those questions in a presentation. Make notes but do not write the answers down.

C PRESENT Give your presentation to the class. While you are listening to the other presentations, listen carefully and be ready to ask questions.

D REFLECT Work in groups and discuss the questions.

1 What did you learn from the presentations? What surprised you?

2 Will you use rhetorical questions again in your presentations or writing?

◯– Plan and conduct an interview
◯– Use rhetorical questions in a presentation

1.3 Welcome back

F– ask for, offer and respond to help   P– intonation and stress

COMPREHENSION

A ▶ Watch the video. Complete the sentences with the names in the box.

> Gaby   Milly   Neena   Sam   Zac

1 _____Sam_____ owns a café.
2 _____Milly_____ runs a vintage clothes shop.
3 _____Zac_____ is Sam's best friend.
4 _____Neena_____ lives with Gaby and Zac.
5 _____Zac_____ is meeting Milly's mum tomorrow.
6 _____Sam_____ agrees to lend Zac some clothes.
7 _____Gaby_____ falls over and hurts her arm.

B Work in pairs and discuss the questions.

1 Why is Gaby taking pictures?   For Sam's website
2 Why does Sam say 'Oh no Zac, I'm so sorry …'?
  thinks Milly's mum died
3 Why does Zac need to borrow some clothes?
  meeting Milly's mum
4 Why is Sam surprised when Zac asks for pants?
  pants are underwear
5 Why is Gaby worried about tomorrow?
  has a photoshoot, broken arm

C Imagine you wanted to borrow the items in the box. Who would you ask and why? Tell your partner.

> €10   €500   a belt   a book   a ladder   a scarf
> a suitcase or rucksack   some shoes or boots

FUNCTIONAL LANGUAGE
Asking for, offering and responding to help

A Complete the phrases with the correct form of *give*, *help* or *need*.

Asking for help

Could you [1] __help__ me out?
Would you mind [2] __giving__ me a hand?
Do you think you could [3] __help__ me out?
I [4] __need__ a favour. Can you lend me some clothes? Please? ☐1

Offering to help

I can [5] __give__ you a hand with that. ☐2
I'd be happy to [6] __help__ you with that.
Can I [7] __help__ you with that?
Shall I bring some stuff round to the flat later? ☐4
Do you [8] __need__ a hand? ☐6
Do you need any [9] __help__ ?

Responding to help

Thank you so much, that would be great. ☐3
That would be awesome. ☐5
If you wouldn't mind.
I can manage. I'm OK. ☐7
It's OK – I can do it myself.
Listen, let me [10] __help__ you. ☐8

B ⦿ 01:01–03:40 Watch the last part of the video. Mark the eight phrases you hear in the order in which you hear them.

MILLY

SAM

NEENA

ZAC

GABY

USEFUL PHRASES

A Match the useful phrases (1–6) with the phrases which show the meaning (a–f).

1 I'm really busy at the moment.
2 I don't know how to say this.
3 Good luck with that!
4 You're a legend!
5 I owe you one.
6 There you go.

a That isn't going to be easy.
b You are amazing!
c I must return the favour.
d I can't talk to you at the moment.
e I've finished.
f This is difficult for me to talk about.

B How do you say these useful phrases in your language?

PRONUNCIATION
Intonation and stress

A Listen and repeat the two questions in the table.
Complete the headings with *falls* or *rises*.

1 Asking for help: intonation _____rises_____.	2 Offering help: intonation _____falls_____.
Can you lend me some clothes?	Can I help you with that?
Could you help me out?	Do you need any help?
Would you mind giving me a hand?	Shall I give you a hand?

B Listen, repeat and write down each question in the correct column. Practise the stress and intonation.

SPEAKING

A Work in pairs. You are going to write and perform a conversation where you ask a friend for help. Think about the following things:

• What sort of help do you need?
• Why do you need help?
• When do you need help?
• Who do you ask?

B PRESENT Write and practise your conversation. Then perform it for the rest of the class.

○ Ask for, offer and respond to help

➤ Turn to page 156 to learn how to write a report about trends.

1.3 Welcome back

LEAD-IN

Ask students to think about the last time they asked for or offered help. Ask them to give details about who, what, when and where. Give students a minute to make notes. Give an example of your own.

COMPREHENSION

A ▶ Explain that students are going to watch an episode of a video series. Tell students they will need to complete the sentences with the name of a character. Ask them to read through the sentences before listening.

B Tell students to discuss the questions in pairs.

C Tell students who you would ask to borrow €10 from, and model the question you would ask. Do the same for €500, using a more indirect question (as it's a larger amount and a bigger favour). Students then do the same in pairs with the other items.

FUNCTIONAL LANGUAGE

A Focus students' attention on the phrases. Tell students some of them come from the video they've just watched and ask them to complete the spaces with *give*, *help* or *need*. Point out that they will need to change the form of the verb in some of them. Check answers and refer back to the language the students used in the previous task, commenting on any similarities or differences between them.

B ▶ 01:01–03:40 Point out the boxes which follow eight of the phrases. Tell students these are the phrases that appear in the video. Tell them to watch again and number the phrases in the order they hear them.

USEFUL PHRASES

A Tell students the useful phrases were all in the video. Ask them to match each one with its meaning. Model and drill pronunciation of each phrase as you check the answers.

B Ask students to think how they would say these phrases in their language. For monolingual classes, students can decide together on the best translations. In multilingual classes, students can compare how similar or different the equivalent phrases in their languages are.

PRONUNCIATION

A 1.12 Play the audio and tell students to repeat, paying careful attention to whether their voice falls or rises at the end of the questions. Tell students to complete rules 1 and 2. Emphasise the importance of sounding friendly and polite when asking for or offering help. You could demonstrate this to humorous effect by asking the questions again yourself with flat, uninterested sounding intonation and eliciting how effective that would be.

B 1.13 Play the other questions and tell students to repeat. Students then copy the questions in the correct column.

SPEAKING

A Tell students to work in pairs and imagine a situation where they would ask a friend for help. Give them time to discuss the questions.

B Tell students to write out a script of their conversation. Monitor again to help with language input. Tell students to practise their conversation in pairs, especially the rising or falling intonation. Tell each pair to perform their conversation to the class.

▶ VIDEOSCRIPT

S = Sam   G = Gaby   Z = Zac   M = Milly

S: Hey, I'm Sam. This is my café. This is Milly. She runs a clothes shop. She's dating Zac. He's my best friend.
This is Neena. She's a lawyer and she lives with Zac and … GABY! This is Gaby. She likes taking photos …

G: … And smile. Smile. Smile more … even more … EVEN MORE!

S: How's this?

G: Urgh, TOO MUCH! Stop. Good. Good! Perfect! These photos'll look great on your website.

S: Zac? Zac, hey, look I'm really busy at the moment, so …

Z: Sam, Sam! It's Zac!

S: Yeah I know! Look, I better get on …

Z: Sam! It's big news! Really big!

S: What is it?

Z: It's Milly's mom … I don't know how to say this, uh, she's … uh … she's …

S: Oh, no. Zac, I'm so sorry …

Z: She's coming to London. Tomorrow.

S: Oh, OK. You haven't met her yet, have you?

Z: No! We're meeting for lunch. Tomorrow!

S: OK, well. Good luck with that! Look, I better go now. I've got a lot of stuff to do.

Z: Wait! Listen, I need a favour, can you lend me some clothes? Please? I need to borrow a shirt, a smart jacket, some pants …

S: Pants?

Z: Oh, OK – trousers.

M: And a tie!

Z: Did you hear that?

S: What?

Z: And a tie! And some shoes.

S: You don't have any shoes?

Z: Well yeah, but … I need some smart shoes … Do you think you could help me out?

S: Sure, I can give you a hand with that.

Z: Thank you SO much, that would be great – you're a legend!

S: I am. Shall I bring some stuff round to the flat later?

Z: That would be awesome. I owe you one.

S: You owe me more than one. Gaby! Are you OK? Do you need a hand?

G: No, I can manage. I'm OK.

S: Listen, let me help you.

G: OK … I think it's OK.

S: Does this hurt?

G: No.

S: How about this?

G: ARGH!

S: There you go. Should be OK in a few days.

G: A few days … Oh, no! I've got a photo shoot tomorrow. What am I going to do?

1 Writing ⬤—Write a report about trends

W— using formal language in reports

A Work in groups of three. Discuss the questions and complete the *Me*, *Partner 1* and *Partner 2* columns in the table.

1 How much time do you spend doing each activity in the table each week?

2 Are you spending more (↑), less (↓) or the same (↔) time on each activity at the moment, compared to last year?

	Me	Partner 1	Partner 2	Average
	hours	hours	hours	hours
checking social media				
sending instant messages				
studying online				

B Now work out the average number of hours spent doing each activity. Are people spending more or less time on each activity compared to last year? Complete the *Average* column of the table in Exercise A.

C Read the *Report about online trends* and answer the questions.

1 What trends did the writer find? Did you find the same trends?

2 What was different?

3 What is the writer's main prediction for the future?

Report about online trends

¹These days, online communication is more and more important in our daily lives. ²But are we actually spending more time online? ³<u>This report examines</u> the number of hours that people spend on <u>various</u> online activities and explores some recent trends. ⁴I interviewed eight members of my English class about their online habits.

How much time do you spend checking social media?

The average number of hours in my group is just over one hour per day. This is surprising, as I expected the total to be higher. <u>One possible reason is that</u> several popular social media sites are showing more adverts these days.

How much time do you spend sending instant messages?

The average number of hours here is <u>approximately</u> 1.5 hours per day. Almost everybody said that this number is increasing for them. <u>It seems that</u> many people are using instant messaging services for conversations that they had on social media before.

How much time do you spend studying online?

The average number of hours here was 4.3 per week. Two people in my group never study online, and this trend is not changing. Two people study online a lot: 12 and 15 hours a week. This trend is also not changing, as these people both study on long-term courses. However, the other three people's answers were <u>especially</u> interesting: they all spend two to three hours a week studying, but this is increasing very fast, from zero last year. They all use language learning apps to study for pleasure.

Conclusion

<u>There certainly seems to be</u> a trend away from social media and towards messaging apps. <u>However,</u> the main trend I noticed is the increase in online studying, especially the use of language apps. I expect this trend to continue into the future.

156 WRITING

D Look at the introduction to the *Report about online trends*. Match the sentences (1–4) with the descriptions (a–d).

4 a Explain where you got your information, e.g. *Who did you ask?*

2 b Ask a rhetorical question to make the reader think about the topic.

3 c Present your reason for writing the report: what does the report do?

1 d Start by introducing the general topic of your report.

E Look at the box and complete the tips about using formal language in reports. Then find examples of each tip in the report.

> **Using formal language in reports**
>
> We *use /*don't use* contractions (e.g. *there's, isn't*).
> In general, most sentences are quite *long/ short*.
> Most sentences have *a human subject, e.g. I, Two people / a non-human subject, e.g. It, This trend.*

F Match the formal phrases (1–7), which are underlined in the *Report about online trends*, with the less formal phrases (a–g).

d 1 This report examines …   a but

f 2 various   b more or less

c 3 One possible reason is that …   c Maybe this is because …

b 4 approximately   d In this report, I look at …

e 5 It seems that … / There certainly seems to be …   e I think …

g 6 especially   f a few different

a 7 However, …   g very

WRITING

A PREPARE You are going to write a report about current trends in communication. What trends do you notice? You can use the ideas in Exercise A or your own ideas.

B PLAN Choose two or three points to include in your report. These will be your main paragraphs.

C WRITE Write your report (150–200 words). Remember:

- to start with an introduction.
- when you present numbers, show what they mean and how they're connected together.
- to use formal language.
- to end with a conclusion.

D REVIEW Work in groups. Share your reports. Who found the most interesting information? Were you surprised by any of the trends he/she found?

Answers

1 The writer found that the average amount of time people are spending on social media is one hour per day. The trend is that people are spending less time using social media. The average amount of time people are spending sending instant messages is 1.5 hours a day. People's usage is going up. The average amount of time people are spending studying online is 4.3 hours per week. For most people, there's no change, but for some people, the number is increasing fast. So overall, there's a small increase.

3 That people will use more and more online study, especially language-learning apps.

> Refer students to this report as a model for the writing task.

> Ask students to compare their reports in small groups.

WRITING

On the left-hand side of the board, write the following words randomly in a circle: *social, instant, study, messaging*. Then on the right-hand side of the board, write the following words in random order in another circle: *media, messages, online, app*. Give students a few moments to pair the words up to make collocations (*social media, instant messages, study online, messaging app*). Then ask students to tell their partner if they do use these things and how much time they devote to them.

A Start by giving your own personal answers to the questions. Then put students into groups of three to discuss the questions and complete the table.

B Check students understand the meaning of *average*, then ask them to complete the *Average* column of the table. Ask students to discuss any interesting findings.

C Check students remember the meaning of *trends* from earlier in the unit and elicit an example of one. Tell students they're going to read a report about trends. Check understanding of *a prediction*, then ask students to read and answer the questions.

D Tell students to read the introduction (first paragraph) of the text again and to match the sentences labelled 1–4 to the descriptions a–d.

E Focus students' attention on the tips for using formal language in reports. Elicit the first answer and an example from the class. Tell students to complete the remaining tips and to find further examples of each in the report.

F Tell students that all the formal phrases are used in the report. Tell them to match each with the less formal equivalent.

WRITING TASK

A Give students some time to choose a trend to write about.

B Tell students to choose two or three main points to include. They should also write an introduction.

C Tell students to write their report.

D Put students into groups to share their reports. Finish with feedback on the content, organisation and language in the reports.

GRAMMAR

A Complete the social media update with the present simple or present continuous form of the verbs in brackets.

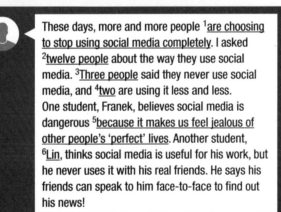

I'm in Moscow! As you can see in the picture,
I [1] _'m having_ (have)
a coffee with some of my new friends.
I [2] _'m studying_ (study)
here on a two-week intensive language course.
I [3] _'m really enjoying_ (really enjoy)
it so far.
I [4] _don't speak_ (not speak)
very much Russian at all, so it was
really difficult on the first day, but now it
[5] _'s getting_ (get)
easier every day, and my teachers are excellent.
Why Russian? Well, firstly, I
[6] _think_ (think)
it's a beautiful language, and secondly,
I [7] _'m considering_ (consider)
studying at university here next year.

B Read part of a report about social media trends. Then write questions about the underlined information in the report. Use the prompts to help you.

These days, more and more people [1]are choosing to stop using social media completely. I asked [2]twelve people about the way they use social media. [3]Three people said they never use social media, and [4]two are using it less and less. One student, Franek, believes social media is dangerous [5]because it makes us feel jealous of other people's 'perfect' lives. Another student, [6]Lin, thinks social media is useful for his work, but he never uses it with his real friends. He says his friends can speak to him face-to-face to find out his news!

1 What / more and more people / do / these days?
   What are more and more people doing these days?

2 How many people / the writer / ask / about the way they use social media? _How many people did the writer ask about the way they use social media?_

3 How many people / say / they never use social media?
   How many people said they never use social media?

4 How many people / use / social media less and less?
   How many people are using social media less and less?

5 Why / Franek / believe / social media is dangerous?
   Why does Franek believe social media is dangerous?

6 Who / think / social media is useful for work?
   Who thinks social media is useful for work?

VOCABULARY

A Complete the sentences with the correct form of the verbs in the box.

hear   listen   look   see   sound   watch

1 **A:** 'I think we should go soon.'
   B: 'Yes, that _sounds_ like a good idea.'

2 I prefer normal phone calls to video calls – it's better when the other person can _hear_ you, but they can't _see_ you!

3 Excuse me. I _'m looking_ for my dog. I can't find him anywhere. Have you seen him?

4 I usually _listen_ to podcasts while I'm travelling to work.

5 Can I call you back later? I _'m watching_ a TV programme and I don't want to miss the end.

B Choose the correct words to complete the conversation.

A: Ah, this is nice, just sitting outside a café and relaxing. I think it's really interesting to [1]_observe_ / recognise / stare all the people in the street.

B: Yes, but be careful. It looks like you're [2]noticing / spotting / _staring_ at other people a bit too much. It's quite rude.

A: Don't worry! They're too busy to [3]_notice_ / observe / recognise me! They're all looking at their phones, anyway!

C Read about five English-speaking friends. Then answer the questions.

Angela only speaks English and no other languages.

You can hear that **Brian** is from New Zealand because of the way he pronounces *ed*.

When **Eryk** is speaking English, he doesn't make many mistakes.

Francesca speaks English as well as Italian.

George loves using phrases like 'use it or lose it' and 'plan B'.

1 Who speaks accurately?   _Eryk_
2 Who's monolingual?   _Angela_
3 Who likes idioms?   _George_
4 Who's bilingual?   _Francesca_
5 Who has a strong accent?   _Brian_

FUNCTIONAL LANGUAGE

Complete the dialogues with the words in the box.

busy   could   favour   hand   help   mind   want

1 **A:** Hey, Gary, I need a _favour_. Have you got a few minutes?
   B: Sorry, Paul, I'm really _busy_ right now.

2 **A:** Do you think you _could_ help me write this?
   B: Sure, I can give you a _hand_ with that.

3 **A:** Do you _want_ me to have a look at that?
   B: If you wouldn't _mind_.

4 **A:** Hi, Sam. If you aren't busy, I could use your _help_ with my application letter.
   B: Sure.

2 Experiences

2 EXPERIENCES

Experience (n) something that happens to you or a situation that you are involved in. Synonyms: situation (n), circumstance (n)

Nothing is a waste of time if you use the experience wisely.

Auguste Rodin

Skydiver in mid-air over Southern Australia.

The quote for this unit is about learning from your experiences, whether they are positive or negative, and gaining wisdom as a result.

Auguste Rodin (1840–1917) was a French sculptor, most famous for the sculpture *The Thinker*. His style and ideas were ahead of their time, and he was involved in a lot of controversy during his life and career.

OBJECTIVES

- talk about past experiences and things you want to do
- talk about a life-changing decision
- talk about an inspirational person
- talk about solving a problem
- ask for, give and refuse permission
- write an informal email

Work with a partner. Discuss the questions.

1 Look at the picture. What do you think of the activity the person is doing?

2 Read the quote. What do you think it means?

3 Tell your partner about experiences you have had that were:

- incredible
- unusual
- risky
- memorable
- eye-opening
- thrilling

EXPERIENCES 13

OBJECTIVES

Read the unit objectives to the class.

UNIT OPENER QUESTIONS

With books closed, write the word *experience* on the board and elicit collocations. You could give an example of *an amazing experience*. When you have a few more on the board, put students into pairs to think of an example of each type of experience.

1 Focus students' attention on the picture and elicit their reactions. Have they ever done the activity shown? If so, did they enjoy it? Would they do it again? If not, would they like to try it? Why / Why not?

2 Tell students to read the quote and discuss in pairs what they think it means. Elicit answers, encouraging students to interpret the quote for themselves and in their own words. Ask if students agree with the idea expressed in the quote.

3 Check students understand the adjectives. Give examples to help them understand where necessary. Tell students to tell their partners about their own experiences. Elicit ideas in open class. Pay attention to how confidently and accurately students use past simple and present perfect. This will indicate if students need a lot of clarification or just some consolidation when studying the grammar later in the unit.

WORKSHEETS

Lesson 2.1 Important decisions

Grammar: Present perfect simple and past simple (W5)

Vocabulary: Collocations: making big decisions (W6)

Lesson 2.2 You can do it!

Grammar: Present and past ability (W7)

Vocabulary: Dependent prepositions (verb/adjective + *for/of*) (W8)

2.1 Important decisions

● Talk about past experiences and things you want to ○
● Talk about a life-changing decision

G — present perfect simple and past simple   P — 's and 've   V — collocations: making big decisions
S — listening for the main idea

READING

A Match the different types of lists (1–5) with the examples (a–e).

c **1** list of favourite things, e.g. films, songs   e **4** list of pros and cons

a **2** shopping list   d **5** bucket list

b **3** everyday to-do list

a
- bananas
- cheese
- yoghurt

b
1 Phone Mum
2 Email the bank
3 Pay rent

c
1 Toy Story
2 X-Men
3 Beauty and the Beast

d
1 Swim with dolphins
2 Learn to surf
3 Do a parachute jump

e
For: cheaper / easy to find
Against: poor quality / ordinary

B SPEAK Work in pairs. How often do you make lists? What types of lists do you make? Why?

C READ FOR GIST Read *Not yet? No more!* and answer the questions.

1 Which sentence summarises the blogger's opinion?

   a A bucket list is a great idea, but remember that you probably can't do all those things in your lifetime.

   (b) Make a list of things that are possible to do rather than a list of dreams.

   c People write bucket lists just for fun and to dream a little, not in order to actually do those things.

2 How many of the people commenting on the blog agree with the writer? two people - the first and third

Not yet? No more!

About me / Recent posts / Archive

posted by Julia
16th November | Leave a comment

Have you ever written a bucket list? If so, have you done many of those incredible things on your list? I certainly haven't.

I wrote mine on New Year's Day five years ago, and I chose 50 things, like swimming with dolphins and climbing Mount Everest. However, after all these years, I've only done one thing on that list. Last year, I watched the sun rise and set on the same day. I still haven't swum with dolphins. I still haven't climbed Everest. And, I think I never will!

The problem is that you need an infinite amount of time and money to do all those incredible things or to learn those skills. I've simply never had that time and money. What is the point in making an unachievable list? How does that improve your life?

So, this is my achievable bucket list blog. The aim is still to do unusual things that are positive and life-enhancing, but without needing to be a millionaire or to have all the time in the world to achieve these goals.

Here's the start of my list. I haven't done any of these things yet, but I think I can in the future. What do you think? Achievable? Life-enhancing?

- Plant a tree.
- Do a charity walk or run.
- Write a poem.
- Learn how to make a fire in the wild.
- Ride a horse.
- Eat nothing but fresh food for a week.
- Stop using social media for two weeks.
- Learn and perform a magic trick.

Comments:

Yuka W

Thanks! Before I read this, my bucket list was only expensive travel ideas. I've just written a new list of interesting but doable things!   Ex C Q2

dream_catcher77

Actually, I think a bucket list should be about amazing things. I wrote mine last year and I've already done half of it. This year, I've seen lions in the wild and I've done a parachute jump. Next month, the Pyramids! All because they're on my list.

Robin Stannard

Also, sometimes those incredible things are not so great. I've swum with dolphins. It was rubbish! I'd rather swim with   Ex C Q2
my friends. Keep it simple – it's still special ;-)

LEAD-IN

Elicit one example of a type of list. Tell students to think of as many more examples as they can in one minute.

READING

A Tell students to open their books and to see if any of their ideas are the same as those listed. Tell them to match the type of lists with the examples.

B Put students into pairs to discuss how often they make lists and which kind. Monitor and encourage students to explain why they do or don't make certain kinds of lists.

C Set a time limit. Make it clear that students don't need to read and understand everything at this stage. Students should just choose the correct summary and find out how many comments agree with the writer.

TEACHING IDEA by David Seymour and Maria Popova

Topic: Life plans

Use this activity to extend the topic.

Look at this pattern and write some more sentences that are true for you, e.g. *When it stops raining, I'll go out. As soon as he phones, I'll let you know.*

when	
as soon as	+ present future
until	
before	

Write some more examples using these verbs.

> arrive, end (this lesson), start work, get up, finish job, go out, finish, be ready, get married, have dinner, do homework

In pairs, tell each other about your own expectations using *going to* for plans, e.g. *As soon as my English is good enough, I'm going to go back home and get a good job.*

In pairs, continue this sequence, e.g. *As soon as I pass my exams, I'll go to college. When I leave college, I'm going to go travelling. I'll keep travelling until my money runs out …* Try to make it go somewhere interesting, e.g. *into an extremely adventurous life, a lucky one*, etc.

pass exams –> leave college –> go travelling –> live in India …

GRAMMAR HUB

2.1 Present perfect simple and past simple

	Positive	Negative	Question
Present perfect simple	**Wilhelm has climbed** Mt Everest before. **We've visited** the Pyramids already.	**I haven't been** sailing before. **Paula hasn't made** a bucket list yet.	**Have you** ever **met** a movie star? **Have they** already **bought** the flight?
Past simple	**Wilhelm climbed** Mt Everest last month. **We visited** Yosemite National Park a year ago.	**I didn't go** sailing last weekend. **Paula didn't move** out of her parents' house a week ago.	**Did you meet** a movie star yesterday? **Did they buy** the flight?

- We use the present perfect simple for actions completed during a period of time that continues to now.

  Juan has been in Asia for three months so far.
  = He's still there.

- We also use the present perfect simple for actions completed before now when we don't say exactly when.

  She has already written out a bucket list.
  NOT She already wrote out her bucket list.

- We often use time expressions such as *before, already, just* and *yet* with the present perfect simple.

  Have you finished your exams yet?

- We use the past simple for actions completed during a finished period of time or at a specific time in the past.

  Did you stop using your social media account last week?

- We often use time expressions such as *yesterday, two days / a week, a month ago,* or *last week/month/year* with the past simple.

- If we use a specific time reference, we usually use the past simple.

  She's just won a free holiday. BUT She won a free holiday a moment ago.
  Henri has already booked a flight to India. BUT Henri booked a flight to India yesterday.

D Tell students to read the text again more slowly and carefully and then answer the questions.

E Put students into pairs to share their opinions about the text. Monitor and draw out any different views students have and encourage them to expand on them.

GRAMMAR

A Tell students the sentences are all from the blog they've just read. To check students are familiar with the terminology, ask them to underline the past simple verbs and circle the present perfect simple verbs. Explain that identifying the structures is, of course, not as important as understanding why they're used. Tell students to match the sentences to the timelines. In feedback, check students understand what the different parts of the timelines represent. A lot of students find timelines very helpful, but some can find them confusing. The key thing is to make sure the connection between the events in the sentences and the way they're represented on the timelines is explicit.

B Tell students to look back at the blog and find the adverbs of time from the box. Tell students to look at the way the adverbs are used in context to help them match them with the definitions.

C Tell students to look back at the example sentences, timelines and definitions from Exercises A and B to help them complete the rules. In feedback, elicit which sentences from Exercises A and B are examples of each rule.

D Direct students to the **Grammar Hub** on pages 124 and 125 (see TB14 and below). Use the **Grammar Worksheet** on W5 for extra practice.

PRONUNCIATION

🔊
2.1
Tell students to listen carefully to the pairs of sentences to identify which one is in the present perfect simple. If students find this difficult, ask why. Elicit that the contracted auxiliaries *'s* and *'ve* are unstressed and hard to hear. Play the audio again if necessary to give students more practice at picking up the sounds. Drill pronunciation with the students.

SPEAKING

A Put students into pairs and tell student A to turn to the **Communication Hub** on page 148 and student B to turn to page 153. Tell students to find out if their partner has done any of the things on their list, and if so, to find out more details. Model the task and elicit the questions students will need to ask such as *Have you ever …?* for the initial question followed by *Where / When / How did you …?* to find out more information.

B Tell students they're now going to write their own achievable bucket list. Tell students to choose eight things, either from the lists they've just read or using their own ideas. Remind students that they must be achievable but also positive and life-enhancing. You could give examples of absurd or mundane ideas and elicit if these would be appropriate, so students are clear what not to include. Monitor to check students are on task and to help with language if necessary.

C Put students into bigger groups to compare their ideas. Tell them they must agree on ten things for their group bucket list. If students have very different ideas, encourage them to argue the case for the inclusion of theirs, but also make sure students realise that they are aiming to reach a consensus so compromise may be necessary. Monitor as they do this, noting errors and good language use to highlight in feedback.

D Put students into new groups containing one representative of each previous group. Tell them to explain their lists to each other and justify their choices.

Extra activity

You can keep the bucket lists in the classroom and use these as a spring board for further activities. Writing tasks can involve students recording their experiences of completing a task on the bucket list, or even recording them on a blog.

Students can also report back on their experiences at the start of a class. You can ask them how they felt before, during and after doing something from the list.

GRAMMAR HUB

2.1 Present perfect simple and past simple

A Choose the correct option.

1 I (have swum) / swam with dolphins before.

2 Martin (dreamt) / has dreamt about the pyramids last night.

3 We (haven't climbed) / didn't climb Mt Everest yet.

4 Did you hear / (Have you heard) Leon's good news already?

5 (Did Zac learn) / Has Zac learnt how to make a fire at camp last summer?

6 (Have you ever taken) / Did you ever take a trip abroad?

B Correct the mistakes in each sentence. Use contractions where possible.

1 She ~~has seen~~ a beautiful sunset last week. *saw*

2 They ~~made~~ a short film already. *'ve* (inserted)

3 Molly ~~didn't prepare~~ a list yet. *hasn't prepared*

4 Mohammed ~~travelled never~~ around Asia before. *'s never travelled*

5 ~~Did you deal~~ with a serious problem before? *Have you dealt*

6 He ~~has come~~ up with a smart plan yesterday. *came*

C Complete each sentence with the correct form of the verb in brackets.

1 Giralt _has never been_ (never / be) to America.

2 Dan _has just finished_ (just / finish) a charity walk.

3 Katerina worked hard but she **didn't achieve/did not achieve** (not / achieve) her goal.

4 When the time was right, the chess champion ___put___ (put) his plan into action.

5 _Have you read_ (you / read) other people's bucket lists before?

6 I ___'ve/have already done___ (already / do) two parachute jumps this year.

➤ Go back to page 15.

D READ FOR DETAIL Read again. Answer the questions.

1 How many things on her first bucket list has the writer not done? 49

2 Why is it not possible to do all the things on a typical bucket list? You need a lot of time and money.

3 How is her new list similar to her original list?
It has positive activities.
4 How many outdoor activities are there on her new list? Four

E SPEAK Work in pairs. Read again and discuss the questions.

1 Are the writer's choices good ideas for an achievable bucket list?

2 Which choices do you like most and why?

GRAMMAR
Present perfect simple and past simple

A WORK IT OUT Look at the sentences (1–4) from *Not yet? No more!* Underline the verbs in the past simple and circle the verbs in the present perfect simple. Then match each sentence with a diagram (a–d).

1 I wrote mine on New Year's Day five years ago. b

2 (I've only done) one thing on that list. a

3 This year, (I've seen) lions in the wild. d

4 Last year, I watched the sun rise and set on the same day. c

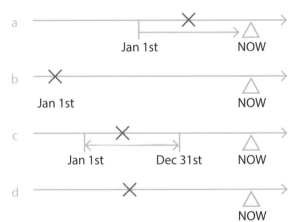

a ⟶ ✕ ⟶ △
   Jan 1st   NOW

b ✕ ⟶ △
   Jan 1st   NOW

c ⟶ ✕ ⟶ △
   Jan 1st   Dec 31st   NOW

d ⟶ ✕ ⟶
              △
              NOW

B Look at the adverbs of time in the box. Can you find them in the blog? Match the adverbs with the definitions (1–5).

> already   just   never   not yet   still

1 at no time in the past ____never____

2 a short time ago ____just____

3 a situation has not changed or not completely ended ____still____

4 not happened before now, but will probably happen ____not yet____

5 happened before a point in time, perhaps sooner than expected ____already____

C Complete the rules with *present perfect simple* or *past simple*.

Present perfect simple and past simple
For actions that we completed:

during a finished period of time, we use the
1 _____past simple_____.

during a period of time that continues to now, we use the
2 _____present perfect simple_____.

at a specific time in the past, we use the
3 _____past simple_____.

before now, but we do not say exactly when, we use the
4 _____present perfect simple_____.

We often use adverbs of time with these tenses, but we do not use *yet* and *already* with actions in the
5 _____past simple_____.

D Go to the Grammar Hub on page 124.

PRONUNCIATION
's and 've

🔊 Listen to the pairs of sentences (1–6). Which sentence (a or
2.1 b) is in the present perfect simple?

1	b	3	b	5	a
2	a	4	b	6	a

SPEAKING

A Work in pairs. You are going to write an achievable bucket list. Student A – read the bucket list on page 148. Student B – read the list on page 153. Has your partner done any of the things on your list? If they have, find out more details.

B Work in pairs. Choose eight things to put on your achievable bucket list. Use the ideas on the lists and your own ideas. They should be positive, life-enhancing and achievable.

C Work in groups. Compare your lists and choose ten things for a group bucket list.

D Compare your list with another group. Are their ideas the same or different?

a cruise along canals, freshwater, houseboat

b cross oceans, saltwater, yacht

LISTENING

A Match the words and phrases in the box with the pictures (a–b).

> cross oceans cruise along canals
> freshwater houseboat saltwater yacht

B SPEAK Work in pairs and discuss the questions.

1 Have you ever been on a boat? If so, what kind?

2 Which of the two boats in the pictures would you prefer to travel on?

C LISTEN FOR GIST Look at the pictures (a and b) and
2.2 listen to a podcast interview with Emma. Complete the sentences with *a* or *b*.

1 Picture _b_ shows Emma's ultimate dream.

2 Picture _a_ shows Emma's current reality.

D Listen again. Which of the phrases (1–8) from the podcast
2.2 are the main ideas of Emma's story? Use the strategies in the box to help you.

1 I love swimming

2 yachts are very expensive

③ to make a decision to put a plan into action

4 it won't take me around the world

⑤ to stay motivated and not lose heart

6 learning to live in a small space

⑦ doing something similar to my dream, it's a start

⑧ the hardest part of any journey is the first step

Listening for the main idea

To help you catch the main ideas of a conversation, listen out for common expressions that we use to introduce a main idea.

- *The most important thing here …*
- *Well, it is important to note …*
- *And I stress the importance of …*

Listen out for common words and phrases that we use to talk about things generally.

- *in general, overall, on the whole*

We often speak more slowly or loudly when we want to emphasise a main idea.

E LISTEN FOR DETAIL Listen again. Find and correct six
2.2 mistakes in the summary of Emma's story.

> 35
> Emma is 33 and she works in the sailing industry.   advertising
> She loves swimming and fishing. For the last few   diving
> years, she's been learning how to sail. Her dream is to
> live on a yacht and sail around the world. She hasn't
> bought a yacht yet because she can't find one that   they are expensive
> she likes. She sold her house and bought a houseboat.
> The houseboat is an opportunity for Emma to learn to
> live on the sea and move from place to place. She is   water
> happy with her decision to buy a houseboat because it
> means that she has 'made the break' from the water to
> the land.   the land to the water

F SPEAK Work in groups and discuss the questions.

1 Do you agree that living on a houseboat will help Emma to achieve her ultimate dream? Give reasons.

2 What are the pros and cons of living on a houseboat compared to living on land?

2.1 Important decisions

LEAD-IN

With books closed, ask students to write down as many words connected to water as they can. You could help by giving prompts, e.g. types of water, ways of travelling on water, etc.

LISTENING

A Tell students to open their books and check if any of the words are the same as those the students thought of. Focus students' attention on the pictures and ask them to match the words and phrases to picture a or b. Check answers as a whole class. Drill pronunciation of *oceans, canals* and *yacht*.

B Put students into pairs to discuss the questions. Encourage them to ask follow-up questions to show interest in each other's comments and opinions. Do the same when you get feedback from the class.

C Tell students the pictures are related to a podcast. Ask them to listen and match the pictures to the sentences.

D Point out listening strategies to help understand the main idea of a conversation. Tell students some of the expressions were used in the podcast, so they should listen out for them to help with the task. Ask students to read through the phrases and try to remember the main ideas of the story before they listen to the podcast again and check. In feedback, elicit not just the answers but what made the students decide they were the main ideas. You could drill pronunciation of these phrases, highlighting the intonation used. This will raise students' awareness of these features and start to build their confidence to use them in their own speaking.

E Tell students to read the summary and correct the six factual mistakes in it. They can then listen once more to check before you check answers as a whole class.

F Put students into groups to discuss the questions. Encourage them to give reasons to support their opinions. In feedback, record useful language that comes up on the board.

AUDIOSCRIPT

 2.2

Listening, Exercise C
I = Interviewer   E = Emma

I: Welcome to Dreams Come True, the podcast that finds out about people's life-long dreams and how they've turned them into reality. My guest in the studio today is Emma Sykes from Kent.

E: Hello, thanks for having me!

Ex E **I:** Glad you could be here. Now, Emma, you are 35 Ex E and you are the owner of a successful advertising agency, is that right?

E: Yes, that's right.

I: So you've already had a lot of success in your life.

E: Yes, you could say that. I've worked very hard and the agency is doing well, but I still have dreams – well, one dream anyway.

I: And I believe that dream involves big plans on water! Tell us a bit more about it.

E: That's right, John. Ever since I was young, I've been
Ex E fascinated by the water. I love swimming and diving, and for the last few years I've been learning how to sail. My ultimate dream, the thing I've wanted to achieve my whole life, is to live on a yacht and sail around the world.

I: Wow, that's quite a dream! And it doesn't sound easy. Tell us, just how have you made this dream a reality?

E: Well, that's the thing … I haven't. Not yet. Not completely.

I: So, you haven't sailed around the world?

E: No, I haven't. It's just not practical at this time in my
Ex E life. Yachts are very expensive. I've raised quite a bit of money, but not enough yet. Plus, I don't have enough skills or knowledge yet to go sailing on my own across the oceans.

I: Well, that does sound quite complicated! So how do you keep going with your plan when it seems so far away?

Ex D **E:** For me, the most important thing is to make a decision to put a plan into action. Once you've made the decision, you can set short-term and long-term goals that will help you achieve your dream.

I: I see. Yes, that's a good point. So what are some of your short-term goals? How are you going to work towards that ultimate goal?

E: Well, there's the sailing lessons, obviously. But actually, I've turned one part of the dream into reality already.

I: Really? What's that?

E: A year ago, I sold my house and used some of the money to buy a houseboat. It isn't a yacht, and it won't take me around the world, but it's a home and it's on the water. OK, I'm on freshwater, not saltwater, but I now live on a boat.

I: Wow, that is already quite a big change! But does living on a houseboat really prepare you for sailing around the world?

Ex D **E:** Yes, I think so. The important thing here is to stay motivated and not lose heart, and this step helps me to do that.

I: And of course, you're getting some experience of what it's like to live on the water.

Ex E **E:** Exactly! I'm learning to live in a small space, and I'm also finding out what it's like to live in a home that can move from place to place. OK, I'm cruising along
Ex D canals, not crossing oceans, but doing something similar to my dream – it's a start.

I: And now that you've made that start, do you think your plan to sail around the world is more achievable?

Ex D **E:** Absolutely. On the whole, I think the hardest part of any journey is the first step. Now that I've made the break from the land to the water, I'll be able to take the next step of my journey with more confidence.

I: Well, thank you for coming to talk to us, Emma. I hope you can join us again once you've achieved your ultimate dream. Will you do that?

E: Yes, of course. I look forward to it.

I: Thank you, Emma. Now, next up, I'll be speaking to …

VOCABULARY

A Tell students to look at the verbs and phrases and explain that they were all used in the podcast. Tell students to match each verb to a phrase and point out that one verb can be used twice. Check answers as a whole class, ensuring students understand the meaning of the phrases. The best way to do this would be to refer back to how they were used in the *Listening* to provide useful context to help students grasp the meaning. Tell students that these are all collocation words which are commonly used together. There isn't a rule for why certain words go together. Students should record collocations from here and elsewhere. They could experiment in recording them in different ways to see which method is most effective for remembering them.

B Tell students to look at the photos of the three people talking about a life-changing decision they've made. Tell students to complete the gaps in the stories with the collocations from Exercise A.

C Play the audio for students to check. In feedback, use these new stories for further context to consolidate understanding of any items that students found difficult to understand at first. Drill pronunciation of the collocations either by modelling them yourself or using the recording.

2.3

D Put students into pairs to discuss which they think are the most and least achievable decisions. Monitor and encourage debate if students have different opinions. Use the **Vocabulary Worksheet** on W6 for extra practice.

SPEAKING HUB

A Tell students to think about a life-changing decision they have made, using either the ideas provided or their own. Check they all understand the vocabulary, e.g. *fitter* and *retrain*.

B Give students time to plan what they're going to say, making notes about each of the prompts. Be clear that students shouldn't write out what they're going to say word for word. Monitor to help with language input. Tell fast finishers to rehearse what they're going to say in their heads, referring to their notes.

C Tell students to interview their partner about their decision. Elicit how students can turn the prompts into questions to ask during the interview. Remind students about the methods of highlighting the main ideas of a story from the *Listening*. If time permits, change partners and tell students to interview each other again. Repeating a speaking task can build students' confidence. Students refine the language they use and speak more fluently once their ideas are consolidated.

D Put students into new groups to tell each other the decisions they heard about. When they have all shared the stories, ask them to decide which was the most life-changing and why. If a group reaches a consensus early, they can rank all the decisions. Monitor and get the class to share in any really positive experiences, giving them time to ask each other any questions they may have.

METHODOLOGY HUB by Jim Scrivener

Guidelines for listening skills work in class

- Keep the recording short: two minutes of recorded material is enough to provide a lot of listening work.

- Play the recording a sufficient number of times. (This is one point that teacher trainers and supervisors often comment on when they observe teachers' lessons: the teachers did not give the students enough opportunities to hear the recording. The students found the material a lot more difficult than the teacher realised.)

- Let students discuss their answers together (perhaps in pairs).

- Don't immediately acknowledge correct answers with words or facial expressions; throw the answers back to the class: What do you think of Claire's answer – do you agree?

- Don't be led by one strong student. Have they all got it?

- Aim to get the students to agree together without your help, using verbal prodding, raised eyebrows, nods, hints, etc. Play the recording again whenever they need to hear it, to confirm or refute their ideas, until they agree.

- Play little bits of the recording (a word, a phrase, a sentence) again and again until it's clear.

- Give help if they are completely stuck – but still with the aim of getting them to work it out if at all possible (e.g. *There are three words in this sentence* or *Listen to what she says here*) rather than giving them the answers.

- Consider giving the students control of the recording – to listen when and to what they wish.

- Don't cheat them by changing your requirements halfway, i.e. don't set one task, but then afterwards ask for answers to something completely different!

- Don't let them lose heart. Try to make sure the task is just within their abilities. It should be difficult, but achievable. The sense of achievement in finishing a task should be great: *It was difficult, but we did it!*

VOCABULARY
Collocations: making big decisions

A Match the verbs (1–8) with the phrases (a–i) to make collocations that Emma used in her interview. One verb can be used twice. Use the audioscript on **page 167** to help you.

1 lose   **a** a decision
2 make   **b** a plan into action
3 put   **c** short-term and long-term goals
4 set   **d** towards a goal
5 stay   **e** a dream into reality
6 take   **f** motivated
7 turn   **g** the break/change
8 work   **h** the next step
    i heart

B Read the information from the people (1–3) about a life-changing decision. Complete the gaps with collocations from Exercise A in the correct form.

C Listen and check your answers.

D SPEAK Work in pairs. Which decision in Exercise C do you think is the most achievable? Which is the least achievable? Give reasons.

SPEAKING HUB

A Think about a life-changing decision that you have made. Use the ideas below to help you.

- moving home (changing cities/countries)
- studying (a new course, retraining, learning a new skill)
- a lifestyle change (becoming healthier, fitter, more relaxed)
- turning a dream into reality

B PLAN Make notes about your decision. Think about:

- why you made the decision.
- how you put it into action.
- short-term/long-term goals.
- how you feel about the decision now.
- any advice you can give related to your decision.

C SPEAK Work in pairs. Interview your partner about his/her life-changing decision. Use your ideas in Exercise B to help you. Take turns.

D REFLECT Work in groups. Tell the group about your partner's decision. Then discuss all of the decisions. Whose decision was the most life-changing?

1

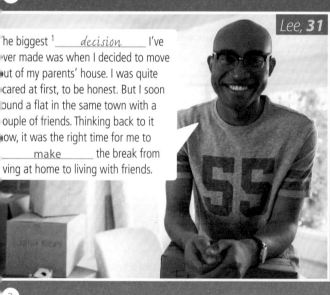

The biggest ¹ _____decision_____ I've ever made was when I decided to move out of my parents' house. I was quite scared at first, to be honest. But I soon found a flat in the same town with a couple of friends. Thinking back to it now, it was the right time for me to _____make_____ the break from living at home to living with friends.

Lee, 31

2

Three years ago, I decided to climb El Capitan in Yosemite National Park. It was always one of those things on my bucket list. Since I started to put the ³ _____plan_____ into action, I've learnt a lot about climbing and myself. My advice? Never ⁴ _____lose_____ heart! If you are ⁵ _____working_____ towards a goal, you'll achieve it in the end. I haven't got to Yosemite yet, but I know I will!

Maki, 25

3

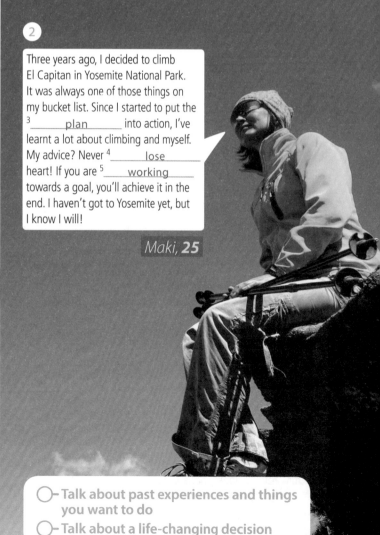

Alessandra, 35

When I was a teenager, I wanted to be a famous film star. But it didn't happen. My dream now is to be a chef. I've learnt that the best way to _____turn_____ a dream into reality is to be realistic. Set short-term _____goals_____ to help you _____stay_____ motivated. Becoming a chef is going to be difficult, but I've already started a course and cook regularly for friends and family.

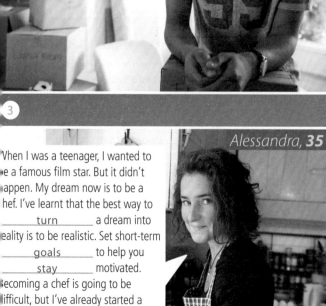

○– Talk about past experiences and things you want to do
○– Talk about a life-changing decision

2.2 You can do it!
● Talk about an inspirational person
● Talk about solving a problem

Ⓥ— dependent prepositions; problems and solutions
Ⓖ— present and past ability

Ⓟ— word stress: verbs with two syllables
Ⓢ— deducing the meaning of unknown words from context

READING

A SPEAK Work in pairs and discuss the question.

How do retired people typically spend their time in your country?

B Read the advert taken from a local newspaper. Then answer the questions.

1 What is unusual about the advert?

2 Why do you think he has written the advert?

3 How do you think people reacted to the advert?

C READ FOR GIST Read *89-year-old seeks job* and check your answers to Exercise B.

D Look at the words in bold in the article. What do you think they mean? Use the strategies in the box to help you. Then work in pairs and compare your ideas.

1 seeks   3 spotted   5 role

2 snaps him up   4 enable him to   6 taking on

> ## WORK WANTED
> Senior citizen 89 seeks employment in Paignton area. 20hrs+ per week. Still able to clean, light gardening, DIY and anything.
>
> I have references. Old soldier, airborne forces.
>
> *Save me from dying of boredom!* ©LW

89-year-old **seeks** job: café **snaps him up**

An 89-year-old has found a job after putting an advert in his local paper asking for part-time work to stop him 'dying of boredom'. Joe Bartley, from Paignton, south Devon, is due to start working in a café next week in the town after the owners of the family-run business **spotted** his advert.

'Whatever your age or your background, you deserve a chance,' said Cantina Bar and Kitchen's co-owner Sarah Martin. 'Most people have got something to offer, and Joe is someone who is keen, who is putting himself out there. What is not to like about that? A lot of people who come here don't just come for coffee – they come for a chat – so Joe is perfect.'

Ex B Q 2 Bartley has lived alone since his wife, Cassandra, died a couple of years ago, and he has been lonely. 'I miss my wife dreadfully, when you live on your own there is no one to speak to. I like reading, and I'll watch a bit of television, but there's a lot of rubbish on these days. I just got bored stiff with nothing to do. I thought even though I am 89, I can still work. I can clean tables, do some gardening – anything really.'

Bartley put his advert in the *Herald Express* last month. 'The owner phoned me and she asked me to come in. So I arrived at the café, we had a bit of a chat and shook hands.' He is now looking forward to earning his own money to **enable him to** pay his rent. 'I can't believe it really. I feel great about it,' he said.

Ex B Q 3 Bartley told *The Guardian* that the media reaction has been incredible, adding that he is in danger of becoming a celebrity. 'When I first put in the advert, I thought it was just an old guy looking for work – I don't really see what is strange about that,' he said. 'But have I now reached celebrity status? That might worry some people, but it doesn't worry me.'

His new **role** in the café was not the only job offer he got. Glenn Rodgers, an independent baker in Barnstaple, north Devon, offered him a job, but the bakery was too far away for Bartley to travel.

Rodgers wanted to offer the pensioner a job to put a 'smile on his face'. 'More employers should think about **taking on** older staff,' he added. 'Why not give him a chance? Also, it works both ways: employers are getting experienced reliable staff who really want to work.'

Bartley will get a lift to work with his new employer on Sundays, but will take a bus the rest of the week. 'He is delighted and we are looking forward to it,' said Martin. 'We think about these things all the time. We are never going to be rich, but we like to give something back to society.'

2.2 You can do it

LEAD-IN

Write the word *Work* in the middle of a circle and then draw some lines branching off in different directions. Put students into groups and give them three minutes to think of as many related words as they can. Elicit a couple of ideas (*job, part-time, full-time*) as a whole class to clarify the task.

READING

A Do this stage with books closed to prevent students from being distracted or influenced by the pictures. Put students into pairs and ask them to discuss how people in their country typically spend their time when retired. You could ask extra questions as well, e.g. *What age do people usually retire in their country, Are students looking forward to retiring (and why / why not)?* Get some feedback here, encouraging students to go beyond the most obvious or stereotypical ideas.

B In the likely event that students didn't say that they expect retired people to be looking for a job, pique their interest in the text by telling them they're going to read an unusual story about a retired person. Tell students to open their books, look at the advert and picture and discuss the questions. Get some feedback on students' predictions, but don't confirm or deny anything yet.

C Tell students to read the news article and check how accurate their answers in Exercise B were. Let students compare in pairs after reading, changing their answers together if necessary, before whole-class feedback.

1 It is a little unusual for someone to place an advert looking for work. It is also unusual in the UK for that person to be 89 years old. The final sentence is very unusual in an advert related to work.
2 He wrote the advert because he was lonely and bored after his wife died. He felt he was still able to work.
3 People were impressed by the advert. He received two job offers. The media reported on the story. People wanted to help him. It was an opportunity for other people to do something positive and generous by offering him work.

D Point out the strategies in the box for deducing the meaning of unknown words from context. Go through the first word *seeks* as an example, asking students each of the questions from the box before encouraging them to suggest what they think it means. Students can then work in pairs and follow the same steps for the other words. In feedback, ask students to tell you how they worked out the meaning of the words, again referring back to the questions in the box.

1 looks for
2 employs him/gives him a job
3 saw/noticed
4 make it possible for him to
5 job
6 employing/giving someone a job

TEACHING IDEA
by David Seymour and Maria Popova

Topic: Job interview

Use this activity to extend the topic.

If you do not already know about the students' professions or future career plans, ask them to tell you the job they do, or the one they would like to do. Choose two or three students who do, or would like to do, the same kind of work and put them together to prepare for a job interview for a specific position of your choosing. They should write a list of their relevant skills and strengths.

The rest of the class works in two or three groups to write interview questions for this position. Applicant A is interviewed by the first group, while B is interviewed by the second. Then they swap places.

Interviewers: Who had the best qualifications and experience? Who was the most relaxed and friendly during the interview? Who gets the job?

Applicants: How did you each feel about your interview? What did you think about the attitude of the different interviewers? Do you think you'll get the job?

TEACHING IDEA
by David Seymour and Maria Popova

Topic: Project

Use this activity to extend the topic.

Look in the situations vacant section of a newspaper and find a job advertisement to bring to the next lesson. In class, have a look at everybody else's advert and agree the three or four most interesting ones. Work in groups, one advert for each group. Agree a list of the skills and strengths needed for the job and discuss what research you could do on the company and the job before applying.

Write a letter of application for the job. (Elicit the layout and conventions for this kind of letter. Decide if the letter should simply request an application form, enclose a CV or give additional information.)

Write your own CV in English and bring it to class. Include the following information:

personal details, personal profile, education and qualifications, employment history, other skills, hobbies/interests, referees

In class, work in pairs or small groups. Look at another student's CV and make suggestions for improving it.

E Tell students to read the comments and discuss which ones they agree or disagree with. You could also encourage them to discuss if they could imagine this situation happening in their country, and, if so, what people's reactions would be.

VOCABULARY

A Tell students that all the phrases come from the article and the comments they've just read. Check students understand the meaning of the words in bold, and which ones are verbs or adjectives. Tell students to try to complete each gap with a preposition. Students can then look back at the article and find the phrases to check their answers. Encourage students to think about how they would say the phrases in their own language and to notice any similarities or differences in the prepositions used.

B Tell students to complete the gaps in the questions with a verb or adjective from Exercise A. You could make this more challenging by telling students to cover A while they do this, then uncover it to check when they've finished. Check answers as a whole class. Highlight that in question 4 *prepare for* was used as a verb in the comments, but here it's an adjective, *prepared for*.

C Tell students to discuss the questions with a partner. Encourage them to ask each other follow-up questions and to expand on their answers. These questions should produce interesting answers. Monitor and get students to share any particularly interesting answers with the whole class. Use the **Vocabulary Worksheet** on W8 for extra practice.

SPEAKING

A Tell students that they're going to choose someone to receive an award for inspiring others because of their special or unusual achievements. Give a personal example to further model the task. Tell students to work alone and think of three people who they think should receive the award.

B Tell students to work in pairs and explain who the people they've chosen are and what they've done to deserve the award. Tell students they have to agree on the one person who they think is the most inspirational and who they will nominate for the award.

C Put students into larger groups to give a presentation about their inspirational person and reasons why this person should win the award. Monitor and listen out for good examples of language used and errors that you could look at later in feedback. Once all students have made their presentations, tell them to vote in their group for who should win the award.

D Get feedback as a whole class. Each group should explain who their winner was and why they chose that person. If you have time, you could have a vote for the whole-class winner. Finish with some feedback on students' language use during the task. With some classes, peer feedback on language and delivery can be a useful way to round off a presentation activity. You should always handle this kind of feedback sensitively, though. One approach is to give students some areas to focus and make notes on: for example, pace, organisation, etc. Ensure that feedback always focuses on some positive aspects of each presentation.

AUDIOSCRIPT

🔊 **2.4**

Listening, Exercise B
M = Matt   S = Suzanna   N = Nancy   R = Roberto

M: You know, when you move away from home, arrive in a new place, there are loads of different challenges, and for me the biggest one was eating.

Ex C Q1   Well, not eating, but cooking. I mean, I could make a salad or a sandwich, but not cook anything, like, I couldn't boil an egg. I know that sounds silly, but I simply had no idea. Anyway, I looked at some books

Ex C Q2   and also found some excellent 'how to cook' videos online. To be honest, the books didn't help, but I started to teach myself with the videos. I wasn't very good at first – the first time, I didn't manage to make anything at all; I just watched the video and then ordered a takeaway! But, I never gave up. I kept practising. And when my parents came to see me six months later, I managed to cook them a really tasty meal. They were so surprised.

S: I really hate standing up in front of people to give

Ex C Q3   a talk or a presentation. So, when my brother asked me to make a speech at his wedding, I didn't know what to do. I couldn't say no to him. Luckily a friend of mine, an actor, helped me. Basically, we created a character for me to play when giving the speech, so that I didn't think it was actually me standing up

Ex C Q4   to speak. Also, I learnt my speech by heart so that I didn't need to use any notes. Just like an actor. On the big day, I wasn't able to stop my hands from shaking, but I remembered everything and I played that character. And, incredibly, I was able to complete the speech. That was a big day for me, as well as for my brother.

N: I worked as a volunteer in a village school in China for about six months, and the language was my

Ex C Q5   biggest problem. I was able to speak very basic Chinese, but I couldn't remember many new words. I studied each day, but didn't achieve much – the words went in one ear and then straight out the other! Then, I had a great idea. I had my guitar with me, so I started to write simple songs with all the new words. They were kind of like children's songs. I asked a Chinese friend to check my grammar was correct, and then tried to learn the songs. And, you know what, it worked. Each day, I was able to remember those new words, and I even started singing the songs to the kids. I was actually pretty

Ex C Q6   nervous the first time I sang to them, but I managed to do it without mistakes, although I think my pronunciation was pretty poor, from the way the kids were laughing at me.

Ex C Q7   **R:** When I was a child, I never learnt to swim, and, when I started going on beach holidays, I really regretted that. My friends spent ages swimming in the sea, but I wasn't able to swim. All I could do was sunbathe! So, I asked my sister to teach me. She was very patient, but, after a few months, I gave up because I still couldn't swim. Then, after another holiday just sitting on the beach, I decided to try again. This time, I paid for lessons at the local pool. And yes, after a few more months, I finally managed to swim 50 metres. That felt so good. And then, that next

Ex C Q8   holiday, I was finally able to swim in the sea with my friends – that felt incredible. A real achievement!

Deducing the meaning of words from context

When you do not know the meaning of words and phrases, you can use their context to help you understand them.

Think about:

- What type of word or phrase is it (noun, adjective or verb)?
- Does it have a prefix (*un-, im-*) or suffix (*-ment, -ion*)?
- Where is it in the sentence and what other words are near it?
- How does the word relate to the paragraph?
- What possible meanings of the word suit the topic of the sentence, paragraph and text?

E SPEAK Work in pairs. Look at the readers' comments on the article. Do you agree or disagree with them? Why?

Comments

Smart1
Joe is an inspiration to us all! He should be very proud of himself for getting a job that some would say is more suitable for a younger person.

ID2
If no one had replied to the advert, Joe could have thought about volunteering. Mind you, even those roles are hard to find these days!

Jan1003
The government should be more aware of this problem and work with communities to help people like Joe. Loneliness is a big problem nowadays.

4Kent
Though quite typical of this newspaper, it's great that this issue is in the news. We need to prepare for our retirement now, so we can retire comfortably, not serve coffee in our old age.

VOCABULARY
Dependent prepositions (verb/adjective + *for/of*)

A Look at the phrases from *89-year-old seeks job* and from the comments. Are the words in bold verbs or adjectives? Complete each phrase with *for* or *of*.

verb **1** look ___for___ work

verb **2** prepare ___for___ retirement

adjective **3** typical ___of___ this newspaper

adjective **4** suitable ___for___ a younger person

adjective **5** proud ___of___ himself

adjective **6** aware ___of___ this problem

verb **7** work ___for___ a café

verb **8** ask ___for___ part-time work

B Complete the questions with a verb or adjective from Exercise A.

1 What do you _____look_____ for in an ideal job?

2 Do you think age ever makes people more or less _____suitable_____ for some jobs?

3 Which of your achievements are you most _____proud_____ of?

4 What big changes in your life are coming soon? How can you _____prepare_____ for them?

C SPEAK Work in pairs. Ask and answer the questions in Exercise B.

SPEAKING

A Think of three people who should receive an award for inspiring others because of their special or unusual achievements.

B Work in pairs. Discuss your choices and choose the most inspirational person. Make notes of your reasons for choosing that person.

C Work in groups. In pairs, give a short presentation about your inspirational person, explaining why the person should win the award. As a group, vote for who should win the award.

D Tell the class about your group's choice. Why did the group feel the person was special? Did everyone in the group agree with the vote?

LISTENING

A **SPEAK** Work in pairs. Look at the pictures (1–4). What are the people doing? What problems could they have when they do these things?

B **LISTEN FOR MAIN IDEA** You are going to listen to four people talking about a challenge or problem. Complete the sentences (1–4) with the phrases in the box. There are four extra phrases.

2.4

> ~~by pretending to be a different person~~
> by spending a lot of money ~~by taking classes~~
> ~~by using a different skill~~ by using books during a holiday
> ~~on his/her own~~ with the help of his/her family

1 Matt solved a problem _____on his own_____.
2 Suzanna solved a problem <u>by pretending to be a different person</u>
3 Nancy solved a problem ___by using a different skill___.
4 Roberto solved a problem ___by taking classes___.

C **LISTEN FOR DETAIL** Listen again. Choose the correct words to complete the sentences.

2.4

1 Matt *knew* / *didn't know* how to cook simple hot food.
2 He found useful advice on *the internet* / *TV*.
3 Suzanna needed to give a speech at *work* / *a family event*.
4 She *read* / *didn't read* her speech aloud from a script.
5 Nancy *knew a little* / *didn't know any* Chinese.
6 She *made several* / *didn't make any* mistakes when she first sang to the children.
7 When Roberto was a child, he *tried* / *didn't try* to learn to swim.
8 He *has* / *still hasn't* swum in the sea.

D **SPEAK** Work in pairs and discuss the questions.

1 Which of the four challenges do you think is the hardest?
2 What advice could you give to someone who can't do those things well?
3 Have you had any of these challenges yourself? What did you do to deal with them?
4 Is it more important to solve problems yourself or ask for help?

PRONUNCIATION
Word stress: verbs with two syllables

A Work in pairs. Look at the verbs from the listening below. Take turns saying the verbs and marking the stress.

1 ach<u>ie</u>ve   3 compl<u>e</u>te   5 regr<u>e</u>t
2 arr<u>i</u>ve   4 cre<u>a</u>te   6 st<u>u</u>dy

B Does the stress normally come on the first or second syllable? the second syllable

C Now listen to the verbs. Check and repeat.

2.5

GRAMMAR
Present and past ability

A **WORK IT OUT** Look at the sentences (1–9). Write *a* if they are about having (or not having) a general ability or skill in the past. Write *b* if they are about doing something (or not doing something) on a particular occasion in the past.

1 I was able to speak very basic Chinese. _____a_____
2 I managed to cook them a very tasty meal. _____b_____
3 I was able to complete the speech. _____b_____
4 I couldn't boil an egg. _____a_____
5 I could make a salad. _____a_____
6 The first time, I didn't manage to make anything. _____b_____
7 I wasn't able to swim. _____a_____
8 I wasn't able to stop my hands shaking. _____b_____
9 I couldn't say no to him. _____b_____

B Choose the correct words to complete the rules.

Present and past ability

1 When we talk about ability or skills in general in the present, we <u>use</u> / *do not use* can/can't or (not) be able to.
2 When we talk about ability or skills in general in the past, we <u>use</u> / *do not use* could, couldn't or (not) be able to.
3 When we talk about ability to do a specific task on a particular occasion in the past, we <u>use</u> / *do not use* (not) manage to, (not) be able to or couldn't. We do not usually use could.

C Go to the Grammar Hub on page 124.

2.2 You can do it

LISTENING

A Point out the pictures and ask students to discuss the questions about what the people are doing. To encourage students to give more detailed answers, you could split the class into pairs or four groups and give each group or pair just one picture each to discuss. Get whole-class feedback, eliciting as many ideas from everyone as you can. Elicit the word *challenge* in relation to these activities at some stage during feedback.

B Tell the students they can now check their ideas as they're going to hear the people in the pictures talking about a challenge or problem they faced. Tell students to complete the sentences with the phrases from the box. Make sure students realise that they only need to use four of the phrases, and the other four don't match with any of the speakers. Check answers as a whole class but don't go into any more detail yet.

C Tell students they're going to listen again but before they do try to complete the sentences from memory. Students then listen again to check. This time, elicit more detail in feedback and ask students to explain their answers.

D Put students into pairs to discuss the questions. Discuss the questions as a whole class, encouraging students to expand on their answers, especially if they have personal experience of any of these situations.

PRONUNCIATION

A Tell students the verbs are all from the *Listening*. Model the first one then tell students to pronounce them in pairs and mark where they think the stress is.

B Tell students to look over their answers and notice where they think the stress normally comes.

C Tell students to listen and check. Check answers as a whole class.

2.5

GRAMMAR

A Elicit that the sentences are all about ability. Use the first two sentences as examples to make sure students understand the difference between general ability and ability to do something on a particular occasion in the past. Then ask them to look at the other sentences.

B After checking the answers in Exercise A, tell students to use the sentences to help them complete the rules.

C Direct students to the Grammar Hub on pages 124 and 125 (see below and TB21). Use the Grammar Worksheet on W7 for extra practice.

GRAMMAR HUB

2.2 Present and past ability

can

	Positive	Negative
I/you/he/ she/it/we/they	**Rosa can ride** a horse.	**They cannot drive.** **They can't drive.**

Question	Positive short answer	Negative short answer
Can you fish in the lake?	Yes, **I can.**	No, **I can't.**

be able to **(present simple)**

	Positive	Negative
I/you/he/ she/it/we/they	**I am able to book** a taxi online.	**Sven isn't able to fly** a plane.

Question	Positive short answer	Negative short answer
Are Tomas and Jaime able to work as volunteers?	Yes, **they are.**	No, **they aren't.**

manage to **(present simple)**

	Positive	Negative
I/you/he/ she/it/ we/they	**He manages to remember** new words every day.	**We don't manage to meet** our friends very often.

Question	Positive short answer	Negative short answer
Does Laura manage to stay calm when she presents?	Yes, **she does.**	No, **she doesn't.**

- We use *can*, *can't*, *(not) be able to* and *(not) manage to* talk about our ability or skills in general in the present.

could

Subject	Positive	Negative
I/you/he/ she/it/ we/they	**I could cook** when I was young.	**Paolo couldn't take on** more work.

Question	Positive short answer	Negative short answer
Could your cousin swim as a baby?	Yes, **he could.**	No, **he couldn't.**

- We use *could*, *couldn't* or *(not) be able to* when we talk about our ability or skills in general in the past.

- We use *couldn't*, *(not) be able to* and *(not) manage to* when we talk about our ability to do a specific task on a particular occasion in the past. We usually do NOT use *could*.

  We couldn't solve the problem at that time.
  BUT NOT We could solve the problem at that time.
  We were/weren't able to solve the problem at that time.
  We managed / didn't manage to solve the problem at that time.

- When a verb is followed by *-ing* or *to* + infinitive, we can't use *can*. We use *be able to* instead.

  Sebastian enjoys being able to cook.
  NOT Sebastian enjoys can cook.

D Model the game with your own personal example sentences before students write their own. Get some feedback on the most interesting stories.

VOCABULARY

A–C Put students into pairs to complete the exercises.

D Direct students to the **Vocabulary Hub** on page 142 for further practice of vocabulary related to problems and solutions.

E Tell students to complete the personality test for themselves. They should then check the **Communication Hub** on page 148 to see what their answers say about them.

SPEAKING HUB

A Elicit from students what typical questions they think are asked at job interviews. Tell students they're going to prepare to answer a question like this and ask them to read it.

B Tell students to work individually and make notes to prepare their answer. Monitor to provide language. Make sure students are not scripting their answer word for word.

C Tell students to ask and answer the question in pairs, making notes about their partner's answer as they listen.

D Put students into new pairs to tell each other their previous partner's answer. Tell students to decide which answer they think was best and why. Conclude by discussing answers as a whole class. Focus on content and the language used.

GRAMMAR HUB

2.2 Present and past ability

A Complete the sentences with the words in the box.

can could couldn't manage managed wasn't

1 She didn't _____manage_____ to make it to the interview on time.
2 Amazingly, Diego _____could_____ read when he was two and a half years old.
3 They _____managed_____ to find a solution to the complicated problem.
4 We were discussing something important, so I _____wasn't_____ able to answer my phone.
5 Francisco _____couldn't_____ stop his hands from shaking because he was so nervous.
6 Michela is amazing because she _____can_____ do three jobs and not be tired.

B Put the words in order to make sentences.

1 can't / Helena / egg / an / boil
_____Helena can't boil an egg._____
2 a / manage / I / cook / meal / didn't / tasty / to
_____I didn't manage to cook a tasty meal._____
3 our / we / goals / long-term / were / to / able / achieve
_____We were able to achieve our long-term goals._____
4 system / very / can / quickly / analyse / the / data
_____The system can analyse data very quickly._____
5 manage / speech / to / give / Aisha / her / did / ?
_____Did Aisha manage to give her speech?_____
6 couldn't / easier / suggest / an / plan / they
_____They couldn't suggest an easier plan._____

C Choose the correct option.

1 Marina _____ raise enough money for her trip.
   a wasn't able b didn't manage **c couldn't**
2 Olaf _____ paint great pictures of animals.
   a can b manages c is able
3 I _____ watch TV all day as a kid.
   a was able b can **c could**
4 They _____ to deal with any more problems.
   a couldn't **b weren't able** c can't
5 Hana _____ to find a good cooking video.
   a can't **b didn't manage** c couldn't
6 She forgot her lines, but she _____ stay calm.
   a could **b managed to** c was able
7 She _____ to find the theatre with the help of her app.
   a was able **b manages** c can't
8 Fred _____ sing to other people – he gets too nervous.
   a couldn't b manages **c can't**
9 Poppy _____ work and study, but she's often tired.
   a manages to b able to c can't
10 I _____ sit my English exam because I was on holiday.
   a couldn't b didn't manage c wasn't able

➤ Go back to page 20.

D SPEAK Work in pairs. Play *True or false?* Follow the instructions.

1 Write two sentences for each idea (a–c). One sentence should be true and one should be false.

  a something you can do now, but which you couldn't do five or ten years ago

  b a problem you had because you weren't able to do something

  c a particular time that you managed to do something that was difficult

2 Listen to your partner's sentences. Ask questions to find out more information, then guess which sentences are true. Take turns.

VOCABULARY
Problems and solutions

A SPEAK Work in pairs. How good are you at solving problems? Give yourself a score out of five. Explain your score to your partner.

B Look at the personality test. Complete the sentences with *problem(s)* or *solution(s)*.

How do you feel about difficult situations and problems?

Use this personality test to find out. How true are the following statements for you on a scale of 1–5?

1 = False　　　　　　4 = Mostly true
2 = Mostly false　　　5 = True
3 = Sometimes true /
　　Sometimes false

1 If I can't **solve** a difficult ____problem____, I don't give up. I keep trying until I find a ____solution____
1 **2 3 4 5**

2 I always try to **deal with** ____problem____ because ignoring them only **causes** more ____problems____.
1 **2 3 4 5**

3 When working in groups, I **suggest** lots of ____solutions____ to any ____problems____.
1 **2 3 4 5**

4 When I have a ____problem____, I look at it from different angles to **come up with** the best ____solution____.
1 **2 3 4 5**

5 When I deal with a complicated ____problem____, I **analyse** the possible ____solutions____ with lists of their pros and cons.
1 **2 3 4 5**

6 I prefer to discuss a ____problem____ with other people. Then we can **agree on** a ____solution____ together.
1 **2 3 4 5**

C WORK IT OUT Match the verbs in bold in the personality test with the definitions (1–7).

1 to think of something such as an idea or a plan　come up with

2 to study or examine something in detail in order to understand or explain it　analyse

3 to decide together what will be done and how it will be done　agree on

4 to offer an idea or plan for someone to consider　suggest

5 to take action to do something　deal with

6 to find a solution to something that is causing difficulties　solve

7 to make something happen, usually something bad　cause

D Go to the Vocabulary Hub on page 142.

E SPEAK Take the personality test. Go to the Communication Hub on page 148 to see what your answers may show about you. Then work in pairs and discuss your answers.

◯ SPEAKING HUB

A You are going to answer a question that employers often ask in job interviews to find out about problem-solving skills.

> Can you tell us about a time when you faced a challenge or a difficult problem that you successfully dealt with?

B PLAN Make notes about:
- the situation.
- what action you took to deal with the situation.
- what you learnt from trying to deal with the situation.

C SPEAK Work in pairs. Ask and answer the question. Make notes about your partner's answer.

D REFLECT Tell a classmate what your partner said. Think about what you both heard. Whose answer was best?

◯– Talk about an inspirational person
◯– Talk about solving a problem

COMPREHENSION

A 🔘 00:00–00:50 Watch the first part of the video. What wakes Gaby up? Someone knocking on the door.

B Work in pairs. The actual photo shoot is not successful. Look at the stills and predict the difficulties that Gaby has.

C ▶ 00:51–04:00 Watch the second part of the video and check your ideas. Then complete the sentences with *Gaby* or *Eric*.

1 _____Gaby_____ gets _____Eric_____'s name wrong.
2 _____Eric_____ is in a hurry.
3 _____Gaby_____ can't set up the tripod.
4 _____Gaby_____ gets _____Eric_____'s name wrong again.

5 _____Gaby_____ drops the camera.
6 _____Eric_____ fixes the camera onto the tripod.
7 _____Eric_____ suggests more light on the bowl.
8 _____Gaby_____ suggests putting fruit in the bowl.

FUNCTIONAL LANGUAGE
Asking for, giving and refusing permission

A Eric was in a hurry and wanted to start the photo shoot straight away. Tick (✓) the phrase he used.

Asking for permission	
	Least formal
Can we start …	☐
Could we start … straight away?	☐
May we start …	☐
Is it all right if we start …	✓
Would it be OK to …	☐
Would you mind if we started …	☐
	Most formal

Giving and refusing permission	
Sure, I don't see why not.	I'm sorry, but …
No problem.	I'd like to help, but …
Yes, of course.	I'm afraid that isn't possible.

MILLY

SAM

NEENA

ZAC

GABY

B Write down phrases asking for permission in the following situations. Choose an appropriate level of formality.

1 It's very hot in the classroom. You want to open a window. Ask your classmates.

_____

2 You have a dental appointment tomorrow. You want to leave work early. Ask your boss.

_____

3 You are chairing a business meeting. You want to start. Ask everyone in the meeting.

_____

4 It's a beautiful day and you're in a park. You want to sit on the grass. Ask the park warden.

_____

5 You're in front of somebody's house. You want to park your car there. Ask the house-owner.

_____

6 You're in a lecture with 200 other people. You want to ask a question. Ask the lecturer.

_____

USEFUL PHRASES

A Choose the correct alternatives to complete the useful phrases. Watch the video again if necessary.

1 *Call* / *Name* me Gaby. = Please use the name 'Gaby' when you talk to me.

2 I can't thank you *enough* / *at all*. = I am very grateful to you.

3 You *must* / *should* be Derek. = I am sure your name is Derek.

4 I haven't got *this* / *that* long. = I have very little time.

5 We're *almost* / *quite* there. = We have nearly finished.

B How do you say these useful phrases in your language?

PRONUNCIATION
Intonation and stress in questions

A Listen and repeat the questions. Does the intonation rise or fall after the main stress in the sentence?
2.6

1	Could I open the <u>win</u>dow?	rises
2	Can I leave work <u>ear</u>ly?	falls
3	Is it all right if we <u>start</u> now?	falls
4	Would it be OK to sit on the <u>arm</u>chair?	rises
5	Would you mind if I parked my <u>car</u> here?	rises
6	May I ask you a <u>ques</u>tion?	rises

B Practise the stress and intonation in the questions in Exercise A.

SPEAKING

A Work in pairs. You are going to write a conversation in which you ask permission for something.

• Decide on the situation: why do you need permission and who from?

• Decide on the level of formality.

• Write your conversation.

B PRESENT Practise your conversation. Then act out your conversation for the class.

○– **Ask for, give and refuse permission**

➤ Turn to page 157 to learn how to write an informal email.

2.3 Picture this

LEAD-IN

Give students three minutes to think of as many words related to photography as they can. Elicit answers on the board and try to elicit *tripod* and *photo shoot*.

COMPREHENSION

A ▶ 00:00–00:50 Point out the pictures of the characters and elicit what they can remember about each. Students then watch and answer the question.

B Tell students to look at the pictures and predict what is going to happen, particularly why the photo shoot is unsuccessful.

C ▶ 00:51–04:00 Students watch the rest to check their ideas. Let students compare in pairs after watching to complete the sentences. Play again if difficult.

FUNCTIONAL LANGUAGE

A Point out the phrases in the table, highlighting that they move from informal to formal. Ask students if they remember Eric's phrase.

B Tell students to imagine being in the situations and do the first one as a whole class. Students then discuss the others in pairs. Highlight to students that there may be several different correct answers for each situation.

USEFUL PHRASES

A Tell students all phrases were in the episode. Ask them to complete phrases with correct options. Play the video again if difficult.

B Tell students to think about how they would say these phrases in their own language.

PRONUNCIATION

A Tell students to listen and repeat, paying attention to intonation after the main stress. Point out that the main stress in a sentence is usually the final stressed syllable.
2.6

B Students practise asking the questions in pairs. Tell students to listen to their partner's stress and intonation and decide if it would make them likely to agree to the requests.

SPEAKING

A Students discuss the questions in pairs and then write the conversation. Remind them to refer to the phrases for permission as well as the useful phrases.

B Tell students to practise their conversations, paying special attention to their intonation. Students then act out their conversations for the class.

▶ VIDEOSCRIPT

C = Client   G = Gaby

C: These are excellent Gabriela. Excellent!

G: Please Derek, call me Gaby.

C: Yes of course, of course. Gaby – thank you. You've managed to capture the bowl perfectly. This is exactly what we were looking for! I can't thank you enough!

G: Come in. Hello. You must be Derek.

C: It's Eric actually.

G: Sorry, sorry! Of course. Eric. I'm Gaby.

C: Hi Gaby, nice to meet you. Is it alright if we start straight away? I haven't got that long.

G: Of course. No problem.

C: What's happened to your arm?

G: I fell over yesterday and hurt my wrist.

C: Oh no.

G: I've just got to set up the tripod and camera. It won't take long …

C: Erm … Can I do anything?

G: No, I'm fine.

C: I'm happy to help.

G: Actually, that would be great. Would you mind helping me with this?

C: Not at all. There you go.

G: Thanks, Derek.

C: Eric.

G: Eric! Sorry!

C: Are you okay?

G: Yes, I'm fine. Do you think you could help me with the camera as well?

C: Sure, no problem. That's all done.

G: Thank you so so much, it looks like we're ready to begin!

C: Would it be OK to have the light slightly brighter on this side?

G: Yes, of course.

C: These are definitely better. I think we're almost there. I feel like something's missing though. The shot feels a bit … Umm …

G: Empty …?

C: Yes.

G: How about adding some fruit?

C: Yes. Good idea. That would solve the problem. Yes, I think that looks good.

G: Maybe a few more grapes?

C: No, I think it's probably okay like that …

G: Come on. Just … one … more …

Z: Hey Gaby, how was the shoot?

G: A total disaster! I'm not sure photography is for me.

Z: I'm sure it wasn't that bad, I'll pick up some Pizza Roma to cheer you up!

G: Thanks, Zac.

Unit 2 Writing

2 Writing ● Write an informal email

W – informal writing

A SPEAK Work in pairs. Read the email from Sophie to Marta. What is their relationship?

a family members   c primary school friends

b new friends   d business colleagues

To: Marta
Subject: Hello and good news

Hi Marta,

How are you? I hope everything has been OK since you left London. Did you have a good holiday with your family? I guess you're back at uni now. Studying or partying hard? ¹ _b_ ☺

Sorry I haven't written sooner – I can't believe it's been two months since our course finished! I really miss London. My English really improved, and I loved getting to know you, Sato and the others. ² _c_

Anyway, I've got some good news! I've got a new job and I've moved to Paris. I'm working for a web design agency. I'm so pleased. It's only a small company, but everyone's really nice and ³ _a_

So, how about coming to Paris to visit me? Would you like to? I remember that you haven't been to Paris before, so now's your chance. Come for a weekend and stay at my place – it's easy to get here from Rome! What do you reckon? ⁴ _e_

Let me know what you think, and let me know when you finally get on Facebook – ⁵ _d_

Hugs and all the best.

Sophie

B Read again. Answer the questions.

1 Where did Sophie and Marta meet each other? _London, on a course._

2 When did they last see each other? _Two months ago_

3 Where do they live? _Sophie–Paris, Marta–Rome_

4 How has Sophie's life changed recently? _She got a new job; moved to Paris_

5 What does Sophie want Marta to do? _To visit her in Paris._

C Complete Sophie's email with the sentences (a–e).

a I'm enjoying the work.

b Or both?

c Have you heard from anyone else from our class?

d I can't believe you haven't done that yet!

e I'd love to see you.

D Put the sections in the order they appear in Sophie's email.

telling Marta about what she has done recently	3
making a suggestion/plan for the future	4
asking about Marta's life	1
talking about a shared experience	2

E Look at the box. Find and underline features of informal writing in the sentences (1–4).

Informal writing

In emails and letters to friends and family, we often use an informal writing style. We use:

- contractions, such as *You'll* …
- incomplete grammar, such as *How you doing?*
- informal words and phrases, such as *mate* (= *friend*).
- informal punctuation, such as *! , –* .
- emojis/emoticons, such as ☺ .
- informal opening and closing expressions, such as *Hi, Hugs*.

1 I'm going on holiday soon – can't wait!

2 I've just passed my driving test ☺ .

3 All fine here. It's great to be back at uni!

4 Big hug and say hi to your mum.

WRITING

A PREPARE You are going to write an informal email to a friend. Think of a friend you want to write to or imagine you are writing to a new friend.

B PLAN Make notes:

- what can you ask your friend about?
- what shared experience can you write about?
- what news have you got? What have you done recently?
- what suggestion or request can you make?

C WRITE Write your email (150–200 words). Use Sophie's email and the skills box to help you.

D REVIEW Work in pairs. Read your partner's email. Ask for more information about his/her news.

> Refer students to this email as a model for the writing task.

> Remind students to use features of informal writing to make their emails sound more natural.

Answers

1 contractions: I'm, can't
   incomplete grammar: can't wait

2 contractions: I've
   emojis/emoticons: ☺

3 contractions: It's
   incomplete grammar: All fine here.
   informal words: uni

4 incomplete grammar: big hug
   informal closing expression: big hug

WRITING

With books closed, ask students to think of all the people they write emails to and the reasons they write to them. Ask the class to share some of their answers.

A Tell students to open their books and look at the photo of Sophie and Marta. Ask students what they think the relationship between them is. Tell students to read the email and check. Tell them to ignore the gaps in the email for now.

B Tell students to read the email again and answer the questions.

C Tell students to complete the gaps in the email with the phrases. In feedback, elicit that the email is written in an informal style.

D Tell students that even though the email is informal, it is still well organised. Tell students to read it again and to put the sections in the order that they appear in the email. Point out that each of the first four paragraphs of the email is a section.

E Point out the features of informal writing in the box. Tell them to underline examples of these features in the sentences. In feedback, ask students if informal writing in their language follows similar conventions.

WRITING TASK

A Tell students to think of a friend they would like to write an informal email to. It could be a real friend or an imaginary new one.

B Tell students to make notes about the questions. Monitor to help with language input.

C Tell students to use their notes to write the email. Remind them to divide the email into paragraphs, one for each of the questions from Exercise B. Tell students to look back at Sophie's email and the features in the *Informal writing* box as well.

D Tell students to read each other's emails. Encourage them to ask each other questions to find out more information. Tell students to think about how well written the emails are in terms of style and organisation. Finish with feedback both on the content of the emails and how successfully the students think the emails were written.

GRAMMAR

A Complete the comments (1–2) about achievable bucket lists with the correct form of the verbs in brackets.

● ● ● ⟨ ⟩   🔍 🏠

Comments

1 Maybe the best bucket list is a mixture of easy and hard to achieve . I ¹ __'ve done__ (do) both simple activities and bigger adventures. Both ² __have given__ (give) me great memories. I once ³ __learnt__ (learn) to bake a cake in the morning, and then ⁴ __(I) did__ (do) my first bungee jump in the afternoon. The cake ⁵ __tasted__ (taste) great after that! I ⁶ __haven't done__ (do) a bungee jump since, but I ⁷ __'ve made__ (made) plenty of cakes!

2 How about awesome adventures that also benefit other people or society? A few years ago, I ¹ __wanted__ (want) to ride an elephant, so I ² __found__ (find) a position as an international volunteer at an elephant conservation park. I ³ __stayed__ (stay) there for two months. It ⁴ __was__ (be) great to help a charity and do something on my bucket list. Since then, I ⁵ __'ve done__ (do) loads of similar things.

B Find and correct the mistakes in five of the sentences.

1 When I was a kid, I could ~~to~~ swim. I learnt as a baby.
2 They ~~wasn't~~ **weren't** able to score a goal. What a boring game.
3 I managed to finish everything. **correct**
4 I couldn't ~~to~~ ride a bike until I was 19.
5 I am able **to** dance quite well.
6 I'm afraid you didn't ~~managed~~ **manage** to pass. You'll have to retake it.

VOCABULARY

A Match the sentence beginnings (1–5) and endings (a–e).

1 I don't believe in setting   _d_
2 It's easy to stay   _b_
3 I'm sorry you didn't get the job, but don't lose   _e_
4 When I moved to the countryside, I   _c_
5 I was nervous about taking   _a_

a the next step, but I knew it was the right time to make the change.
b motivated when you really enjoy what you do.
c turned my dream into reality!
d long-terms goals – I prefer to focus on my weekly plans.
e heart – there will be other opportunities.

B Complete the sentences with the correct form of the words in the box and *for* or *of*.

ask   aware   look   prepare
proud   suitable   typical   work

1 We're lost. We need to __ask for__ help and get directions.
2 I __'m looking for__ a new job. I check a few online agencies each week.
3 This behaviour is __typical of__ Jane. She has always been difficult.
4 She's giving a presentation tomorrow. She needs to __prepare for__ that tonight.
5 Is this film __suitable for__ young children? I'd like to watch it with my niece.
6 We have both __worked for__ the same company all our lives. That's quite unusual.
7 Is your boss __aware of__ all the problems with the project?
8 I'm very __proud of__ my achievements. It's never too late to learn something new.

C Choose the correct words to complete the results of a personality quiz about problem solving.

The results show that when you try and ¹**deal** / **solve** a problem, you like to make quick decisions. This can be helpful, but sometimes you should take more time to ²**analyse** / **come up with** the problem first. This will help when you have to ³**deal with** / **suggest** complicated situations and need to ⁴**come up with** / **cause** many different solutions.

The results also show that when you work in a team, you expect to ⁵**solve** / **agree on** solutions quickly, and if you don't, you often lose interest. However, if you don't take the time to look at the pros and cons of your solutions, this might ⁶**cause** / **suggest** more problems.

FUNCTIONAL LANGUAGE

Put the dialogue in the correct order.

A: Alright, no problem. In that case could you lend me your phone?   _3_
A: Hey there, Pete. Would you mind if I borrowed your laptop?   _1_
B: I'm afraid I can't do that either – I'm expecting an important call.   _4_
B: I'm not sure to be honest – I've got a lot of work to do today and I need it.   _2_
A: Yes, Arsenal are playing and I want to check the score!   _7_
A: OK, never mind.   _5_
B: Is it for something urgent?   _6_

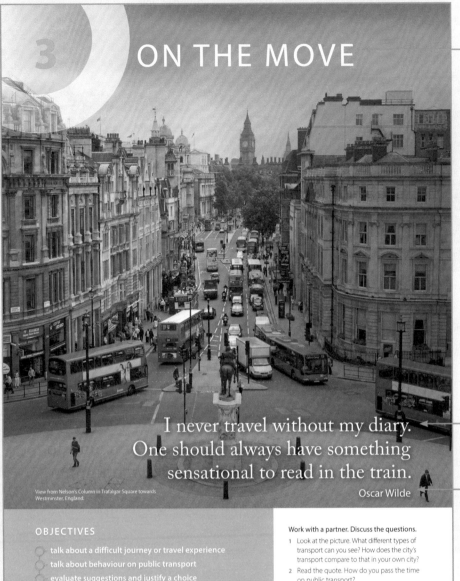

ON THE MOVE

> On the move (phrase) travelling from place to place.
> Synonyms: go (v), ride (v), commute (v)

> I never travel without my diary. One should always have something sensational to read in the train.
>
> Oscar Wilde

View from Nelson's Column in Trafalgar Square towards Westminster, England.

> The quote for this unit is humorous with Wilde implying that there is nothing more exciting to read than the story of his life while he is travelling.

> Oscar Wilde (1854–1900) was an Irish poet and playwright. He wrote poetry and stories but is best known for his plays such as the comedy *The Importance of Being Earnest*.

OBJECTIVES

- talk about a difficult journey or travel experience
- talk about behaviour on public transport
- evaluate suggestions and justify a choice
- talk about why a plan didn't work
- tell a story
- write an email of complaint

Work with a partner. Discuss the questions.

1 Look at the picture. What different types of transport can you see? How does the city's transport compare to that in your own city?

2 Read the quote. How do you pass the time on public transport?

3 Which types of transport would you describe with the adjectives in the box?

> convenient dangerous essential
> exciting expensive free fun noisy
> relaxing safe stressful tiring

ON THE MOVE 25

OBJECTIVES

Read the unit objectives to the class.

UNIT OPENER QUESTIONS

With books closed, write on the board *An advanced city is/has …* Put students into pairs and ask them to discuss different ways in which they would complete the sentence. Elicit students' ideas and write them on the board. Put students back into pairs to discuss which idea they agree with the most.

1 Tell students to look at the picture and elicit the different types of transport shown (i.e. *bus, coach, car, motorbike*). Write the vocabulary on the board and drill pronunciation if needed. Put students into pairs to discuss how similar or different the public transport in the city in the picture is to that in their own city, or nearest city.

2 Tell students to read the quote and discuss what they do while they are travelling. Share any interesting answers.

3 Check students understand the adjectives, especially *convenient* (easy to use), *essential* (necessary) and *tiring* (making you feel tired). Drill pronunciation of all the adjectives. Ask students which methods of transport they would describe with those adjectives. Elicit a couple of ideas as a whole class before students discuss them in pairs.

WORKSHEETS

Lesson 3.1 Travel experiences

Grammar: Narrative tenses: past simple, past continuous, past perfect simple (W9)

Vocabulary: Collocations: travel information (W10)

Lesson 3.2 Travel smart

Grammar: Articles and quantifiers (W11)

Vocabulary: Gradable and ungradable adjectives (W12)

3.1 Travel experiences

— Talk about a difficult journey or travel experience
— Talk about behaviour on public transport

G— narrative tenses   V— collocations: travel information; nouns ending in -ion
P— word stress in nouns ending in -ion   S— skim-reading to build a map of a text

LISTENING

A SPEAK Work in pairs and discuss the questions.

1 What types of transport do you use? How often do you use them?

2 Which do you prefer and why? Which is your least favourite?

3 What problems might there be for each one?

B LISTEN FOR GIST Listen to a radio phone-in
3.1 programme. What is the topic of today's discussion?

a bad or unusual journeys to work

ⓑ bad or unusual journeys in general

c bad or unusual journeys on national holidays

C LISTEN FOR DETAIL Are the sentences true (T) or
3.1 false (F)? Correct the false sentences. Then listen again and check your answers.

Junko's experience
                                    it was New Year's Day
1 There were no trains because ~~of the bad weather.~~   F

2 She didn't sit at the bus stop for a long time.   T
   The police car stopped to ask if she needed help.
3 ~~She stopped a police car to ask for help.~~   F
              took her to her friend's house
4 The police ~~found a taxi for her.~~   F

5 She arrived at her friend's house in time for dinner.   T

Alan's experience
   The train was cancelled.
6 ~~He missed the first train because the taxi was slow.~~   F

7 The second train stopped moving after half an hour.   T

8 When the train reached its destination, he was
   an hour
   ~~already two hours~~ late for the interview.   F
                          had to get out of
9 Because the traffic was heavy, he ~~walked from the~~   F
   the taxi and walk to the office.
   ~~station to the office.~~
   The interviewer
10 ~~Another job candidate~~ was late because of the   F
   train problems.

D SPEAK Work in pairs and discuss the questions.

1 What mistakes did Junko and Alan make? Who made the worst ones?

2 Who had the worst or most unusual journey? Why?

GRAMMAR
Narrative tenses

A Look at the pairs of sentences from the radio phone-in programme. In each pair, who is the speaker? Write J (Junko) or A (Alan). What tenses are the underlined verbs?

        past continuous   past simple
1 A: It <u>was raining</u> when I <u>left</u>.   A
        past continuous
   B: It <u>was snowing</u>.   J
      past simple
2 A: I <u>got</u> the next train, but after about 30 minutes,
        past simple
   that train <u>broke down.</u>   A
        past simple   past simple
   B: I <u>found</u> a bus stop and <u>sat down</u>.   J
                    past continuous
3 A: A police car <u>was driving</u> past, when it suddenly
      past simple
   <u>stopped.</u>   J
        past continuous   past simple past simple
   B: We <u>were still not moving</u>, so I <u>got out</u> and <u>walked</u>.   A
         past simple
4 A: We <u>arrived</u> about two hours late, and that
         past perfect simple
   meant <u>I'd already missed</u> the interview.   A
   past perfect simple
   B: <u>I'd arranged</u> to go to a classmate's house
      for dinner.   J

B WORK IT OUT Complete the rules with *past simple*, *past continuous* or *past perfect simple*.

Narrative tenses

When we tell a story, we use a range of past tenses.

1 We use the _____ past simple _____ to describe the main events in a story, in the order that they happened.

2 We use the _____ past continuous _____ to describe a longer action that is interrupted by a shorter event. We also use it to describe a longer action that is not a main event in the story, such as the weather.

3 We use the _____ past perfect simple _____ to describe an event that happened before the main events in the story.

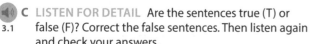

LEAD-IN

Elicit an example of a reason why people make a journey. Write this on the board, then put students into pairs to think of more.

LISTENING

A–C Students work and check in pairs to complete the exercises. Monitor and encourage students to explain their opinions.

AUDIOSCRIPT

 3.1

Listening, Exercise B
B = Presenter (Bobby)   J = Junko   A = Alan

B: Right, our first caller is Junko. Hello, Junko.

J: Hello, Bobby. Well, my story happened some time ago, when I first came to the UK to study English. I was only 18 then.

B: OK. Can I ask, where are you from, Junko?

J: Japan.

B: Japan? OK, but you aren't calling from there, are you?

J: No, no. I've lived here for ten years now.

B: OK. Well, Junko, thank you for calling. Tell us your story. What problem did you have?

J: Well, the problem was a public holiday. New Year's Day to be exact!

B: New Year's Day was a problem? That is pretty unusual. What happened?

J: Well, I'd arranged to go to a classmate's house for dinner. Of course, I knew it was a holiday. But what I didn't know was there was no public transport. So in the afternoon, I went to the underground station. It was snowing, not very heavily, but it was really cold. Anyway, the station was shut when I got there, so I couldn't get a train. I thought it was because of the snow, but the roads were OK, so I decided to try to get a bus.

Ex C Q1

B: But there were no buses either?

J: Mmm, exactly. But I didn't know. Anyway, I found a bus stop and sat down to wait.

B: Oh, no! Did you wait for long?

J: Actually, not so long. I was very lucky.

B: You got a taxi?

Ex C Q3 **J:** Not exactly. A police car was driving past when it suddenly stopped and one of the officers got out. She asked me if I was OK and explained there were no buses today. I felt so embarrassed and stupid. But then, guess what?

B: What?

J: She told me to get in the car. I was worried. Had I done something wrong? But they were both smiling, so I just asked why.

B: So then what?

Ex C Q4 **J:** They took me to my friend's place.

B: What? Like a taxi?

J: Exactly. I couldn't believe it. So kind. You know, we went right across the city. When I arrived, my friends hadn't started dinner. So, I wasn't late at all. Perfect!

B: How lovely, Junko. I guess it was a quiet day for everyone, even the police. A lovely example of the New Year's spirit in action. Thank you. Right, now let's hear from Alan. Hello, Alan. Tell us your story.

A: Sure. Hi, Bobby. Yeah, so, I'd been out of work for a few months when I got this interview for a job in another city. I really needed the job, so I decided to leave really early – you know, I didn't want to be late and all that.

B: Not for an interview, no!

A: Right! Well, it was raining when I left, so I ordered a taxi to the station. That didn't take long, but when I got there, I found out that they'd cancelled my train. I wasn't too worried though – the next one was in half an hour, and I had plenty of time. So I got the next train, but after about 30 minutes, that train broke down and we were just stuck there. Not moving or anything. And, stupidly, I'd left my phone at home. Yes, I'd changed jacket just before I left, and my phone was in that first jacket, so I couldn't even call the company.

Ex C Q6

B: How unlucky, Alan. So how long were you stuck there?

A: About an hour! And all that time I was getting more and more stressed. The train got moving in the end, but really slowly, and we arrived about two hours late, and that meant I had already missed the interview by over an hour. So, I jumped in a taxi, but that only made things worse.

Ex C Q8

B: In what way?

A: The traffic was awful – you know, it was still raining. We ended up stuck in a traffic jam. After about 20 minutes, we were still not moving, so I got out and walked. So, when I finally got to the office, I was really late, stressed and wet from the rain. I looked a right mess.

Ex C Q9

B: I can imagine. Nightmare! Did they still interview you?

A: Well, that's the funny thing. I was standing at the reception desk, waiting to make my excuses to the receptionist when this guy stepped in front of me. I was about to complain when the receptionist said 'Mr Hammond, you've arrived. At last'. And, can you guess who he was?

B: Another candidate?

Ex C Q10 **A:** Oh, no, not another candidate. He was the manager, the interviewer! It turned out he'd been on the same train as me! I introduced myself immediately, and we had a bit of a laugh about the whole journey.

B: Amazing! What a coincidence. And so I have to ask: did you get the job?

A: Well, after all that bad luck, things had to change, and yes, I got the job.

GRAMMAR

A Do the first one as an example to make sure students are familiar with the terminology.

B Tell students to use the example sentences from Exercise A to help them complete the rules. Use the **Grammar Worksheet** on W9 for extra practice.

3.1 Travel experiences

C-D Put students into pairs to check when they have completed the exercises.

E Direct students to the **Grammar Hub** on pages 126 and 127 (see below).

F Direct students to the **Communication Hub** on page 149.

VOCABULARY

A-B Students check answers in pairs after completing the exercises.

C Direct students to the **Vocabulary Hub** on page 142 for further practice of vocabulary related to travel information.

D Put students into pairs to discuss the questions. Use the **Vocabulary Worksheet** on W10 for extra practice.

SPEAKING

A-C Students plan, share and decide on the best stories.

GRAMMAR HUB

3.1 Narrative tenses

	Positive	Negative	Question
Past simple	They **went** to Spain last year.	The train journey **didn't take** long.	Where **did** you **go** on holiday?
Past continuous	It **was raining** when we left the house.	Anna **wasn't enjoying** the journey.	Where **were you going** when I saw you yesterday?
Past perfect simple	I **had just arrived** at the hotel. We **had missed** the train.	Ben **hadn't arrived** at the office.	What time **had** they **left** the house? **Had** you ever **been** there before?

- We use the past simple to talk about finished actions or situations, and things that happened one after another.

  I waited at the bus stop until my bus came.
- We use the past continuous to describe the background to a story.

  It was snowing and the traffic was moving very slowly.
- When we are talking about two events in the past, we use the past perfect to show that one event happened before the other.

- We use the past continuous for actions or situations that were unfinished at a past time and which were interrupted by shorter events (described using the past simple).

  While we were going through town, the bus started making a strange noise.

past ◄──────────────────────────► present
　　I had left the train station when I saw a bus.

I left the train station. ↑　　　　　　　　↑ I saw a bus.

3.1 Narrative tenses

A Complete each sentence with the correct form of the verb in brackets.

1 We got to the station but we *had already missed* (already / miss) the train.
2 When I arrived at the station, my cousin *was waiting* (wait) for me.
3 The car left the road and *hit* (hit) a tree.
4 *Had you been* (you / go) to Berlin before or was it your first time?
5 What *did your friend say* (your friend / say) when you finally arrived?
6 We *had just arrived* (just / arrive) at the station when we saw our train coming in.

B Choose the correct option.

1 We were excited because we *didn't visit* /(*had never visited*) South America before.
2 *Did anyone wait* /(*Was anyone waiting*) for you when you got there?
3 Tom arrived at the hotel and *had gone* /(*went*) straight to his room for a sleep.
4 The reason we were lost was that we *were taking* /(*had taken*) the wrong underground line.
5 What(*did you do*)/ *had you done* when you realised you'd lost your ticket?
6 Didn't you know the train *was being* /(*had been*) cancelled?

C Correct the mistakes in each sentence.

1 The accident happened because the driver had ~~fell~~ *fallen* asleep at the wheel.
2 I was late, but luckily for me the meeting ~~wasn't starting.~~ *hadn't started*
3 We missed the start because we ~~were getting~~ *were / had got* stuck in a traffic jam.
4 They had already ~~went~~ *been* to Paris so they decided to go somewhere else.
5 I was worried because I ~~wasn't hearing~~ *hadn't heard* from my brother for several hours.
6 The traffic ~~didn't move~~ *wasn't moving* at all so we got out of the taxi and walked.

➤ Go back to page 27.

TB27　**ON THE MOVE**

C Match the timelines (a–d) with the rules (1–3) in Exercise B.

2 a

1
2
NOW

1 b
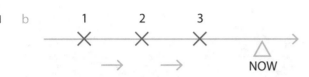
1 2 3
NOW

2 c
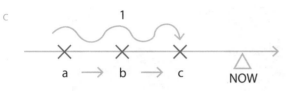
1
a → b → c
NOW

3 d
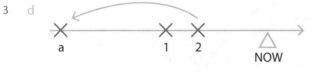
a 1 2
NOW

D PRACTISE Complete the stories with the correct form of the verbs in brackets.

It ¹____was raining____ (rain), and I ²____was driving____ (drive) at night in the countryside when a wild animal suddenly ³____jumped____ (jump) in front of me. I ⁴____managed____ (manage) to avoid hitting the animal, but I ⁵____went____ (go) off the road into a field and I couldn't move the car. Unfortunately, I ⁶____'d/had forgotten____ (forget) to charge my phone, so I couldn't call for help. That was a long walk home!

I ⁷____was travelling____ (travel) to work on the train when a ticket inspector ⁸____asked____ (ask) to see my ticket. I ⁹____looked____ (look) everywhere, but I had no idea where I ¹⁰____'d/had put____ (put) it. I emptied out my pockets but it ¹¹____had disappeared____ (disappear) completely. There were two kids opposite me, and while I ¹²____was paying____ (pay) the inspector, I ¹³____noticed____ (notice) they ¹⁴____were smiling and laughing____ (smile and laugh). They got off at the next station, and my ticket ¹⁵____was____ (be) on their seat. They ¹⁶____had found and hidden____ (find and hide) it.

E Go to the Grammar Hub on page 126.

F Work in pairs. Go to the Communication Hub on page 149.

VOCABULARY
Collocations: travel information

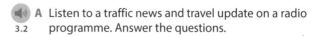

A Listen to a traffic news and travel update on a radio programme. Answer the questions.
3.2

1 How many types of transport do they mention?
three: cars, underground/subway trains, trains
2 Which has the fewest problems?
the underground

B LISTEN FOR KEY WORDS Listen again. Choose the correct words to make the collocations used in the travel update.
3.2

1 rush _hour_ / job
2 traffic _lights_ / _jam_
3 road _sign_ / _works_
4 severe _delay_ / problem
5 slight _delay_ / interest
6 good conditions / _service_
7 underground station / _line_
8 cancel _a train_ / an event
9 heavy _rain_ / _traffic_
10 overcrowded _trains_ / buses

C Go to the Vocabulary Hub on page 142.

D SPEAK Work in pairs and discuss the questions.

1 When was the last time you were stuck in heavy traffic?
2 What do you think about travelling during rush hour?
3 Which is worse: being on an overcrowded train or in a traffic jam?

SPEAKING

A You are going to tell a story for a radio show. Think of either an interesting or a difficult journey that you have made. Make notes to help you plan your story. Think about:

- Background information (When? Where? Why?)
- What was the weather like?
- What happened on the journey?
- How did it finish?

B Work in groups. Share your stories. Ask and answer questions about the stories.

C Which story do you think would be best for the radio show? Which was the most interesting, unusual or difficult journey? Which was the funniest story?

READING

A SPEAK Work in pairs. Look at the pictures (a–c) and discuss the questions.

1 What are the people doing?

2 Which activities do you like / not like doing when you are travelling?

B SKIM Read the article quickly and answer the questions. Use the strategies in the box to help you build a map of the text.

> ### Skim-reading to build a map of a text
>
> You can build a map of a text by identifying the main topic and the paragraph topics.
>
> Read the title and the first paragraph to find out what the main topic is.
>
> Read the first sentence of each paragraph to find out what the paragraph's topic is. Make a note of the paragraph topics.

1 What is the main topic or idea in this text?
  Talking to strangers on public transport.

2 Match the headings (a–f) with the paragraphs (1–6).

4 **a** The details of what the research discovered

5 **b** Epley's conclusions regarding the research

6 **c** How the research changed Epley's life

1 **d** Avoiding conversations and reasons not to

3 **e** How the research was carried out

2 **f** The reason why Epley and Schroeder did the research

⚛ DAY2DAY SCIENCE   Your source of science news

Is it time to start talking to strangers?

1 Using your mobile phone. Putting on your headphones. Staring out of the window with a blank look on your face. Those are all classic ways to avoid talking to strangers on public transport. **Ex B Q1** However, this may not be the best thing to do for your well-being. Recent research by Nicholas Epley, a professor of behavioural science at the University of Chicago, and Juliana Schroeder, a PhD student, reveals that people are happier when they chat with other passengers rather than ignoring them. **Vocabulary, Ex A**

2 The inspiration for the research came from Epley's own daily commute. Humans are, by nature, social animals, and being social is key to our happiness. However, the commuters that Epley saw every day were behaving in very antisocial ways, avoiding all communication as if they were sitting next to a rock. He wondered why nearly everyone acted against their social nature in this situation. Is talking to a stranger on a train truly less pleasant than sitting in silence? Or is everybody wrong?

3 To find out, Epley and Schroeder designed two experiments. In the first, Epley simply asked people to imagine starting a conversation with another passenger. Would it be a pleasant thing to do? Would they feel happy afterwards? In the second study, they asked commuters to actually start conversations with strangers on their journey, and then to complete a survey about the experience.

4 His studies revealed a difference between people's expectations of talking to strangers and the reality. In the first study, people generally said it would neither be a pleasant thing to do nor increase their happiness. In addition, they felt that most strangers would not want to chat.

In contrast, the second experiment showed that people enjoyed their commute more when they talked to a stranger and their general level of happiness increased. It also revealed that the reaction of their conversation partners was positive because they all took part in the conversations, even though they were not aware it was an experiment.

5 Based on the findings, Epley feels that train carriages filled with silence, blank expressions and little eye contact are the result of basic misunderstandings and false expectations. Despite what everyone thinks, strangers are happy to chat and chatting makes you happier. Once people make the decision to start a conversation, they find this connection to others improves their own lives.

6 Since publishing the research, Epley has put his findings into action and changed his own commuting behaviour. He no longer uses his mobile phone and he starts conversations with opening lines as simple as 'I like your hat'. He often finds himself sitting next to someone he has talked to before, which 'just makes it more pleasant'. As Epley says, 'Other people are people too, and it turns out they'd like to get to know you.'

3.1 Travel experiences

READING

A Tell students to look at the pictures and discuss the questions in pairs. In feedback, elicit what they have in common – that they show people in public transport and that the people aren't speaking to each other. Ask students if they think this is typical in their country and encourage them to share examples from their own experiences with the class, either travelling in their country or when travelling abroad.

B Tell students to read the strategies for skim-reading to build a map of the text. Ask students if they do any of these things already, either when reading in English or in their own language. Tell students to use these strategies to read the text and answer the questions. Students should work alone at this point but you can monitor and assist, particularly to ensure students have understood the box and are referring to it when answering the questions.

C Tell students to compare their answers in pairs and to discuss how much more information they can remember after their skim-reading. In feedback, elicit as much detail as you can about the text. Ask students if they found the skim-reading strategies effective. You can also ask them if they think they will use them again in the future.

D Put students into groups to discuss what they think about the results of the research described in the text. Encourage them to share their own experiences. If there is time you can let groups share their ideas with another group. Then discuss answers as a whole class and ask students to expand on their responses.

VOCABULARY

A Tell students that the article they've just read contains eight nouns that share the same suffix. Try to elicit what this is. Tell students to underline all eight examples in the text.

B Tell students to use the context in which the words appear in the article to help them work out the meaning of the nouns as they match them to the definitions. Do the first one as an example with the whole class.

C Direct students to the **Vocabulary Hub** on page 143 for further practice of nouns ending in -*ion*.

D Put students into pairs to discuss the sentences and to change them so they are true for them if they disagree. Monitor and encourage students to express different opinions.

Extra activity

As a way of extending the discussion about the topic, you could ask the following questions:

1 Have you ever chatted to other passengers on public transport?

2 What advice would you give to someone who would like to speak more often to other passengers?

3 Rank the following activities you can do while travelling in order of which you prefer most:

> read a book or magazine, phone friends or family, work or study, talk to other passengers, daydream, watch a film, eat and drink, listen to music, sleep

TEACHING IDEA
by David Seymour and Maria Popova

Topic: Reading habits

Use this activity to extend the topic.

How important is storytelling in your culture? Do you think it is important to tell young children stories? Why (not)? Find out about your partner's reading habits. Here are some questions to help you.

1 Are you reading a book in your free time? What's it about?

2 What kind of books do you usually read? Why?

3 What's the best book you've ever read? Why did you like it so much?

4 Are you a fast reader?

5 Do you read magazines or comics? Which ones?

6 What do you think of e-books? Will they ever replace traditional books?

Estimate how much time you spend reading every day and how much time you spend watching TV. Note the times down on a piece of paper. Below that draw a pie chart including the following kinds of reading:

novels, 'quality' newspapers/magazines, other press/comics, signs/hoardings, instructions, study books, computer screens

Mingle with the rest of the class and compare your notes and pie chart with other students.

TEACHING IDEA
by David Seymour and Maria Popova

Topic: Public transport

Use this activity to extend the topic.

How does the public transport system here compare with the system in another city you know well? How do you travel to class?

In small groups, discuss the advantages and disadvantages of cycling and driving to work.

Agree a list of ten transport policies for a smoggy, congested, over-populated city. You will need to find a way of encouraging people out of their cars and onto public transport.

METHODOLOGY HUB by Jim Scrivener

Creating a positive learning atmosphere

Below are some features that may be important in creating a positive relationship and a positive learning atmosphere. Decide which items are inborn and which could be worked on and improved. In a positive learning atmosphere the teacher . . .

> really listens   shows respect   is fair
> has a good sense of humour
> gives clear and positive feedback   inspires confidence
> is, by and large, authentically her/himself   is patient
> empathises with students/people   trusts people
> does not complicate things unnecessarily
> is well organised   is honest   is approachable

PRONUNCIATION

A Tell students to listen carefully to the pronunciation of the words and to underline the stressed syllable in each one. If students struggle with this, play the audio again.

3.3

B When students have correctly underlined the stress, play the audio again and tell students to repeat them and think about how the stress pattern is similar. Ask students what is the same about the pronunciation of the final syllable of each word. Ensure that the students are pronouncing the nouns correctly. If necessary, correct and model the pronunciation.

3.3

The penultimate syllable is always stressed. The final syllable has a weak vowel sound: /ə/.

C Tell students to look at the nouns and underline where they think the stressed syllable will be. Play the audio for students to check and tell them to repeat the words as they hear them. Make sure students are repeating the words correctly. If necessary, model them again yourself. Check students have noticed all nouns follow the pattern identified in Exercise B.

3.4

D Tell students to practise the pronunciation further in pairs and encourage them to correct each other if necessary. To provide more context, you could encourage students to put the words into sentences as they do this.

SPEAKING HUB

A Tell students to turn to the **Communication Hub** on page 154. Check understanding of *litter, coughing and sneezing, queuing, to board* and *to give up your seat*. Tell students to work individually first to rank the behaviour on public transport from one to ten in terms of how annoying it is for them personally.

B Put students into groups to compare their lists, explaining and justifying their reasons to each other. Tell students that their group is going to have to agree on the top three, so they need to try to persuade each other that their choices should be included. If some groups agree more than others, ask them to try to add more ideas to the list of annoying behaviour on public transport.

C Tell the groups that they need to agree on their top three most annoying things. If different groups have very different ideas, you could change groups again and encourage further debate. Ask groups to reveal their top three to the class. As a whole class, discuss further until a definitive top three is agreed on.

Put students back into groups to think of ways to stop the annoying behaviour from the top three. Elicit an example with the whole class, then monitor to help with language. When groups have their ideas, re-group students again to explain their ideas and again to try to agree on the best idea for each one. Finish with some discussion as a whole class with students explaining their choices. You could ask if students really believe this behaviour can be changed. Finish with some feedback on students' language use during the task, focusing both on successes and errors.

METHODOLOGY HUB by Jim Scrivener

Give collocations rather than definitions

When a student wants to know what the difference is between *late* and *delayed*, it's often hard to give a clear distinction of meaning. But there are clearly certain collocations and chunks that one is more likely to fit into than the other. When you want to make a sentence, knowing the typical collocations – and learning them, phrasebook-like – is probably going to be of more use than trying to select between two very similar meanings.

There are many games and activities specifically aiming to work on collocational understanding. Here are three of my favourites:

Quick choices

Choose two or three nouns, e.g. food, cooking and meal, that have a number of (possibly confusable) collocations. In this case, the list might include baby, fast, slow, health, dog, home, evening, delicious, light, balanced, three-course, French, vegetarian, frozen, cat. Tell the students that you will read out the list item by item and they must indicate which of the two (or three) words is the best collocate, or if the item goes with more than one word. Decide on how students will indicate their choices. You could go for quiet ways, e.g. students write their answers in a list; noisy ways, e.g. students call out their choice

of words; physical ways, e.g. students point at the words written on wall notices; action ways, e.g. designate different parts of the room for different words and students run to the right part of the room (or between parts).

Guess the collocation

Divide the class into three or more teams. In each team, students are given a common word (e.g. town) and have to prepare a list of five common collocations (e.g. planning, hall, home, market, centre). Each team has a different starter word. When everyone is ready, students read their lists out one item at a time and the other teams try to guess the original word. If the word is guessed immediately on the first clue, both teams (list-makers and word-guessers) get ten points; for each extra word, the points go down by one. This scoring scheme encourages list-makers to find the most likely and distinctive collocations.

Chunk watching

Students work in groups of three, two of whom face each other. The teacher gives them a topic to talk about and they simply chat naturally for a few minutes. The third person sits out of their line of sight and takes no part in the conversation, but listens carefully and takes notes of as many 'chunks' as she can catch. At the end of the time, the listener shows her list to the speakers and they go through and discuss the items.

C Work in pairs. Compare your answers to Exercise B. What other information can you remember from your skim-reading?

D SPEAK Work in groups. What do you think of the results of the research?

VOCABULARY
Nouns ending in -ion

A WORK IT OUT Look at *Is it time to start talking to strangers?* again. Find and underline eight nouns that end with *-ion*.

B Complete the definitions with the nouns from Exercise A.

1 to have an ___expectation___: to have a belief about what something will be like or what will happen

2 to have a positive ___reaction___: to feel good as a result of something that happens

3 to make a ___decision___: to choose something after thinking carefully

4 to have a ___connection___: to have a relationship to something

5 to have a confused ___expression___: to look like you don't understand something

6 to be in a difficult ___situation___: to be doing something that is not easy

7 to be in ___communication___: to be sharing information, ideas and feelings

8 to be an ___inspiration___: to give you new ideas or the enthusiasm to create something with them

C Go to the Vocabulary Hub on page 143.

D SPEAK Work in pairs. Do you agree or disagree with the statements below. If you disagree with them, change them so they are true for you.

1 Communication with other passengers is a waste of time. I don't know them and I might never see them again.

2 How far you choose to live from work is a very important decision. There is a connection between everyday happiness and the length of your commute.

PRONUNCIATION
Word stress in nouns ending in -ion

 A Listen to the pronunciation of the nouns ending
3.3 in *-ion* and underline the stressed syllables. Some words may have two stressed syllables.

1 action 2 connection 3 communication

B Listen again and repeat the words. How is the
3.3 stress pattern similar?

C Underline the stressed syllables of the nouns
3.4 ending in *-ion*. Then listen and check your answers. Repeat the words.

1 decision 4 inspiration

2 expectation 5 reaction

3 expression 6 situation

D SPEAK Work in pairs. Practise saying the words. Listen and check your partner's pronunciation.

SPEAKING HUB

A Go to the Communication Hub on page 154.

B SPEAK Work in groups. Compare your lists and explain your reasons to each other.

C DISCUSS Decide on the top three most annoying things. Discuss ways of stopping that behaviour. Compare your ideas with another group.

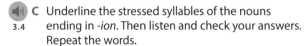
○– Talk about a difficult journey or travel experience
○– Talk about behaviour on public transport

- Evaluate suggestions and justify a choice
- Talk about why a plan didn't work

G — articles and quantifiers   P — sentence stress: quantifiers   V — gradable and ungradable adjectives
S — listening for signposting

READING

A SPEAK Work in pairs and discuss the question. Do you think there are too many cars on the road where you live or study?

B READ FOR MAIN IDEA Read *Whatever happened to Helsinki's Kutsuplus transport scheme?* Match the headings (a–e) with the paragraphs (1–5).

a The advantages of Kutsuplus
b The disadvantages of Kutsuplus
c How Kutsuplus worked
d Was Kutsuplus a success?
e What was Kutsuplus?

Whatever happened to Helsinki's *Kutsuplus* transport scheme?

1 e

A few years ago, Helsinki, Finland, decided it had a problem: there were **too many cars**. So the Helsinki Regional Transport Authority decided to hold a three-year trial of an on-demand minibus scheme <u>designed to</u> Ex C Q1 <u>reduce the number of cars on the road</u>. It was called *Kutsuplus* and it allowed passengers to choose where they wanted to go.

2 c Ex C Q2

<u>Passengers went online and selected a start and end point for their journey.</u>Rule 4; They then paid online and went to their nearest bus stop. **A minibus** arrived Rule 1 and took them to <u>the chosen end point</u>. If other **people** wanted to go to <u>the</u> Rule 2 <u>same area</u> at <u>the same time</u>, no problem: there was **plenty of** space and they Rule could share **the minibus**! Even if **people** often wanted to go to different places in Rule 2,4 <u>the same area</u>, **the online service** was able to choose <u>the best route</u> available, Rule 3 so everybody was happy!

3 a

For passengers, the key benefits of *Kutsuplus* were convenience and cost. They could choose where they wanted to go and they didn't have to wait long for the bus to arrive. During the time of the trial, the average *Kutsuplus* journey cost €5. In comparison, the average cost of a taxi journey started from €6, but could be much more expensive for longer journeys. Surely this would make *Kutsuplus* a great success! Well, not quite …

4 b

Although it was more convenient than a normal bus or the metro, unlike a taxi, the minibus wasn't able to take people exactly where they wanted to go. Passengers had to use the nearest bus stops as the start and end points of their journey. Another major problem was that there were very few buses in operation. <u>By the end of the trial,</u> Ex C Q3 <u>Kutsuplus had 21,000 registered users</u>, but only 15 buses. This would have a big effect on the result of the trial.

5 d

<u>In general, Helsinki residents had positive feelings about</u> Ex C Q4 <u>the scheme. A **lot of** them felt that it was convenient</u>, especially for people who lived in areas where there wasn't **enough** public stignsport. However, with **not enough** buses in operation, it wasn't convenient for everybody. <u>In the end, city officials decided not</u> Ex C Q5 <u>to continue the scheme.</u>

LEAD-IN

With books closed, elicit from students one positive thing and one negative thing they associate with cars and write these on the board. Put students into pairs to think of more before sharing answers as a whole class. Record useful ideas and language on the board.

READING

A Tell students to open their books and discuss the question. Monitor and make note of any errors for correction at the end of the lesson. Open the discussion to the whole class. Call on each pair to give their opinions. Encourage other members of the class to agree or disagree with the opinions given.

B Tell students to look at the pictures and tell them they are going to read an article about the Kutsuplus transport scheme in Helsinki, Finland. Then tell students to read the article and match the five headings with the five paragraphs. Set a time limit to prevent students from reading in too much detail at this point, but tell them that they will have the chance to read again for more detail. Check answers as a whole class but don't go into in-depth discussion of the article yet.

C Tell students to read the article again in more detail to answer the questions. Encourage students to underline the parts of the text that help them find each answer. Ask students to justify their answers with reference to the parts of the text they underlined.

D Tell students to discuss the questions in pairs. You could also ask if they think the scheme would be popular in their country and if they think it could work.

GRAMMAR HUB

3.2 Articles and quantifiers

Articles

a/an, the, no article

a/an	We use *a/an* the first time we talk about a singular noun.	I've got **a ticket** for the train. There was **an accident** on the main road.
the	We use *the* when we have already mentioned the person or thing.	There was an accident. **The accident** wasn't serious.
	We use *the* with singular nouns when it is clear what we are talking about or when there is only one.	I usually take **the bus** that leaves at 6.15.
	We use *the* with plural nouns when it is clear what we are talking about.	**The trains** that leave in the mornings are overcrowded.
no article	We use no article with the names of people, companies, cities and countries (except *the UK*, *the USA*, *the Netherlands*).	My cousin's name is **Sam**. He recently flew to **Colorado**, which is in **the USA**.
	We use no article when we talk about things in general.	Do you like **travelling**? **Buses** are sometimes faster than **trains**.

- We use *an* before a vowel sound. We use *a* before a consonant sound, even if the word begins with *a, e, i, o* or *u*.

  an hour, an expensive journey, a university town
- We sometimes use *the* before a type of transport.

  We always take the bus / the train / the plane.

- We use *the* before the names of seas and rivers and countries whose names are plural.

  the Atlantic Ocean / the River Nile / the United States / the Philippines

Quantifiers

	Countable nouns	Uncountable nouns
Question	**How many people** use the underground?	**How much traffic** was there on the road?
Positive number	There are **a few people** on the train.	There is **a little ice** on the roads so drive carefully.
	There are **a lot of / lots of people** waiting for the bus.	There is **a lot of / lots of information** in this booklet.
	There are **enough seats**.	There is **enough space**.
	There are **plenty of buses**.	There is **plenty of time**.
Negative number	There are **few people** on the train.	There is **little chance** of us getting there on time.
	There aren't **many people** here.	There isn't **much traffic** today.
	There aren't **enough seats**.	There isn't **enough space**.
	There are **too many people** on this train. It's **too small**.	There's **too much noise** on the train. It's **too noisy**.

3.2 Travel smart

GRAMMAR

A Tell students to focus on the words in bold in the second paragraph of the text, and elicit that the connection between them is the use, or lack of use, of articles. Tell students to refer to these examples to help them complete the rules.

B Tell students to find and underline more examples of articles in the same paragraph of the text and to match each to the rules.

C Direct students to the **Grammar Hub** on pages 126 and 127 (see TB30 and below).

D–F Discuss as a whole class after students complete the exercises.

G Direct students to the **Grammar Hub** on pages 126 and 127 (see TB30 and below).

H Begin the task by giving some personal examples, modelling how you can use quantifiers in your answers. Use the **Grammar Worksheet** on W11 for extra practice.

PRONUNCIATION

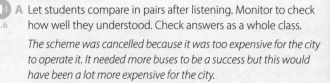

A–C Put students into pairs to discuss their answers and practise.

3.5

SPEAKING

A Let students compare in pairs after listening. Monitor to check how well they understood. Check answers as a whole class.

3.6

The scheme was cancelled because it was too expensive for the city to operate it. It needed more buses to be a success but this would have been a lot more expensive for the city.

B Put students into pairs to discuss what they think about the reasons given and if they agree with the decision.

C Put students into bigger groups to compare ideas. Ask students to expand on their ideas in feedback.

D Tell each group to discuss how they would either continue or adapt the scheme, either in Helsinki or in their own country. Finish with some feedback on students' use of language during the task.

> **Extra activity**
> For homework, students can research other ideas that cities or towns have used to solve car or traffic problems. Ask them to make notes on: key benefits, problems with the schemes, how residents felt about them. Review and discuss their research at the start of the next class.

GRAMMAR HUB

3.2 Articles and quantifiers

A Find eight more mistakes with articles and correct them.

  The journey from my house to my office only takes me
  about half ^an hour. There is ~~the~~ ^a quicker way – I could take
a/the bus – but I prefer to walk. There are many reasons for this.
  Firstly, ~~the~~ walking is healthy and I find it puts me in ^a good
  mood. I usually arrive at ^the office awake and ready for work.
  Going by ~~the~~ bus, on the other hand, leaves me feeling tired
  and stressed before ^the ~~a~~ day begins!

B Write one word in each gap. Sometimes more than one answer is possible.

1 How __much__ time have we got before the train comes?

2 Sometimes we take _____a_____ taxi and share the cost between us.

3 There weren't very __many__ passengers on my bus this morning. I wonder why.

4 I find that cycling is __an/one__ easy way to get through traffic jams.

5 Very _____few_____ people in the village have cars, so the bus service is really important to them.

6 There aren't __enough/__ places to park, and that's why
   there are traffic problems. __many__

C Tick (✓) the sentences that are correct. Write *of* in the right place in the sentences that are incorrect.

1 There are very few buses that go near my house. ✓

2 It will take a little time for the public to get used to the new system. ✓

3 Not enough people used the bus service so they stopped running it. ✓

4 A lot ^of passengers complain of overcrowding on the buses.

5 I don't often take taxis because they cost too much money. ✓

6 There are plenty ^of people who take their cars to work every day.

7 There are lots ^of taxis where I live.

8 There's plenty ^of money to improve the bus system.

9 There were few free seats on the train today. ✓

10 Is there too much traffic on our streets? ✓

➤ Go back to page 31.

C READ FOR DETAIL Read again. Complete the sentences by choosing a, b or c.

1 The long-term aim of *Kutsuplus* was to encourage people to stop …
   (a) driving cars.   c hiring minibuses.
   b using the metro.

2 Passengers could choose the start and end point of their journeys by …
   a asking at the bus stop.   (c) using the internet.
   b calling the driver.

3 There were … registered users by the end of the trial.
   a a small number of   (c) a lot of
   b not enough

4 Overall, people who lived in Helsinki thought the scheme was …
   (a) useful.   b expensive.   c unfair.

5 The local … stopped the scheme.
   a businesses   (b) government   c residents

D SPEAK Work in pairs. Do you think the *Kutsuplus* service was a good idea? Why/Why not?

GRAMMAR
Articles and quantifiers

A WORK IT OUT Look at the words in bold in paragraph 2 of *Whatever happened to Helsinki's Kutsuplus transport scheme?* Then complete the rules with *a/an*, *the* or – (no article).

Articles
1 We use _a/an_ the first time we mention a person or thing.
2 We use _the_ the second time we mention the person or thing.
3 We use _the_ when it is clear who or what we are talking about.
4 We use _–_ when we talk generally about people or things.

B Find and underline other uses of *a/an*, *the* or – (no article) in the same paragraph and match them with the rules (1–4) in Exercise A.

C Go to the Grammar Hub on page 126.

D PRACTISE Choose *a*, *the* or – (no article) to complete the questions.

1 How long does *a* / _the_ / – journey from where you live (or are staying) to where you study usually take?

2 Would you like to go by _a_ / *the* / – different type of *a* / *the* / _–_ transport? If so, which one?

E SPEAK Work in pairs. Ask and answer the questions in Exercise D.

F WORK IT OUT Look at the quantifiers in **red** in the text. Then choose the correct words to complete the rules.

Quantifiers
1 We use quantifiers to talk about **_amounts_** / *qualities*.
2 Quantifiers go **_before_** / *after* nouns.

G Go to the Grammar Hub on page 126.

H SPEAK Work in pairs. What is the public transport system like in your town? Does your town need more or fewer buses, trains or taxis? Why? Tell your partner.

PRONUNCIATION
Sentence stress: quantifiers

A Listen to the sentences from the article. Tick (✓) the sentences you hear. Which words are stressed?
3.5

1 a A <u>lot of</u> them felt that it was convenient.   ✓
  b A lot of <u>them</u> felt that it was convenient.   ☐

2 a There were very few <u>buses</u> in operation.   ☐
  b There were very <u>few</u> buses in operation.   ✓

B WORK IT OUT Listen again and repeat the sentences. Do we usually stress the main noun or the quantifier?
3.5

C SPEAK Work in pairs. Practise saying the sentences. Listen and check your partner's pronunciation.

SPEAKING

A Listen to an expert explaining why the *Kutsuplus* scheme was cancelled. What reasons does the expert give?
3.6

B Work in pairs and discuss the reasons. Do you think the local officials were right to stop the scheme? Why/Why not?

C Work in groups. Summarise your discussion. Explain your opinions and listen to the opinions of others.

D Work in groups. Plan how you could continue the scheme or do it differently.

LISTENING

A **SPEAK** Work in pairs. Look at the poster and discuss the questions.

1 What event is the poster advertising?

2 What happens during that event?

3 Why do cities and towns hold these kinds of event?

4 Does your city or town hold similar events?

 B **LISTEN FOR GIST** Listen to a city council meeting
3.7 about a Car-Free Day and answer the questions.

1 What is Alfred Shaw's view of the Car-Free Day?

2 Do the others at the meeting agree with him?

3 What is Alfred's opinion of cars generally?

4 What two events does Alfred suggest holding instead?

5 What reason does Alfred give for being at the city council meeting?

Glossary

ban (v) to say officially that someone is not allowed to do something

campaign (n) a series of actions intended to produce social change

pedestrian (n) someone who is walking, especially in a town or city, instead of driving or riding

 C **LISTEN FOR DETAIL** Listen again and choose the
3.7 correct answers.

1 Why don't annual Car-Free Days reduce the amount of traffic?

 a The city has little public transport.

 (b) Cars are the most effective type of transport.

 c You need more than ten Car-Free Days a year.

2 How do Car-Free Days affect the pollution levels?

 a They decrease the amount of pollution.

 b They increase the amount of pollution.

 (c) They do not change the amount of pollution.

3 What might increase the number of people buying electric cars?

 a Providing free electricity-charging stations.

 (b) Providing opportunities for people to test drive them.

 c Providing online videos showing their advantages.

4 Why do people prefer travelling by car rather than by bus?

 a There are not enough buses.

 b The buses are too slow.

 (c) The buses are dirty.

5 Why doesn't this city provide bicycles that people can rent?

 a The roads are not very safe.

 (b) The council has not discussed the idea.

 c It would be too expensive to do.

GREEN EVENTS

CAR-FREE DAY IS BACK!

Walking, jogging and cycling welcome.
Leave the car at home.

Join us for street market, competitions, music, picnic and play area.

Saturday 18th November

D Read the information in the box. Now listen again. For 1–7, put
3.7 the signposting language you hear in the correct position.

Listening for signposting language

When giving a short talk, speakers use signposting language to show the order of points and make their argument easy for people to follow.

- First, I want to talk about the problems.
- ¹ First of _____ all _____ …
- Firstly, …
- Finally, …

They can use it to introduce a new topic:

- Now, let's turn to the solutions.
- Moving on, I'll now discuss my ideas in more detail.
- ² _____ Let's _____ look at …
- ³ I'll now _____ move _____ onto …

They can use it to introduce an extra point:

- In addition, …
- ⁴ Here's another _____ reason _____ why …
- ⁵ And _____ another _____ thing, …
- Also, …

They can also use it to finish a section of a talk or to finish the talk:

- That's all I want to say on that. Any questions?
- In conclusion, …
- ⁶ In _____ short _____ , …
- ⁷ OK, to sum _____ up _____ …

E **SPEAK** Work in pairs. Discuss Alfred's arguments and claims. Do you agree or disagree with Alfred?

LISTENING

A Tell students to look at the poster and discuss the questions in pairs. In feedback, elicit students' opinions about Car-Free Days. Do they think they are a good idea? Would it work in their country? Why / Why not?

B Tell students they're going to listen to a city council meeting about a Car-Free Day. Check students understand that the *council* is the local government. Tell students not to worry if they don't understand everything as they just have to answer the two questions for now. However, draw their attention to the vocabulary in the glossary and check students understand the concept of *ban* and *campaign* by eliciting examples of both.

1 *He thinks it is useless and won't solve the traffic problems.*
2 *No, they disagree.*
3 *He thinks they are fantastic.*
4 *An e-car festival and Use Public Transport Week.*
5 *He wants the city to be a brilliant place to live.*

C Tell students to read the questions and to try to choose the correct answer from memory. Play the audio again for students to check. Check answers as a whole class and ask students to justify their answer with reference to exactly what was said during the meeting.

D Point out the strategies for listening for signposting language in the box. Explain that signposting language is used to organise a spoken or written text in order to make it easier to follow. Highlight the examples already filled in the box. Tell students to read the strategies and try to add any words or phrases they remember hearing in the audio in the correct places. Then play the audio again for students to listen and check.

E Elicit Alfred's arguments against Car-Free Days from the class. If students find this difficult, they could look at the audioscript and identify the arguments there. Once the arguments are all clear, put students into pairs to discuss the question. Discuss the students' opinions as a whole class and encourage any further debate.

AUDIOSCRIPT

 3.7

Listening, Exercise B
C = Chairperson   A = Alfred   C1 = Councillor 1
C2 = Councillor 2

C: OK, everyone, before we make our final decisions on this year's Car-Free Day, I'd like to invite some members of the public to give their views. First, let me introduce Alfred Shaw, a lecturer in business studies.

A: Thank you. OK, well, it's clear what most of you think about a Car-Free Day. An absolutely wonderful idea, right? However, I'm here to disagree. Actually, it's a really terrible idea.

C1: What? You can't be serious!

C2: Nonsense, it's an excellent idea.

A: OK, you say that, but it really isn't. Let's look at the facts. First of all, they don't solve the traffic problem. And, anyway, cars are, quite simply, fantastic.

C2: Fantastic? Come off it! We know they cause some awful problems.

Ex C Q1 **A:** OK, some things about cars are fairly bad, but they're clearly the best way to get around, and so they're never going to disappear. We've held this Car-Free Day 15 times before, but the rush-hour traffic jams have not gone away. Car-Free Days have a really tiny effect on driving habits, if any at all.

C1: But it's still better than doing nothing.

A: Is it? Here's another reason why we should think again. Car-Free Days don't even help the environment. Think about it. Although there may be
Ex C Q2 no cars in the city centre for that one day, those cars are still out there on the roads, just on different roads. So, all you're doing is moving the pollution. And another thing, the Car-Free Day causes massive traffic problems in the city, as drivers have to find other ways to go. Remember what happened last year, when that lorry got stuck under the railway bridge because we'd closed the main road? Because of that, there was an absolutely enormous traffic jam, trains were cancelled and thousands of pounds of damage was caused. People were furious about that, and rightly so.

In short, Car-Free Days are absolutely useless because they change nothing, and they create huge problems, not solutions. I'll now move onto what we should do instead.

C1: About time!

C2: Like what? A pedestrian-free day?!

C1: Ha ha. That's very funny.

A: Hmm, hilarious. You're clearly missing my point. We shouldn't ban anything, we should just improve everything.

Firstly, we should start a campaign to encourage people to buy greener cars. Let's get more people using electric and hybrid cars. This may be extremely difficult, but it isn't impossible. We could hold an
Ex C Q3 e-car festival and give people a chance to try the cars out in order to see their benefits. That would be a superb way to change things.

Also, we need to improve public transport and get people using it. We need more buses, and cleaner
Ex C Q4 buses – some of our old buses are really filthy, so it's no wonder people choose cars first. Let's invest some money, and then, why don't we run a 'Use Public Transport Week', instead of banning cars for a day?

C1: Actually, that's a really good idea.

A: Thanks – an extremely good idea, I'd say. Finally, we should encourage a healthier and greener lifestyle all year round, rather than just for one day a year. Let's get people back on bikes. Let's teach people of all ages how to cycle safely. Other cities have got
Ex C Q5 city bike hire schemes – why haven't we? We haven't even had a meeting to discuss it because you're too busy planning for Car-Free Day.

OK, to sum up, there are alternatives to Car-Free Days that are actually better for the environment and that actually reduce car use. Let's try them out, instead of holding another useless Car-Free Day. Right, any questions?

C2: Erm, isn't it true that your brother runs an electric car dealership? Perhaps that's …

A: Hey, what's that got to do with anything? Really! I just want our city to be a brilliant place to live, that's all.

3.2 Travel smart

VOCABULARY

A Tell students the sentences here all come from the meeting they listened to. Tell students to underline the adjective in each sentence.

B Go through the information about gradable and ungradable adjectives in the box with the students. Use *bad* in sentence 1 as an example, eliciting from students that it's possible to say *fairly, very, extremely, a bit, really bad*, and that it has a comparative form (*worse*), so therefore it is a gradable adjective. Tell students to look at the other adjectives from Exercise A and do the same to decide whether they are gradable or ungradable.

C Tell students to complete the gaps with the adjectives from Exercise A. Do the first one as a whole class to make sure students are clear on the relationship between the adjectives in each pair.

D Tell students that there can be more than one ungradable adjective for a gradable adjective. Elicit that *wonderful* is a synonym of *excellent* from Exercise C, as both mean very good. Tell students to match the others.

E Direct students to the **Vocabulary Hub** on page 143 for further practice of gradable and ungradable adjectives.

F Put students into pairs and tell them to use ungradable adjectives to describe a recent experience, as in the example. To provide a clear reason to listen, you could tell students not to say what they're describing so that their partner has to guess. Use the **Vocabulary Worksheet** on W12 for extra practice.

SPEAKING HUB

A Check understanding of *mayor* and drill pronunciation. Tell students the local mayor has decided to cancel the city's Car-Free Day and now wants a new project and campaign to reduce the traffic problems and pollution. Tell students they are going to read three proposals that have been put forward. Turn to the **Communication Hub** on page 151.

B Tell students to read through the proposals in groups, then discuss the advantages and disadvantages of each one. Tell students to make notes as they do this, as they'll need to refer to them when they share and explain their ideas later. Encourage students to add more of their own ideas to each proposal as well.

C Tell students that they have to decide which proposal would be the best. Give each group time to decide and prepare to justify their choice.

An alternative way to do this would be to divide the class into three groups, assign one of the proposals to each group and tell them that they have to prepare to argue for their proposal to be chosen as the best.

D Ask students to share their ideas with the class and see how similar their thinking was. Encourage students to explain their reasons, and if there is disagreement, encourage debate. If the alternative option was chosen above in Exercise C, each group could present their ideas, either to the whole class or in smaller groups containing one or two members of each previous group. Tell students to put forward as many reasons as they can for why their proposal should be chosen. Finish with a whole-class vote on who had the best justifications for their choice; students can't vote for their own group!

TEACHING IDEA by David Seymour and Maria Popova

Vocabulary: Gradable and ungradable adjectives

Use this activity to practise the grammar.

In pairs, match an adjective from the first list with one from the second. What is the difference between the two lists? (Write the words from each box in two columns on the board. Re-order the adjectives in the second box when you write them up; they appear here in the correct order.)

> good, clever, small, hot, happy, excellent, cold, ugly, tired, difficult, hungry, funny, interesting, large

> excellent, brilliant, tiny, boiling, thrilled, freezing, hideous, exhausted, impossible, famished, hilarious, fascinating, gigantic

Compare your answers with another pair.
Look at this conversation.
(Model the emphatic stress and ask the students to repeat it.)

A: This bedroom is rather small, isn't it?

B: Small? It's absolutely tiny!

In pairs, write similar short conversations with the words from the matching activity.
Invite pairs to read out some of their conversations.

Monitor and provide feedback on the emphatic stress. You can get pairs to swap their conversations for further practice. Finish with a class vote on the funniest conversation.

VOCABULARY
Gradable and ungradable adjectives

A Underline the adjectives in the sentences from the council meeting about the Car-Free Day.

1 Some things about cars are fairly <u>bad</u>.
2 That's very <u>funny</u>.
3 That's a really <u>good</u> idea.
4 This may be extremely <u>difficult</u>.
5 Car-Free Days have a really <u>tiny</u> effect on driving habits.
6 There was an absolutely <u>enormous</u> traffic jam.
7 People were <u>furious</u> about that.
8 Some of our <u>old</u> buses are really <u>filthy</u>.

B Look at the adjectives in Exercise A. Which are gradable? Which are ungradable? Use the information in the box to help you. G: bad, funny, good, difficult, old
U: tiny, enormous, furious, filthy

Gradable and ungradable adjectives

Gradable adjectives can be made stronger and weaker. We can use a range of adverbs to change their strength (*fairly, very, extremely, a bit, really*). They have a comparative form.

Ungradable adjectives cannot be made weaker. They already mean *very* + adjective. We can use some adverbs to emphasise the adjective (*extremely, absolutely, completely, really*). They do not have a comparative form.

C Write the adjectives from Exercise A in the correct place.

1 very ___good___ → excellent
2 very small → ___tiny___
3 very ___bad___ → terrible
4 very angry → ___furious___
5 very ___difficult___ → impossible
6 very dirty → ___filthy___
7 very ___funny___ → hilarious
8 very big → ___enormous___

D Match the ungradable adjectives (a–g) with some of the adjectives (1–8) in Exercise C.

a wonderful ___very good___
b huge ___very big___
c fantastic ___very good___
d brilliant ___very good___
e awful ___very bad___
f superb ___very good___
g massive ___very big___

E Go to the Vocabulary Hub on page 143.

F SPEAK Work in pairs. Describe something you have bought, seen, eaten or done recently using ungradable adjectives.

I saw an awful play last weekend. The lead actor was absolutely terrible. He kept forgetting his words!

SPEAKING HUB

A Go to the Communication Hub on page 151.

B DISCUSS Work in groups. Discuss the proposals and make notes of their advantages and disadvantages. Think of other ideas you can add to each proposal.

C PLAN Decide which proposal would be the best for the city and its people as well as being the best value for money.

D REFLECT Share your ideas with the class. Was your thinking similar or different?

- Evaluate suggestions and justify a choice
- Talk about why a plan didn't work

3.3 Getting there

F– tell a story P– intonation in responses

COMPREHENSION

A Complete the personal information with *Milly* or *Zac*.

Name:	1 Zac	2 Milly
Nationality:	American	American
Home town:	Seattle	Seattle
Address:	London	London
Job:	makes video games	owns a clothes store
Hobbies:	playing video games	cycling

B Look at the picture. Where do you think Milly and Zac are going today?

C Watch the video and check your ideas. Then answer the questions.

1 Which famous people does the cabbie say have been in the back of his cab? Beyoncé, Jay-Z, Prince Harry, Wayne Rooney, Gérard Depardieu, Cristiano Ronaldo, guy out of Coldplay, all of One Direction

2 Why are Milly and Zac amazed at the cabbie's story about his American girlfriend? It is identical to their story.

3 How does the cabbie react when Milly asks, 'Are you sure this is the right way?' He's offended.

D Work in pairs. Discuss the last time you took a taxi.

- Where did you go from and to?
- How much did it cost?
- What did you talk about?

FUNCTIONAL LANGUAGE

Telling a story in five stages

A Work in pairs. Complete sentences (1–8) in the grey box with the endings (a–h). Then watch the video again and check.

a ... went out with an American girl.
b ... what happened the other day.
c ... I was putting on a shirt and tie.
d ... got my cab licence.
e ... I miss you, Molly.
f ... who I had in the back of my cab the other week.
g ... she loved cycling.
h ... she stopped answering my calls.

Telling a story in five stages

Introduction

1 You'll never guess ... b

2 You won't believe ... f

3 I once ... a

Background

4 It was a few years ago now, when I ... d

The funny thing was she hated driving.

5 It turned out ... g

This is the best part: she used to run this fantastic little vintage clothes shop.

Problem

Well, a couple of months later, everything was going great, then one day, while I was watching the football, she said to me ...

6 Before I knew it c

All of a sudden things started to change.

Resolution

7 In the end ... h

Comment

8 I still love that girl ... e

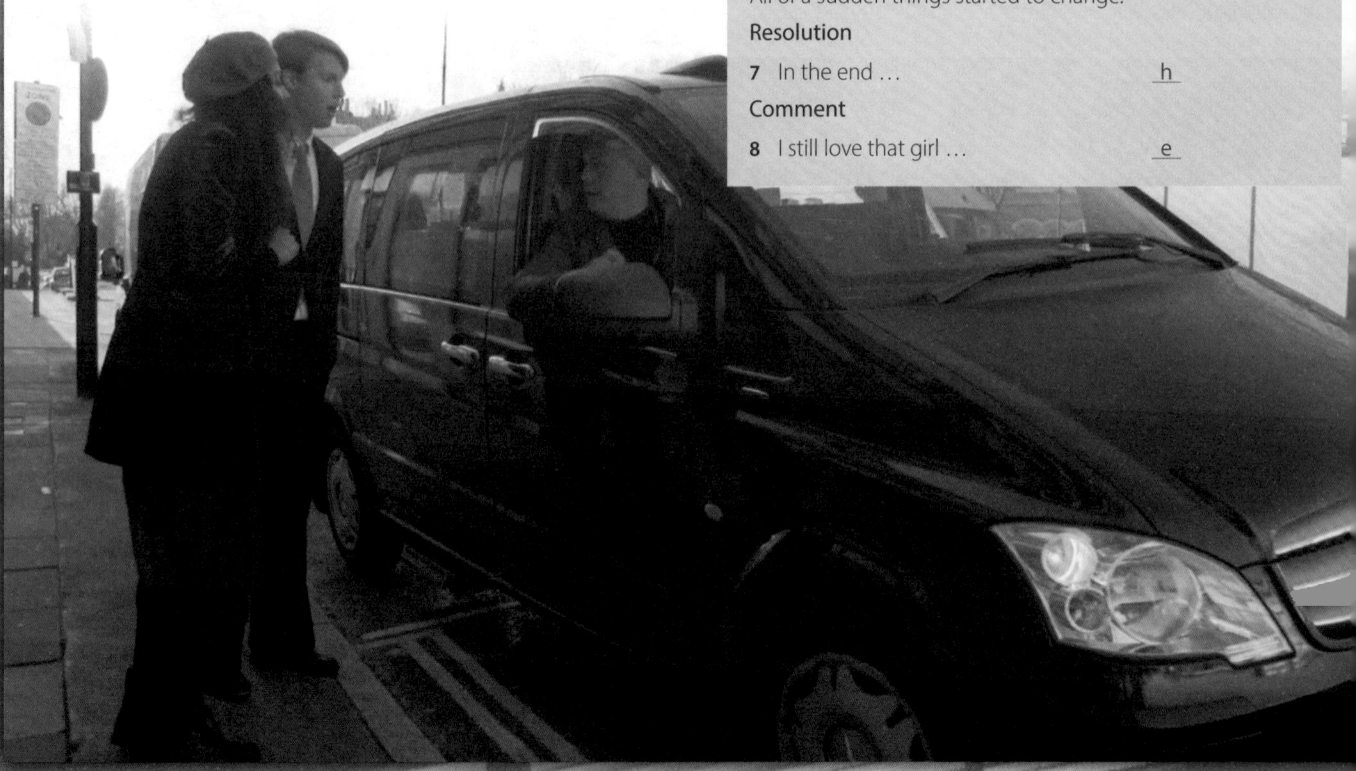

MILLY   SAM   NEENA   ZAC   GABY

B Work in pairs. Look at Milly and Zac's responses in the box. Student A – retell the cabbie's story. Student B – use the responses at an appropriate moment.

> No way!   Really? That's awesome!   Really? You're kidding!
> So what happened?   That's tough.

USEFUL PHRASES

A Complete the useful phrases with the correct form of the verbs in the box. There are two verbs you do not need.

> ~~be~~ do ~~have~~ ~~joke~~ ~~jump~~ ~~let~~ make ~~take~~

1 Whatever, _____**jump**_____ in the back, Jack.
2 Go on, _____**have**_____ a guess.
3 Only _____**joking**_____!
4 I'll _____**take**_____ a short cut.
5 _____**Are**_____ you two an item?
6 _____**Let**_____ me tell you something.

B How do you say these useful phrases in your language?

PRONUNCIATION
Intonation in responses

A Listen and write the responses in the table below. Then listen and repeat the responses. Copy the stress and intonation.

B Which two types of responses have similar intonation?

Something is very good	Something is difficult	Something is surprising
eally? That's awesome!	That's tough.	*I don't believe it!*
eally? That's amazing!	That must be	
ow! That's impressive.	hard to take.	Really? You're kidding.
	That's bad news.	No way!

C Work in pairs. Student A – use a prompt from the box or your own ideas to begin a conversation. Student B – respond appropriately.

> I found €50 in the street.   I got full marks in English.
> I got tickets to see my favourite band.   I won a prize.
> My dog died.   My father lost his job.

SPEAKING

A You are going to tell your partner about somebody you used to spend a lot of time with, but now you do not. Answer the questions.

● Who is this person – a childhood friend, a neighbour, a relative?
● When and how did you meet him/her?
● How often did you use to see him/her?
● What sort of things did you use to do / talk about?
● Why did you stop seeing him/her so much?
● When was the last time you saw him/her?
● What is he/she doing now?

B DISCUSS Work in pairs. Take it in turns to talk about the person. Use the functional language to structure your story, and if you are listening, respond in an appropriate way.

◯– Tell a story

➤ Turn to page 158 to learn how to write an email of complaint.

LEAD-IN

Ask students if they can remember a story and tell it to their partner.

COMPREHENSION

A Tell students to match the names with the fact files.

B Elicit a few ideas before students watch the video to check.

C ▶ Students discuss the questions in pairs.

D Tell the students about a taxi journey you've had, then ask them to discuss the questions in pairs.

FUNCTIONAL LANGUAGE

A ▶ Put students into pairs to complete the sentences, then play the video for students to watch again and check.

B Students retell the story, while their partner responds with the phrases. Then swap roles.

USEFUL PHRASES

A Ask students to complete the spaces with the correct form of the verbs. There are two verbs they won't need.

B Tell students to think about how they say the phrases in their own language. Are taxi drivers like that in their country?

PRONUNCIATION

3.8

A Play the responses to the story for the students to repeat, and put into the table.

B Check which two categories require similar intonation (*something is very good* and *something is surprising*).

C Tell students to practise with a partner by responding to the prompts in the box.

SPEAKING

A Tell students to think about the questions and make notes. Remind students to use some of the phrases for telling a story in five stages.

B Students talk about the person they chose with their partner. Remind them to respond appropriately while listening.

▶ VIDEOSCRIPT

M = Milly   Z = Zac   C = Cabbie

M: Come on! We don't want to be late – You're meeting my mom for the first time …

Z: OK OK! I'm coming!

C: Jack?

Z: Zac.

C: Oh whatever, jump in the back, Jack. Afternoon! Americans?

Z: Uh, yeah …

C: Lovely! Let's go! You'll never guess what happened the other day? Go on then, have a guess … Only joking! So anyway. You won't believe who I had in the back of my cab the other week: Beyoncé and Jay-Z!

M: Really? You're kidding?

C: I'm not! They didn't say much though. I asked them to write a song about me. They stopped talking after that.

Z: Well …

C: I've had everyone you can think of in the back of my cab. I've had Prince Harry, Wayne Rooney … who's that French bloke er Gérard Depardieu … who else? Cristiano Ronaldo, that guy out of Coldplay, and even all of One Direction …

Z: You had Prince Harry in your cab?

C: Well … it looked like him. Probably was.

Z: Right.

C: Hmmm. Traffic jam. There'll be a slight delay, I'm afraid. Hang on, I'll take a shortcut. So, er, are you two an item?

M: A what?

C: IS HE YOUR BOYFRIEND?

M: Oh, err, yeah.

C: Luverly. Lovely stuff. I once went out with an American girl. It was a few years ago now, when I got my cab licence. The funny thing was that she hated driving! She wouldn't get into my cab!

M: No way!

C: Well, it wasn't too bad – it turned out she loves cycling. Everywhere. Absolutely. Everywhere. Even in the rain! Ah, she was hilarious … She actually taught me to cycle!

Z: Really? That's awesome.

C: Yeah … and this is the best part – she used to run this fantastic little vintage clothes shop. It was amazing, full of colour – and she used to get me all these clothes! It was brilliant!

Z: So what happened?

C: Well, a couple of months later, everything was going great. Then one day, while I was watching the football, she said to me: 'I want you to meet my mum.' Before I knew it, I was putting on a shirt and tie and meeting up for lunch. She never liked me. Didn't even laugh at one of my jokes. Not even one of them!

Z: That's tough.

C: Yeah … all of sudden things started to change. She wasn't interested in me anymore – in the end, she stopped answering my calls. I still love that girl. I miss you Molly.

M: Milly?!

C: MOLLY. From Seattle.

M: Are you sure this is the right way?

C: Young lady, let me tell you something – I've been a cabbie all my life. My dad's a cabbie, my grandad was a cabbie, my great great … oh great! Here we are. That's er £9 please. Thank you. There you go.

M: Don't worry about it.

C: Have a lovely holiday!

Z: But we're not on holiday. Well then. Time to meet your mom. Let's do this …

3 Writing ● Write an email of complaint

W— using adverbs to give emphasis

A Work in pairs. Add to the list of common causes of complaint for travellers.

- litter on buses and trains
- poor quality in-flight entertainment
- a lack of space
- delays due to technical problems

B Work in pairs. Have you experienced any of the problems you wrote down in Exercise A? Did you make a complaint? Why/Why not?

C Read Asaf King's email of complaint. Are the sentences true (T) or false (F)? Correct the false sentences.

1 When he made the booking, Asaf paid more money to guarantee his seat. **T**

2 Asaf went quickly to check-in because he didn't have much time left. he arrived early **F**

3 There were no seats available on the flight to London. **T**

4 Asaf was not able to travel to Bangkok. took a new flight **F**

5 Asaf did not tell the airline staff about his seat reservation. staff ignored his reservation **F**

6 He wants the airline to give his money back and to pay extra for his problems. **T**

To: LuxAir Customer Services
Subject: A serious complaint:
Booking Reference No. 589RT

Dear Sir or Madam,

a I am writing to complain about the mistakes your airline made with my booking that meant I missed two flights and lost important business.

b On 17th April, I made a reservation with your airline for flight Y33 from Dublin to London on 23rd May. I also paid extra to reserve my seat.

c I arrived at Dublin airport two hours before the flight and immediately went to the check-in desks. As I had arrived early, I certainly wasn't expecting any problems, but sadly this was not the case. At check-in, I was told that the flight had been overbooked and was completely full, which meant I couldn't board the plane.

d This was extremely disappointing and incredibly inconvenient because it meant that I also missed my connecting flight, an international departure from London to Bangkok. The new flight to Bangkok cost me £500, and I missed an important meeting.

e The simple fact is that I had paid in advance to confirm my reservation, but you failed to hold my seat. I found your customer service at the airport completely unsatisfactory as your staff totally ignored my seat reservation.

f Because of the extra flight costs, my lost time and the effect on my business, I would like to ask for a full refund for my flight and for additional compensation.

I hope to hear from you soon regarding this matter.
Kind regards,
Asaf King

D Match the descriptions (1–6) with the paragraphs (a–f) in Asaf's email.

1 a detailed description of the main events **c**
2 the reason why you are writing the email **a**
3 the result you want from your email **f**
4 the key dates and places **b**
5 a summary of the main complaint **e**
6 the effects of the event and problems it caused **d**

E Look at the box. Then match the adverbs (1–3) with those that have a similar meaning (a–c). Use the email to help you.

Using adverbs to give emphasis

In the email, the writer uses adverbs to make a word stronger. An adverb usually goes before the adjective or verb that it describes.

- The flight … was **completely** full.
- This was **extremely** disappointing.

1 certainly — a incredibly
2 extremely — b totally
3 completely — c definitely

WRITING

A PREPARE Choose one of the situations to write an email about.

- Your recent flight was terrible.
- A member of staff gave you the wrong information.
- You experienced a long travel delay.

B PLAN Write detailed notes about what happened. Think about:

- where and when did it happen?
- what result do you want?

C WRITE Write a semi-formal email of complaint (150–250 words).

- Use Asaf's email and Exercise D to help you.
- Use adverbs to explain your problem.

158 WRITING

> Remind students to use adverbs of emphasis to make their writing more powerful.

> Refer students to this email as a model for the writing task.

> If students don't have a real experience to write about, they could invent one.

WRITING

With books closed, elicit *complain* and *make a complaint* in relation to what people do when they aren't satisfied with a service. Put students into pairs to discuss if they have ever made a complaint about anything. If they have, how did they complain and what was the result? If not, why not? Ask students to share their most interesting stories. You could tell them that for British people, making a complaint can be quite embarrassing, and ask if it is the same in the students' cultures.

A Tell students to look at the picture and elicit that it shows a bad travelling experience. Show students the list of common causes for complaint for travellers and ask them to add more. Discuss with the class and write any extra ideas elicited on the board.

B Give a personal example and then tell students to discuss in pairs if they have experienced any of the problems in the list. Ask them to also say if they made a complaint and why or why not.

C Tell students that they're going to read an email of complaint. Tell them first to decide if the sentences about the email are true or false and to correct the false ones.

D Tell students to read the email again, this time thinking about the way it is organised. Tell them to match the descriptions to the paragraphs.

E Point out the box and explain that adverbs are often used to give emphasis. Make sure students realise that the adverbs here are all used in the email. Tell them to look at how they are used to help them match those with a similar meaning.

WRITING TASK

A Tell students they're going to write their own email of complaint, either about a real experience they have had or an invented one. Tell students to choose one of the situations to write about.

B Tell students to plan their email by making notes about the questions. Tell them that the notes should be detailed but stress that they shouldn't start writing out the email in full yet.

C Tell students to write their emails, using their notes and referring back to the paragraph structure and use of adverbs for emphasis from Asaf's email. If there are any fast finishers, tell them to read each other's emails and comment on how effective they are. Do they think the email would achieve the desired result, and why or why not?

GRAMMAR

A Complete the story with the correct form of the verbs in brackets.

We left home early in the morning because it
¹_____was snowing_____ (snow) heavily.
After we had found a parking space at the airport, we
²_____went_____ (go) straight to
the check-in desks. That was when Kenny realised he
³_____had forgotten_____ (forgot) his passport.
He thought he ⁴_____had left_____ (leave)
it on the kitchen table!

I ⁵_____decided_____ (decide) to travel
without him, but this made me nervous because
I ⁶_____hadn't flown_____ (not fly)
on my own before. Luckily, when
I ⁷_____was waiting_____ (wait)
in the queue at security control, Kenny
⁸_____phoned_____ (phone) me with
some excellent news.

He ⁹_____had found_____ (find) his passport
in the car and ¹⁰_____was walking_____ (walk)
back to the check-in desks.

B Correct the mistakes in the following passage by using *a*, *an*, *the* or – (no article).

Japan has ~~the~~ᵃ famous network of bullet trains. ~~A~~ The network
is the world's busiest and connects the major cities of the
country. Like many ~~the~~ major train networks, it gets very busy
at peak times. It is mainlyᵃ transport system for long distances.

C Choose the correct quantifiers to complete the sentences.

1 The town centre is full of traffic jams during the day. There are just *too much* / **too many** cars on the road.

2 Our city has a bicycle-sharing scheme. But at peaks times it is difficult to get a bike because there are **not enough** / *too little*.

3 Overall, our town does not invest enough in transport schemes. This is because the council has *few* / **little** money for this.

4 How *many* / **much** of what the council says about the scheme is actually true?

VOCABULARY

A Choose the best words to complete the traffic reports.

Storm Anna is over, but there are still problems affecting roads and public transport. You should only travel if it is essential. The central railway station is closed, and they have ¹**cancelled** / *delayed* all trains to and from there. Better news below the roads for the ²**bus service** / *underground lines*. There ³**is a good service** / *are overcrowded trains* on all lines except for line 3. On that line, there are ⁴*severe* / **slight** delays of about ten minutes.

Traffic is building up on Bank Street due to the ⁵**roadworks** / *rush hour* at the corner of Bank and Church Street. You can expect ⁶*heavy delays* / **heavy traffic** all day there, and probably a ⁷*slight delay* / **traffic jam** during ⁸*heavy rain* / **rush hour**. That's certainly what happened yesterday. Nothing moved after 5 pm. So, avoid that route if you can.

B Complete the sentences with the nouns in the box.

communication connection decision
expectation inspiration situation

1 I don't like to make a ____decision____ too quickly as I may regret it later.

2 It is important to see the ____connection____ between the job you want and your own experience and knowledge.

3 Many jobs need strong ____communication____ skills because talking and writing to people is essential.

4 When your ____expectation____ is realistic, you are less likely to be disappointed.

5 When you cannot change a ____situation____ you are in, you can learn to accept it.

6 You can waste time waiting for ____inspiration____ to produce something. Sometimes it's best to take action.

C Find and correct the mistakes in four of the sentences.

1 Tell Stan that joke about the self-driving car. It's ~~very~~ hilarious.
_____

2 I'm very angry. The train is late again!
_____correct_____

3 This road is very bad. They need to repair it.
_____correct_____

4 Sometimes, the old buses are ~~very~~ filthy.
_____

5 These timetables are ~~very~~ impossible to understand.
_____

6 The London bus tour was ~~very~~ excellent.
_____

FUNCTIONAL LANGUAGE

Complete the dialogue with the words in the box.

~~awesome~~ ~~best~~ ~~couple~~ ~~dear~~ ~~guess~~
~~kidding~~ ~~sudden~~ ~~turned~~ ~~way~~

A: You'll never ¹____guess____ what happened on my last holiday with Kate. We got lost up a mountain without a map.

B: Really? You're ²____kidding____!

A: No, I'm not! It was a ³____couple____ of months ago in Patagonia. I left the map in our hotel.

B: Oh ⁴____dear____!

A: And even worse, it was dark when we got to the top. Then all of a ⁵____sudden____ Katie remembers she left the torch at the hotel, too.

B: No ⁶____way____! I can't believe she did that.

A: Yeah, we were a bit stupid. But we were lucky. We met two locals and they helped us get back. And you know the ⁷____best____ part?

B: What? Tell me!

A: They invited us for dinner. And it ⁸____turned____ out they owned the most expensive restaurant in town!

A: That's ⁹____awesome____.

4 Change

> There is nothing permanent
> except change.
> — Heraclitus

Old and new buildings contrast in modern day Hong Kong.

Change (n) a situation in which one person or thing is replaced by another.
Synonyms: replacement (n), substitution (n)

The quote suggests that change is central to reality and is the only constant.

Heraclitus (c. 535–475 BCE) was a Greek philosopher. His work mainly survives as fragments that are quoted by other authors. He is known for his doctrine of universal flux – everything is constantly changing. His ideas were influential in philosophy.

OBJECTIVES

- talk about resolutions and plans
- talk about a life-changing book or film
- make and discuss predictions
- discuss problems, reasons and consequences
- clarify and ask for clarification
- make and deal with complaints
- write a short essay

Work with a partner. Discuss the questions.

1 Look at the picture. What change does it show? Is it positive or negative?
2 Read the quote. Do you agree with it?
3 What have been the most important changes in your life?

CHANGE 17

OBJECTIVES

Read the unit objectives to the class.

UNIT OPENER QUESTIONS

With books closed, ask students what they associate with the word *change*. Are these associations generally positive or negative, and why?

1 Tell students to open their books and look at the pictures. Elicit what kinds of change are shown. Ask students to discuss with their partner whether they think these changes are positive or negative. Monitor and provide language input. Elicit any interesting ideas and language on the board at the end of the activity. Is the class generally optimistic or pessimistic about how the world is changing?

2 Tell students to look at the quote and think about whether they agree or disagree with it. Give them a few moments before speaking to write down a few ideas. They can also use this as an opportunity to request any new vocabulary.

Ask students to discuss their opinion in small groups. Monitor and encourage debate if students have different opinions.

3 Tell students to tell each other about the most important changes in their own lives. Before they start, elicit a few ideas on the board of areas of change they could discuss (e.g. communication, fashion, shopping, studying, transport, family, etc). Monitor to hear which students have experienced the most significant changes. Ask one or two to share them with the class.

WORKSHEETS

Lesson 4.1 Personal change

Grammar: Future forms: decisions, intentions and arrangements (W13)

Vocabulary: Collocations: goals and resolutions (W14)

Lesson 4.2 Social change

Grammar: Making predictions (W15)

Vocabulary: Prefixes: *dis-, mis-, over-, re-, under-* (W16)

4.1 Personal change
● Talk about resolutions and plans
● Talk about a life-changing book or film

G— future forms
V— collocations: goals and resolutions
P— intonation for attitude and mood
S— summarising

LISTENING

A SPEAK Work in pairs and discuss the questions.

1 Is New Year's Eve an important celebration:
   - for you?
   - in your country?

2 How do people celebrate the New Year in different parts of the world?

3 Why do people celebrate the New Year?

🔊 **B LISTEN FOR GIST** Listen to a video call between Julia
4.1 and Shireen. Then answer the questions.

1 What is their relationship and where are they?

They <u>are good friends. Julia is in Spain (Madrid)</u>. Shireen is in the UK (London).

2 Tick (✓) which of these topics they talk about.

a	their New Year's Eve activities	✓
b	moving house	☐
c	buying new clothes	✓
d	making new friends	☐
e	changing jobs	☐
f	learning a language	✓

3 What do you think a New Year's resolution is?

It's <u>a promise to yourself to make a positive change</u> in your life.

🔊 **C LISTEN FOR DETAIL** Listen again. Are the sentences
4.1 true (T) or false (F)? Correct the false sentences.

1 The weather was cold on New Year's Eve in London. **T**
He has decided to try to be more romantic in the future.
2 ~~Julia's boyfriend has always been very romantic.~~ **F**

3 Julia wants to do more physical exercise. **T**
She can speak Spanish, but wants to improve.
4 ~~Julia can't speak Spanish.~~ **F**
She has found a new teacher already.
5 ~~Julia is looking for a new teacher.~~ **F**

6 Shireen thinks Julia reads too many advice books. **T**
She agrees to eat less.
7 ~~Shireen agrees to stop eating chocolate.~~ **F**

D SPEAK Work in pairs and discuss the questions.

1 Look at the list of the ten most common New Year's resolutions. Which do you think are the top three? Go to the **Communication Hub** on **page 147** to check your answers.
   - get fit and healthy
   - get organised
   - enjoy life to the fullest
   - change the food you eat
   - quit unhealthy habits
   - help others achieve their dreams
   - fall in love
   - spend less, save more
   - learn something exciting
   - spend more time with family

2 What could people do to achieve these resolutions?

3 Which do you think are the hardest to achieve?

GRAMMAR
Future forms

A WORK IT OUT Look at the sentences (1–7) from the conversation between Julia and Shireen. Tick (✓) the sentences in which the speaker made a decision or plan before this conversation.

1	Oh! Oops! I'll do it now. Hold on.	☐
2	I've decided to get fit this year, so I'm going to join a gym.	✓
3	I did get pretty cold. I'm going to look for a new hat tomorrow.	✓
4	Sophie's coming here to have lunch.	✓
5	I'm meeting a new teacher on Thursday.	✓
6	Make your mind up now!	☐
7	OK, OK. I'll stop eating it every day.	☐

4.1 Personal change

LEAD-IN

Put students into pairs to discuss which is their favourite day of the year and why. Share any interesting answers.

LISTENING

A Tell students to look at the picture and elicit where it is (Sydney Opera House / Sydney Harbour) and what is happening (New Year's Eve fireworks' display). Put students into pairs to discuss.

B Tell students they're going to listen to a video call between Julia and Shireen. Focus them on the questions and tick boxes.

C Play the audio again. Students should correct any false sentences.

D Tell students to look at just Question 1 first. Encourage discussion in pairs and as a whole class before telling students to turn to the **Communication Hub** on page 147 to check their answers.

GRAMMAR

A Tell them to tick the sentences in which the speaker has made their decision or plan before speaking.

B Tell students to look at the sentences again and elicit the different ways they express the future. Tell students to look at the rules for using them and to complete the gaps with the phrases, referring to their answers to Exercise A to help them.

C Direct students to the **Grammar Hub** on page 128 (see TB39).

D Give students a chance to personalise the language by discussing the questions with their partner. Give a few personal examples to model the structures you would use to answer each question. Use the **Grammar Worksheet** on W13 for extra practice.

AUDIOSCRIPT

 4.1

Listening, Exercises B and C
J = Julia   S = Shireen

J: Hi, Shireen.

S: Hi, Julia. I can't see you; I don't think you've clicked the video button.

J: Oh! Oops! I'll do it now. Hold on. There we go.

S: That's better. Good to see you. Happy New Year!

J: And happy New Year to you!

S: How's everything going in Spain?

J: Great. We had a lovely time on New Year's Eve; there's a real party atmosphere in Madrid. We were at a house party, and then out on the streets at midnight, eating grapes, dancing and drinking hot chocolate – just lovely!

S: Well, lucky you! Sounds better than mine. We went to see the fireworks at the London Eye.

J: But that sounds amazing!

S: Oh, I'm sure they were – it's just we never actually saw them.

J: Oh no! What happened? You didn't get lost again, did you?

S: Not exactly – we just weren't early enough. There was a massive crowd and we got stuck in a small road. We could hear it OK, but couldn't see a thing.

J: Oh! I bet it was freezing, too. I'm glad I was at that party and had that hot chocolate at midnight.

S: Yeah, I can imagine. We were outside for hours, and I lost my hat. To be honest, I did get pretty cold. I'm going to look for a new hat tomorrow; Sophie's coming here to have lunch, and then we're going sales shopping.

J: That's nice. Is that one of your New Year's resolutions? Are you going to finally buy some new clothes? No more going out in your sister's old ones?

S: Haha, very funny. Actually, I've not made any resolutions yet.

J: Haven't you? I've made quite a few.

S: Really? What've you decided?

J: Try and guess.

S: OK, OK! Let me see. So, are you going to get married this year? Time to copy me?

J: Ooh, that's a big question to ask! No, no plans yet, but Alberto's said he's going to buy me flowers every

Ex C Q2   month. He's going to try to be more romantic, for a change.

S: That's great. He sounds sweet. Let's hope he keeps that one. So, what are yours?

J: Well, I've decided to get fit this year, so I'm going to join a gym, and I'm going to study Spanish more seriously. I find it quite hard to follow Alberto's friends.

Ex C Q4   S: That's a surprise! I always thought your Spanish was really good.

Ex C Q5   J: Well, not good enough. In fact, I'm meeting a new teacher on Thursday, for one-to-one lessons.

S: Really? That's quick!

J: Well, there's no point in putting things off. Just get started and then stick to the plan. I was reading a self-help book about this the other day: *How to reach your goals and change your life.*

S: Another self-help book? I reckon you should make a resolution to stop reading them.

J: Well, I think you should read some. It'd be good for you.

S: Really? I'll leave that to you, I think.

J: Oh, come on – now's the time to make some resolutions. What do you want to achieve this year? Or change? What about your chocolate habit? Resolutions are a great way to quit bad habits.

S: My chocolate habit? What do you mean?

J: You eat some every day, don't you?

S: Well, just a little. At work, you know.

J: Shireen, I really think you should cut it out of your diet. I was reading about how we've all become sugar addicts and …

S: That's a surprise! Another book! But, yeah, I know what you mean. It's just that I get really bored at

Ex C Q7   work. I don't think I can totally quit, but I'll cut down on the amount I eat. Happy now?

J: Cut down by how much? There's no escape – make your mind up now!

S: OK, OK, I'll stop eating it every day. I'll have chocolate on Fridays only, as a treat.

J: Great, and I'll make sure you don't break that resolution.

S: Great, and how are you going to do that? Going to come to work with me each day?

J: Hmm, I'll put a webcam on your office desk.

S: Well, at least you can see how boring my job is then.

4.1 Personal change

PRONUNCIATION

🔊 A–C Monitor and give feedback as students complete the exercises.

4.2; 4.3
D Put students into pairs and tell student A to turn to the Communication Hub on page 148 and student B to turn to page 153. When they seem ready, tell students to have the conversation and think carefully about their intonation.

VOCABULARY

A–B Put students into pairs to check answers before whole-class feedback.

C Direct students to the Vocabulary Hub on page 143 for further practice.

D Give a personal example as a model and then ask students to discuss the questions with their partner. Use the Vocabulary Worksheet on W14 for extra practice.

SPEAKING

A Put students into pairs and tell them to imagine they have agreed to make eight resolutions together. Tell student A to turn to the Communication Hub on page 149 and student B to page 150.

B Tell students to follow the instructions, first making resolutions about their own topics, then making further resolutions about their partner's topics.

C Make bigger groups and encourage pairs to exchange ideas and discuss which resolutions will be easy or hard to keep.

GRAMMAR HUB

4.1 Future forms

• We use *will* when we make a decision at the time of speaking.

I'll get my coat and we can leave now.

I won't buy this dress because it's too small.

• We use *be going to* for our intentions (the things we want to do or have already decided to do).

Salma is going to cut down on the amount of chocolate she eats.

We aren't going to have a New Year's party this year.

Are you going to keep your New Year's resolutions?

• We use the present continuous when we have made an arrangement for a certain time in the future, often with another person.

Aisa is going shopping with her sister tomorrow.

He isn't coming out with us tonight.

What are you doing on New Year's Eve?

Be careful!

• We don't use the present continuous for intentions that haven't been arranged yet. We use *be going to*.

I'm going to write a book one day.

NOT ~~I'm writing a book one day.~~

4.1 Future forms

A Match the sentences (1–6) to the answers (a–f) to make short dialogues.

1 The phone's ringing! — d
2 Are you staying at home tonight? — f
3 Would you like anything else? — e
4 Josh is having a fireworks party tomorrow. — c
5 I've lost my wallet! — a
6 What time are you meeting the others? — b

a Oh no! What are you going to do?
b Sometime tomorrow morning.
c Sounds amazing. Can I come?
d OK. I'll get it!
e Yes, I'll have a coffee, please.
f No, I'm having dinner with Kate.

B Choose the correct option.

1 A: 'I've just heard it's Dan's birthday today.'
   B: 'Oh! *I'll get* / I'm getting him a present at lunchtime, then.'

2 Next year, I'm *going to try* / trying to keep my New Year's resolutions.

3 It's all arranged. We'll move / *We're moving* house next Tuesday.

4 I made a big decision last week. I'll / *I'm going to* look for a new job.

5 A: 'I don't think I'll ever fall in love.'
   B: 'Don't be silly. It's happening / *going to happen* soon, I'm sure.'

C Complete the dialogue with the correct form of the words in brackets. Sometimes more than one answer is possible.

Ashanti: What are you doing at the weekend, Camilla?

Camilla: I ¹am/'m not doing (not / do) anything special. Why?

Ashanti: Well, I'm going on a two-day self-help course. Come with me!

Camilla: Self-help?

Ashanti: Yes. I've decided I ²am/'m going to change (change) my life.

Camilla: It doesn't sound like my kind of thing. What time ³are you leaving / (leave) tomorrow? are you going to leave

Ashanti: Early – at about eight o'clock.

Camilla: In that case, I definitely don't want to come! Tomorrow's Saturday and I ⁴am/'m not working (not / work). I ⁵am/'m going (sleep) until eleven to sleep o'clock and then have breakfast in bed!

Ashanti: All right. If you're sure. In that case, I ⁶ will/'ll call (call) you on Sunday evening and tell you all about it.

Camilla: OK. Have a good time!

➤ Go back to page 39.

B Complete the rules with the phrases in the box.

> already   at a certain time in the future
> at the time of speaking

Future forms

1 When we talk about future actions and events, we use *be going to* when we have _____ already _____ decided to do something.

2 We use *will* when we make the decision _____ at the time of speaking _____ .

3 We use the present continuous when we have a planned arrangement ___ at a certain time in the future ___, often with another person.

C Go to the Grammar Hub on page 128.

D SPEAK   Work in pairs and discuss the questions.

1 What are you doing tonight?

2 Have you got any plans or arrangements for the weekend?

3 What do you intend to do over the next few months?

4 Imagine you have just realised you left your wallet at home. What will you do?

PRONUNCIATION
Intonation for attitude and mood

Intonation for attitude and mood

We change the tone of our voice to communicate our feelings about or attitude towards something. For example, interested/uninterested, surprised/unsurprised, positive/negative.

Our tone of voice can be in a high, mid or low position.

As we speak, our tone may rise and fall to show mood and attitude.

A Listen and write down the five words and phrases that you hear. They are in a neutral tone.   1. OK, OK.   2. Great.   3. Really?   4. Well, …   5. That's a surprise.

B Listen to the same five words and phrases. Each phrase is said in two different tones. Match each tone (*a* or *b*) with the moods and feelings below.

1 very positive   a
  not very positive   b

2 excited   b
  unexcited   a

3 interested and surprised   a
  not interested   b

4 serious/determined   b
  unsure   a

5 quite surprised   a
  not surprised at all (sarcastic)   b

C Listen again and repeat the sentences.

D SPEAK   Work in pairs. Student A – go to the Communication Hub on page 148. Student B – go to the Communication Hub on page 153.

VOCABULARY
Collocations: goals and resolutions

A Match the phrases (1–6) with phrases with a similar meaning (a–f).

1 make a resolution   a do less of something
2 keep a resolution   b achieve something
3 break a resolution   c set (yourself) a goal
4 quit a bad habit   d not do what you promised
5 reach a target   e stick to a plan
6 cut down on   f stop doing something
  something   that is not good for you

B Choose the best words to complete the sentences.

1 I've made a resolution *to learn* / *of learning* ten English words a day.

2 He managed to keep his resolution *by* / *in* using a fitness app.

3 He quit *smoking* / *smoke* last year.

4 She wants to cut down on *drink* / *drinking* coffee.

5 His goals are not very *realistic* / *real*. They're too hard to achieve.

6 Stick to your plan *until* / *when* you reach your target.

C Go to the Vocabulary Hub on page 143.

D SPEAK   Work in pairs. Discuss your experiences of making resolutions and achieving goals. Find out:

• about resolutions your partner has made, kept and broken.

• how your partner managed to achieve his/her goals and stick to his/her plans.

• if your partner has ever quit, or cut down on, doing something.

SPEAKING

A Work in pairs. It is New Year's Eve, and you have agreed with your friend to each make eight resolutions. Student A – go to the Communication Hub on page 149. Student B – go to the Communication Hub on page 150.

B Talk to your partner about your resolutions, and ask them to make a resolution for each of your topics.

C Compare your resolutions with another pair. Do you think the resolutions will be easy or hard to keep?

READING

A Choose the correct sentence endings.

1 Self-help books …

   a contain instructions for doing something, especially operating a machine.

   (b) are designed to help you solve your own problems or improve your life.

2 Self-help books are usually written in …

   a a formal style that is for experts only.

   (b) an informal style for anyone.

B SCAN Read *Life Cycle* quickly. Match the phrases (1–5) with the topics (a–e).

1 Helena Schneiderlin   **a** a journey

2 *Life Cycle*   **b** the author's next book

3 Paris to Moscow   **c** the author's passion

4 cycling   **d** the author

5 *Inner Pedal Power*   **e** the author's first book

Life Cycle: How to find what you love and love what you find

About this book

Ten years ago, Helena Schneiderlin was a hard-working mum with no time for herself. Like many people, she didn't know what Ex B **she really wanted to do with** her life. Today, Schneiderlin is a cyclist who is well known for going on long and difficult journeys. She has ridden from Paris to Moscow by herself. She has also ridden across Australia, and last year she rode from the bottom of South America to the top.

Thanks to her cycling experiences, and the effect they have had on her life, Schneiderlin has also become a leading lifestyle expert. Her talks have been watched millions of times online, and she is often asked to speak at international lifestyle events and conferences.

Ex B In *Life Cycle, which is her first book*, she Ex B describes how finding her true passion changed her life, and explains how you can find yours.

'This isn't a book about cycling,' says Ex A Q1 Schneiderlin. 'It's a book about finding the thing that you enjoy doing most, and helping to make that thing benefit all other areas of your life.'

In *Life Cycle*, Schneiderlin uses her own story as an example for others to follow. She describes how she found her passion for cycling while on holiday with her family, and what it has taught her about commitment, sacrifice and success. She provides valuable advice and life Ex A Q2 lessons that apply to all of us, including chapters on getting rid of the things in life that aren't helping, and how to identify the things that make you feel better about yourself.

Schneiderlin says:

> I believe that everyone has a passion, but they may not know what it is. I also believe that when you find that passion, you should use it to improve every area of your life. In my case, it was cycling – but it could have been anything. What's important is finding the thing that you love, and then using it in the right way.

4.1 Personal change

READING

A With books closed, write the word *self-help book* on the board with some of the letters missing and replaced by a dash, e.g. *s___-h___ b___*. Explain the concept of a self-help book and try to elicit. To check the understanding of the concept, ask students what type of problems you might buy a self-help book to help with. Tell students to open their books and answer the questions.

B Tell students they're going to read about a self-help book. Tell them to look at the images and to predict what they think the book will be about. Elicit some predictions, then tell students to scan the text to match the phrases with the topics. Explain that scanning means reading quickly to find specific information, so students don't need to worry about unknown vocabulary to do this.

C Point out the strategies for summarising in the box and make sure they understand the purpose of a summary. Tell students to read the two summaries and choose which is best and why, thinking about the summarising strategies as they do this. Let students compare answers in pairs before checking answers as a whole class. Ask students to justify their choice with reference to the strategies.

  1 *repeats too many details, and some phrases are copied word for word. It doesn't give a clear overview of all of the information in the description.*
  2 *is the best summary. It mentions all of the most important pieces of information from the book description but it doesn't copy the description word for word.*

D Tell students to discuss with a partner whether or not they would like to read *Life Cycle* and why. Discuss as a whole class and ask if students have ever read any similar books to this. If they have, what did they think of them and would they recommend them.

TEACHING IDEA
by David Seymour and Maria Popova

Topic: Hobbies

Use this activity to extend the topic.

(Arrange the students so that they are standing/sitting in a circle. Stand in the middle. Ask each of these questions to individual students at random. After they answer it, tell them to repeat the question to the next student and make a note of the student's answer. Indicate that they should continue the chain so the question progresses around the class. Meanwhile, introduce the other questions so that in the end there are lots of questions moving around the class.)

> What sports do you play, if any? How much time do you spend watching TV? Have you got a hobby? What hobby would you like to take up? What do you do on Sunday afternoons? How much free time do you have? What do you read for enjoyment? What hobbies did you use to have as a child? When and where did you last go to the seaside? What are the main leisure activities in your family?

Turn your notes into full sentences, e.g. *Maria wants to take up hang gliding.*

In small groups, discuss these questions.

> What are the main leisure activities in the UK/USA and in your country? What about other countries? What do you understand by the expressions quality time, the work ethic and the leisure society? How much quality time do you get? What do you think is the right balance between work and play?

TEACHING IDEA
by David Seymour and Maria Popova

Topic: Leisure survey

Use this activity to extend the topic.

In small groups, find out who:

- watches TV the most
- has the most interesting hobby
- has had the most hobbies
- has been a collector of something

METHODOLOGY HUB
by Jim Scrivener

The importance of skills work

Don't underestimate the importance of skills work. Not every lesson needs to teach new words or new grammar. Lessons also need to be planned to give students opportunities to practise and improve their language skills. Skills work is not something to add in at the end of a five-year course in English. There is no need to wait for extensive knowledge before daring to embark on listening, reading and speaking work. On the contrary, it is something so essential that it needs to be at the heart of a course from the start. Even a beginner with one day's English will be able to practise speaking and listening usefully.

4.1 Personal change

LISTENING

🔊 **4.4**

A Tell students that they're going to listen to four people talking about a book or a film that changed their lives. Tell them to listen and match each speaker to what they talk about. Remind students that they don't need to worry if they don't understand everything the speakers say and that they will be able to listen again for more information after completing this task.

🔊 **4.4**

B Before listening, tell students to look at the summaries of what each speaker said and to try to complete them with the words in the box. Play the audio again for them to check.

C Put students into pairs to discuss which of the books or films they are most interested in and why. Encourage students to tell each other if they have read or seen any similar books or films.

SPEAKING HUB

A Tell students they are going to talk about a life-changing book or film. If students find this a bit daunting, rephrase it to *a book or film that had a big effect* on them. Tell students to read the questions and to make notes to prepare what they're going to say. Remind students specifically about the strategies for summarising and elicit what makes a good or bad summary. Monitor as they prepare, helping with language as required and ensuring that students are just making notes and not scripting exactly what they're going to say.

B Tell students to tell their partner about their chosen book or film and to explain in as much detail as they can why it had such a big effect on them. Encourage students to listen carefully while their partner is speaking and to ask follow-up questions.

For further practice, you could put the students with a new partner to repeat the task. This time give a shorter time limit, but tell students they need to include all the key information. This would force students to think more carefully about the language they use to summarise the book or film, and to be more precise in expressing how it affected them.

Conclude the activity by asking students which of their classmates' recommended books or films they'd most like to read or see and why. Write any book or film recommendations up on the board.

Extra activity

The list could be used to encourage extensive reading, as well as watching films in English outside class. If any of the titles suggested are available in English, they could be added to a class list of reading materials. Also this lesson could be used to introduce any extracurricular book club that is planned. Students can be asked to bring in English books to share and discuss at the next lesson.

Either way as a follow-up activity, students can write up a brief book or film recommendation based on the work they spoke about.

AUDIOSCRIPT

🔊 **4.4**

Listening, Exercise A
A = Announcer   M = Maya   L = Lukas   J = Jody
H = Hassan

A: Maya

M: I never usually bother with self-help books. I usually prefer fiction, especially things like sci-fi and fantasy. But last year, I read a book that totally changed the way I feel about myself. It's called *Life Cycle* and it's by a famous cyclist and lifestyle expert called Helena Schneiderlin. The book explains how you can find

Ex B Q1 the real you and be a happier person when you find your true passion. It gives you advice on how to find the thing that you love and how to use it to improve

Ex B Q1 the quality of your life. I followed the advice in the book, and since then I've become much happier. It's definitely changed how I feel about myself. It's

Ex B Q1 changed my life really. I'm much more confident now.

A: Lukas

L: I think the one thing that changed my life most of all was a book called *The Road*. It's by Cormac McCarthy

Ex B Q2 and it's about a father and son on a journey through a strange and unwelcoming place. It might be the future after a terrible event – the book doesn't say exactly. Really, I think it's about the relationship between the two characters. Even though their situation is very bad, the love they have keeps them strong. I'll never forget the first time I read this book.

Ex B Q2 It made me think about my own relationship with my father. We don't always get on, but I think *The Road* has helped me to understand him better.

A: Jody

Ex B Q3 **J:** There's a book called *Sapiens*. I only read it last year, but honestly, I can't think of another book that has

Ex C Q3 had such a strong effect on me. It's a history book, and it tells the story of the human race – everything, from how we started as hunters, and then became farmers, on to how we developed cities and industry. It's written by Yuval Noah Harari. He talks about

Ex B Q3 religion, money, countries, law – everything. It's a very impressive piece of work, and it really helped me to see things in context. I feel I've got a better understanding about who we are now I've read that book.

A: Hassan

H: Seeing the film *Hoop Dreams* was a life-changing moment for me.

Ex B Q4 It's a documentary about two teenagers in Chicago who want to be professional basketball players. It follows six years of their lives, as they try and make it to the top. Both boys come from poor backgrounds,

Ex B Q4 and the film is about a lot more than just basketball. It's about society, and it's about how a life can change in an instant. I was really into basketball when I was young, and I went into the cinema that day wanting to be a basketball player, but by the time I walked out of the cinema, I wanted to be a film-maker instead. And that's what I am now. *Hoop Dreams* inspired me to make documentaries.

C SUMMARISE Read the two summaries of the book *Life Cycle*. Which is the best summary? Why? Use the strategies in the box to help you.

Summarising

A summary gives a brief explanation of the most important parts of the text.

To write a summary, first identify the details in the original text that don't need to be included in a summary. Then find the main points in the original text. Finally, put these together to make a summary, but try not to copy word for word.

1 Helena Schneiderlin has gone on a lot of long bicycle journeys. Once she rode from Paris to Moscow. Another time she rode across Australia. She has also ridden all the way up South America. She is a mum. She is a lifestyle expert and lots of people watch her talks on the internet. This is her first book. This book is about lifestyle changes. This book is about finding the thing you enjoy doing most. It is not about cycling, but she does talk about how she found her passion for cycling while she was on holiday with her family. This book is also about improving your life.

2 Helena Schneiderlin is a top lifestyle expert and a well-known cyclist who has ridden across continents. In this, her first book, she explains how cycling led to a life change and self-discovery, and gives advice on how to find your true passion. Using her own story as a guide, the author explains what she has learnt from cycling, and discusses how these 'life lessons' can apply to all of us, in all aspects of life.

D SPEAK Work in pairs. Would you like to read *Life Cycle*? Why/Why not?

Since being published last year, *Life Cycle* has become the fastest-selling self-help book in modern times. Now available as an e-book, this edition also includes the first chapter of Ex B Schneiderlin's next book.

Inner Pedal Power: How I found myself on two wheels.

LISTENING

A LISTEN FOR GIST Listen to four people talking about books or films that changed their lives. Write *Maya*, *Lukas*, *Jody* or *Hassan*.

4.4

Who talks about …

1	a non-fiction film?	Hassan
2	a fiction book?	Lukas
3	doing what the book suggested?	Maya
4	the whole of human history?	Jody

B LISTEN FOR MAIN IDEA Complete the summaries (1–4) with the words in the box. Then listen again and check your answers.

4.4

> advice   characters   confident
> documentary   father   history   impressive
> journey   passion   society   sport   recently

1 Maya read a self-help book about finding your true ___passion___. She followed the ___advice___ in the book and now she feels happier and more ___confident___.

2 Lukas read a book about two ___characters___ on a ___journey___ in a strange place. The book made him think about his own relationship with his ___father___.

3 Jody learnt a lot about the ___history___ of the human race in a book she read ___recently___. She thinks the book is very ___impressive___.

4 Hassan saw a ___documentary___ set in the USA. He feels that the story is about more than ___sport___; he thinks it also has an important message about ___society___.

C SPEAK Work in pairs. Which book or film from the listening are you most interested in? Why?

○ SPEAKING HUB

A PLAN You are going to talk about a life-changing book or film.

1 Choose a book or film that had a big effect on you.

2 Think about how you can summarise the book/film:
   • What kind of book/film is it?
   • Who wrote/made it?
   • What is it about?

3 Think about how it affected you:
   • When did you read/see it?
   • Why did you read/see it?
   • How did it change the way you think/feel?
   • Who else do you think should read/see it?

B SPEAK Work in pairs. Tell your partner about the book or film that changed your life. Listen to his/her description. Ask and answer questions.

○– Talk about resolutions and plans
○– Talk about a life-changing book or film

4.2 Social change

- ● Make and discuss predictions
- ● Discuss problems, reasons and consequences

G – making predictions

P – contraction of *will*; linking final consonant and first vowel sounds

V – prefixes: *dis-, mis-, over-, re-, under-*

S – paraphrasing

READING

A **SPEAK** Work in groups. Have you ever predicted something that later came true?

B Look at the headline of the article. Which word means:

   a a person who has detailed knowledge about a subject? expert

   b a person who talks about future events and situations? forecaster

C **READ FOR GIST** Read *How super-forecasters could replace professional experts*. Then choose the best summary.

   1 Philip Tetlock carried out a study into why experts are good media guests, but make predictions that are generally less accurate than those made by most ordinary people.

   2 Philip Tetlock carried out a research project to show that ordinary people who have particular thinking skills often make better future predictions than experts.

How super-forecasters could replace professional experts

Katy Macnab

'Five minutes left, and Brazil are leading by three goals. They're going to win the World Cup again.' Apart from situations like this, the only certain thing about the future is that our predictions will probably be wrong.

In his early research, Philip Tetlock, of the University of Pennsylvania, showed that professional experts are only slightly better at predicting the future than monkeys. However, his most recent study is more hopeful.

This project involved thousands of ordinary people making predictions about social change. They used the internet, but they did not have detailed knowledge of a topic or access to secret data. Despite this, Tetlock found that 2 per cent of them were rather good at it – better than both monkeys and professional experts. These 'super-forecasters' are clever, but not geniuses. However, they do have good thinking skills that anyone can develop.

Ex D Q2 Super-forecasters are analytical thinkers who update their opinion when they get new information, and they don't let their personal hopes affect their thinking. Importantly, they listen carefully to

different views that they then use in their forecast. This perhaps explains why they make their most accurate predictions when working in teams of super-forecasters. Ex D Q3

Surprisingly, professional experts often lack these qualities. They tend to work alone and have strong personal opinions that guide their thinking. They speak with great confidence, stressing they are totally certain: 'I'm sure all cars will be driverless', 'Robots are going to replace office workers', 'We won't have an early election'. This means they are great TV guests and bloggers, but not the best forecasters. Ex D Q1 Ex D Q4 Ex D Q6

Super-forecasters don't speak in a way that suits TV. They are more cautious: 'There may be an early election', 'People might stop reading newspapers', 'Chinese could become a global language'. They also use percentages to show how likely something is: 'I think this has an 80 per cent chance of happening'. In this way, the team can discuss different ideas easily and make a final prediction. Ex D Q5

Tetlock also identified three useful techniques, namely looking at current trends, comparison with past events and exploring the possible effects of a prediction: 'If everyone uses electric cars, how will we produce enough electricity?'

In the future, we will definitely develop better computers to make accurate predictions about our society. For now though, teams of super-forecasters are the best crystal balls we have.

Glossary

analytical (adj) using a method of separating things into their parts in order to examine and understand them

genius (n) someone who is much more intelligent or skilful than other people

tend (v) to usually do a particular thing

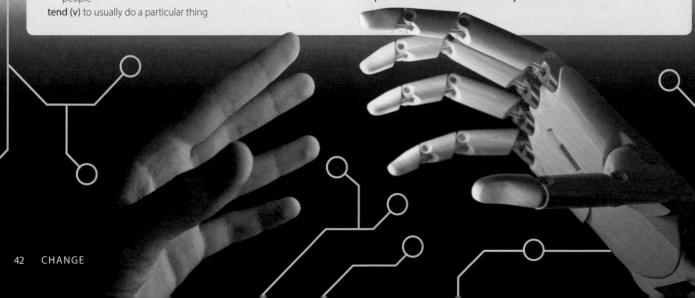

4.2 Social change

LEAD-IN

With books closed, ask students some simple questions about what they think will happen in the immediate future in relation to the weather, or a sporting event or any other topical issue they will know about. Elicit *prediction* by asking if their ideas are things that will definitely happen, or just their opinion.

READING

A Tell students to open their books and to discuss the question in groups. Share any interesting answers.

B Tell students they're going to read an article about predictions. Tell them to look at the headline and answer the questions.

C Set a time limit and tell students to read the article quickly and choose the best summary of it. Remind students that they don't need to read in detail or worry about unknown words at this stage. Reassure them that they will get a chance to read it again more carefully.

1 is a weak summary as it has the experts as the main topic, when in the article the ordinary people are the focus. Also, he was not studying why experts are good media guests. It's also incorrect that experts are not worse at predicting than most ordinary people.

2 is the best summary as it identifies which ordinary people are good at predictions.

D Tell students they can now read the text more closely and decide if the sentences refer to professional experts (PE) or super-forecasters (SF). Tell students to underline the text that helps them to decide. Encourage students to check their answers with their partner. Check answers as a whole class, eliciting which sections of the text helped answer the questions.

E Look at the three different situations. For each situation, elicit some ideas on the board of things you would need to consider to help predict these things. For example, for the winner of a football competition, you might elicit ideas such as how many goals a team has scored this season, if their star player is injured, will they be playing at home or away, etc. Put students into pairs to discuss how easy it is to predict these things accurately and then to rank them. Elicit students' opinions.

b This is probably the easiest to predict because data on numbers of births allows sensible predictions.

a There may be a clear favourite, but in football you never know! There are plenty of examples of the underdog winning a tournament or competition.

c This is probably the hardest to predict accurately simply because of the length of time. However, it is sometimes surprising to note how little changes, even over 100 years.

TEACHING IDEA by David Seymour and Maria Popova

Grammar: Making predictions

2099

Write *2099* on the board. Ask students to imagine what the world will be like then. Offer some prediction of your own (People will live on Mars; Robots will do all the work; The seas will be dead.) then get them to make predictions themselves.

Help with sentence starts (All children will …) or key vocabulary (extinct) where needed.

TEACHING IDEA by David Seymour and Maria Popova

Fortune-telling

Hand out a list of possible personal predictions (You will meet a tall handsome stranger; You will win a lot of money.) and check that students understand them. Make pairs – A is a fortune-teller and B is a visitor. A tells B their fortune, using ideas from the list and adding to them where possible.

GRAMMAR HUB

4.2 Making predictions

- When we are certain about a future event or situation, we can use either *be going to* or *will*.

  Panit is going to keep his New Year's resolutions.
  The company won't reach its sales target this month.
  Will the forecaster's predictions be accurate?

- Although there is often little difference between the use of *be going to* and *will* for predictions, if there is strong evidence or a good reason for our prediction, we often use *be going to* rather than *will*.

  Caitlyn is going to have a baby.
  NOT ~~Caitlyn will have a baby.~~

- To add even greater certainty to our prediction, we can use the adverb *definitely*.

  The other team have a lot of points – they're definitely going to win.

- We can use the adverb *probably* to show that we are not completely certain.

  I'll probably stay at home on New Year's Eve.

- We often use these phrases with *will* when we're making a prediction: *I (don't) think …, I expect …, I'm sure …*

  I don't think the media experts will predict the election results accurately.

- When we feel that a future event is possible, but we are not completely certain, we use *could, may* or *might*.

  You could make some new friends by joining the gym.

Be careful!

- We put the adverbs *definitely* and *probably* after the auxiliary verb in sentences with *be going to* or *will*.

  They're definitely going to win the World Cup.
  NOT ~~They're going to definitely win the World Cup.~~
  I'll probably take part in the project.
  NOT ~~I'll take part probably in the project.~~

4.2 Social change

GRAMMAR

A Use sentence 1 to elicit that the speaker is 100 per cent sure about this prediction before students complete the task.

B Tell students to look back at the sentences from Exercise A to complete the rules. Elicit which sentences from Exercise A are examples of each rule.

C Direct students to the **Grammar Hub** on pages 128 and 129 (see TB43). Use the **Grammar Worksheet** on W15 for extra practice.

PRONUNCIATION

A Elicit from students how *will* is usually said in natural, connected speech. Then play the audio for students to notice which sentence in the pair uses *'ll*.
4.5

B Tell students to listen again and repeat. Correct and drill the pronunciation again yourself if they need extra practice.
4.6

C Tell students to turn to the **Communication Hub** for Exercise A on page 148. Tell one student to say a sentence, and their partner has to point at which one they think they heard.

SPEAKING

A Ask students to look at the topics in the box and choose three. They should then make two predictions for each topic. Next to each prediction, they should write a percentage to represent how likely they think their predictions are to come true. Ask students to make some note about their reasons.

B Explain that students are now a team of super-forecasters. Put students into pairs to discuss their predictions.

C Tell pairs to choose what they consider to be their four strongest predictions. When they have agreed on these, put two sets of pairs together to explain their predictions to each other. Tell them to think about how similar or different their predictions are, and if they agree with each other's ideas. Discuss these ideas as a whole class.

METHODOLOGY HUB by Jim Scrivener

Will: watch out for these problems …

Students at a low level overuse *will* as an 'all-purpose future' to the avoidance of all other ways of talking about the future:
✗ *It will rain.*

This is because it is met early on, it is quickly learnt and then it is easy to place the single word into any sentence where they wish to convey a future meaning. Even if grammatically incorrect, it may often be a sufficiently successful piece of communication to encourage students to use it again and again.

GRAMMAR HUB

4.2 Making predictions

A Reorder the words to make sentences.

1 the future / for our children / is / going to / what / be like / ?
What is the future going to be like for our children?

2 probably / at university / study / Modern Languages / Gareth / will
Gareth will probably study Modern Languages at university.

3 going / she / buy / definitely / to / a new smartphone / is
She is definitely going to buy a new smartphone.

4 soon / will / he / sure / be here / I'm
I'm sure he will be here soon.

5 will / don't / to the party / Dimitris / I / come / think
I don't think Dimitris will come to the party.

6 Jamie / going / is / a new suit / to buy / for the interview / ?
Is Jamie going to buy a new suit for the interview?

B Write a word from the box in each gap to complete the sentences. Sometimes more than one answer is possible.

could   definitely   is   might   think   won't

1 The score is 4-0 – they're __definitely__ going to lose.
2 She __could/might__ make a lot of money one day – anything's possible!
3 Don't worry – you __won't__ have any problems.
4 She __is__ going to compete in a national sports competition.
5 I __think__ she will need some help moving house.
6 The weather's bad today; some people __could/might__ arrive late.

C Choose the correct option.

1 I'm sure people _____ fewer hours in the future.
   a are working   **(b) will work**

2 Hundreds of people _____ their jobs when the factory closes.
   a are losing   **(b) are going to lose**

3 Look out! That driverless car _____ crash!
   a will   **(b) is going to**

4 People _____ reading newspapers in the future, perhaps, but I don't think they'll stop reading books.
   a are stopping   **(b) will stop**

5 I think Magda _____ a good mother when she's older.
   (a) is going to be   b is being

6 I don't expect that he _____ get good marks as he never studies.
   (a) will   b won't

➤ Go back to page 43.

D READ FOR DETAIL Read again. Match the sentences (1–6) to the professional experts (PE) or the super-forecasters (SF).

1 They generally work individually.	PE
2 They change their ideas when they learn something new.	SF
3 They make better predictions when in groups.	SF
4 Their personal beliefs influence their thinking.	PE
5 They use percentages to show how certain they are.	SF
6 The way they speak shows they are really certain.	PE

E SPEAK Work in pairs. How easy is it to accurately predict these things? Put them in order (1 = easiest, 3 = hardest). Give reasons for your decisions.

2 **a** the winner of a football competition

1 **b** the number of schools we will need in ten years' time

3 **c** what life will be like in 100 years' time

GRAMMAR
Making predictions

A WORK IT OUT Look at the words in bold in the sentences from *How you could become a super-forecaster*. Which words show that the speaker is less than 100 per cent sure of a prediction? Which show that the speaker is 100 per cent sure?

Language that shows you are 100 per cent sure of a prediction:
1 Brazil are leading by three goals. They**'re going to** win the World Cup again.

Language that shows you are less than 100 per cent certain of your prediction:
2 There **may** be an early election.

1, 3, 5, 7

prediction: 2, 4, 6, 8

3 I'm sure all cars **will** be driverless.

4 Our predictions **will probably** be wrong.

5 Robots **are going to** replace office workers.

6 Chinese **could** become a global language.

7 We **will definitely** develop better computers.

8 People **might** stop reading newspapers.

B Choose the correct words to complete the rules.

Making predictions

1 When we feel certain about a future event or situation, we *use* / *don't use* be going to, will or *won't*.

2 To show stronger certainty, we can add *definitely* / *probably*.

3 To show we are confident, but not completely certain, we can add *definitely* / *probably*.

4 There is little difference between *will* and *be going to* for predictions. However, if the present provides strong evidence or reasons for our predictions, we often use *be going to* / *will*.

5 When we feel a future event or situation is possible, but are not completely certain, we *use* / *don't use* could, may or might.

C Go to the Grammar Hub on page 128.

PRONUNCIATION
contraction of *will*

 A Listen to five pairs of sentences. In each pair, which sentence (a or b) uses *'ll*?

4.5

1	a	2	b	3	a	4	b	5	b

 B Listen and repeat the subject pronouns + *'ll*.

4.6

C SPEAK Work in pairs. Look at the audioscript for Exercise A on **page 148**. Student A – say a sentence. Student B – point to the sentence. Take turns.

SPEAKING

A Follow the instructions.

1 Make two predictions for three of the topics in the box – one prediction for life in ten years' time, the other for life in 50 years.

> education   housing and domestic life
> leisure time   national culture
> technology   the environment
> transport   work and employment

2 Give each of your predictions a percentage mark to show how likely you think it is.

3 What are the reasons for your predictions and percentages? Make notes.

B Work in pairs. Imagine you are a team of 'super-forecasters'. Explain and discuss your predictions. Practise using super-forecasting language from *How super-forecasters could replace professional experts*.

C Decide on your pair's strongest four predictions. Compare your predictions with another pair.

LISTENING

A SPEAK Work in pairs. Student A – describe picture a. Student B – describe picture b. Ask and answer the questions.

1 What are the positive things about living in this place?

2 What are the negative things about living in this place?

B LISTEN FOR GIST Listen to a current affairs radio programme. Which is the best description of the programme's main topic?

4.7

1 They are revealing why a negative prediction, about life in the countryside disappearing, is not very accurate.

2 They are describing the advantages and disadvantages of living in the countryside, in order to understand why the rural population is decreasing.

③ They are reporting on how we can increase the number of people living and working in the countryside in order to stop villages from dying out.

Glossary

expense (n) an amount of money that you spend in order to buy or do something

resident (n) someone who lives in a particular place

C LISTEN FOR DETAIL Listen again. Complete the summaries with the missing word(s) and/or number(s).

4.7

Kamiyama, which is ¹_____far away_____ from the city, offers a ²_super-fast internet_ to attract new businesses. service
Toshi Asaka thinks working in Kamiyama doesn't have any
³_drawbacks or disadvantages_____ and life is less expensive. Kamiyama is replacing old-style business with ⁴_____modern_____ companies.

Nakanoshima fishing village provides opportunities for ⁵_foreign visitors_ to live and work there for ⁶_____six months_____ and to discover a more traditional lifestyle. They get inexpensive accommodation and ⁷_____part-time_____ jobs with farmers and fishermen. Because of this programme, residents start new businesses, and that helps keep ⁸_local (young) people_in the area.

Mishima Island gives money to ⁹_____single_____ people to pay for romantic dates in the hope that they will stay on the island if they get married and start a family. All ¹⁰_new residents_ receive a young cow. The meat is valuable (it costs ¹¹_____$500_____ per kilo), and these cows are ¹²_in danger of_ disappearing completely.

D Match the phrases (1–4) with phrases with the same meaning (a–d). Use the strategies in the box to help you.

Paraphrasing

When explaining and describing things, we sometimes paraphrase, which means that we repeat a point, but use different words. We paraphrase for various purposes:

• As the speaker, to make a point clear or to give it extra emphasis.

• As the listener, to check, or show that you understand the speaker's point.

• Both the speaker and the listener may paraphrase to sum up a few points or longer argument.

1 young people are relocating to urban areas

2 offering financial incentives

3 blue-sky thinking

4 these cows are in danger of extinction

a ideas that are different, fresh and unexpected

b they're going to the cities

c offering things like free or cheap housing

d of disappearing completely forever

E SPEAK Work in pairs. Can you think of any other ways to encourage people to move to the countryside?

PRONUNCIATION
Linking final consonant and first vowel sounds

A Complete the sentences from the radio programme. Then listen and check your answers.

4.8

1 Oh yes, such as_____?

2 Tell us_____ more.

3 What's the next idea_____?

4 That sounds like a_____ fun thing to do.

5 But, is it_____ such a good idea?

6 What else_____ did you discover?

7 That isn't a_____ lot of money, is it?

8 That's a_____ lot of money!

B We often link the final consonant sound of a word to the first vowel sound of the next word. Listen and repeat sentences 1 and 2 from Exercise A.

4.8

C Mark the links between the final consonant and first vowel sounds in Exercise A. Then listen again and check your answers. Repeat the sentences.

4.8

D SPEAK Work in pairs. Practise saying the sentences. Listen and check your partner's pronunciation.

4.2 Social change

LISTENING

A–D Check answers and students' understanding in whole-class feedback as they complete the exercises.

E Ask each pair to share their best idea with the class.

AUDIOSCRIPT

🔊 **4.7**

Listening, Exercise B
R = Rita Costa   J = John Malone   T = Toshi Asaka

R: Hi, I'm Rita Costa, and this is Rethinking the Future, when we look at how we can stop pessimistic predictions coming true.
OK, so, today's prediction is that rural life has no future. Many villages and small towns are going to disappear, or only have older residents because young people are relocating to urban areas – that is, they're going to the cities to find work and a new, modern life. We've talked before about overpopulation in urban areas, but what about the problem of under-population in rural areas? Like many countries, Japan faces that problem, but it is trying to deal with it. Our reporter John has been there to find out more. Hi, John.

J: Hi, Rita. Yes, I visited several places and saw some great ideas for repopulating small villages, for getting people to change their life in the city for one in the country.

R: I guess that means offering financial incentives, you know, offering things like free or cheap housing, low business taxes and relocation expenses.

J: Yes, and some local governments are certainly doing that, but I'm talking about examples of blue-sky thinking, and by that I mean ideas that are different, fresh and unexpected.

R: Oh yes, such as?

J: Well, the fresh thinking involves foreigners, the internet, cows and love.

R: That sounds fascinating. Tell us more.

J: Sure. My tour started in the small mountain town
Ex C Q1 of Kamiyama, where the city feels far away. At first, it all seems very traditional and underdeveloped – you know, there are very few signs of modern life. However, to encourage companies to relocate from
Ex C Q2 urban areas the town council provides a super-fast internet service, faster than Tokyo's. And now, if you look inside some of those traditional buildings, you'll see signs of a growing digital start-up economy, teams of young designers and programmers working away on their computers.

R: Do you mean like small digital design and app companies? Like in those urban creative business centres?

J: Exactly. Here's Toshi Asaka, the owner of one.

T: I decided to move here from Tokyo because of the internet service. I can do my work anywhere, and
Ex C Q3 here the quality of life is wonderful. There are no drawbacks, no disadvantages, about living here– my staff don't feel underpaid now!

Ex C Q4 **J:** Kamiyama Council has managed to reinvent the local economy, moving from traditional to modern digital business.

PRONUNCIATION

🔊 **A–D** Play the audio for students to check answers, listen and repeat.
4.8   Help with and correct pronunciation where appropriate.

R: Right, using modern technology to create opportunities for young people. That makes sense. What's the next idea?

J: Well, other places are using tradition rather than technology to change their future. The small fishing village of Nakanoshima has its eye on young people, too, but not young Japanese. They offer special
Ex C Q6; Q5 six-month Working Holiday Visas to foreign visitors who want to experience a truly traditional Japanese lifestyle. You stay in cheap, shared accommodation,
Ex C Q7 in a traditional building and do part-time agricultural work, that is, you have a job in the farming or fishing industries.

R: That sounds like a fun thing to do. But is it such a good idea? I'm not sure it really helps the village to grow. I mean, the visitors only stay six months.

J: But then, new businesses like restaurants, cafés and language schools open up, and that encourages
Ex C Q8 local young people to stay and not go to the city, so the visitors are an opportunity for the locals.

R: OK, so the experience of the foreign visitors is only half the story. What else did you discover?

J: My final stop was Mishima Island. Like the other places, they provide financial help like cheap accommodation and relocation expenses, but if you
Ex C Q9 are single and looking for romance, they will also pay for your dates.

R: Pay for your dates? Cute, but, that isn't a lot of money, is it?

J: Well, perhaps you've misunderstood the aim of this plan, its intention. It isn't about attracting new people; it's about keeping them. What I mean is, they want people to move to their village, and to then stay forever. What better way to do that than to help them to find love and perhaps start a family. Isn't that both sweet and smart?

R: OK, I get it now, but what about married couples? It doesn't help them, does it?

Ex C Q10 J: Not really, no, but they also give every new resident a young cow.

R: A cow? I'm not sure that will get me moo-ving there.

J: Oh, not just any cow. Mishima cows are extremely rare, and their beef is incredibly expensive, with a
Ex C Q11 kilogram worth $500.

R: That's a lot of money! I can't believe it.

J: Yeah, but it really is that expensive. And the thing is,
Ex C Q12 just like the village life, these cows are in danger of extinction, of disappearing completely forever, so they're another thing the new residents are helping to save.

R: The thing I love about the Mishima Island approach is that it creates emotional bonds to a place. What I mean by that is people soon make a strong connection to their new home, either through finding love or bringing up a cow. Definitely blue-sky thinking.

VOCABULARY

A Point out the information about using prefixes in the box, and check students understand that certain prefixes have a particular meaning. Elicit the meaning of the three prefixes in the box. Tell students to look at the sentences from the *Listening* and to underline the prefixes.

B Tell students to look at the sentences from Exercise A again to help them match the prefixes with their meanings.

C Tell students to think about the meanings from Exercise B to help them add the correct prefixes to the words in bold.

D Direct students to the Vocabulary Hub on page 143 for further practice of prefixes.

E Tell students to look back at the sentences in Exercise C and think if they are true for them. If they aren't, tell students to rewrite them so that they are. Monitor and help with language if necessary here. Put students into pairs to compare their sentences and explain why they wrote what they wrote. Use the Vocabulary Worksheet on W16 for extra practice.

SPEAKING HUB

A Tell students to read the predicted future problems. Check they understand them, and check pronunciation of *damage* and *privacy*. Tell students to think about the questions and to make notes about their ideas. Monitor and help with language if necessary.

B Put students into groups to compare their ideas and choose the best two solutions for each predicted problem.

C Regroup students so each new group has one or two representatives from a previous group. Tell the new groups to compare their solutions and to think about how similar or different their ideas are. Check students understand the meaning of *blue-sky thinking* (creating completely new and highly original ideas). Tell them to try to agree on the best examples of blue-sky thinking. Conclude by briefly discussing their solutions as a whole class and giving some feedback on good language usage and any errors made during the task.

METHODOLOGY HUB   by Jim Scrivener

Analysing connected speech

In connected speech, the following things tend to happen:

- Unstressed syllables tend to have weak vowel sounds.
- Sounds get dropped (this is known as elision).
- Sounds get changed (this is known as assimilation).
- There may be additional sounds (linking or intrusive sounds) for bridging the space between words.

Your students probably need to be able to recognise and understand such sentences even if you don't want them to produce language like this. In fact, it's worth remembering that one of the main problems learners have with listening to English is that they can't recognise pronunciations that are entirely different from what they are expecting. For example, if a student expects to hear /wɒt ɑː(r) juː/ but instead hears /'wɒtʃə/, they may well not register at all that it represents the same words. So a key point to remember is that it's vital to teach pronunciation – not just for the students' own speech production but to help them listen better.

METHODOLOGY HUB   by Jim Scrivener

Ways of recording lexis

The action of noting down a list of lexical items is no guarantee that remembering will take place. Remembering involves four things:

putting into storage, keeping in storage, retrieving, using

The following are alternative methods of recording items:

Lexical items lists

The table shows an alternative lexical item list that provides more information.

Lexical item	Pronunciation	Translation	Grammar	Collocations	Example
motorcycle /	'məutə(r)ˌsaɪk(ə)ɪ/	pikipiki	noun	ride a ~, get on my ~, ~maintenance, ~ race, ~ courier	She's just bought a 600cc Suzuki motorcycle.

Labelling

Another way involves grouping of words so that a set is learnt together. This is often more effective than studying unrelated individual words. For example, you could present a set of words connected with kitchens by using a picture of a kitchen; the students each have a copy of the picture and write the words on it as they learn them.

Word or topic webs

A similar idea is to build a **word web** (or memory map or mind map) where connections in meaning or use between different words are visually indicated in the structure of the diagram.

Word page: collocations and chunks

This page is for recording lexical items that typically go together in patterns with a single keyword. The learner writes the keyword in the centre box and then uses the columns before and after the box to write in phrases, sentences, chunks, etc.

Lexical item page: lexical item collector

This page can be used to record lexical items and then collect and relate items, classified as different grammatical types. For example, if the student has found *happy*, they could then go on to find and record *happiness* and *happily*.

VOCABULARY
Prefixes: *dis-*, *mis-*, *over-*, *re-*, *under-*

> ### Using prefixes
> We can add a prefix to a verb, noun or adjective to change its meaning. We use prefixes to show the opposite, to indicate a size or to show repetition. For example:
> - *do – **un**do*   *circle – **semi**circle*   *organise – **re**organise*

A Underline the prefixes in the sentences from the radio programme.

a Hi, I'm Rita Costa and this is <u>Re</u>*thinking the Future*.

b Many villages and small towns are going to <u>dis</u>appear.

c We've talked before about <u>over</u>population in urban areas …

d You've <u>mis</u>understood the aim of this plan.

e My staff don't feel <u>under</u>paid now!

B Match the prefixes in the box with their meanings (a–e).

> dis- mis- over- re- under-

a bad or wrong mis-

b opposite dis-

c too little or too small under-

d again, but perhaps in a different way re-

e too much over-

C Complete the words in bold with the correct prefixes.

1 There are many things I ___dis___**like** about where I live. I'd like to move.

2 I know someone who often ___over___ **works**. They should relax more.

3 I often ___mis___**place** things and waste time trying to find them.

4 There are some terrible buildings in my town that they should knock down and ___re___ **build**.

5 I often ___dis___**agree** with my parents, which sometimes leads to arguments.

6 I think that football players are ___over___ **paid**. Some get millions of pounds a year. In contrast, I think nurses are ___under___ **paid**.

D Go to the Vocabulary Hub on page 143.

E SPEAK Work in pairs. Rewrite the sentences in Exercise C so they are true for you. Then compare your ideas with your partner.

⬭ SPEAKING HUB

A Look at the predicted problems. Think of solutions to these problems. How can we stop this from happening? What could we do? How can we create a better future?

1 The use of robots and artificial intelligence will create massive unemployment because many jobs will disappear.

2 Across the world, air pollution will continue to increase and damage human health.

3 Using social media and digital services will lead to a near total loss of privacy, as companies and governments store and use all the data.

B DISCUSS Work in groups. Discuss your ideas. Choose the best two solutions for each problem.

C REFLECT Compare your group's solutions with another group. Are they the same or different? Which ideas are good examples of blue-sky thinking?

b

⬭– **Make and discuss predictions**
⬭– **Discuss problems, reasons and consequences**

Café Hub

COMPREHENSION

A ▶ 00:00–02:30 Work in pairs. Watch the first part of the video without sound and guess the answers to the questions.

1 How is Gaby feeling?
2 What does Sam suggest?
3 How does Gaby respond?
4 What do they decide?
5 What misunderstanding do they have?

B ▶ 00:00–02:30 Watch the first part of the video with sound and check your ideas in Exercise A. What is the main reason Sam gives for taking Gaby on?

C ▶ 02:30–04:49 Watch the second part of the video and answer the questions.

1 What does the customer complain about?
  the coffee and croissant
2 What does the customer want Gaby to do?
  give her her money back
3 How does Gaby react to the situation?
  apologises but then she becomes angry
4 Why does the customer ask to speak to Sam?
  complain about the service
5 How does Sam deal with the situation?
  Sam supports Gaby

FUNCTIONAL LANGUAGE
Clarifying and asking for clarification

A ▶ 01:48–04:49 Complete what Gaby says with the correct form of *get*, *say*, *lose* or *catch*. Then watch the clip and check your answers.

Clarifying and asking for clarification
1 What did you _____ say _____?
2 Sorry, I didn't _____ catch _____ that.
3 I don't _____ get _____ what you're saying.
4 So you're _____ saying _____ you want me to …
5 You've _____ lost _____ me.
6 Why didn't you just _____ say _____ that?

B You are going to roleplay a similar situation. Invent a conversation.

Student A: You are Sam. Begin with '… And remember to put the plates under here.'

Student B: You are Gaby. Ask for clarification and use phrases from Exercise A.

| MILLY | SAM | NEENA | ZAC | GABY |

Making and dealing with complaints

C 02:30-04:49 Put the words or phrases in brackets in the correct position to complete the sentences. Then watch the second part of the video to check.

Making a complaint	Finding out about a complaint	Apologising
¹I'm sorry to bother you, but _I'm afraid_ there's a problem with … (*I'm afraid*) I want my money back, please. ²I'm not happy with the service. (*really*)	³What is the problem? (*exactly*) What seems to be the problem?	I'm sorry to hear that. ⁴That's no problem. I'm sorry about that. (*so*) ⁵I'm sorry for the inconvenience, madam; it won't happen again. (*terribly*)

USEFUL PHRASES

A Match the useful phrases in the box with the phrases before or after them from the video (1–6).

> How dare you!   How's your first day going?
> Leave it to me.   Something good will come along.
> The customer is always right.   What's up?

1 _____ What's up? _____ / I don't know, Sam.

2 __Something good will come along.__ / It always does.

3 ____How's your first day going?____ / Great so far.

4 Excuse me! Hello? Excuse me! / _____ Leave it to me. _____

5 __The customer is always right.__ / Unless the customer is wrong.

6 _____ How dare you! _____ / I want to speak to the manager.

B How do you say these useful phrases in your language?

PRONUNCIATION
Intonation and stress

A Listen and write down three versions of the question 'What's the problem?'
4.9

1 exactly

_____ What exactly is the problem? _____

2 seems

_____ What seems to be the problem? _____

3 appears

_____ What appears to be the problem? _____

B Practise the questions in Exercise A. Copy the stress and intonation.

SPEAKING

A Work in groups of three: the customer, the waiter, the manager. The customer makes one of the following complaints. Write a funny conversation.

• The soup is cold. (The customer has eaten the soup.)

• The steak is tough. (The customer has eaten the steak.)

• The pasta is too salty. (The customer has eaten the pasta.)

B PRESENT Perform your conversation in front of the class.

◯— Clarify and ask for clarification
◯— Make and deal with complaints

➤ Turn to page 159 to learn how to write a short essay.

4.3 Part-time

LEAD-IN

Elicit the verb *complain* and the corresponding noun *complaint*. Ask the students if they have ever made a complaint in a restaurant or a shop and why.

COMPREHENSION

A ▶ 00:00–02:30 Tell students that they're going to watch part of the video without sound and to try to answer the questions. Let them compare ideas.

Possible answers:
1 miserable
2 That Gaby works part-time in the café.
3 She is apprehensive.
4 Sam will train her to work in the café.
5 Sam tells Gaby to put the glasses on top of the dishwasher, but he means on the top shelf of the dishwasher.

B ▶ 00:00–02:30 Play the video with sound for students to watch and check their ideas and to answer the extra question.

Sam was already thinking about advertising for some part-time help.

C ▶ 02:30–04:49 Tell students to watch the rest of the episode and to answer the questions.

FUNCTIONAL LANGUAGE

A ▶ 01:48–04:49 Ask students to complete the gaps with the correct form of *get, say, lose* or *catch*. Play the video again for students to check. Elicit that the phrases are fairly informal.

B Put students into pairs and tell one to be Sam and the other to be Gaby. Tell the student playing Sam to give instructions and the students playing Gaby to ask for clarification.

C ▶ 02:30–04:49 Tell students to look at the words and to put the word in brackets in the correct position. Watch the appropriate part of the episode again to check.

2 I'm really not happy with the service.
3 What exactly is the problem?
4 That's no problem. I'm so sorry about that.
5 I'm terribly sorry for the inconvenience, madam; it won't happen again.

USEFUL PHRASES

A Point out the useful phrases and tell them to match each one with the phrase that came just before or after it.

B Tell students to translate the phrases into their own language. Ask students how often they use those phrases.

PRONUNCIATION

A Tell them to listen and to write down the question, putting the word given in the correct place. Elicit that adding the extra words makes the question softer and more indirect. (4.9)

B Tell students to listen to the questions again and to copy the stress and intonation.

SPEAKING

A Put students into groups of three and tell them to choose a role each. Tell the groups to choose one of the situations given and to write a funny conversation about it. When the groups have finished writing their conversations, tell them to practise performing them.

B Tell each group to perform their conversation for the class. Tell the other groups to watch and note down something that they thought was really good about each conversation.

▶ VIDEOSCRIPT

S = Sam   G = Gaby   C = Customer

S: Hey.
G: Hey.
S: What's up?
G: I don't know, Sam. I don't have much work on at the moment and I'm totally broke …
S: Gaby! You're such a good photographer – the website photos you did for me are amazing! Something good will come along – it always does.
  I've got an idea – why don't you help me out here? It's been very busy recently and I was already thinking about advertising for some part-time help.
G: Are you sure? I sometimes … drop … things …
S: Yeah … you do … but you're great with people! I'll train you! It'll be like the film *Rocky*, but with more coffee and less boxing.
G: OK! Let's do this.
S: … And remember to put the glasses on top.
G: What did you say?
S: Remember to put the glasses …
G: Sorry … I didn't catch that …
S: … on top …
G: On top of what? I don't get what you're saying?
S: The dishwasher.
G: So you're saying you want me to put the glasses on the top of the dishwasher? You've lost me.
S: No! On the top shelf of the dishwasher.

G: Ah! Sure, why didn't you just say that? Err, do you have any … glue?
S: So how's your first day going?
G: Great so far!
C: Hello? Excuse me!
G: Leave it to me!
C: Hello. I'm sorry to bother you, but I'm afraid there's a problem with the coffee AND with the croissant.
G: I'm sorry to hear that – what exactly is the problem?
C: I don't know! They just don't taste good. I want my money back please.
G: That's no problem. I'm so sorry about that, perhaps we … oh … but you finished them … both.
C: Well, yeah.
G: So they weren't that bad then?
C: What happened to the customer is always right?
G: The customer is always right. Unless the customer is wrong. Like now.
C: How dare you! I want to speak to the manager NOW!
G: Sam! You remember when you said I was good with people?
S: What seems to be the problem?
C: I'm really not happy with the service, this woman …
S: I'm terribly sorry for the inconvenience madam, it won't happen again.
C: Good.
S: … Because if you don't like it here, then you really don't need to come back. Thank you and have a nice day.
C: I have never … ever … ever … ever … ever … ever … ever.

4 Writing ● Write a short essay

ⓌⒸ using linking words to introduce reasons and consequences

A Read the advert for a competition. What can you win? How can you win it? TINTO X mobile phone; write a short essay.

Happy New Year with Digital Express and Tinto Phones

Enter our New Year competition and win a TINTO X mobile phone.

Digital technology has already changed our lives in many ways, and this is going to continue in the future. We want to know how you think digital technology is going to change our lives over the next 20 years.

Write a short essay describing a change that digital technology will bring to our lives, explaining why this will happen and any consequences it will have.

The five winning entries will be published online.

B Read a competition essay entry. Put the paragraphs (a–d) in the correct order (1–4).

1 introduction (what the writer thinks the change will be) **b**
2 reason 1 **d**
3 reason 2 **a**
4 conclusion **c**

a Secondly, digital technology supports a sharing economy, and that means people will not need to buy so many things. Owning a car will not be necessary **as** you will simply use an app to book a driverless car when you need one. People will share things like bicycles and gardening equipment within their local community by using an app to find what they need. **As a result**, people will own fewer things, but they will have more contact with other people.

b People are always buying things **because** they want to get the latest products. However, in the future, people will probably buy fewer things **because of** the development of digital technology.

c To sum up, digital technology will definitely continue to change our lives, and one of those changes will be that we won't need to own so much stuff.

d In the past, new inventions brought many products into our houses, but digital technology often replaces these things with a single device. For example, your mobile phone can now be your television, radio, music player and alarm clock. In the future, children may play all their games on a phone or tablet, **and so** traditional board games will disappear. **Consequently**, people will have less stuff in their house, although they will spend a lot on digital services.

C SPEAK Work in pairs. Read again and discuss the questions.

1 What two reasons are given for why people will own fewer things?
2 How many examples illustrate each reason?
3 What other things will happen?
4 What do you think of the predictions?

D Look at the linking words in bold in the essay. Write them in the correct column.

Introduce a reason	Introduce a consequence
because	As a result
as	Consequently
because of	and so

E Look again at the linking words in bold in the essay. Write them in the correct place in the box. Use each of them twice.

Using linking words to introduce reasons and consequences

We use linking words and phrases to show the relationship between information and ideas.

1 Some linking words connect ideas inside one sentence. For example, ___because___ , ___as___ , ___and so___ , ___because of___ .
2 Some connect ideas across two sentences. For example, ___As a result___ , ___Consequently___ .
3 Some linking words are followed by a clause (subject + verb). For example, ___as___ , ___as a result___ , ___because___ , ___and so___ , ___Consequently___ .
4 Others are followed by noun phrases (such as the increase in pollution). For example, ___because of___ .

F SPEAK Work in pairs. Complete the sentences with your own ideas. Then **compare** your answers with a partner.

1 All cars should be electric because …
2 Children are using social media. As a result, …
3 Every year, more people are only paying for things electronically. Consequently, …
4 Cities are unhealthy places to live because of …
5 People are watching less TV as …
6 Online shopping continues to increase, and so …

WRITING

A PLAN Make a prediction about how digital technology will change the future. Think of the reasons why this change will happen and any consequences it will have.

B WRITE Write your competition entry (150–200 words).

C REVIEW Work in groups. Read and discuss your essays. Have a vote to decide on the two winning entries.

Answers

1 *Digital technology often replaces these things with a single device; digital technology supports a sharing economy.*
2 *Two examples per reason*
3 *People will spend a lot on digital services; they will have more contact with other people.*

Refer students to this essay as a model for the writing task.

Tell students to think about how the use of signposting language, such as linking words and phrases, can help them to transition between points.

WRITING

Ask students to tell their partner if they've ever entered a competition and if they've ever won anything.

A Tell students to look at the advert and answer the questions.

B Tell them to read and put the paragraphs in the correct order according to the paragraph structure given.

C Tell students to look back at the competition entry and to discuss the questions with a partner.

1 *Digital technology often replaces these things with a single device; digital technology supports a sharing economy.*
2 *Two examples per reason*
3 *People will spend a lot on digital services; they will have more contact with other people.*

D Tell students now to look at the words in bold in the essay. Elicit that they are all linking words. Tell students to look back at the essay to help them work out the meaning of the linking words and to write them in the correct column.

E Tell students to look again at how the linking words are used in the essay and to complete the box.

F Tell students to work individually to complete the sentences with their own ideas before they compare.

Possible answers:
1 *They are better for the environment.*
2 *They are not doing enough exercise.*
3 *Cash will disappear.*
4 *The pollution.*
5 *They are spending time online and on social media.*
6 *Traditional shops in town centres will close.*

WRITING TASK

A Tell students that they are going to write their own competition entry essay. Elicit some ideas from the class. Tell students to choose one of the changes and make some notes.

B Tell students to look back at the structure of the competition entry to help them organise their essay. Remind them to use but not overuse some of the linking words.

C Put students into groups and tell them to pass their essays around so everyone can read each other's.

GRAMMAR

A Choose the best verb form to complete the sentences.

1 I can't tonight, I'm busy. I can't call you tomorrow either. I *'m visiting* / *will visit* my parents all day. I *'m calling* / *'ll call* you when I'm free.

2 He *'s going to* / *'ll* do that this afternoon. It's next on his to-do list.

3 Can I borrow some money? You *'re getting* / *'ll get* it back tomorrow, if that's OK?

4 Well, let me check. Yes, I *'m going to* / *'ll* lend you £20. Here you are.

5 We're going now. We *'re meeting* / *'ll meet* Asif for dinner at seven. Bye!

6 Oh, look – it's raining. Change of plan! I *'m not cycling* / *won't cycle* today; I think I *'m going to* / *'ll* take the underground instead.

7 My sister's decided to go to Italy for her holiday this year. She *'s going to* / *'ll* visit Rome, Florence and Venice.

B Choose the correct words to complete the dialogues.

1 **A:** This match is rubbish. Come on – let's go early.

  B: No, let's wait to the end.

  A: But there's no point staying. We're losing 5–0. We ¹ *aren't going to* / *probably won't* win.

  B: But we ² *might* / *will* score one at least. You never know!

  A: There's no way that ³ *may* / *will* happen. Come on. Time to give up.

2 **A:** Flying cars? Of course, I can't say it will ⁴ *definitely* / *probably* happen, but it ⁵ *definitely* / *probably* will.

  B: No, it ⁶ *might not* / *won't* happen. I'm sure. Think about it, what would happen if every car were a flying car? It would be too dangerous.

  A: But people are definitely ⁷ *going to* / *might* want them in the future. The technology can't be far away. I'm sure we ⁸ *'re going to* / *could* have flying cars in the future!

VOCABULARY

A Which is the odd-one-out in each set of verb phrases? Why?

1 ⓐ achieve a target because the other two refer to making a plan
  b make a resolution
  c set a goal

2 **a** keep a resolution
  b stick to a plan
  ⓒ cut down on something because the other two refer to following a plan

3 ⓐ do less of something because the other two mean 'stop completely'
  b quit a bad habit
  c stop doing something

4 ⓐ reach a goal because the other two refer to failing to achieve/to not reaching your goal
  b break resolutions
  c not do what you promised

B Look at the words in bold. Are the prefixes correct or incorrect? If they are incorrect, write the correct prefix.

1 The fire destroyed a lot of the building. We'll need to **misbuild** it. *[re]*

2 I'm definitely **overpaid**. Unless I get a pay rise, it'll be time to find a new job! *[under]*

3 Some money has **reappeared**. It's missing. No one is leaving until we find it. *[dis]*

4 Wait, let me help! It's heavy. Don't **overdo** it. I'll lift it with you. *[correct]*

5 And, don't **disbehave**! We want to impress our school visitors. *[mis]*

6 No, I didn't pass my exam, unfortunately. I've got my **overtake** next week. *[re]*

7 The answer is wrong. You made a **miscalculation**. Do the maths again. *[correct]*

8 Urban **underpopulation** isn't a problem now, but it soon will be. The city's population is increasing rapidly. *[over]*

FUNCTIONAL LANGUAGE

Choose the correct words to complete the dialogue.

A: Hi. I'm sorry to ¹*excuse* / *bother* you.

B: Not at all, sir. Please sit down. How can I help?

A: I took one of your courses, 'How to change your life in seven days'. I'm ²*afraid* / *not happy* there is a problem with the course.

B: Oh, I'm sorry. Could I take your name first?

A: Jim Stevens.

B: Sorry, I didn't ³*take* / *catch* the last part.

A: Stevens.

B: Great. What was the problem with the course?

A: I took the course ten days ago. But my life hasn't changed!

B: OK, I'm not sure I ⁴*have* / *get* what you are saying. Do you mean the course was unhelpful?

A: Yes. I expect results for the price. And the teacher was always late.

B: I'm sorry to ⁵*hear* / *catch* that. We will talk to the teacher. That won't ⁶*happen* / *bother* again.

A: And the money?

B: So you're ⁷*saying* / *hearing* you want your money back?

A: Exactly!

B: Ok, just let me check with my manager …

5 WORK AND BUSINESS

A business that makes nothing
but money is a poor business.

Henry Ford

Work (n) activity that involves physical or mental effort.
Synonyms: labour (n), effort (n)
Business (n) the work of buying or selling products or services for money.
Synonyms: commerce (n), trading (n)

Henry Ford (1863–1947) is best known as the founder of the Ford Motor Company. He was also involved in the development of the assembly line, which made mass production possible.

The quote for this unit suggests that the purpose of a business should be to make people's lives better. It could also be interpreted as highlighting the need for social and environmental responsibility in business.

Designers making tough decisions at a studio in Berlin.

OBJECTIVES

- discuss and give advice about employment skills and career interests
- discuss and suggest workplace benefits and changes
- describe and evaluate a small business
- talk about environmental business ideas
- structure a presentation
- write a covering letter for a job application

Work with a partner. Discuss the questions.

1 Look at the picture. What do you think they are doing?
2 Read the quote. Do you agree that a business which makes money can still be poor?
3 What kind of business would you like to work for?

WORK AND BUSINESS 49

OBJECTIVES

Read the unit objectives to the class.

UNIT OPENER QUESTIONS

With books closed, ask students to discuss in pairs what they believe the purpose of a business is. While they're doing this, write on the board *A business that makes nothing but _____ is a poor business.* Highlight the two meanings of *poor* (bad and not rich) that are played on in the quote. Elicit some ideas as a whole class and get them to guess the missing word.

1 Tell students to open their books and look at the picture. What do they think the people are doing? Elicit some ideas as a whole class.

2 Ask students to look at the quote again and discuss with their partner whether they think a business that makes money can still be poor. Monitor and provide language input.

3 Ask students to discuss what kind of business they would like to work for and why. Elicit some useful adjectives on the board for the type of attributes they would like to see in a company and in a boss.

WORKSHEETS

Lesson 5.1 At work

Grammar: Past habits and states: *used to* and *would* (W17)

Vocabulary: Employment skills and qualities (W18)

Lesson 5.2 In business

Grammar: The passive (W19)

Vocabulary: Business collocations (W20)

5.1 At work

- Discuss and give advice about employment skills and career interests
- Discuss and suggest workplace benefits and changes

V – employment skills and qualities; verbs of influence
G – past habits and states

P – intonation and rhythm: holding your turn
S – following reference links in a text

teacher   restaurant manager   engineer   police officer

VOCABULARY
Employment skills and qualities

A SPEAK Work in pairs. Look at the pictures (a–d). What are the people's jobs? What skills do they need to do these jobs?

B SPEAK Work in pairs. Student A – go to the Communication Hub on page 152. Student B – go to the Communication Hub on page 147.

C Read the report about a business survey. Complete the phrases with *be* or *have*.

> Many jobs require very specific skills and experience. However, there are also many skills and personal qualities that all employers are looking for. We surveyed **100 Human Resource Managers** to find out which are the most important general employment skills and qualities.

People should:

1   __be__   reliable. Student B, Q4
2   __have__   good communication skills. Student B, Q1
3   __have__   good digital technology skills. Student A, Q1
4   __be__   good at time management. Student B, Q2
5   __be__   good at team work. Student B, Q3
6   __be__   able to work well under pressure. Student A, Q2
7   __have__   creative thinking skills. Student A, Q4
8   __have__   good people skills. Student A, Q3

D SPEAK Work in pairs. Match the quiz questions in Exercise B with the employment skills in Exercise C.

E SPEAK For each employment skill in Exercise C, give yourself a percentage score to show your strength. For example, 100 per cent = a great strength, no room for improvement. Then work in pairs and explain your answers.

LISTENING

A LISTEN FOR KEY WORDS Listen to the first part of a conversation between Fiona and Michael about work. Choose the correct answer for each question.
5.1

1 What is Fiona's job?
  a Human Resources Manager in a company
  ⓑ a careers adviser
  c a psychologist

2 What is Michael's role in the bank?
  a head of the accountancy team
  b a junior member of the property investment team
  ⓒ a member of the general management team

3 Why is Michael unhappy in his job?
  a He doesn't work closely with other people.
  ⓑ His work doesn't offer enough challenges.
  c He has to meet too many deadlines.

4 In which of these areas hasn't he worked?
  a fashion
  ⓑ sports
  c food and drink

5 Which of these things seem most important to Michael?
  ⓐ team work
  b digital technology skills
  c time management

B LISTEN FOR DETAIL Listen again. Are the sentences true (T) or false (F)? Correct the false sentences.
5.1

1 Michael has worked in ~~five different banks.~~ *the same bank for five years.*   F
2 Michael currently uses the skills that the test showed as strengths.   T
3 ~~Michael sometimes bought the clothes that he modelled.~~ *They often gave him the clothes.*   F
4 Michael enjoyed working ~~as a waiter, but not~~ when it was ~~very~~ busy. *under pressure*   F
5 Michael feels positively about training and coaching.   T
6 Michael ~~is interested in setting up his own~~ company. *wants to work for a good*   F

C SPEAK Work in pairs. Look at the pictures (a–d) again. Which job do you think Fiona will recommend for Michael? Why?

D LISTEN FOR DETAIL Listen to the second part of the conversation. Which job does Fiona suggest? Why?
5.2

LEAD-IN

Put students into pairs and give them three minutes to think of a profession for every letter of the alphabet.

VOCABULARY

A Look at the pictures as a whole class and elicit the jobs shown. Put students into pairs to think of the skills needed for each.

B Tell students to work with a partner. Tell student A to turn to the **Communication Hub** on page 152 and student B to turn to the **Communication Hub** on page 147. Students can then check their answers on page 149.

C–E Monitor the students as they complete the exercises and discuss the answers as a whole class. Use the **Vocabulary Worksheet** on W18 for extra practice.

LISTENING

A Tell students to read the questions and possible answers before they listen and check understanding of *challenges*, *deadlines* and *property investment*.

B Tell students to look at the sentences and to try to remember if they are true or false. Play the audio again to check.

C Tell students to discuss which job Fiona will recommend.

D Tell students to listen to the end of the conversation to check their ideas.

Catering Manager: He has experience of the catering industry. His degree in business is useful for this job. She thinks the work will suit him: planning and running successful events. He has an interest in cooking and food. It should require good people, communication and time management skills. It should have a lot of variety and involve working in a team. It will give a sense of achievement.

AUDIOSCRIPT

 5.1

Listening, Exercise A
F = Fiona   M = Michael

F: Hello, sorry I'm late. You must be Michael. I'm Fiona.

M: Hi, Fiona. Nice to meet you.

F: Nice to meet you, and thank you for coming, and for waiting. I hope we can help you. So, I've had a quick look at your personality test and, in today's session, I'd like you to tell me why you're thinking about changing career, and to find out more about the kind of work that you like doing.

M: Sure.

Ex B Q1 **F:** OK, so you're currently working in a bank. I see you've been there for five years, since leaving university, so why do you want to leave that behind?

M: Well, it's been a good job, but erm, I just feel there's something missing. I studied business and finance at university, and getting a banking job seemed the right thing to do at that time, but I'm not so sure now.

F: I see, and what is it that's missing exactly? Your personality test showed you have good people skills. Does your work involve using those much? And your organisational skills are strong. I'm sure that's important at the bank.

M: Yeah, absolutely. You definitely need to be well organised, to both meet deadlines and manage the money carefully. Erm, I work in a local branch of the bank, so I have to deal with customers face to face, and I've recently been made assistant manager, so those people skills are important, and I do more general planning now, like team planning, you know, to make sure the work gets done – that sort of thing. I think the thing is that basically every day is pretty much the same. I rarely have to think on my feet, or deal with surprises.

F: OK, you want a bit more variety in your work. So, this's been your only job since university. Did you have any part-time jobs before?

M: Well, this may surprise you, but I used to be a fashion model.

F: A fashion model? Well, now you tell me, it isn't so surprising, I mean you look very smart and presentable.

M: Thank you. I didn't do it for long, erm, but it was good fun. I really enjoyed the photo shoots. It's good doing something creative together; the teamwork was good and important. And, well, they'd usually give us some of the clothes after the shoot, which was great for me as a student!

F: I can imagine, and also very different to working in a bank. Erm, anything else?

M: The other thing was working as a waiter. I joined an agency for part-time catering work, so I used to serve food at conferences and events, or I'd work in a café or restaurant for a few days, you know, if their staff were ill or something.

F: Well, that's great experience to have. Did you like doing that?

Ex B Q4 **M:** Oh, yeah, for sure. You have to work hard. At busy times, you would always be under a lot of pressure, but in a good way. I liked helping the customers enjoy the event. I used to be tired but happy at the end of a day. But, you know, that was only student work for me. It did get me into food and cooking though; that's one of my hobbies now – home baking and stuff like that.

F: Well, it's certainly interesting to hear that you liked working under pressure. Erm, you just mentioned hobbies. Do you have any other interests? Anything that might involve skills that you could use in a job?

M: Well, you obviously don't mean going to the cinema. I love skiing. Erm, before university, I was a member of a ski club at a local ski centre. One thing then, I used to help new members, you know, I'd coach them a little, and just help them as they were learning. That was pretty rewarding. There was a nice sense of achievement, you know.

F: Is that feeling missing from your work in the bank?

M: In a way, yes. But I don't want to be a ski instructor,

Ex B Q6 you know, that's just like having your own business. I want a steady job, to have a career in a good company, but, well, just not in a bank.

F: Sure, sure. Well, from what you've said, I do have an early suggestion for you to consider.

M: Already? OK, well, what are you thinking?

Ex B Q3

5.1 At work

AUDIOSCRIPT

 5.2

Listening, Exercise D
F = Fiona   M = Michael

F: Sure, sure. Well, from what you've said, I do have an early suggestion for you to consider.

M: Already? OK, well, what are you thinking?

F: Well, it's clear you like using your people and communication skills, and your personality test shows you're good at organisation and time management.

M: That's all true, I think.

F: Yes, and you're looking for a job that's got a lot of variety. And you enjoy working in a team.

M: Uh huh.

F: So, have you thought about a career in catering? Not as a waiter or chef, but as the person who organises the catering at events. You used to work as a waiter at them, how about running them? A catering manager is a good career, and it requires all those skills.

M: Well, I don't know, erm, sounds interesting, but, I mean, I don't have any training in that area.

F: But you do have experience of those events, and actually catering companies do look for people with a business studies degree.

M: Do they?

F: Uh huh. And I think that planning and running an event should suit you and your skills.

M: And food and cooking is a hobby of mine.

F: Exactly.

M: OK, well, I'm interested. Let's find out more.

PRONUNCIATION

A Tell students to listen to the extracts from the conversation and to answer the questions.
5.3

1 Michael 2 Fiona 3 Fiona: word is longer with rise. Michael: word is shorter with fall.

B Tell students to read the information in the box about holding your turn. Tell them to read the other examples from the *Listening* and to underline the words the speaker makes longer.
5.4

C Tell students to work in pairs to practise saying the sentences with the same intonation as Michael and Fiona used.

GRAMMAR

A–B Allow students to check answers in pairs before whole-class feedback as they complete the exercises.

C Direct students to the **Grammar Hub** on pages 130 and 131 (see below and TB54).

D Give your own example for one of the topics as a model. Use the **Grammar Worksheet** on W17 for extra practice.

SPEAKING HUB

A Tell students that they're going to give and receive some careers advice. Tell them to work alone and think about the questions, then to write down three jobs they would like to do.

B Tell students to prepare some interview questions that would be useful to find out about their partner's employment skills, interests and experience. Direct students to the **Audioscript** on page 171 to help them.

C Tell students to take it in turns to interview their partner and make notes of their answers.

D Tell students to work alone. Tell them to look at their notes about their partner and to write down three jobs that they think would be suitable for them. Then tell students to show their partners the jobs they chose for them. After they've done this, students can tell their partners how similar the list is to the one they wrote in Exercise A.

GRAMMAR HUB

5.1 Past habits and states

	Positive	Negative
I/you/he/she/it/we/they	**I used to be** a waiter in a restaurant.	**They did not use to work** here. **They didn't use to work** here.

Question	Positive short answer	Negative short answer
Did you use to work from home?	Yes, **I did**.	No, **I didn't**.

- We use *used to* to talk about past situations that do not exist now. These include past habits and past states.

  *Past habit: We **used to meet** at the station on the way to work.*

  *Past state: He **used to be** a manager but he left his job.*

- We use *use to* with the auxiliary verb *did*.

  *I didn't **use to** work here.*
  NOT I didn't used to work here.

  *Did you **use to** do voluntary work?*
  NOT Did you used to do voluntary work?

- In the negative, we can also say *never used to*.

  *I didn't **use to** work here. OR I **never used to** work here.*

- We can use *would* when we talk about past actions. We do not use it for permanent states in the past.

  When I was younger, I would visit London regularly on business. NOT When I was younger, I would live in London.

- We often use *would* when we are telling a story or talking fondly about the past.

  Every year, the boss would take us all out for a meal.

- When talking about the past, we rarely use *would* in the negative or question form.

  I didn't use to like it here. NOT I wouldn't like it here.

  Did you use to work part time? NOT Would you work part time?

PRONUNCIATION
Intonation and rhythm: holding your turn

A Listen to Michael and Fiona saying *Nice to meet you.* Then answer the questions.

1 Who sounds like they have finished speaking?

2 Who sounds like they are going to continue speaking?

3 What is the difference in how they say *you*?

Holding your turn

We can show that we are going to continue speaking by making a word longer, and sometimes, by using a rising intonation.

We show that we have finished speaking by using a falling intonation on our final word.

B Read the box. Now listen to more examples from Michael and Fiona's conversation. Underline the words the speaker makes longer to show they want to keep speaking.

1 I see you've been there <u>for</u> five years.

2 <u>Well</u>, it's been a good job, but erm, I just feel there's something missing.

3 I see, <u>and</u> what is it that's missing exactly?

4 I've recently been made assistant manager, <u>so</u> those skills are important.

5 I mean, you look <u>very</u> smart and presentable.

C SPEAK Work in pairs. Practice saying the sentences in Exercise C. Listen and check your partner's pronunciation.

GRAMMAR
Past habits and states

A WORK IT OUT Look at the sentences from the conversation between Fiona and Michael. Which underlined verbs are state verbs and which are action verbs? Which words are used to show repeated actions and events in the past?

1 I used to <u>be</u> a fashion model.
  State verb
2 They'd usually <u>give</u> us some of the clothes after the shoot.
  Action verb
3 I used to <u>help</u> new members.
  Action verb
4 At busy times, you <u>would</u> always <u>be</u> under a lot of pressure.
  State verb
5 I used to <u>be</u> tired but happy at the end of each day.
  State verb

B WORK IT OUT Choose the correct words to complete the rules. Then match the rules (2–5) with the sentences in Exercise A.

Past habits and states

1 We use *used to* and *would* to describe actions and states in the *present /* (*past.*) These are likely to be actions and states that are finished.

2 To talk about repeated actions in the past, we can use *used to* (*and*) */ but not would*. 2, 3

3 To talk about temporary repeated states in the past, we can use *used to* (*and*) */ but not would*. 4, 5

4 To talk about permanent states in the past, we use *used to and / * (*but not*) *would*. 1

5 We often use adverbs of frequency with *used to /* (*would.*) 2, 4

C Go to the Grammar Hub on page 130.

D SPEAK Work in groups. Discuss some of these topics.

* your childhood holidays
* your grandparents' younger lives
* how you have changed over the years

SPEAKING HUB

A You are going to give and receive some careers advice. Think about your employment skills, interests and experience. Then write down three jobs you would like to do.

* What strengths do you have?
* What skills have you used in work, college or your hobbies?
* What is important for you in a job or career?
* What types of work do you like doing?

B PLAN Write some interview questions that will help you find out about your partner's employment skills, interests and experience. Use the audioscript on page 171 to help you.

C SPEAK Work in pairs. Interview your partner. Listen carefully and make a note of his/her answers. Take turns.

D DISCUSS Choose three jobs that you think match your partner's skills and experience. Are they the same jobs that your partner wrote down before?

READING

A SPEAK Work in pairs. Look at the pictures (a–c) and discuss the questions.

1 Which offices would you like to work in? Why?

2 Which wouldn't you like to work in? Why?

B READ FOR MAIN IDEA Read *Are we in the middle of a workplace revolution?* Which is the best subtitle? Why?

1 Why digital technology companies are so successful

2 Why office life is changing and how to manage it

3 Why modern offices and unusual benefits are bad for business

Are we in the middle of a WORKPLACE REVOLUTION?

Pool tables, nap-pods and free food. **They** sound like things at an all-inclusive holiday resort rather than in an office. However, digital tech companies have redesigned the office and provided unusual benefits to make the workplace a more pleasant and productive place to be. **Ex D Q1**
5 Need a massage to help reduce stress? Want to bring your pet to work? No problem. For these companies, the days of individual cubicles where people would work on their own for eight hours a day are no more.

10 This trend is now spreading outside Silicon Valley. Bob Randell, director of MiCareer, says, 'Everyone's realising that tech companies don't provide fancy perks or games areas in order to seem cool and trendy. They want their staff to feel good **Ex D Q1** about themselves and their jobs. Happy employees are less
15 likely to leave to work for a competitor and, most importantly, they are more productive.'

This new kind of workplace also encourages people to **Ex D Q1** collaborate and to be creative. Playing table tennis with a colleague you rarely work with can lead to new ways of
20 working and fresh thinking. Thinking over a problem while lying in a hammock might be the best way to find **its** solution.

However, this doesn't mean employers should immediately offer free ice cream, replace desks with sofas or let staff bring pets to work. 'Firms have to make sure their perks are of real **Ex D Q2**
25 interest to their employees, and that **they** can afford them **Ex D Q2** for the long term. If a company stops offering a perk, staff **Ex D Q2** happiness goes down and people are less satisfied,' says Anna Tang, head of HR at DigitalForest.

'We advise our managers to monitor the effects of the perks
30 carefully. We now offer free breakfasts instead of free lunches. **This** persuades people to arrive early and to start work with good energy levels, which makes **them** more productive. Large free lunches just made them feel sleepy.'

This revolution in the workplace is unlikely to slow down.
35 As Randell says, 'All businesses can improve by increasing creativity, collaboration and happiness at work. The most successful ones do exactly **that**, and which companies don't want to be successful?'

5.1 At work

READING

A With books closed, ask students what they think of when they think of offices. Do they generally have positive or negative associations for the students? Tell students to open their books, to look at the pictures and to discuss the questions. In feedback ask students if they were surprised by anything in the pictures.

B Tell students to look at the pictures in the article. Elicit what type of offices the students think the article will be about. Then tell students to read quickly and to choose the best subtitle for the article. Set a time limit and remind students that they don't need to read too closely or worry about unknown vocabulary in order to get the main ideas. Explain that students don't need to focus on the words in bold at this stage.

2 The article describes how trends have spread from digital technology company culture and the reasons for those trends. It also describes potential disadvantages and the need to think carefully before introducing these kinds of changes.

C Point out the tips for following reference links in a text. Look at the first word in bold in the text together as a whole class to demonstrate the reference link, then tell students to do the same with the rest. Check students' understanding by carefully eliciting how the words link back to the previously mentioned people, things or ideas.

D Tell students to read the article again, more closely this time, and to answer the questions. Tell students to underline the part of the text that helped them find their answers and elicit this when you check answers. If some students finish much faster than others, put the faster finishers together to prepare more comprehension questions for each other about the article.

E Elicit an example of one innovation or perk mentioned in the article (e.g. nap-pods, free food). Put students into groups to find and underline more and discuss what they think of them. Encourage students to expand on their answers by asking them the following questions: *Would you like to work in the types of offices described in the article? Why / why not? Are there offices like that in your country? If not, do they think there will be in the future?*

GRAMMAR HUB

5.1   Past habits and states

A Complete the sentences with *used to* or *would* and the verb in brackets. If both options are possible, write both.

1 When I was younger, I __used to dream / would dream__ of running my own business. (*dream*)

2 In my old job, I ___would plan___ events. (*plan*)

3 The office has moved. It ___used to be___ closer to my home. (*be*)

4 I __didn't use to think__ that management skills were important. (*not think*)

5 Joel ___used to love___ his job but he hates it now. (*love*)

6 Work ___used to start / would start___ at eight and nobody dared to be late! (*start*)

B Make questions with *used to*.

1 you / live / London / ?
  Did you use to live in London?

2 Sally / work / restaurant / ?
  Did Sally use to work in a restaurant?

3 things / be better / in the past / ?
  Did things use to be better in the past?

4 where / you / spend / your childhood holidays / ?
  Where did you use to spend your childhood holidays?

5 what / you / do / in your old job / ?
  What did you use to do in your old job?

6 when you walked to work / how long / it / take you / ?
  When you walked to work, how long did it use to take you?

C Make sentences with *used to*. Put a tick (✓) or a cross (✗) to show whether the same idea can be expressed with *would*.

1 when / I / be / younger / I / have / my own business
  When I was younger, I used to have my own business. ✗

2 in the past / our manager / not have / good communication skills
  In the past, our manager didn't use to have (such/very) good communication skills. ✗

3 every afternoon / I / try / finish / all the letters
  Every afternoon, I used to try to/and finish all the letters. ✓

4 years ago / people / laugh / at the idea / computers in the home
  Years ago, people used to laugh at the idea of computers in the home. ✓

5 you / enjoy / your job / more / ?
  Did you use to enjoy your job more? ✗

6 often / we / not have / a summer holiday
  Often, we didn't use to have a summer holiday. ✓

➤ Go back to page 51.

5.1 At work

VOCABULARY

A Tell students to look at the sentences and explain that they were said by Sophia, the boss, to her employees Simon and James. Work through the first one as an example, eliciting which meaning is the correct description of what Sophia said. Tell students to do the same with the others.

B Direct students to the **Vocabulary Hub** on page 144 for further practice of verbs of influence.

C Show students the table. Give one or two personal examples about when you were younger to demonstrate how to create sentences, taking something from each column. Encourage students to ask you follow-up questions about your sentences, then ask them to do the same with their partner. Monitor to check students are using the verbs correctly, especially that they're using the infinitive <u>without</u> to after *let* and *make*. Share answers as a whole class and ask students to tell the class how similar or different their childhood and their partner's was and why. Use the **Vocabulary Worksheet** on W20 for extra practice.

SPEAKING HUB

A Tell students to look at picture b on page 52 and to imagine that they all work in an office similar to this. Tell them that they're going to have a meeting to discuss how to improve the workplace and employee motivation by redesigning the office and giving employees new perks. Elicit a couple of ideas from the group. Tell students to work alone and add more ideas to their list.

B Put students into groups to compare and explain their ideas. Encourage them to give as many reasons for their ideas as possible.

C Tell each group to agree on the best ideas and then to make a plan of their office redesign and list their chosen perks. Tell students to prepare to explain their ideas to the class. Monitor and help with language input if necessary.

D Tell each group to present their ideas to the class. Encourage the other groups to ask questions at the end of each presentation. Once all the presentations have been given and there are no further questions, tell students to vote on the best plan. Finish by giving some feedback on students' language use during the presentations.

TEACHING IDEA by David Seymour and Maria Popova

Topic: The job market

Do people spend too much of their lives working? What is the employment situation like in your country? What are the effects of globalisation on the job market?

In small groups, tell each other about these jobs:

1 the best / worst / most interesting / most dangerous job you have done

2 the best / worst / most interesting / most dangerous job in the world

TEACHING IDEA by David Seymour and Maria Popova

Topic: Job description

Here are some important aspects of a job:

duties, pay, the boss, benefits, training, holidays, health and safety, promotion, hours of work, experience, overtime, unions, job security

Ask me questions about these aspects of my job. (Pretend only to hear the grammatically correct questions.)

In pairs, use similar questions to interview your partner about his/her job. (If fewer than half the students are in work, put them in small groups. If no one is working, ask them to imagine a job they would like.)

TEACHING IDEA by David Seymour and Maria Popova

Topic: Globalisation

Work in two groups of six. (If the class does not divide, make one or more groups smaller and take away one of the roles below.) Each of you choose a different number from 1 to 6. You are going to discuss the building of a clothes factory in a poorer country. I'm going to give you a role according to the number you chose.

In the richer country:

1 Businessman/investor

2 Anti-capitalist protestor

3 Factory worker

In the poorer country:

4 Unemployed factory worker

5 Politician

6 Environmentalist

Take turns to say if you are in favour of the factory and how it will affect your life and the country if it is built. Assuming that the factory is going ahead, talk together as a group to negotiate the best possible deal for everybody concerned.

METHODOLOGY HUB by Jim Scrivener

Lexis and skills work

A great deal of lexis work in class occurs in relation to reading and listening tasks. There are definite advantages in this, most importantly because learners meet the language in realistic contexts and see how the items fit into the meaning and style of a whole text.

The text that immediately surrounds a lexical item is referred to as *co-text*. Co-text provides important exposure for learners to samples of language being used. This suggests why texts are often more useful for teaching lexis than lessons that focus on lexis as separated, stand-alone items without such surrounding language.

When using reading or listening texts, a focus on lexis may occur before, while or after the students read or listen.

C Read again. What do the words in bold refer to? Use the strategies in the box to help you.

> **Following reference links in a text**
>
> We use pronouns (for example *it*, *them*, *this*) instead of repeating the same word many times. They usually refer to a person or thing, but they can also refer to ideas.
>
> In order to improve your understanding of a text, it is important to understand which idea or thing the pronouns refer to.

1 Line 1: They ____*pool tables, nap-pods and free food.*____

2 Line 21: Its ____a problem____

3 Line 25: they ____firms____

4 Line 31: This ____offering free breakfast____

5 Line 32: them ____people____

6 Line 37: that <u>increasing creativity, collaboration and</u> happiness at work

D READ FOR DETAIL Read again. Answer the questions.

1 According to the article, which of the following are advantages of modern office design and attractive perks?

  (a) increasing the quality of work that people do

  b attracting high quality people to the company

  (c) encouraging sharing ideas with different people

  (d) stopping people leaving their jobs

2 What should companies who want to update their benefits and office design do?

  (a) provide benefits that employees really want

  (b) consider the future costs of extra benefits

  (c) avoid cancelling benefits

  d offer different perks to other companies

E SPEAK Work in groups. Find and underline the innovations and perks in the article. What is your opinion of them?

VOCABULARY
Verbs of influence

A Look at what Sophia, the boss, said to her employees Simon and James. Match the pairs of sentences with the correct meanings (a or b).

1 Yes, of course, you can do that. a

2 Do it now! b

  a She allowed him to do it.

  b She told him to do it.

3 Of course, no problem. Feel free to do it. b

4 I'll explain why it's a good idea, and then you might change your mind. a

  a She persuaded him to do it.

  b She let him do it.

5 You must do it. If you don't, I will sack you! a

6 I think you should do it this way. b

  a She made him do something.

  b She advised him to do something.

7 Don't worry, I'm sure you are good enough. Try to do it. a

8 I would like you to do it, not her. b

  a She encouraged him to do it.

  b She wanted him to do it.

B Go to the Vocabulary Hub on page 144.

C SPEAK Work in pairs. Talk to your partner about when you were younger. Use the ideas below to help you.

When I was younger, …		
my parents	didn't let	me …
a friend	used to make	us …
my teacher	encouraged	my parents …
I	advised	a friend …

◯ SPEAKING HUB

A Look at picture b on page 52. Imagine that you work in an office similar to this. You are going to a meeting about improving the workplace and employee motivation. Make a list of ideas to take to the meeting.

B DISCUSS Work in groups. Compare your ideas, giving explanations for each one.

C ORGANISE Choose the best ideas and make a simple plan to show your office redesign and list your chosen perks.

D PRESENT Show your plan to the class. Then have a class vote to decide which plan is the most popular.

◯– Discuss and give advice about employment skills and career interests

◯– Discuss and suggest workplace benefits and changes

5.2 In business
— Describe and evaluate a small business
— Talk about environmental business ideas

G— the passive   V— business collocations   P— silent consonants   S— listening for examples

READING

A SPEAK How much extra do you think you pay when you buy these products? Match the products (1–3) with the percentages in the box. There are two extra percentages. Then work in pairs and compare your answers.

> 40 per cent   300 per cent   600 per cent
> 1200 per cent   4000 per cent

1 bottled water rather than tap water   4000 per cent
2 pre-cut vegetables and fruit rather than uncut   40 per cent
3 take-away espresso coffee rather than making it at home   300 per cent

B SPEAK Work in pairs and discuss the questions.

1 How often do you buy the items in Exercise A?
2 What's your opinion of these products and the prices charged for them?

C PREDICT You are going to read an article about a new company, Aethaer. Before you read, answer the questions below. Then work in pairs and compare your answers.

1 Look at the picture and the title of the article. What product does Aethaer sell?

2 Which four of the following topics do you think will be in the article?

a personal information about the owner of Aethaer
b the production method
c Aethaer's business model – product, price and target customers
d full details of how to order, including delivery costs
e information about other similar businesses
f why people buy the product

D READ FOR GIST Read *The new bottled water?* Check your answers to Exercise C. 1. It sells fresh air in jars.
2. b, c, d, f

Business Business

News and views on the business of doing business

The new bottled water?

Dorset, Great Britain

AETHAER

At *Business Business*, we are always looking for the next bottled water, and we think we have found it – bottled air.

Ex E Q1 Businessman Leo de Watts is selling jars of fresh air from the British countryside to the residents of polluted cities around the world. He claims Britain has 'designer quality' **Ex E Q2** fresh air, and he sells Aethaer as a luxury product. Each jar costs a breathtaking £95.

Ex E Q3 The business was launched two months ago. Orders can **Ex E Q4** be made online only, and already 200 jars have been delivered to China. Not many small businesses achieve sales of £16,000 in their first months, and none have a **Ex E Q5** product that is so cheap to produce. With plans to start marketing Aethaer in India, Watts could be made a **Ex E Q6** millionaire by selling almost nothing, nothing but air. **Ex E Q7** 'Air-farming' is incredibly easy. The air is collected from different places in the countryside, from the seaside to the mountains, from the green hills to the forests. The glass jars are held high in the air, and are closed after a few minutes. That's it – the simplest production process ever. **Ex E Q8** Next, a label saying where the air comes from is put on

the jars. Then, after they have been packed for delivery, they are sent overseas. Job done. There are currently 15 different 'airs' in the product range. Watts claims that each one has different qualities, depending on where they were collected. While some **Ex E Q9** customers do buy the air to inhale, many people buy the jars as gifts that will be kept and won't be opened. Aethaer air is sold as a luxury item for wealthy people, but other new businesses have started selling cans of compressed air for everyday or sports use. Each can **Ex E Q10** contains 200 breaths of air, and they come with a face mask for efficient and easy use.

People laughed when bottled water was first sold in convenience stores, but now everyone buys it. With urban air pollution increasing, it may not be long until you buy a can of clean air as well as a bottle of water every day.

LEAD-IN

With books closed, ask students to think of a product that they consider to be good value for money, and one that they consider bad value for money. Ask students to explain their answers and try to elicit what students think it is that makes something good value for money.

READING

A Tell students to open their books and discuss the questions. Check the meaning of *pre-cut* and *uncut* and highlight the use of prefixes to create different meaning.

1 4000 per cent
2 40 per cent
3 300 per cent

B Tell students to discuss the questions with their partner. Ask students why they think people pay so much extra for these products and if they consider them value for money despite now knowing the price-percentage increases they saw in Exercise A.

C Tell students they're going to read an article about a new company called Aethaer. Tell them to cover the article below the title at first and just to look at the picture and title while they discuss the questions. Share students' predictions as a whole class before they read but don't confirm or deny anything yet.

D Tell students to uncover the article and to read it quickly to check their answers. Set a time limit to ensure students don't try to read in too much detail at this stage.

METHODOLOGY HUB by Jim Scrivener

Reading for detail

A lot of in-class reading work has traditionally been 'reading for detail' – or 'intensive reading', i.e. reading texts closely and carefully with the intention of gaining an understanding of as much detail as possible. Often this is so that the student can answer comprehension questions (e.g. *Why did the three men go into the office?*). This is typically a stop/start kind of reading, involving going back over small pieces of the same text a number of times to find out more and more about it, making sure that the words have been correctly interpreted. This is how a competent language user might read an instruction manual for a piece of flat-pack furniture or a leaflet with guidelines on whether they have to pay income tax or not. It's not the way she would typically read a chapter from a novel or a magazine article, although, in classrooms, it is often how students are asked to process such material (with true/false and other comprehension questions to check if they can pick up specific points).

In everyday life, we tend to do much more extensive reading, i.e. fluent, faster reading, often of longer texts, for pleasure, entertainment and general understanding, but without such careful attention to the details. When we don't understand words or small sections, we usually just keep going, maybe only coming back when there has been a major breakdown in our understanding.

There is certainly a place for intensive reading in class, helping students to uncover and accurately understand details in a text – but this is by no means the only strategy that a good reader needs. Being able to read fast and fluently is also very important.

GRAMMAR HUB

5.2 The passive

	Positive	Negative	Question
Present simple	**I am expected** to work at weekends.	**You are not allowed** to take time off. **You aren't allowed** to take time off.	**Is he paid** a lot of money?
Present continuous	**The goods are being delivered** now.	**The workers are not being trained** at the moment. **The workers aren't being trained** at the moment.	**Is the product being sold** at full price?
Past simple	**I was told** to wait in Reception.	**They were not asked** to work at weekends. **They weren't asked** to work at weekends.	**Were you given** instructions?
Past continuous	**The product was being used** all over the world.	**She was not being paid** very much. **She wasn't being paid** very much.	**Was bottled water being sold** here 30 years ago?
Present perfect	**The product has** just **been launched**.	**Your order has not been received.** **Your order hasn't been received.**	**Have the workers been told**?

- We use the passive when we don't say who or what causes the action (usually because the person or thing is not known, not important or obvious).

  *The business **was launched** last year.*

- We can sometimes say the same thing in the active or passive voice. The choice often depends on the topic we are talking about.

  *Active: The company **sells** the product as a luxury item. (The topic is the company.)*

  *Passive: The product **is sold** as a luxury item. (The topic is the product.)*

- We use *by* when we know who does/did an action and we want to mention it.

  *This product was bought **by** both young and old customers.*

- We can use the passive with modal verbs.

  *Orders **can be made** online or at one of our stores.*

  *The product **might be launched** in the New Year.*

- We don't use *by* + the agent unless it is important, useful information.

  The product is sold all over the world. NOT ~~The product is sold by shopkeepers all over the world.~~

E Ask students to read through the sentences, filling in any gaps with information that they remember and querying any unknown vocabulary. Then tell students to read the article again, more carefully this time, and to complete the sentences with a word or phrase from the article. Encourage students to compare answers when they've finished and to explain where in the text they found their answers. If students finish this task at very different times, monitor and check that the faster finishers have got the correct answers and can explain how they found them. These faster finishers can then become your deputies, monitoring other pairs or groups and prompting them towards the answers. Elicit how and where students found the answers to ensure students have a good understanding of the text and the reading processes.

F Put students into pairs to discuss the questions. Encourage students to explain and expand on their opinions. Ask if they agree with the final sentence and if they think that fresh air in jars will one day become as popular as bottled water.

GRAMMAR

A Elicit that the sentences all come from the article the students have just read. Tell them to underline the main verb and to think about whether the sentences tell us who did the action. Do the first one together to check students understand the task.
Sentences 1 and 5 say who did the action.

B Tell students to look back at the sentences in Exercise A to help them complete the rules. Check the answers as a whole class, referring back to the examples to check students understand why the passive is used in each case. Ask students if they have a similar structure in their language and, if so, how often they use it. Point out that the passive is very common in English and used more often than it is in many other languages.

by Jim Scrivener

C Direct students to the **Grammar Hub** on pages 130 and 131 (see TB54 and below).
A way to make one of these exercises more fun would be to make it competitive. Divide the class into pairs or teams of three. Photocopy, and enlarge if possible, the exercise so there is one for each team. Have each one on different colour paper as well if possible. Cut the exercise into strips to separate the questions, and attach them to a wall in the classroom, or in a corridor outside. Tell each team to choose one person who will be the runner. The runner has to run to their team's exercise, tear off the strip for question 1 and take it back to their team. They answer the question together and write the answer on the strip, then the runner brings it to you. If it is correct, tell the runner to take the next question from the wall and repeat. If it is incorrect, send the runner back to their team to try again. The first team to finish wins. Use the **Grammar Worksheet** on W19 for extra practice.

SPEAKING HUB

A Tell half the pairs to be student A and the other half to be student B and to turn to the **Communication Hub** on page 152.

B Tell students to look at their company profile and to work together to make notes to help them present the information to a new partner later. Monitor and help if needed.

C Re-pair students, so each pair contains one student A and one student B. Tell them to present their company to their new partner in as much detail as possible. Encourage them to ask each other questions if they don't understand something.

D Ask students first to discuss in pairs which of their companies should win the award, or whether Aethaer should win. Open this up to a whole-class discussion before holding a vote to establish the overall winner. Feedback on students' language.

GRAMMAR HUB

5.2 The passive

A Correct the mistakes in each sentence.

1 The office ~~is~~ located in the centre of Manchester. *is*
2 The business was ~~start~~ by two brothers in Cape Town in 2018. *started*
3 The company is ~~knowing~~ for its luxury goods and excellent website. *known*
4 Is the plan ~~been~~ considered at the moment or is there a delay? *being*
5 The items you have ordered can ~~delivered~~ within two working days. *be*
6 The managers agreed. A decision was taken ~~by them~~ yesterday.

B Choose the correct option.

1 When will we _____?
   a paid   **(b) be paid**   c paying
2 My order _____ yesterday.
   (a) was made   b is make   c made
3 We _____ what to do.
   a haven't told   b didn't tell   **(c) weren't told**
4 When you phoned me, I _____ for a job.
   (a) was being interviewed   b was interviewed   c am interviewing
5 The food for tonight _____.
   a has been delivering   **(b) has just been delivered**   c was been delivered
6 Is everything _____ in the box?
   a provide   **(b) provided**   c providing

C Rewrite the sentences in the passive. Use *by* only when necessary.

1 They usually give us our tasks in the morning.
   We are usually given our tasks in the morning.

2 The manager is studying Rob's business plan.
   Rob's business plan is being studied by the manager.

3 They started the business last year.
   The business was started last year.

4 They have only delivered three jars.
   Only three jars have been delivered.

5 Matt presented details of the plan.
   Details of the plan were presented by Matt.

6 When I started, they were making some big changes.
   When I started, some big changes were being made.

➤ Go back to page 55.

E **READ FOR DETAIL** Read again. Complete each sentence with a word or phrase from the article.

1 Aethaer's customers usually live in _____ polluted cities _____.

2 Aethaer air costs £95 per jar because it is a _____ luxury product _____.

3 Leo de Watts started the business _____ two months ago _____.

4 If you want some Aethaer air, you must buy it _____ online _____.

5 There aren't any other businesses with such _____ cheap _____ production costs.

6 He may become _____ a millionaire _____ in the future.

7 Collecting the air is _____ incredibly easy _____ to do.

8 Before he puts the jars in boxes, Leo adds _____ a label _____ to each jar.

9 _____ Some costumers _____ want to breathe the air, but _____ many people _____ never open the jars.

10 Aethaer's competitors want people to buy air for their _____ everyday _____ lives or when they are playing _____ sports _____.

F **SPEAK** Work in pairs and discuss the questions.

1 Why does the article say bottled air is the new bottled water?

2 What do you think of the idea of buying a jar of air for £95?

GRAMMAR
The passive

A **WORK IT OUT** Look at the sentences from *The new bottled water?* and underline the main verb. Which sentences tell us who did the action?

1 Leo de Watts <u>sells</u> Aethaer as a luxury product.

2 The business <u>was launched</u> two months ago.

3 Orders <u>can be made</u> online only.

4 The air <u>is collected</u> from different places in the countryside.

5 Other businesses <u>have started</u> selling cans of compressed air.

B Choose the correct words to complete the rules.

> **The passive**
>
> We form the passive with **be** + the past participle of the main verb.
> We use the passive when:
>
> **a** we *know* / **don't know** or it is *important* / **not important** who or what did the action.
>
> **b** it is *obvious* / **not obvious** who or what did the action.
>
> **c** we *want* / **don't want** to focus on the person or thing affected by the action.

C Go to the Grammar Hub on page 130.

A You are going to choose a business idea as the winner of the *Business Business* Low-cost Business of the Year Award. Read the information about *Autumn Memories* below, then compare it to the *Arctic Diamond* on page 152.

SPEAKING HUB

A You are going to choose a business idea as the winner of the *Business Business* Low-cost Business of the Year Award. Read the information about *Autumn Memories* below, then compare it to the *Arctic Diamond* on page 152.

B **PLAN** Write notes to help you present the information in the company profile.

C **PRESENT** Work in pairs. Present the company to your partner. Then listen to your partner's presentation and take notes of the key information.

D **REFLECT** Have a class vote to decide which company (including Aethaer) should win the Low-cost Business of the Year Award.

Basic information

Country:	Canada
Business name:	Autumn Memories
Slogan:	'Bring nature's beauty into your home'
Founded by:	Jessica Malone
Products:	Autumn leaves in a gift box (Three leaves: 1 red, 1 yellow, 1 mixed)
Price:	$30

Production process

picked by hand / dried and pressed for ten days / wrapped in tissue paper / packed in a gift box

Sales

Online business:	130 orders in first three days / $12,000 in first year of business
Current customers:	People from hot, dry states in the USA, e.g. Nevada, Texas
Future markets:	India / Saudi Arabia / Dubai

Autumn Memories

REPAIR, REUSE OR RECYCLE

LISTENING

A SPEAK Work in pairs and discuss the questions.

1 How often do you buy new clothes?

2 Have you ever bought second-hand clothes?

3 Why do you think some people prefer to buy second-hand clothes?

B LISTEN FOR GIST Complete the sentences (1–3) with the words in the box. Then listen to the *Business Business* podcast and check your answers.
5.5

marketing   outdoor   second-hand

1 Patagonia is an _____outdoor_____ clothing company.

2 They launched a _____marketing_____ campaign called 'Worn Wear'.

3 It encouraged people to return old clothes and buy _____second-hand_____ clothes.

C LISTEN FOR MAIN IDEA Listen again. Are the sentences true (T) or false (F)? Correct the false sentences.
5.5

1 Patagonia makes ~~things~~ clothes that people ~~only~~ can wear ~~when they are at work or at home.~~ and use outdoors. F

2 Patagonia is one of many companies in this sector. T

3 'Worn Wear' is a campaign that persuades people to ~~make their own~~ buy second-hand clothes. F

4 Customers are encouraged to give their old clothes to be sold second-hand. T

5 ~~'Worn Wear' is the only time Patagonia has launched an environmental campaign.~~ F
They also took out a full-page ad in The New York Times in 2011 encouraging people not to buy one of their jackets.

6 As a company, Patagonia is concerned about its effect on the environment. T

D LISTEN FOR EXAMPLES Listen again. Complete the sentences (1–5) with the missing words and phrases. Use the strategies in the box to help you.
5.6

Listening for examples

In longer talks and discussions, speakers give examples to support their claims.

Here are some words and phrases that we often use to introduce an example:

- *For example, …*   • *… like …*   • *… such as …*
- *As the survey(s) / results / sales figures show …*
- *Another instance …*

Paying close attention to the examples that follow these words will give you a fuller understanding of the speaker's main ideas.

1 There are lots of others, _____such as_____ North Face, Berghaus and Columbia.

2 'Worn Wear' encourages customers to buy second-hand Patagonia clothes, _____like_____ old jackets and T-shirts.

3 _____As the results show_____, their sales have increased because of campaigns like 'Worn Wear'.

4 _____For example_____, they made record profits on Black Friday.

5 _____Another instance_____ of this is when Patagonia took out a full-page ad in *The New York Times*.

E SPEAK Work in pairs and discuss the questions.

1 Why do you think the 'Worn Wear' and 'Don't Buy This Jacket' campaigns were a success for Patagonia?

2 Would campaigns like these encourage you to buy a company's products? Why/Why not?

3 Can you think of any other environmental business ideas like these campaigns? Give examples.

5.2 In business

LEAD-IN

With books closed, ask students to tell you one thing they would buy second-hand and one thing they would never buy second-hand. Put students into pairs to think of more. Monitor and encourage students to ask questions or expand on their answers, especially if there are differences of opinion in the class.

LISTENING

 A–D Allow students to check answers in pairs before whole-class feedback as they complete the listening exercises. Then encourage them to share their opinions and talk about their own experiences in whole-class feedback.

E Put students into pairs to discuss the questions.

AUDIOSCRIPT

🔊 **5.5**

Listening, Exercise B
C = Clive   E = Ella

C: Welcome to the Business Business podcast. Today, we're discussing environmental business ideas, and we're starting with the retail sector. I'm talking to our retail expert Ella Stevens.

E: Hello, Clive.

C: Ella, I understand you're going to tell us about a clothing company with some very unusual marketing ideas.

E: Yes. I'm talking today about Patagonia. It's an outdoor activities clothing company based in the USA. It was started by Yvon Chouinard in 1973. He used to be a rock climber, and at first, Patagonia made climbing equipment. Since then, it has changed its focus to outdoor clothing.

C: So they make and sell clothing for activities like hiking and skiing, as well as climbing?

Ex C Q1   E: That's right. Patagonia is one of the largest brands in the outdoor clothing sector, but there are lots of others, such as North Face, Berghaus and Columbia. These brands are now so popular that you see people wearing their clothes all the time, not just when they are out in the countryside.

C: So what's different about Patagonia?

E: Well, a few years ago, the company launched a new marketing campaign called 'Worn Wear', which

Ex C Q3   encourages customers to buy second-hand Patagonia clothes like old jackets and T-shirts.

C: That is an unusual way to run a business. It's difficult for a clothing company to make a profit selling new clothes if everyone chooses to buy second-hand instead.

E: That's a good point, Clive, but Patagonia go even further. They also actively encourage their customers to give them their old Patagonia clothes so that they can then sell them as second-hand items.

C: Really? Why are they doing this? There must be a good reason.

E: Well, Patagonia strongly believes in looking after the environment.
They've built a brand based on respecting nature, and they are trying hard to reduce the negative impact that the company has on the world we live in. They believe that by encouraging people to repair their clothes and return them so they can be bought second-hand, they are helping the environment.

C: And is this strategy working for them?

E: Yes, it is, Clive. Patagonia is doing a good job of attracting new customers. As the results show, their sales have increased because of campaigns like 'Worn Wear'. For example, they made record profits on Black Friday a few years ago, and they donated the whole amount to environmental organisations.

C: That's incredible! And I imagine this helped them to make even more money in the long term.

E: It's certainly made their brand more attractive to customers who are concerned about the environment.

C: Is 'Worn Wear' the first time Patagonia has used such an unusual marketing campaign?

Ex C Q5   E: No, it isn't. Another instance of this is when Patagonia took out a full-page ad in *The New York Times* that encouraged people NOT to buy one of their jackets because of the damage it would do to the environment. Consequently, they got a lot of media attention.

C: I can imagine – that seems quite a risky strategy. Did they sell more jackets?

E: Probably, but there's no doubt that the company has helped to increase people's knowledge about the effect the clothing industry can have on the environment.

C: And it's a very interesting approach to building a brand. Thank you for coming in to talk to us today, Ella. Next on the podcast we're looking at …

5.2 In business

VOCABULARY

A Elicit that all the sentences are from the podcast. Tell them to choose the correct verb to complete the collocations, either from memory or according to which they think sounds right. Highlight that there is often no rule or reason why certain words are frequently used together so students will just need to memorise collocations. You could briefly discuss different ways of recording vocabulary and get students to think about which methods are most effective for them.

B Highlight that these sentences are also from the podcast. Tell them to match the beginnings of the sentences with the endings. After checking answers, get students to work in pairs to test each other, with one student reading the beginning of the sentence and their partner trying to say the ending from memory. They can also test each other on the collocations from Exercise A, with one student closing their book and their partner reading the sentence without the verb. The student whose book is closed has to listen and say the missing verb.

C Direct students to the **Vocabulary Hub** on page 144 for further practice of business collocations.

D Students discuss the questions with a partner. Elicit some examples of companies that students will all be familiar with to get students started. Use the **Vocabulary Worksheet** on W20 for extra practice.

PRONUNCIATION

A Tell students to listen to the sentences from the podcast and to complete the missing word in each. Write the words on the board and ask students what the pronunciation of the two words has in common. Elicit that they both have silent letters. Elicit which consonant is silent in each one.

B Tell students all the words have a silent consonant. Ask them to underline which one they think it is in each word. Play the audio for students to check.

C Tell students to look at the sentences and to find and correct the spelling mistake in each one. Do question 1 together as a whole class. Elicit that the missing letter in each word will be a silent consonant like the *b* in *doubt*.

SPEAKING HUB

A Put students into pairs and make each one student A or student B. Ask student A to look at the box on the page and ask student B to turn to the **Communication Hub** on page 153. Tell them they're going to make a podcast and talk about an environmental business idea.

B Tell each pair to prepare and plan their talk by making notes and thinking about all the points listed. Monitor and help with language input.

C Put students into new pairs with one student A working with one student B. Tell students to take it in turns to present their idea as if they were presenting a business podcast. Encourage students to ask each other further questions about each idea.

D Tell each pair to discuss which idea they think is the best and why. Discuss as a whole class and ask students to explain their ideas and encourage further discussion here. Conclude the class with feedback on students' use of language during the task. Write on the board any interesting vocabulary that was requested earlier in the lesson.

> **Extra activity**
> For homework, students can research other environmental business ideas online. They should come prepared to share these ideas at the start of the next class.

TEACHING IDEA
by David Seymour and Maria Popova

Topic: Public consultation meeting

Use this activity to extend the topic.

A paper factory is planned for your town, which is very beautiful but high in unemployment. There are concerns from the local community about pollution and the destruction of an ancient forest nearby.

In groups of eight, you are going to roleplay a public consultation meeting to listen to local views. (Allocate these roles. If the class does not divide into groups of eight, drop one or two of the roles.)

In favour of the factory: the mayor, a representative of the paper company, the building contractor, an unemployed person.

Against the factory: a member of the Green Party, an environmental scientist, a local craftsman, a local hotel owner.

Before the meeting, discuss your arguments with the people who share your views, considering pollution, visual impact, tourism, jobs and effects on other businesses. Roleplay the meeting.

TEACHING IDEA
by David Seymour and Maria Popova

Topic: Eco-warrior

Use this activity to extend the topic.

What is an 'eco-warrior'? What kind of issues do they fight for and how do they fight for them?

In pairs, imagine a motorway is being built through an area of outstanding natural beauty.

How would you oppose it if you were an eco-warrior?

What arguments would you make?

What arguments would you expect from the developer?

Roleplay an interview between a journalist and an eco-warrior chained to a tree. Discuss the planned development, how long he/she has been there and what he/she plans to do when the bulldozers arrive.

PRONUNCIATION
Silent consonants

🔊 **A** Listen to the sentences from the podcast. Complete the
5.6 missing words. Which consonant is silent?

1 Patagonia strongly believes in looking after the
e<u>nvironment</u>. Silent consonant: the second n

2 Is 'Worn Wear' the first time Patagonia has used such an
unusual marketing c<u>ampaign</u>? Silent consonant: g

🔊 **B** Underline the silent consonants in each word. Then listen
5.7 and check your answers.

1 clim<u>b</u>ing	3 hig<u>h</u>	5 <u>k</u>nowledge
2 desi<u>g</u>n	4 <u>h</u>onest	6 <u>w</u>rite

C Find and correct the mistakes in the sentences.

1 There's no ~~dout~~ the company sold a lot more clothes
   doubt
   as a result of the magazine ad.

2 It's ~~rong~~ to say that all businesses are only interested
   wrong
   in profits.

3 To understand advertising, you need to understand
   people's ~~sychology.~~ psychology

4 You can buy second-hand Patagonia clothes at any
   of their stores with a 'Worn Wear' ~~sain.~~
                                        sign

VOCABULARY
Business collocations

A Choose the correct verbs to complete the business
collocations in the sentences from the podcast.

1 The company *landed* / **launched** a new marketing
campaign called 'Worn Wear'.

2 That is an unusual way to **run** / *do* a business.

3 It's difficult for a clothing company to *have* / **make** a
profit selling new clothes.

4 They've *run* / **built** a brand based on respecting nature.

5 Patagonia is doing a good job of **attracting** / *adapting*
new customers.

B Match the beginnings of sentences (1–5) with the
endings (a–e).

1 Over the last few years,
the company has **built**

2 When we **attract**

3 The company tries to
launch

4 Like any business,
we **make**

5 The best way to **run**

a new **investors**, we'll
have more money.

b **money** by selling our
products for a profit.

c its **reputation**
successfully.

d a **company** is to hire
good people.

e at least one new
product every year.

C Go to the Vocabulary Hub on page 144.

D SPEAK Work in pairs and discuss the questions.

1 What can a retailer do to attract new customers?

2 What campaigns have companies that you know
launched recently?

⭘ SPEAKING HUB

A You are going to talk about an environmental
business idea in a podcast. Student A – read the box
below about the company *REI stores*. Student B – go
to the Communication Hub on page 153.

B PLAN Plan your talk:

• explain the idea.

• include examples and business collocations.

• be prepared to answer questions.

C SPEAK Work in pairs. Roleplay presenting a
business podcast. Listen to your partner and ask
questions about his/her idea. Take turns.

D REFLECT Work in pairs. Which idea do you think is
the best? Why?

Student A

Company:	REI stores, USA
Retail sector:	Outdoor clothing and equipment
Environmental idea:	Close all stores on Black Friday (the busiest shopping day of the year in the USA). Staff are paid to take the day off.
Reason:	To encourage people to spend more time outdoors.
Result:	700 organizations, and 8 million people supported the campaign via social media in its first few years.

⭘– Describe and evaluate a small business
⭘– Talk about environmental business ideas

COMPREHENSION

A Work in pairs. Which of the following factors are most important for a successful business presentation?

- be smartly dressed
- have neat, organised handouts
- show interesting slides
- have a clear, confident voice
- be fit, well and relaxed
- be punctual

B ▶ 00:00–02:48 Watch the first part of the video. What problems does Matthew Williams have with his presentation?

C Predict what happens next. Do *Jobs, Jobs, Jobs and Jobs* get the contract?

D ▶ 02:48–04:53 Watch the second part of the video and check your ideas. Why does Neena smile at the end?

FUNCTIONAL LANGUAGE
Structuring a presentation

A Put the phrases in the box into a logical order in the table.

> Do you have any questions?   So first of all, I'd like to talk about
> So, the next question is   That brings us to
> Today's presentation is all about

Structuring a presentation

Welcome

Good morning and thank you for coming.

Introduction

1 <u>Today's presentation is all about</u>   how we can work together in Brazil.

Main points

2 <u>So first of all, I'd like to talk about</u>   the benefits.
Let's take a look at the first slide.
We have a great deal of experience in the jobs marketplace.

3 <u>So the next question is</u>   how to market ourselves in Brazil.

4 <u>That brings us to</u>   the end of the presentation.

Questions

5 <u>Do you have any questions?</u>

Summary

Great. So to sum up, we see an exciting future …

B ▶ 00:00–02:48 Watch the first part again and check your answers.

C At what stage of a presentation would you expect to hear sentence beginnings 1–5? Use the headings in the box.

1 Let's move on now to look at …	<u>Main points</u>
2 In conclusion, …	<u>Summary</u>
3 The purpose of today's presentation is …	<u>Introduction</u>
4 I'd like to finish with …	<u>Summary</u>
5 The next point I would like to explore is …	<u>Main points</u>

MILLY   SAM   NEENA   ZAC   GABY

USEFUL PHRASES

A Rewrite the useful phrases from the presentation less formally. Use the words and phrases in the box.

> agree   loads   write / straight away

1 We have a great deal of experience …

   We have loads of experience …

2 If we can come to an agreement …

   If we can agree …

3 We can put the contract together immediately.

   We can write the contract straight away.

B How do you say these useful phrases in your language?

PRONUNCIATION
Ordering adverbs

A Listen and write the ordering adverbs in the correct space.

1	Firstly	4	Fourthly
2	Secondly	5	Fifthly
3	Thirdly	6	Finally

B Work in pairs. Practise the adverbs in Exercise A. Student A – say a number. Student B – say the adverb.

SPEAKING

A You are going to give a presentation about a personal possession and explain why it is a good one to have. Choose from the personal possessions in the box or your own ideas.

> my bag   my bicycle   my car   my coat
> my laptop/computer   my mobile phone

B Prepare your presentation. Make presentation slides if possible and think about the following:

- Give a 'history' of your personal possession – when, why, how did you get it?
- Talk about the advantages (and any disadvantages) of owning it.
- Say why it has been a good personal possession to have.
- Use at least six examples of functional language.

C PRESENT Give your presentation to the rest of the class.

○— Structure a presentation

➤ Turn to page 160 to learn how to write a covering letter for a job application.

5.3 Major presentation

LEAD-IN

Ask students to tell their partner about a presentation they gave. If they haven't done one, tell them to discuss what they think would make a successful business presentation.

COMPREHENSION

A Ask students to decide on which are the most important factors.

B ▶ 00:00-02:48 Tell students to watch the video and think about what problems there are with the presentation.

He's untidy.
He is unwell. He is coughing and losing his voice.
He arrives a bit late and is not relaxed.

C Put students into pairs to predict what will happen next. Elicit some ideas but don't confirm or deny anything yet.

D ▶ 02:48-04:53 Tell students to watch the video to check their predictions and answer the question.

Neena thinks she is going to get a pay rise.

FUNCTIONAL LANGUAGE

A Tell students to put the phrases in a logical order in the table.

B ▶ 00:00-02:48 Play the video for students to check their answers.

C Tell students to look at the sentence beginnings and decide what stage of a presentation they should be used in.

USEFUL PHRASES

A Tell students to rewrite the presentation phrases so they are less formal using the words and phrases in the box.

B Tell students to translate the useful phrases into their own language. Ask students in what situations they would use them.

PRONUNCIATION

A Tell students to listen and write the words they hear. Check answers as a class. Elicit the correct order they should be used in.

B Put students into pairs to practise saying the adverbs with one student saying the number from Exercise A and the other saying the corresponding adverb.

SPEAKING

A Tell students they can choose from one of the items in the box or use an idea of their own for their presentation.

B Make sure students follow the suggested steps as they prepare and remind them to use the phrases for structuring a presentation and the ordering of adverbs from earlier.

C Tell students to give their presentation, either in groups or to the rest of the class. Encourage the other students to listen carefully and to ask questions at the end of each presentation. Give feedback on students' language use, focusing on the organisation of the presentations, pronunciation and any other useful language.

▶ VIDEOSCRIPT

Ma = Matthew   N = Neena   Ms = Ms Santos

Ma: Oh Neena! I'm so sorry I'm late!

N: That's okay. Are you alright?

Ma: Yes, yes, I'll be fine. Just a bit of a cold and a …

N: We're all ready to go and here's all the information. Ms Santos will be here in about five minutes. Erm … tie?

Ma: What? Oh, yes, of course. Thank you. Good morning and thank you for coming. My name is Matthew Williams, I am a Director here at Jobs, Jobs, Jobs … Jobs. We've been finding jobs for people here in the UK since 2003 and we hope to do the same for people in Brazil in the future. Today's presentation is all about how we can work together in Brazil. So first of all, I'd like to talk about the benefits … Let's take a look at the first slide. We have a great deal of experience in the jobs marketplace … So, the next question is how to market ourselves in Brazil. Here at Jobs, Jobs … and Jobs … That brings … That bri …

N: That brings us to the end of the presentation … Do you have any questions?

Ms: Yes, thank you, Ms …

N: Patel, Neena Patel.

Ms: Ms Patel. And thank you, Mr Williams, of course. First of all, what market share do you expect to have after the first year?

N: Well, from our forecasts, we expect around a 12% share of the market after the first year.

Ms: Really?

N: Yes, I can email you all the data this afternoon.

Ms: That's very good news. And secondly, how soon could you be ready to launch?

N: Realistically, by September, but perhaps earlier if we can come to an agreement in the next week or two.

Ms: Good. That's all the questions we have for now.

N: Great. So to sum up, we see an exciting future working closely together with Empregos, Empregos, Empregos e Empregos.

Ms: Thank you, Ms Patel. Er … Can we have a moment to discuss?

N: Of course. Please say yes, please say yes!

Ms: Thank you for waiting. So moving onto my final question … when can we begin?

N: That's wonderful news! We can put the contract together immediately.

Ms: Perfect. I will send you an email later to sum up what we have decided today.

N: Thank you. We'll be in touch.

Ma: Well done, Neena. That was excellent work, excellent. Well, I'm sorry, I think I need to go home now.

N: Err … just a moment Matthew.

Ma: Yes.

N: Would now be a good time to talk about a pay rise?

Ma: No, now isn't a good time to talk about anything. Let's talk about it first thing in the morning!

5 Writing   ○— Write a covering letter for a job application

Ⓦ— paragraph structure

A Read the job advert. Is it the type of work you are interested in? Why/Why not?

Events Team Assistant (Ref: 783G)
ICE: International Charity Events
This is an exciting opportunity to join our lively and dynamic Events Team. We organise and promote fundraising events and programmes for charities across Europe. Typical events include sports, cultural events and adventure challenges and tours.
Essential requirements:
- excellent organisational, communication and marketing skills
- a great team player
- good digital technology skills
- able to meet deadlines

Desired experience:
- experience of working internationally

To apply, email a covering letter and CV to Marta Safin: M.Safin@ice.nett

B Read Peter O'Malley's application. In which paragraph (1–4) does he cover each topic (a–d)?

a why he is a good candidate for this job   2
b when he is able to attend an interview   4
c why he wants to work for this company   3
d what job he is applying for and why   1

Ex C

To: Ms. Safin
Subject: Events Team Assistant (Ref: 783G)

Dear Ms. Safin

1 I am writing to apply for the position of Events Team Assistant, currently advertised on Euro_Recruit.com (Ref: 783G). I have attached my CV. I recently graduated with a degree in Marketing, and I wish to start a career in events organisation.

2 The experience and skills that I gained from university make me the perfect candidate for this role. I was a member of the Student Social Committee and I was responsible for our International Food Festival. This demanded excellent organisational skills and demonstrated my ability to meet deadlines. I also improved the marketing for the event, which led to the largest ever attendance at the festival. In addition, I attended frequent meetings, which required good communication skills and the ability to work in a team.

3 Working for your company would be a great opportunity for me to begin my career. I am interested in the wide range of events that you organise and I would love the opportunity to work for an international company.

4 Thank you for considering my application. I am available for interview at any time, and I look forward to hearing from you.

Yours sincerely,
Peter O'Malley

C Look at the advice about writing a covering letter. Find and underline examples in Peter O'Malley's covering letter.

Writing a covering letter

Write in a professional, formal style that suits a business letter. Do not use informal language such as contractions. Follow a clear structure:
- If possible, address the letter to a named person. Use Dear Mr/Mrs. Do not use the person's first name.
- State where you saw the job advert and give its reference number.
- Show your interest in the position on offer and the company.
- Describe the key skills and experience that you have for the role and give examples to support your claims.
- Use standard closing sentences.

D Look at the box. Then read paragraphs 2 and 3 of the covering letter again. Identify the topic sentence and examples for each paragraph.

Paragraph structure

The paragraphs in the main body of a covering letter should focus on a single topic and be carefully organised and well structured. Always:
- start with a topic sentence that makes a clear, relevant point.
- support that point with examples to show how your skills and experience meet those listed in the job advert, or to show your genuine interest in the role.
- only add extra points if they relate to the topic sentence.

WRITING

A PLAN You are going to write a covering letter for the job advert below. Think about:
- what language style you need to use.
- the best way to organise the letter.
- what your topic sentences will be and how you will structure each paragraph.

Catering Management Assistant (Ref: 812C)
SCC: Superior Conference Catering
High quality catering for events and conferences in the UK and mainland Europe
Essential requirements:
- excellent organisation and time management skills
- excellent communication and team-working skills
- strong digital technology skills

Desired experience and interests:
- event organisation   • food and drink
- languages

B WRITE Write the letter (150–200 words).

C REVIEW Work in pairs. Read your partner's letter. Has he/she covered the key points in the advert and organised the letter well?

> This stage could also be modified to allow students to write covering letters for jobs they are interested in.

> Refer students to this letter as a model for the writing task.

> 1. Digital technology often replaces these things with a single device; digital technology supports a sharing economy.
> 2. Two examples per reason
> 3. People will spend a lot on digital services; they will have more contact with other people.

> Tell students to think about how the use of signposting language, such as linking words and phrases, can help them to transition between points.

WRITING

With books closed, ask students what they would do and where they would look if they were trying to find a job. Elicit as many ways or places to find work as possible and write any interesting vocabulary on the board.

A Before they read, check students' understanding of *dynamic* and *fundraising*. Tell students to read the job advert and to discuss with a partner if they would be interested in the job and why or why not. Monitor and check students understand all the information about the job.

B Tell students to read the application for the job and to match the topics (a–d) with paragraphs (1–4) in which they're mentioned.

C Point out the advice about writing a covering letter in the box. Ask students to find and underline examples of each tip in the letter from Exercise B.

D Point out the box about paragraph structure and check students understand what a topic sentence is by eliciting an example from the letter. Tell students to read the letter again and identify the topic sentences and the examples that support them in paragraphs 2 and 3.

WRITING TASK

A Tell students they're going to write a covering letter for the job shown in the advert. Tell them to plan their letter, thinking about style, organisation and structure as suggested. Monitor and help with language input.

B Tell students to write their letter. Monitor and provide help if requested.

C Tell students to swap letters with a partner and to read each other's. Tell them to give each other feedback on how successful the letter is in terms of style, organisation and structure. Ask students if they think their partner would get an interview as a result of their covering letter.

VOCABULARY

A Complete the interviewer's comments with the phrases in the box.

communication skills   creative thinking skills   people skills
reliable   teamwork   time management

1 Well, he arrived late, so he isn't very good at
_____ time management _____ .

2 I'd say she has poor _____ creative thinking skills _____
– she didn't offer any fresh ideas.

3 Her presentation showed she doesn't have good
_____ communication skills _____ – it wasn't
engaging, and her voice was rather flat.

4 I wasn't impressed by his
_____ people skills _____ ; sometimes he
looked annoyed by the questions, and he was a bit
rude once.

5 But will he be good at
_____ teamwork _____ ? He's only been
self-employed before, as a gardener. Not much group
work there.

6 I don't think she is _____ reliable _____ .
She's left her last few jobs after only two months.

B Choose the best verbs to complete sentences. Use the correct tense.

At first, I didn't [1]_____ want _____ (tell / want) him to
go on the rollercoaster, but he kept asking, and finally
he [2]_____ persuaded _____ (persuade / advise) me to buy his
ticket. I certainly didn't [3]_____ encourage _____ (encourage /
make) him to do it, and I [4]_____ told _____ (tell / let) him
to be careful. In the end, it was fine and he enjoyed it, so I
[5]_____ let _____ (let / persuade) him have another go.
My boss [6]_____ made _____ (let / make) my colleague
work over the weekend. I couldn't believe it, but the
boss is the boss. I [7]_____ advised _____ (advise / let) him to
do it this time, but to say no the next time. My boss has
[8]_____ allowed _____ (allow / let) him to have two days off
later in the week, so it isn't so bad. Personally, I think that if
they [9]_____ want _____ (want / make) us to work overtime,
they could [10]_____ persuade _____ (advise / persuade) us by
offering extra money!

C Complete the sentences with the nouns in the box.

customers   business   profit   campaign

1 The company made a big _____ profit _____ last year so
employees received a bonus.

2 The key to running a successful _____ business _____ is to
find the right employees.

3 The gyms have attracted _____ customers _____ because
they offer excellent facilities.

4 The health shops launched a _____ campaign _____ about
healthy eating.

GRAMMAR

A Find and correct the mistakes in the sentences.

1 A few years ago, I would be an accountant. I loved that job.
_____ A few years ago, I was an accountant. _____

2 I'd to arrive early most days. I liked it when the office
was quiet.
_____ I'd arrive early most days. _____

3 So I use to have long lunch breaks.
_____ So I used to have long lunch breaks. _____

4 He didn't used to be such a relaxed boss.
_____ He didn't use to be a relaxed boss. _____

5 They would being very quiet when I returned to the office.
_____ They would be very quiet when I returned to the office. _____

B Complete the text with the correct form of the verbs in brackets.

Parmesan cheese, *Parmigiano-Reggiano*,
[1] _was created_ (create) over 1500 years ago.
It [2]_____ has _____ (have) a
strong and complex savoury taste, and its name
[3]_____ has been protected _____ (protect) by EU
law since 1955.

Parmesan cheese
[4]_____ is made _____ (make) from cow's
milk. The cows [5]_____ are milked _____
(milk) in the morning, and the milk
[6]_____ is put _____ (put) into a large
metal container. Key ingredients, such as whey,
[7]_____ are added _____ (add), and then
the mixture [8]_____ is heated _____ (heat)
to 35°C. After 15 minutes, the temperature
[9]_____ is raised _____ (raise) to 55°C for
an hour.

FUNCTIONAL LANGUAGE

Complete the conversation with the missing words.

Ian: So, moving on to the next item on the agenda: the
new office design. [1]_____ First _____ of all, does
anyone [2]_____ have _____ any questions about the
design? No? OK, so …

Kim: Erm, just a [3]_____ minute _____ . I just want to say that
we should think again. Do we really need a table
tennis table?

Ian: I think we've heard enough, Kim. So moving
[4]_____ on _____ to the next agenda item …

Kim: One moment – I've got more to say!

Ian: Sorry, it's time to decide. Before we vote, let's
[5]_____ sum _____ up what we decided. We're saying
keep the table, but forget the fish tank, for health
reasons and cost reasons. Who agrees?

Kim: No, Ian, you can't make decisions like this. And that
[6]_____ brings _____ me to the next topic we need to
discuss: how to make these meetings better.

SPORTS AND HOBBIES

6

> You can discover more about a person in an hour of play than in a year of conversation.
>
> Richard Lingard

A surfer rides the inside of a wave at End of the road Beach, Tahiti.

Sport (n) an activity in which players or teams compete against each other, usually an activity that involves physical effort.
Synonym: games (n)
Hobby (n) something that you enjoy doing when you are not working.
Synonyms: activity (n), amusement (n)

The quote for this unit is taken from *A Letter of Advice to a Young Gentleman Leaving the University Concerning His Behaviour and Conversation in the World*, and suggests that the way someone reacts to winning or losing, and what they will do in order to win, reveals their true character.

Richard Lingard (1598–1670) was a professor of Divinity at the University of Dublin.

OBJECTIVES

- describe a sport or game
- give a short, persuasive talk
- talk about hobbies and free time activities
- discuss trying new things
- express your opinion
- write an article for a magazine

Work with a partner. Discuss the questions.

1 Do you agree with the quote?

2 Look at the picture. Why do some people take part in sports like this?

3 How interested are you in these free time activities?

team sports   running   music   collecting

SPORTS AND HOBBIES   61

OBJECTIVES

Read the unit objectives to the class.

UNIT OPENER QUESTIONS

With books closed, elicit an example from the class of a good way to get to know what someone is really like. Put students into pairs to think of more ideas. Share answers as a whole class and elicit any useful language on the board.

1 Tell students to open their books and to read the quote. Ask students to discuss if they agree with it. Encourage students to support their opinions with reference to their own experiences.

2 Focus students' attention on the picture and elicit the name of the sport (*surfing*). Elicit a couple of reasons why people take part in sports like these, then put students into pairs to think of more reasons. In whole-class feedback, write any more useful language that students use to talk about sports on the board.

3 Tell students first to work individually to rank the free-time activities in order of preference, then to compare their lists with a partner. Find out which is the most and least popular activity for the group and why.

WORKSHEETS

Lesson 6.1 Take part!

Grammar: Modals of obligation (W21)

Vocabulary: Adjectives ending in *-ive* (W22)

Lesson 6.2 Hobbies

Grammar: *had to / needed to* (W23)

Vocabulary: Hobbies and free-time activities (W24)

6.1 Take part!

● Describe a sport or game
● Give a short, persuasive talk

G— modals of obligation   V— adjectives ending in -ive; sport   P— rhythm: pausing
S— listening for main and supporting points

COMPETITIVE SNOWBALL FIGHTING HITS SCOTLAND!

Ex C **If you think snowball fights are just for school kids, think again.** **Competitive** snowball fighting (*Yukigassen*) is a sport for grown-ups that has just arrived in Scotland.

Ex C It began as an official sport in Japan in 1987 and since then it has spread to countries such as Canada, Australia, Norway and Sweden. And this weekend sees the first ever matches in Scotland.

Angus Campbell, the captain of the Glasgow Ice Warriors, says 'I think *Yukigassen* is going to be **massive** here. We have the snow and it's a fun and **inexpensive** sport that's **attractive** to everyone. Each match only lasts nine minutes, so you don't have to be super fit to take part in a game.'

The snowball fights take place on a small court (40 m x 10 m)
Ex C between two teams of seven players – each team must include male and female members. To win a game, a team has
Ex C to capture the other team's flag or take out all their opponents with direct snowball hits. If a player is hit, he or she has to leave the game.

The rules are fairly simple, but Angus insists that having an **effective** strategy is the key to success. 'You must work together as a team, be **decisive** and keep calm when under pressure from your opponents. You shouldn't just run for the flag – you'll soon get hit and be out. You need to be more **creative** than that. Your team only has 90 snowballs, which the referee gives you before the game. You mustn't make any more during the game.'

Six teams are taking part in the event this weekend, and there will be taster sessions for anyone who wants to try it out. 'It looks a little **aggressive** at first, but you needn't feel nervous. It's only snow, and all players have to wear a helmet, which we'll provide. However, you should bring some warm gloves!'

If you fancy trying something **active** on these cold winter days, you simply must go. The games are **impressive** to watch, and great to play. After all, what's more fun than playing in the snow? The first game starts at 2 pm, on Saturday, in the city park. Entrance is free. Families are welcome.

READING

A SPEAK Write down the names of the different sports you know in pictures 1–4. Then check with another student. What do you know about these sports? Tell your partner.

B READ FOR GIST Read *Competitive snowball fighting hits Scotland!* Where do you think the article comes from? Why?

a a national newspaper

b a sports science academic journal

c a local news and information website

d a travel blog

C READ FOR DETAIL Put the sentences in the order the information appears in the article.

a New players do not need to bring any safety equipment.   6

b There are two ways to beat the other team.   4

c There are men and women in every team.   3

d Generally, people think children, not adults, have snowball fights.   1

e A good game plan is important.   5

f Several countries play competitive snowball fighting.   2

D SPEAK Work in pairs. What is your opinion of *Yukigassen*? Would you like to play it?

6.1 Take part!

LEAD-IN

Ask students to write down one interesting fact about themselves (that no one in the class knows about them) on a piece of paper. Tell students to screw up their pieces of paper and imagine they're snowballs. Students have a snowball fight, first throwing their snowball at another student, then picking up and throwing another one. After one minute, tell students to pick up the nearest snowball to them and to read it. Students then have to find whose snowball they have by mingling and asking questions.

READING

A Tell students to look at the pictures and discuss the questions. Monitor and provide any vocabulary that is requested. Find out if any of the students have done any of these sports.

1 ice skating
2 ski jumping
3 ice hockey
4 snowboarding

B Tell students to read the article quickly and to decide where they think the article comes from. Tell students that they only need to skim the text in order to do this, but encourage them to think about the style in which it is written. Look at the four options (a–d) and quickly elicit what style of writing these would be.

c – The style and register is appropriate for this context, and the final sentence, with a reference to the city park, but not naming the city, suggests a local information site.

C Tell students to read the text again more carefully this time, so that they understand it in more detail. Tell them to look at the sentences and put them in the order the information appears in the article. Go through the example with the whole class, demonstrating how the information in the first paragraph is paraphrased in sentence d. Students then continue with the rest. Tell students to compare in pairs before feedback. Ask students to refer to the text to explain where they found their answers.

D Put students into pairs to discuss the questions. Encourage students to expand on their answers by monitoring and providing any language input they need.

TEACHING IDEA by David Seymour and Maria Popova
Grammar: Getting ready

Set the situation that a group is preparing to go on an expedition to the South Pole. They are discussing what they must do before they leave. Get students to talk and fill in endings for some written sentences (*We have to take …; The ship must …; We ought to tell …; We mustn't forget …; We will have to go …*).

TEACHING IDEA by David Seymour and Maria Popova
Grammar: Design the sign

Ask students to design a new notice for placing somewhere in the school premises where they are studying. Most notices/signs contain implied modality (*No running = You must not run*) rather than explicit ones. Get students to think of a notice where they might need to spell out detailed rules saying what must/mustn't be done.

GRAMMAR HUB

6.1 Modals of obligation
should

	Positive	Negative
I/you/he/she/it/we/they	**I should choose** the best team.	**We shouldn't shout** at the players.

must

	Positive	Negative
I/you/he/she/it/we/they	**They must find** a better place to train.	**You mustn't be** so aggressive on the field.

have to

	Positive	Negative
I/you/we/they	**You have to wear** a helmet.	**They don't have to play** the game on the computer.
he/she/it	**She has to perform** well today.	**He doesn't have to win** every match.

- We use *should/shouldn't* when we describe what is or is not a good idea now, in the future or generally.
- We use *must* and *have to* when we describe rules and situations that are necessary.
- There is sometimes no difference between them. However, we often use *must* and *mustn't* in written rules, and *have to* in speech.
- We use *mustn't* when we describe something that is not allowed.
- We use *don't/doesn't have to* when we describe things that aren't necessary, but you may still do them.
- There is a difference in meaning between *mustn't* and *don't have to*.

  mustn't = not allowed
  don't have to = not necessary
- In questions, we use *have to* instead of *must*.
- We can also use *needn't* or *don't/doesn't need to* instead of *don't/doesn't have to* when we describe things that aren't necessary.

  She doesn't need to buy a ticket in advance. She can buy one at the gate.

6.1 Take part!

GRAMMAR

A Do the first one together as a whole class, eliciting that it describes something 100 per cent necessary so students should write *nc*. Tell students to complete the activity.

B Tell students to look back at the sentences in Exercise A to help them complete the rules. Use these sentences to provide context to check students' understanding.

C Direct students to the Grammar Hub on pages 132 and 133 (see TB62 and below).

D Put students into pairs and tell them to compare and contrast the rules of the sports. Do an example yourself, modelling how you could use modals of obligation to do this. Use the Grammar Worksheet on W21 for extra practice.

VOCABULARY

A Tell students to match the adjective with the definition, using the way the adjectives are used in the text to help them. Do the first adjective, *competitive*, as an example. Students then continue and complete the activity.

B Tell students to practise by completing the questions with an adjective from Exercise A. Check answers as a whole class, then tell students to ask each other the questions. Use the Vocabulary Worksheet on W22 for extra practice.

SPEAKING

A Model the task. Describe a sport with reference to the points listed in the task. Make sure it isn't too easy to guess what the sport is but not impossible either! When students have guessed correctly, tell them to work individually to do the same. Monitor to help with language if needed. Check students have understood that they mustn't say the name of the sport.

B Put students into groups. Tell each student to read their sentences and the other students in the group to guess what the sport is. Tell students that they get six points if they guess correctly after the first sentence, five points if they guess correctly after the second sentence, four points after the third sentence and so on. Any fast finishers can move on to Exercise C.

C When all the sports have been guessed, tell students to discuss the questions in the same group. Discuss as a whole class and encourage students to expand on their answers. If some students have personal experience of a sport other students would like to try, take advantage of this to encourage further questions and discussion. Finish with feedback on students' language use during Exercises B and C, praising successes and correcting some errors.

GRAMMAR HUB

6.1 Modals of obligation

A Choose the correct option.

1 We *don't have to* / *mustn't* be competitive to have fun at sport.

2 He *must* / *doesn't have to* wear a helmet. It's required.

3 I *must* / *mustn't* eat a massive meal before playing a sport.

4 They *shouldn't* / *don't have to* practise today because the coach isn't going to be here.

5 *Do you have to* / *Needn't you* train every day?

6 She *mustn't* / *needn't* pay for entrance to the game. It's free.

B Complete the sentences with the correct words and phrases from the box.

don't have	doesn't have	has	mustn't	needn't	should

1 You _____needn't_____ buy a ticket. Dad's bought them already.

2 She _____should_____ ask her coach for advice on how to play better.

3 I _____don't have_____ to go to practice today. It's been cancelled.

4 For a helmet to work, it _____has_____ to fit on your head properly.

5 You _____mustn't_____ run while holding the ball. It's against the rules.

6 He _____doesn't have_____ to wear protective gear because his sport isn't dangerous.

C Choose the correct option to complete the dialogue.

Anna: I'm excited about Saturday's match. It starts at 1 pm. I think we [1]_____ meet in front of the entrance, shouldn't we?

Vincenzo: I [2]_____ take my little sister to her lesson first, so I might be a bit late. You [3]_____ wait for me outside. Just go on inside and I'll find you.

Anna: Well, I don't mind waiting for you outside. I [4]_____ be in my seat when the game starts. Besides, it's a big place. We [5]_____ go in together so we don't get lost.

Vincenzo: OK, fine.

	a		b		c	
1	a	needn't	b	must	**c**	should
2	**a**	have to	b	should	c	don't have to
3	a	must	**b**	needn't	c	have to
4	a	should	b	must	**c**	don't have to
5	a	must	**b**	should	c	needn't

➤ Go back to page 63.

GRAMMAR
Modals of obligation

A **WORK IT OUT** Look at the sentences from *Competitive snowball fighting hits Scotland!* Write *nc* (you have no choice, this is 100 per cent necessary) or *c* (you have a choice, this is not necessary) next to each sentence.

1 All players **have to** wear a protective helmet.   nc
2 You **don't have to** be super fit.   c
3 You **should** bring some warm gloves.   c
4 You **shouldn't** just run for the flag.   c
5 Each team **must** include male and female members.   nc
6 You **mustn't** make any more during the game.   nc
7 You **needn't** feel nervous.   c

B Match the beginnings of the rules (1–4) with the endings (a–d).

Modals of obligation	
b **1** We use *must / have to / need to*	a to talk about what is or is not a good idea.
d **2** We use *mustn't* when	b for rules and situations that are necessary (strong obligation).
c **3** We use *don't have to / needn't* when	c we describe things that are not necessary, but you may still do them.
a **4** We use *should / shouldn't*	d we describe something that is not allowed.

C Go to the Grammar Hub on page 132.

D **SPEAK** Work in pairs. Compare the pairs of sports below. How are they similar and different? Think about their basic rules and the qualities of good players and successful teams.

> baseball and cricket   football and basketball
> marathon running and running a 100 metre race   tennis and squash

VOCABULARY
Adjectives ending in -ive

A Look at the adjectives in bold in *Competitive snowball fighting hits Scotland!* Then complete the definitions with the correct adjective.

1 A ____decisive____ person makes choices quickly and confidently.
2 A ____competitive____ sport involves two teams trying to beat each other.
3 If something is ____massive____, it is very big or, in informal English, very popular.
4 An ____attractive____ suggestion or idea is one that people are interested in.
5 An ____effective____ plan works well and produces the result that is wanted.
6 An ____inexpensive____ activity doesn't cost a lot of money to do.
7 Having an ____active____ lifestyle means you do not sit around all day.
8 ____Aggressive____ behaviour includes being rude or angry in order to get what you want.
9 You admire an ____impressive____ performance because it is very good and shows a lot of skill.
10 A ____creative____ person thinks of new or unusual ways to do things.

B **SPEAK** Complete the questions with adjectives from Exercise A. Then work in pairs and interview your partner. Take turns. Give reasons and examples to explain your answers.

1 What is the most _____ sport that you have played?
2 Are you a very _____ person? Why do you say that?
3 Which actors do you think are very _____?

SPEAKING

A You are going to write six sentences to describe a sport or game without naming it. Your classmates will try to guess what it is. Think about:

- reasons why you like it.
- the skills and qualities you need to play it well.
- how it is played and what you need to play it.

B Work in groups. Read your sentences to the group. Can your classmates guess the sport or game?

C Work in groups and discuss the questions.

1 Which of the sports and games described have you played? What do you think of them?
2 Which haven't you played? Would you like to try them?
3 Which is the most popular sport or game?

SPORTS AND HOBBIES   63

LISTENING

A SPEAK Work in pairs and discuss the questions. What are the pros and cons of playing video games?

B LISTEN FOR GIST Listen to a talk about eSports and choose the correct answers.
6.1

1 What is the best title for the talk?

   a Video gaming: is it good for you?

   b Video gaming: the professional sport of the future

   c Video gaming: nothing more than a free time activity

   (d) Video gaming: the next Olympic sport?

2 What is the purpose of the talk?

   a to give general information about eSports

   b to encourage people to watch and play eSports

   (c) to persuade people to agree with the speaker's opinion of eSports

   d to give a balanced analysis of eSports

C LISTEN FOR DETAIL Listen again to the introduction. What is the main idea of the talk? What are the supporting points? Use the strategies in the box to help you.
6.1

Listening for main and supporting points

When giving a talk, speakers often give a main idea and then support it with detailed points, in the form of examples, statistics, names or dates.

Listen carefully to identify the main ideas and the supporting points that follow.

D Listen again to another part of the talk. What is the main idea? What are the supporting points?
6.2

E LISTEN FOR DETAIL Listen again to the whole talk and choose the correct answers.
6.1

1 The speaker thinks that many people in the audience …

   a play video games at home.

   b understand how popular eSports are.

   (c) don't realise that video gaming is played professionally.

2 She says playing video games is a sport because …

   a players practise a lot.

   b the games have clear rules.

   (c) there are winners and losers.

3 She says a great eSports player

   (a) has a strong mind and body.

   b plays other traditional sports.

   c spends all their time training.

4 She says eSports are different to traditional sports because …

   (a) they are growing in popularity.

   b young people like them.

   c people watch them online.

5 The Olympic Games wants to include sports that …

   a involve physical activity.

   (b) young people like.

   c have professional players.

F SPEAK Work in pairs and discuss the questions.

1 In your opinion, what is the difference between a sport and a game?

2 Do you agree with the speaker's arguments? Which of her points do you think are strong or weak?

3 Do you think eSports should be an Olympic sport? Why/Why not?

VOCABULARY
Sport

A Tick (✓) the nouns that refer to people.

1	champion	✓	6	stadium	☐
2	coach	✓	7	supporter	✓
3	final	☐	8	top player	✓
4	league	☐	9	tournament	☐
5	spectator	✓	10	trophy	☐

6.1 Take part!

LISTENING

A Tell students to look at the pictures and elicit their initial reaction to them. Divide the class into two groups. If there are clearly some students who like playing video games a lot, and others who strongly dislike it, group them together at this stage. Give some time for one group to think of pros and the other to think of cons. Monitor to help with language as they do this. Put students together with a partner from the other group and ask them to explain their lists to each other. Conclude by discussing this briefly as a whole class and write any useful language that comes up on the board.

B Tell students they're going to listen to a talk about eSports. Use the pictures from Exercise A to remind students what exactly eSports are. Tell students to listen and to choose the correct answers. Tell students not to worry if they don't understand everything the first time as they're going to listen again.

C Point out the strategies in the *Listening for main and supporting points* box. Tell students to listen again to the introduction and use these strategies to help them identify the main idea and supporting points.

Main idea: Football, basketball, golf and tennis are four of the world's most popular sports.
Supporting points: played by millions, watched by millions more, all in the Olympic Games

D Tell students to use the same strategies again to identify the main idea and the supporting points as they listen to another part of the talk.

Main idea: eSports are played in the same way as any other sport.
Supporting points: professional teams compete in large venues and stadiums, thousands of spectators, millions watch online

E Tell students to read the questions and to try to choose the correct answer from memory. Play the audio again for students to check their answers. Check answers as a whole class and ask students to justify their answers by telling the class exactly what the speaker said.

F Put students into pairs to discuss the questions. Share students' opinions as a whole class. Ask if anyone has changed the opinion they had in Exercise A after listening to the talk.

VOCABULARY

A Tell students to look at the nouns and to tick the ones that refer to people. Check students understand the meaning of the words by eliciting examples of each or an example sentence containing the word. Model and drill pronunciation of the nouns. Draw particular attention to the stress on the second syllable of *spectator* and *supporter* and on the first syllable of *tournament*.

AUDIOSCRIPT

 6.1

Listening, Exercise B

Football, basketball, golf, tennis – four of the world's most popular sports. They are played by millions and watched by millions more, and all four are in the greatest festival of sport, the Olympic Games.

However, there is one sport that is just as popular as those, but it still hasn't been accepted in the Olympics, and indeed, many people say that it is not even a sport. What sport am I talking about? eSports. Yes, electronic sports, or competitive video gaming.

Ex E Q1 Now, I guess many of you think video games are just something people play at home or on their phones. In fact, they are played in the same way as any other sport, with teams competing against each other in large venues and stadiums, in front of thousands of paying spectators and with millions more watching online.

Even if you already know how massive eSports are, perhaps many of you think gaming is not actually a sport. But I hope to persuade you that video gaming has all the features that we see in other sports.

Ex E Q2 First of all, it is clearly competitive. Players and teams compete in national and international tournaments, aiming to win the final, lift the trophy and become the champions. The will to win is a key part of video gaming. Also, playing video games requires incredible mental strength and skill.

You need to focus for long periods of time and the games are very fast. eSports demand clever thinking, quick decision-making and great communication between team members, just like traditional team sports. Of course, some people argue that video gaming is not a real sport because it doesn't require physical

strength. Now, I accept it isn't the same as football or rugby, for example, but, because the games are long and demanding, professional gamers have to be very fit. **Ex E Q3** If your fitness levels are poor, so is your ability to concentrate. This is why the managers and coaches of professional teams make sure their players spend time training in the gym and have a healthy diet. That all sounds like a sport to me.

So, have I changed your mind yet? Do you now feel that eSports should be in the Olympics? If not, remember **Ex E Q5** that when they choose new sports for the games, they are looking for ones that are popular and have strong youth appeal. That sounds like eSports to me. Online eSports platforms have hundreds of millions of users **Ex E Q4** every week. While the numbers of people playing and watching traditional sports are declining, they are rapidly increasing for eSports, and most of those people are young people.

So, eSports are physically and mentally demanding. They attract young people like no other sport. They are popular all over the world, and, of course, anyone can take part. They have already become a professional success story, with famous top players, great teams and enthusiastic supporters.

There is no doubt that eSports should be in the Olympics as video gaming isn't just a sport that will be popular; it is popular now. So please excuse me, but I've got a game to go and play. Thank you.

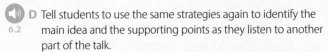 **6.2**

Listening, Exercise D

In fact, they are played in the same way as any other sport, with teams competing against each other in large venues and stadiums, in front of thousands of paying spectators and with millions more watching online.

B Tell students to complete the sentences with the correct form of a noun in Exercise A. Point out that they will need to make some words plural. Elicit the first answer as an example.

C Put students into groups to discuss the questions.

PRONUNCIATION

A Read the information aloud and demonstrate the use of pauses as you do this. Ask students if pauses are used the same way in their language. Tell students to listen to the beginning of the talk about eSports again. Point out how the first two examples of where the speaker pauses have been marked. Tell students to mark the other pauses as they listen and to think about which pauses are longer to add emphasis or drama.

6.3

B Tell students to look at the next part of the talk and to mark where they think the speaker will pause. Then play the audio for students to check.

6.4

C Put students into pairs to practise saying the extracts with the appropriate pauses. Tell them to listen carefully to their partner to check how well they do it.

SPEAKING HUB

A Tell students to choose one of the titles and make some notes about what they're going to say. Monitor to help with language input.

B Tell students to look at the tips for a persuasive talk and check they understand all the points.

C Tell students to give their talks as persuasively as they can. Tell the students listening to make notes.

D Tell students to stay in their groups and to discuss which talks they agreed or disagreed with and which points were the strongest. Discuss as a whole class and encourage students to explain what made some talks especially persuasive. Finish with feedback on how well students organised and delivered their talks. Help them to record any other useful language that came up.

METHODOLOGY HUB by Jim Scrivener

Defining 'genre'

What does the word 'genre' mean? Why might 'genre' be an important consideration when teaching language?

In everyday life, people speak in a variety of ways, depending on who they are with, where they are, the nature of the situation, etc. To take two extreme examples, giving a presentation is a very different kind of speaking from enquiring about car insurance over the phone. These are two different genres.

A genre is a variety of speech (or writing) that you would expect to find in a particular place, with particular people, in a particular context, to achieve a particular result, using a particular channel (e.g. face to face, by phone).

A genre is often characterised by specific choices about style, manner, tone, quantity, volume, directness, choice of words, formality, type of content, etc. Quite apart from the detailed content and specific words of the presentation or the phone call, there is likely to be a generally recognisable 'presentation-ness' about the presentation and an 'enquiry-on-the-phone-ness' about the call. That's not to say that we can't also knowingly choose to ignore or undermine the genre, e.g. by giving a presentation in the style of a comedy sketch (in fact, substituting one genre for another)!

METHODOLOGY HUB by Jim Scrivener

Varieties of speech genre

Make a list of about ten distinctly different real-life types of speaking, e.g. making a public speech. Some possible answers:

- Giving an academic lecture
- Telling a joke
- Greeting a passing colleague
- Making a phone enquiry
- Chatting with a friend
- Explaining medical problems to a doctor
- Negotiating a sale
- Giving street directions
- Making a business presentation

Being more specific about genre

A term such as 'making a public speech' is still relatively imprecise. It could refer to a wide variety of quite different kinds of task, from thanking some colleagues for a birthday present to standing up as best man at a wedding reception to presenting a one-hour talk at a conference of 3,000 people.

It is possible to specify types of speaking more precisely than by simply naming a genre if we add information about **why** the speaking is being done, **where** it is being done and **who** is listening or interacting with the speaker.

METHODOLOGY HUB by Jim Scrivener

Voice settings

One interesting approach to pronunciation may sound a little odd at first. It's based on the idea that, rather than work on all the small details of pronunciation (such as phonemes, stress patterns, etc), it might be better to start with the larger holistic picture - the general 'settings' of the voice. If you think about a foreign language you have heard a number of times, you are probably able to quickly recall some distinctive impressions about how the language is spoken - the sorts of things that a comedian would pick on if they wanted to mimic a speaker of that language; for example, a distinctive mouth position with the lips pushed forward, a flat intonation with machine-gun delivery, a typical hunching of shoulders, frequently heard sounds, a generally high pitch, etc.

Do your students have such an image about British speakers of English? Or Australians? Or Canadians?

One useful activity would be to:

1 watch one or more native speakers on video
2 discuss any noticeable speech features
3 try speaking nonsense words using this 'voice setting' ('comedian' style)
4 practise reading a simple short dialogue in as 'native' a way as they can. (This will probably seem quite funny to your students, who will initially tend to do fairly bland copies, never quite believing that a voice setting may be so different or exaggerated compared with their own language; encourage them to risk looking and sounding really like a native speaker.)

B Complete the sentences with the correct form of the nouns in Exercise A.

1 In the Olympic Games, the winners receive a gold medal, not a ____trophy____.

2 Usain Bolt and Michael Phelps are two of the most famous Olympic ____champions____.

3 The FIFA World Cup is a football ____tournament____ that is held every four years.

4 If you are a Manchester United ____supporter____, you should wear something red to the game.

5 The Camp Nou, in Barcelona, is the largest football ____stadium____ in Europe. It can hold nearly 100,000 ____spectators____.

6 ____Top players____ can earn a lot of money from advertising and sponsorship contracts.

7 If a team loses a lot of matches, the ____coach____ often loses his or her job.

8 Nothing in sport is certain – you don't always see the two best teams in a ____final____.

9 There are 20 teams in the national ____league____. Each team plays the others twice, so each team plays 38 games in a year.

C SPEAK Work in groups and discuss the questions.

1 What are the popular spectator sports and sports tournaments in your country?

2 Who are the top sportsmen and women in your country? What do you know about them?

PRONUNCIATION
Rhythm: pausing

> **Pausing**
>
> We use pauses to support the meaning of what we say, and to help the listener follow and understand.
>
> • Use very short pauses to group words that go together in phrases or clauses. This is similar to using a comma in writing, but can be more frequent.
> • Use short pauses at the end of sentences and paragraphs. This is similar to using a full stop in writing.
> • Make the pauses a little longer to add emphasis or drama.

A Listen to the beginning of the talk about eSports. Mark where the speaker pauses. The first two pauses have been marked (/) to help you. Which pauses are longer to add emphasis or drama?

6.3

Football,/basketball, /golf/tennis/– four of the world's most popular sports./They are played by millions/and watched by millions more,/and all four/are in the greatest festival of sport/the Olympic Games.

B Where do you think the speaker pauses in the next part of the talk? Mark (/) each pause. Then listen and check your answer.

6.4

However,/there is one sport/that is just as popular as those,/but it still hasn't been accepted in the Olympics,/and indeed,/many people say/that it is not even a sport./What sport am I talking about?/eSports./Yes,/electronic sports,/or competitive video gaming.

C SPEAK Work in pairs. Practise saying the extracts in Exercises A and B. Listen and check that your partner pauses in the correct places.

SPEAKING HUB

A You are going to give a short persuasive talk (1–3 minutes). Choose one of the titles and make notes for your talk.

• eSports are not sports and should not be part of the Olympic Games.
• Playing video games is a good activity for children.
• Video games are generally more negative than positive.
• Professional sportsmen and women earn too much money. Their pay should be limited.
• _____ is the best sport to both play and watch.

B PLAN Look at your notes and use these tips on how to improve a persuasive talk.

• Have a good introduction and conclusion.
• Use confident language, e.g. *I strongly believe …*; *It's undoubtedly true that …*
• Use rhetorical questions, e.g. *Why should we do this?*; *I'm sure you agree, don't you?*
• Support your main points with good examples and arguments.
• Practise your pausing and rhythm when giving the talk.

C PRESENT Work in groups. Give your talks. Take notes about the main ideas and supporting points of the other talks.

D REFLECT Work in groups. Did you agree or disagree with the speakers? Which points do you think were strongest?

◯– Describe a sport or game
◯– Give a short, persuasive talk

6.2 Hobbies

- Talk about hobbies and free time activities
- Discuss trying new things

V — hobbies and free time activities   G — present perfect continuous; *had to / needed to*   P — *been*: weak form
S — identifying tone

a   b   c

LISTENING

A SPEAK Work in pairs and discuss the questions.

1 Describe the pictures (a–e). What are the people doing?

2 Which free time activities are you most interested in? Why?

B LISTEN FOR GIST Listen to a radio programme about hobbies and free time activities. Match the pictures (a–e) with the guest speakers (1–5).
6.5

1 <u>d</u>   2 <u>b</u>   3 <u>a</u>   4 <u>e</u>   5 <u>c</u>

C LISTEN FOR DETAIL Listen again. Choose the best answers for each person.
6.5

1 Speaker 1
  a buys and sells new cars.
  (b) spends a lot of money on his hobby.
  c makes enough money from his hobby to pay for his holidays.

2 Speaker 2
  a finds his hobby stressful at times.
  b also works as a photographer.
  (c) is learning how to do something new.

3 Speaker 3
  a wants her husband to spend more time on his hobby.
  (b) says her husband spends a lot of time on his hobby.
  c shares her husband's hobby.

4 Speaker 4
  (a) shares her interest with her friends.
  b has her own social media site about her interest.
  c often stays in hotels in London.

5 Speaker 5
  a usually has a few hobbies at the same time.
  b finds it hard to get interested in things.
  (c) has had many different hobbies.

D SPEAK Work in groups and discuss the questions.

1 Are there any hobbies you would like to try? Which ones?

2 What are the benefits of having a hobby?

VOCABULARY
Hobbies and free time activities

A WORK IT OUT Look at the three sets of verb phrases from the radio programme. Match the beginnings of the phrases with the endings (a–d).

1 join — a interest in a hobby
  be — b a hobby
  lose — c a society
  take up — d my thing

2 be — a into something
  be — b you fit
  keep — c of a singer
  be a fan — d a member of a fan club

3 get — a relaxing
  be — b from daily stress
  collect — c you out of the house
  escape — d something, like stamps or art
  ('get something' is also possible)

B Complete the table with the verb phrases from Exercise A.

Show enthusiasm for a hobby	Something you may do as part of a hobby	Benefits of a hobby	Start a new hobby
<u>be into something</u>	join a society collect <u>something</u> be a member <u>of a fan club</u>	escape from <u>daily stress</u> be relaxing get you out of the house	take something
be my thing			
be a fan <u>of something</u>		<u>keep you fit</u>	
lose interest <u>in something</u>			

C Go to the Vocabulary Hub on page 144.

D SPEAK Rewrite these sentences so they are true for you. Then work in pairs and compare your answers. Give reasons and examples.

1 I'm a big fan of the singer Ed Sheeran.

2 I need to find a way to get myself out of the house more often.

3 I've collected lots of different things during my life.

4 I don't do much to keep fit. I should do more.

5 I've never been a member of a fan club nor joined a society.

6 Cooking isn't really my thing.

7 I've had a few hobbies that I've lost interest in.

8 This year, I've taken up a new hobby.

6.2 Hobbies

LEAD-IN

With books closed, check understanding of *hobbies* and elicit an example. Put students into pairs and give each pair one of the following categories: indoor hobbies, outdoor hobbies, hobbies for young people, hobbies for older people, modern hobbies, traditional hobbies, educational hobbies, creative hobbies, physical hobbies, spiritual hobbies. Tell students to think of as many hobbies as they can for their category. Share ideas with the class and write any useful language that comes up on the board.

LISTENING

A Tell students to look at the pictures and discuss the questions. Elicit the names for the hobbies and free-time activities shown in the pictures.

B Tell students they're going to listen to a radio programme about hobbies and free-time activities. Tell them to listen and match each speaker (1–5) to a picture (a–e) from Exercise A.

C Tell students to look at the questions and to try to choose the correct answer from memory. Play the audio again for students to check. Ask students to justify their answers with reference to exactly what each speaker said.

D Give a personal example answer for question 1, then put students into pairs to discuss the questions. Ask if any students have experience of the hobbies that their classmates would like to try. If they do, they can exchange helpful information.

VOCABULARY

A Elicit that the verb phrases were all used in the radio programme. Tell students to match the beginnings with the endings. Check students understand the meaning of the verb phrases by eliciting how they were used in the radio programme and in relation to which hobby.

B Tell students to put the verb phrases into the correct column in the table. If students have difficulty with this, clarify the meaning of the verb phrases with further examples.

C Direct students to the **Vocabulary Hub** on page 144 for further practice of verb phrases related to hobbies and free-time activities.

D Tell students to look at the sentences and to decide if they are true for themselves. Tell students to rewrite the false sentences so that they are true. Then put students into pairs to compare and explain their answers. Encourage students to expand on their answers and to ask each other follow-up questions. Use the **Vocabulary Worksheet** on W24 for extra practice.

> **Extra activity**
> Divide the class into two groups. Each group should write a list of five sports or hobbies. The groups exchange lists. One person from each group should describe or act out each word for their group to guess. Set a time limit of two minutes.

AUDIOSCRIPT

🔊 **6.5**

Listening, Exercise B
RP = Radio Presenter   S1 = Speaker 1   S2 = Speaker 2
S3 = Speaker 3   S4 = Speaker 4   S5 = Speaker 5

RP: Hobbies. Interests. Pastimes. They're something more than watching TV, and something different to playing sport. I'm Gavin Ross, and in this week's Human Behaviour, we're asking you, the public, about what you like doing in your free time. What hobbies have you got? How long have you been doing them? Why do you have them? Let's hear from some of our listeners out on the streets in London today.

Ex C Q1 **S1:** I'm really into classic or vintage cars. I've been buying them since I was 18, when I first learnt to drive and got my first one, a small 1960s sports car. Obviously, it isn't exactly a cheap hobby, what with buying and then repairing them. It means I don't go on expensive holidays like my friends, but I'm not going to give it up. I've just bought an old Mini, so I'll start working on that tomorrow.

S2: Arts and crafts are my thing – jewellery making, painting, woodwork.

Ex C Q2 I've had this interest since I was a child. For the last six months, I've been going to pottery classes. In fact, I've been working in the studio this afternoon – that's why my hands are so dirty. As a hobby, it's relaxing and a great escape from daily stress, and, you know, it makes time fly – a sure sign I'm enjoying myself.

S3: I don't really have a hobby, but my husband is an enthusiastic cyclist.

Ex C Q3 Actually, I think that cycling is an obsession for him, rather than a hobby. If he isn't out on a ride, he's cleaning the thing, or checking out the latest accessories online. He's been doing it since his teens, so I knew what I was getting when I married him. It isn't really my thing, so I leave him to it; it seems to keep him fit and happy.

S4: I don't know if you can call this a hobby, but I spend most of my time following Danny CJ, the singer – I'm a massive fan. I've been a member of his fan club for ages, I've been to loads of his concerts and I collect everything I can about him: all the music, pictures, posters, calendars. It's great following him on social media, too. He even replied to one of my

Ex C Q4 tweets once. Whenever he comes to London, my mates and I all hang out outside his hotel. He's in there now – we've been waiting here all day, but we haven't seen him yet. Hold on, is that him? Danny! Danny! Over here!

Ex C Q5 **S5:** Do I have a hobby? Well, you might say my hobby is having hobbies. I tend to get really into something, like, at first, I get really obsessed with it, but then I soon lose interest. I don't know why. I've always been like this. Recently, I've been getting into bird watching – I've bought all the kit and loads of books, and I've joined two local societies. No idea how long this'll last though.

I might start cookery classes soon, or take up sailing. Anything that gets me out of the house.

RP: Those are just some of the people I've met while making this programme, and I'd like to hear from even more of you. Visit our programme website to see how you can take part in this series of Human Behaviour. The address is www.radiotalk.nett/ humanbehaviour …

6.2 Hobbies

GRAMMAR

A Do the first one together as a whole class.

B Tell students to look at the sentences in Exercise A again and to complete the rules.

C Direct students to the **Grammar Hub** on pages 132 and 133 (see below and TB68).

D Put students into pairs, one student A and one student B. Tell student A to turn to the **Communication Hub** on page 150, and student B to page 155. As a class, share the most interesting answers and comment on how well students used structures.

PRONUNCIATION

A Tell students to listen to three sentences and to pay special attention to the pronunciation of *been*. Elicit that it rhymes with *thin*, not *seen*. Point out the information in the box, and check students understand that positive auxiliary verbs are not usually stressed, but that negative auxiliaries usually are. Elicit an example of each on the board and then drill pronunciation.

B Tell students to practise by listening and repeating the sentences.

SPEAKING HUB

A Tell students to think about the questions and to make notes. Monitor to help with language input.

B Tell students they're going to interview three or four of their classmates about their hobbies. Tell students to make sure they make notes about each person they speak to. Monitor as they do the interview and make sure both students in each pair get a chance to ask and answer questions.

C Tell students to sit down and then put them into groups with students they haven't worked with before. Tell them to use their notes to tell each other the most unusual/interesting/dangerous/expensive hobbies they heard about.

GRAMMAR HUB

6.2 Present perfect simple and present perfect continuous; *had to / needed to*

Present perfect simple

Positive	Negative	Question
I've joined a sailing club.	**They haven't made up** their minds about joining the league.	**Have you met** your opponent yet?

- We use the present perfect simple for actions completed during a period of time that continues to now.
- We also use the present perfect simple for actions completed before now when we don't say exactly when.
- See Grammar Hub 2.1 for more information about the present perfect simple.

Present perfect continuous

	Positive	Negative
I/you/we/they	**I have been collecting** stamps for years.	**We haven't been doing** our best in every game.
he/she/it	**She's been training** hard every single day.	**Zain hasn't been training** hard enough.

Question	Positive short answer	Negative short answer
Have they been playing tennis for long?	Yes, **they have**.	No, **they haven't**.
Has Anika been watching the sport on TV?	Yes, **she has**.	No, **she hasn't**.

- We use the present perfect continuous to talk about an action that started in the past and continues in the present. It can be a single or a frequently repeated action.

  He has been cooking all afternoon.
  He's been cooking dinner every day.

- We can use both the present perfect simple and the present perfect continuous to describe a recently completed activity.

  She has posted the videos on social media. She has been posting the videos on social media all morning.

- We use the present perfect continuous to find out the duration of an activity.

  How long have you been waiting for your teammates?

- We do NOT use the present perfect continuous with state verbs.

  I have known my coach for years. NOT ~~I have been knowing my coach for years.~~

had to / needed to

	Positive	Negative
I/you/he/she/it/we/they	**They had to** practise for four hours each day. **He needed to wear** safety equipment.	**You didn't have to train** for the snowball fight. **She didn't need to buy** a new helmet.

Question	Positive short answer	Negative short answer
Did you have to take a lesson first?	Yes, **I/we did**.	No, **I/we didn't**.

- We use *had to* and *needed to* to talk about things that were necessary in the past. They mean the same thing.
- We don't use *must* to talk about the past.

  They had to pay for the skiing lessons last winter.
  NOT ~~They must pay for the skiing lessons last winter.~~

- We use *didn't have to* and *didn't need to* to talk about things that were not necessary but possible in the past.

GRAMMAR
Present perfect continuous

A WORK IT OUT Look at the sentences from the radio programme and choose the correct answers.

1 Which sentence describes a single action that continues up to now? b
Which sentences describe an action or activity that is frequently repeated up to now? a, c

   a He's been doing it since his teens.

   b We've been waiting here all day.

   c For the last six months, I've been going to pottery classes.

2 In each sentence, is the main verb a state or an action verb?

   a He's been doing it since his teens.   action verb

   b I've had this interest since I was a child.   state verb

   c I've been a member of his fan club for ages.   state verb

3 What are the recently completed actions in the sentences?
Which sentence focuses on the fact that the action is completed? b
Which sentence focuses on the duration of the action? a

   a I've been <u>working in the studio</u> this afternoon – that's why my hands are so dirty.

   b I've just <u>bought an old Mini</u>, so I'll start working on that tomorrow.

B Complete the rules (1–5) with the words in the box.

continuous   long   now   past   present   repeated   state

Present perfect continuous

1 We often use the present perfect continuous to talk about an action that started in the _____past_____ and is continuing _____now_____. The emphasis is on the unfinished activity.

2 We also use it to talk about a past action that has just finished, but which has a _____present_____ result.

3 We can use it to talk about _____continuous_____ or frequently _____repeated_____ actions.

4 We do not use the present perfect continuous with _____state_____ verbs.

5 We use the present perfect continuous to talk about how _____long_____ something has been happening.

C Go to the Grammar Hub on page 132.

D SPEAK Work in pairs. Student A – go to the Communication Hub on page 150. Student B – go to the Communication Hub on page 155.

PRONUNCIATION
been: weak form

A Listen to three sentences. What do you notice about the pronunciation of *been* in each sentence? Does it rhyme with *seen* or *thin*?
Each time, *been* rhymes with *thin*.
6.6

been

In the present perfect continuous, *been* is an auxiliary verb and it is normally unstressed. We use the weak form /bɪn/. We don't normally use the strong form /biːn/.

The stressed words are usually the main verbs and key information words, not the auxiliary verbs.

B Listen and repeat. Use the weak form of *been*.
6.7

SPEAKING HUB

A Choose one of your hobbies or free time activities and prepare to talk about it. Answer the following questions.

1 When did you take it up and why?

2 How much time and money do you spend on it?

3 What do you like about it?

4 Is there anything you dislike about it?

5 What benefits does it bring to you and your life?

6 Why would someone else enjoy your hobby?

B SPEAK Go around the class and interview three or four of your classmates about their hobbies. Take notes.

C DISCUSS Work in groups. Tell each other about your interviews. Which hobbies were:

• the most unusual?

• the most interesting?

• the most dangerous?

• the most expensive?

READING

A SPEAK Work in pairs. When was the last time you:

- tried a new food or drink?
- listened to a new singer or group?
- visited a new place?

B READ FOR MAIN IDEA Read the first two paragraphs of *My six months of trying new things*. Then complete the summary with a word in the box.

~~interesting~~   relaxing

Candie is not very active. She decided to spend the first six months of this year doing different activities because she wants to find a hobby that will make her free time more ____interesting____.

My **six months** of trying new things
By Candie Carmichael

15th July

I've never been the kind of person who does lots of exciting things in their free time. Paragliding, swimming with dolphins, climbing Mount Everest – not me! My idea of danger is to sit on the sofa and watch the latest crime series on TV. The closest I get to nature is when I 'like' my friends' cat pictures on social media. As for climbing Himalayan mountains – forget it! I'd rather climb the stairs to bed.

But at one point towards the end of last year, I started to feel that my life was becoming a bit … well … boring. I needed to take up a hobby. But which one? There are so many things out there – how do you know what you will enjoy? So I decided to spend the first six months of this year trying out a new hobby each month. I was a complete beginner at every activity I tried.

Here's what happened:

January: Fly fishing

The first thing I learnt was that no flies are harmed in fly fishing. You make a pretty, artificial 'fly' and attach it to a hook on a fishing line. ¹__ When a fish takes a bite you … oh, I don't know. I did NOT do well at this. One month: lots of badly made 'flies', and ZERO fish (apart from the ones I got at the fish and chip shop on my way home).

February: Stamp collecting

Why does anyone do Ex C this? ²__ After a whole four weeks of attaching little squares of paper from around the world into a big book with blank pages, I still have no idea.

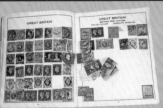

March: Table tennis

This one really surprised me. I'm Ex C actually good at it! I joined a club, and I didn't need to spend a lot of time practising before I started winning games. After only a month, I was already one of the best players in the group. I really can't believe it. ³__

April: Beekeeping

Surely all I had to do was keep some flying insects in a box? ⁴__ About a hundred bee stings later, I realised that a lot can go wrong and beekeeping is a serious (and often painful) business. I think I'll just get my honey from the supermarket in future.

May: Playing the ukulele

The ukulele is like a very small guitar. It has four strings. It makes you look like a giant when you play it. ⁵__ I didn't have to be fit. It wasn't dangerous and it wasn't painful. And at the end of the month, I could play *Rivers of Babylon* all the way through. If that isn't success, I don't know what is!

6.2 Hobbies

READING

A Give a personal example, then put students into pairs to discuss the questions. Share any interesting answers with the class. Ask students to expand on why they tried these new experiences and how it made them feel.

B Tell students they're going to read about a woman called Candie who decided to try lots of new experiences. Tell them to read the first two paragraphs and complete the summary with the correct word.

C Tell students to read the rest of the article and to match the activities with Candie's experiences. Tell them to ignore the gaps in the text at this stage. Ask students to explain which part of the text helped them find the answer.

D Tell students to read the text again and to complete the gaps with the sentences. To make this more challenging for stronger students, tell them to cover sentences a–f and to try to predict the missing sentences. When the other students are almost finished, tell the stronger students to uncover sentences a–f and to put them in the correct gaps, comparing how similar they are to their ideas.

METHODOLOGY HUB by Jim Scrivener

Audience and purpose

When identifying tones, it is important to think about audience and purpose.

In real life, we can judge if our writing was successful by whether it did what we wanted it to do. For example:

- if we wrote a complaint email to an Internet bookshop, we would feel successful if they replied, seemed to understand our problem and took steps to deal with it;

- if we wrote a story about a happy incident in our childhood, we might feel we had succeeded if other people read it and enjoyed it and perhaps wanted to talk to us about it and ask questions or respond with their own stories;

The fact that writing can achieve such things is part of what motivates us to put care into our writing. Good writers need to become careful readers of – and reflectors on – their own work. The existence of audience and purpose are worth bearing in mind in class.

METHODOLOGY HUB by Jim Scrivener

Some alternatives to reading aloud around the class

Here are some alternatives to try:

- You read.

- You read narrative, but students read character conversation.

- You (having read the chapter yourself before class) tell the story in your own words, without notes, in the most spell-binding way you can; later, you get students to do the same with other bits.

- Students read to each other in small groups or pairs, stopping, changing, discussing and helping each other whenever they want to.

- Students read silently, then, without discussion, act out, improvising a scene based on what happened.

- Students silently speed-read a text (say in two minutes), then report back, discussing, comparing, etc before silently reading it more carefully.

GRAMMAR HUB

6.2 Present perfect simple and present perfect continuous; had to / needed to

A Choose the correct option.

1 I've never *played* / been playing squash before. Is it fun?
2 Have you *been watching* / watched sport on TV all day?
3 I've just *finished* / been finishing a really difficult exercise class.
4 Sorry about my appearance. I've run / *been running*.
5 Do you think he's *understood* / been understanding the rules yet?
6 Lee hasn't worked out / *been working out* for a long time but he's already *increased* / been increasing his muscle strength.

B Complete the sentences in the present perfect simple or continuous with the correct form of these verbs. Sometimes more than one tense is possible.

| follow | join | keep | lose | play | spend |

1 Tom has ___lost___ interest in playing football.
2 The coach has __spent / been spending__ a lot of time with the players lately.
3 Have you __been following__ the tennis competition? It's getting good!
4 Georgia has __been keeping__ fit these days using a new exercise programme.
5 Eli and Greta haven't ___joined___ the club yet.
6 I've __been playing__ this video game all day and there's still a lot left.

C Correct the mistakes.

1 He had to ~~left~~ leave the game because he broke his leg.
2 I ~~must~~ had to shout so the other players could hear me.
3 You ~~hadn't~~ didn't have/need to shout. I ~~couldn't~~ could hear you on the field.
4 I didn't ~~needed~~ need/have to tell my friend about the game.
5 **A:** Why ~~they didn't~~ didn't they have to buy a paddle?
   B: Because they already had one.

➤ Go back to page 69.

E Tell students to read the information in the *Identifying tone* box. Tell them to think about this information and to look at the highlighted phrases, words and punctuation in the article to decide what they think the author's tone is. Ask students to explain their answers and if similar techniques are used in their own language. Ask if students know any other ways in which this can be done.

They show us that the article has an informal tone. There are capitalisation for emphasis, exclamation marks and emphasising adverbs and adjectives (still, actually, whole) that indicate the tone of this text is humorous and light-hearted.

F Put students into pairs to discuss which of the activities from the article they would choose to take up, if they had to choose one. If any students already have experience of any of the activities, ask them to share it with the class. Ask students to expand on their reasons for wanting or not wanting to try the activities.

GRAMMAR

A Tell students to read the sentences and to choose the correct words to complete the rules. Check understanding of *didn't have to* carefully by eliciting some personal examples. Ensure students understand that it doesn't have the same meaning as *wasn't allowed to* or *shouldn't have*.

B Direct students to the **Grammar Hub** on pages 132 and 133 (see TB67 and 68).

C Put students into pairs to discuss the questions. Encourage students to expand on their answers. Use the **Grammar Worksheet** on W23 for extra practice.

SPEAKING HUB

A Tell students to think of one or two new activities they have tried.

B Tell students to look at the points in Exercise B and make notes to help them prepare to speak. Monitor to help with language input.

C Put students into pairs to tell each other about their experiences of trying a new activity. Encourage them to show interest in each other's stories and to ask further questions.

TEACHING IDEA by David Seymour and Maria Popova
Grammar: Desert island

Draw a desert island with one long-bearded inhabitant. Add a rescue ship arriving and a rescuer jumping off to greet Robinson Crusoe. Elicit some of their conversation (*How long have you been living here?; I've been eating coconuts for ten years*). Challenge pairs to come up with three more present perfect continuous sentences.

TEACHING IDEA by David Seymour and Maria Popova
Invention

What does the saying `Necessity is the mother of invention' mean?

In small groups, brainstorm a list of ten important inventions. Pass your list to another group. Look at the list your group receives and next to each invention, write a sentence explaining why it was needed, e.g. the wheel – *It was invented because people needed to transport heavy loads.*

TEACHING IDEA by David Seymour and Maria Popova
Historical needs

In small groups, discuss what people needed and didn't need to do at these times, e.g. *People who lived 500 years ago needed to dry a lot of their food for the winter.*

50 years ago, 500 years ago, 5,000 years ago

Compare how things are different these days and make a few notes of your ideas, e.g. *Nowadays we don't need to dry things like fish because we can keep them refrigerated.*

METHODOLOGY HUB by Jim Scrivener
Grammar: Clarification

You have reached a point in your lesson where you want the learners really to focus in on a piece of grammar, to see it, think about it and understand it, to become much clearer on its form, meaning and use. This is what many teachers refer to as *clarification* or *presentation*. However, these are quite broad headings; there is a significant difference between a presentation in which I give you a lecture for 60 minutes and one where I nudge and help you towards discovering much of the same information for yourself via a process of questioning and looking at suggested reference material. We could differentiate three general categories:

1 Teacher explanation
2 Guided discovery
3 Self-directed discovery

An example activity of each category are as follows:

1 Teacher explanation

You tell a story about your weekend. Every time you use a verb in the past simple, you repeat it and write it on the board. At the end, you write 'past simple' on the board and explain that you used all these verbs in the past because the story happened last Saturday.

2 Guided discovery

You hand out a list of 20 *if* sentences. You ask students to work together, discuss and find out what the 'rules' are.

3 Self-directed discovery

Students decide they want to learn about reported speech. They go to the library or on the internet and find out more.

C READ FOR KEY WORDS Read the rest of the article. Match the activities (1–6) with Candie's experiences (a–f).

1 fly fishing
2 stamp collecting
3 yoga
4 beekeeping
5 playing the ukulele
6 table tennis

a This hobby caused her pain.
b She wasn't successful at all.
c She was able to complete a whole song.
d She was surprised by how good she was at this activity.
e She learnt that she is not able to do this kind of thing well because she isn't fit.
f She didn't understand why this is a popular hobby.

D READ FOR DETAIL Read again. Complete the gaps in the article (1–6) with the sentences (a–f).

a Is this really a hobby? 2
b What could possibly go wrong? 4
c Maybe there's a chance for me to get fit after all. 3
d Then you throw the line on the water. 1
e I really enjoyed this. 5
f I am not very flexible. 6

Identifying tone

An essay or serious news article will usually have a formal or serious tone. Other kinds of text, like emails between friends or some web or magazine articles, may have an informal or humorous tone.

You can identify a text's tone from the way it is written and the author's choice of phrases, adverbs and adjectives, capital letters and punctuation.

E Look at the highlighted words and phrases. What do the capital letters, punctuation and word choice tell us about the article's tone?

F SPEAK Work in pairs. If you had to choose one of these activities to take up for a month, which would you choose? Why? Tell your partner.

June: Yoga

Ouch! I thought yoga was relaxing. I didn't realise I had to be super fit and flexible. After one month of downward dogs and (falling over!) tree poses, I learnt some very important things about me: I am not very fit. 6 ___ I do not like yoga.

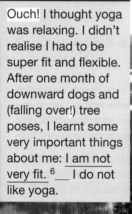

GRAMMAR
had to / needed to

A WORK IT OUT Look at the sentences from *My six months of trying new things*. Then choose the correct words to complete the rules.

I needed to take up a hobby.
All I had to do was keep some flying insects in a box.
I didn't have to be fit.
I didn't need to spend a lot of time practising before I started winning games.

had to / needed to

1 We use **had to** and **needed to** when we talk about things that were necessary in the **present / past**.
2 We use **didn't have to** and **didn't need to** when we talk about things that were **not allowed / not necessary but possible** in the past.

B Go to the Grammar Hub on page 132.

C SPEAK Work in pairs. Tell your partner:
- three things you *had to / needed to* do yesterday. Explain why.
- three things you *didn't have to / didn't need to* do yesterday. Explain why.

SPEAKING HUB

A Think of one or two new activities that you have tried. Use the list to help you or your own ideas.

keep a pet
plant flowers or grow a plant
make a birthday present instead of buying one
try a new form of exercise
take language classes
make a photo album
learn a new board game

B PLAN Think about:
- how and why you did it.
- what was easy/difficult about it.
- the things you had to / needed to do.
- the things you didn't have to / didn't need to do.
- why you stopped/continued doing it.

C SPEAK Work in pairs. Tell your partner about the new activity you tried. Then listen to your partner and ask him/her questions about the activity.

◯– Talk about hobbies and free time activities
◯– Discuss trying new things

Café Hub

F – express your opinion   **P** – intonation for expressing opinions

COMPREHENSION

A Work in pairs. Tell your partner how you prepare for doing exercise or playing sport. What do you do before you start?

B ▶ 00:00–00:32 Watch the first part of the video. Are any of the things you discussed in Exercise A in the video? Who do you think will win the game?

C ▶ 00:33–03:15 Watch the second part of the video. Tick (✓) *Gaby* or *Sam* or both.

Gaby	Sam	
✓		thinks it's unusual to put butter on toast.
	✓	thinks English breakfast is more than buttered toast and milky tea.
✓		thinks Spanish food is better than English food.
		thinks tortilla is boring.
✓	✓	changes their mind at the end.

FUNCTIONAL LANGUAGE
Expressing your opinion

A ▶ Complete the phrases in the table. Then watch the video again and check your answers.

Give an opinion	I ¹ _think_ that's very strange. ² _Don't_ you think that's horrible? I ³ _reckon_ British food is better than ever these days. In my ⁴ _opinion_ , British food is still really bad. If you ask ⁵ _me_ , it's your opinion that's really bad. Spanish food is so much better. Don't ⁶ _you_ agree? Do you know ⁷ _what_ I think? Tortilla is a bit boring.
Give examples to support an opinion	⁸ _For_ instance, … To give you an example, …
Agree with an opinion	I agree. You are probably ⁹ _right_ . Absolutely!
Disagree with an opinion	I disagree. I ¹⁰ _really_ don't think that's true. Nonsense. To be brutally ¹¹ _honest_ , no!

B Work in groups. Decide which are the three countries with the best food in the world.

MILLY

SAM

NEENA

ZAC

GABY

USEFUL PHRASES

A ▶ Match the useful phrases (1–5) with the phrases that come before or after them (a–e). Then watch the video and check your answers.

1 Game, set and match – Sam!
2 Not hugely.
3 Wake up! Say something!
4 I didn't realise you were so passionate about food.
5 British food is average!

a So you don't like Spanish food?
b Sam, are you OK?
c I'm sorry! I got a bit angry.
d I was right!
e Nonsense!

B How do you say these useful phrases in your language?

PRONUNCIATION
Intonation for expressing opinions

A Listen and repeat the extracts from the video. Copy the stress and intonation.

A: In <u>my</u> opinion, <u>Brit</u>ish <u>food</u> is still <u>really</u> <u>bad</u>.

B: Well, if you <u>ask</u> <u>me</u>, it's <u>your</u> opinion that's <u>really</u> <u>bad</u>.

A: Spanish food is <u>so</u> much <u>bet</u>ter – <u>don't</u> you <u>agree</u>?

B: To be <u>brutally</u> <u>hon</u>est, <u>no</u>!

A: Do you want to know what <u>I</u> <u>think</u>? I think tor<u>till</u>a is a bit <u>bor</u>ing.

B: <u>Bor</u>ing!

B Work in pairs. Make similar conversations. Change the information.

SPEAKING

A Complete the statements with opinion phrases from Functional Language Exercise A.

… eat before doing exercise.

If you ask me, you shouldn't eat for one hour before doing exercise.

… do an hour of aerobic exercise every day.

_____

… tennis is more exciting to watch than football.

_____

… the gym is boring.

_____

… female athletes should be paid the same as men.

_____

… running is the best sport in the world.

_____

… boxing is too violent.

_____

… eSports are more exciting than real sports.

_____

B DISCUSS Work in pairs. Take it in turns to read out your statements from Exercise A and agree or disagree with your partner's statements.

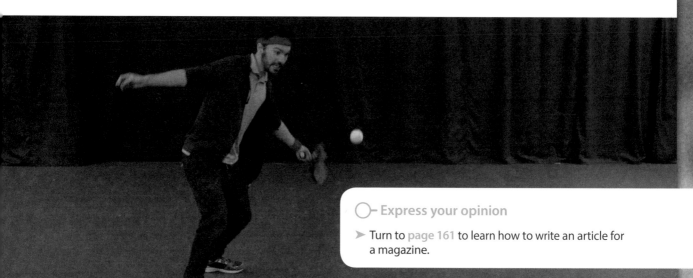

○– **Express your opinion**

➤ Turn to page 161 to learn how to write an article for a magazine.

LEAD-IN

Put students into two teams and give them a time limit of two minutes. They have to come up with a list of as many types of exercises and/or sports as they can. Check answers at the end. The team with the longest (and most accurate) list wins. Concept check any words that are new to the opposing team.

COMPREHENSION

A Elicit a couple of examples from the class and then put students into pairs to discuss the questions. Share ideas as a whole class and write students' ideas and any new or requested vocabulary on the board.

B ▶ 00:00-00:32 Tell students they're going to watch another episode of the video series. Ask students to listen and note down if any of their ideas from Exercise A were mentioned. They can use the list you wrote on the board to support them. They also need to think about who they think will win the game, and why. Check answers as a whole class.

C ▶ 00:33-03:15 Tell students to watch the rest of the episode and to tick the sentences that apply to Sam, Gaby or both of them.

FUNCTIONAL LANGUAGE

A ▶ Tell students to try to complete the phrases from the episode from memory. Tell them not to worry if they can't remember or have no idea, as they're going to watch it again. Monitor to check all students have at least read all the phrases and check the meaning of *brutally* and *nonsense*. Play the video again for students to check their answers.

Make sure students understand that *nonsense* is very direct and informal and not to be used in formal situations or with people they don't know very well!

B Put students into groups to discuss which three countries have the best food in the world. Give students a couple of minutes to prepare their ideas before they speak and tell them to think about using some of the phrases from Exercise A. You could also ask them to try and choose one controversial food to elicit phrases of disagreement!

USEFUL PHRASES

A ▶ Tell students to match the useful phrases from the episode with the phrases that came before or after them. Play the video again for students to check. Check students understand the phrases and how they should be used by referring to context in the video.

B Tell students to think about how they would say the useful phrases in their language. Ask if they use the same tennis reference for number 1. If not, do they use a reference from a different sport? Ask students if they use any other sporting phrases in everyday language.

PRONUNCIATION

6.8

A Play the extracts from the video for students to listen and repeat. Tell students to listen carefully to the intonation and how some words are strongly stressed and to copy this. Ask students if they emphasise words with stress or show how they feel with intonation in the same way in their language.

B Write *In my opinion, British food is still really bad* on the board. Underline *my*, *British food* and *bad* and elicit words from the students that could be used to replace them in the sentence ensuring that it still makes sense. Put students into pairs to make conversations using the structure of the conversation from Exercise A but inserting different information. Monitor as students write their conversations and help them with ideas if they are struggling. Listen for appropriate stress and intonation when students practise their conversations and drill if necessary. Choose one or two confident pairs to perform to the class.

SPEAKING

A Tell students to look at the statements and to complete them with an opinion phrase from *Functional Language* Exercise A. Point out the example and elicit which column it comes from in *Functional Language* Exercise A.

B Put students into pairs. Tell students to read their opinions and to agree or disagree with their partner. Encourage students to support their opinions with examples. If there is time, get students to swap partners and repeat the task. Monitor while students speak, noting down some good language to highlight and some errors for them to correct.

▶ VIDEOSCRIPT

G = Gaby   S = Sam

G: I'm hungry.
S: Really?
G: I haven't eaten anything.
S: I have to eat breakfast before a game of tennis in the morning. You should eat something.
G: I know, I just don't like the food you have for breakfast in England.
S: What? It's great.
G: You put butter on toast! I think that's very strange.
S: Strange? I really don't think that's true.
G: And you put milk … in your tea! Don't you think that's horrible!
S: No! Breakfast isn't just buttered toast and milky tea! People always say that British food isn't very good, but that's not true anymore! For instance, the food in my café isn't horrible, is it?
G: No, it's good – but what I mean is that in general British food is … average …
S: Nonsense! I reckon British food is better than ever these days.

G: In my opinion, British food is still really bad.
S: Well, if you ask me, it's your opinion that's really bad.
G: Ha! Spanish food is so much better, don't you agree?
S: To be brutally honest, no!
G: So you don't like Spanish food?
S: Not hugely.
G: Not even tortilla?
S: Do you know what I think? I think tortilla is a bit boring.
G: BORING!
S: It's just egg and potato.
G: AND … ONIONS! Sam! Are you ok? Sam? Sam! Wake up! Say something!
S: I didn't realise you were so passionate about food …
G: I'm sorry! I got a bit angry.
S: It's OK. I'm sorry, too. Your tortilla is really good.
G: Thanks … and you … are probably right. British food is good these days. What?
S: Haha, you said it – British food is good! I was right! Game, set and match – Sam! Yes.
G: OK. My serve.

6 Writing ● Write an article for a magazine

ⓦ introductory clauses

A Work in pairs. Read the magazine advert. Then look at the free time activities in the box. Which three do you think would be good subjects for an article? Why?

Share your stories with Life & *Style*.

In our Free time section, we're going to publish a new series of reader's articles, called *'Why everyone should …!'*

Send us your short articles about ideas for free time activities and hobbies – things that you think everyone should try doing at least once in their lifetime.

> arts and crafts   playing football   skydiving
> stamp collecting   stargazing (astronomy)
> team video gaming

B Read *Why everyone should … go stargazing!*. Put the sentences (a–f) in the order they are mentioned in the article (1–6).

a It is a good way to meet people.	4
b It is a simple hobby to start.	1
c Stargazing events at night are enjoyable.	6
d Mobile digital technology is useful.	2
e There is a place to go to use good equipment.	3
f You can join a club.	5

Why everyone should … go stargazing!

Wow! That's all I can say as I look at the rings of Saturn, or see a shadow pass across the sun. I'll never regret taking up stargazing.

Besides the wonder of discovering the universe, the great thing about stargazing is that it is an easy hobby to take up. You only have to look up into the sky at night and you've already become a stargazer. The cool thing is that there are many mobile phone apps to help you when you start, telling you exactly what you are looking at.

It is also easy to visit your local observatory. The wonderful thing about going there is that you can use powerful telescopes to see deep into the universe. You'll see the mountains of Mars, the moons of Jupiter and the stardust of the Milky Way.

A nice thing about stargazing is that it is actually very sociable. There are local societies all over the country, and enthusiasts often meet up for 'star parties'. They are like having a picnic at night and are a lot of fun. One thing to remember is that you should bring hot chocolate rather than juice – it's important to keep warm!

Everyone wants to put a little 'wow!' into their lives, and stargazing is a surprisingly simple, inexpensive and enjoyable way to do that. There's so much to discover in the universe, so isn't it time to start exploring?

C Read the tips on writing articles. Then look at the article again. Which tips did the writer follow? Give examples.

Top tips for writing a magazine article

1 In the introduction, clearly give the topic, and grab the reader's attention and interest.
2 Use a more relaxed and personal style than in a newspaper report.
3 Show your passion for the subject.
4 Give each paragraph a clear topic.
5 Use direct quotes from interviews.
6 Use humour.
7 In the conclusion, summarise the key points in the article.
8 Finish with a memorable sentence, giving the reader something to think about.

D Look at the box. Find and underline the introductory clauses in the highlighted sentences in the article.

Introductory clauses

We can begin a sentence with an introductory clause that provides, and draws attention to, the topic for the rest of the sentence.

E Work in pairs. Complete the sentences with information about a hobby, sport or activity that you do. Then compare your answers with a partner.

1 One good thing about _____ is that
   _____.

2 Something that I like about _____ is that
   _____.

3 A good reason to _____ is that
   _____.

4 One problem with _____ is that
   _____.

5 One thing to remember is that
   _____.

WRITING

A PREPARE You are going to write a short magazine article. Choose a hobby, sport or free time activity as the subject of your article. Why do you think everyone should try it?

B PLAN Make notes for your article. Read the tips in Exercise C again to help.

C WRITE Write an article (150–200 words).

D REVIEW Work in groups. Read the other students' articles. Which activities would you choose to do? Why?

WRITING   161

---

1 ✓	Topic: *Stargazing*; Grab attention: *Wow! That's all I can say …*
2 ✓	*I'll never regret …; The cool thing is that …; … isn't it time to start exploring?*
3 ✓	*I'll never regret …; … the great thing about …; … a lot of fun.*
4 ✓	*… it is an easy hobby to take up; It is also easy to visit your local observatory; … it is actually very sociable.*
5 ✗	
6 ✓	*… you should bring hot chocolate rather than juice …!*
7 ✓	*Stargazing is a surprisingly simple, inexpensive and enjoyable way to do that*
8 ✓	*There's so much to discover in the universe, so isn't it time to start exploring?*

Refer students to this letter as a model for the writing task.

WRITING

With books closed, ask students to think of a magazine that they read or have read. Tell students to tell their partner about it.

A Tell students to look at the magazine advert. Point out the pictures and make sure students understand what the activities are. Check the meaning of *stargazing*. Tell students to discuss and choose three free-time activities which would be good subjects for a magazine article.

B Tell students to read the article and to put the sentences in the order they're mentioned.

C Point out the tips in the box for writing a magazine article. Tell students to read the article again and to think about which tips the writer followed and to find examples to back up their answers. Do the first one together as a whole class.

D Point out the information in the box about introductory clauses. Tell students to look at the highlighted phrases in the article and to underline the introductory clause in each.

E Tell students to complete the sentences with information about a hobby, sport or activity that they do.

WRITING TASK

A Tell students to think about a hobby, sport or free-time activity that they think everyone should try and why.

B Tell students to look back at the *Top tips for writing a magazine article* in Exercise C above and to make notes about the content and organisation of their article.

C Tell students to use their notes to write the article. Remind students to use some introductory clauses as well as following the top tips.

D Put students into groups and tell them to read each other's articles. Encourage students to ask each other further questions.

GRAMMAR

A Complete the conversation between a football coach and some new players with the correct modals of obligation.

Coach: The rules say so. You [1]_____mustn't_____ touch the ball with your hands. It isn't allowed.

Player 1: But what about the goalkeeper? He sometimes [2]_____has to_____ use his hand to stop a shot. I've seen it on TV.

Coach: OK, OK! Everyone except the goalkeeper [3]_____must / has to_____ follow that rule. And you all [4]_____must / have to_____ warm up before a game. I insist on that. If you don't warm up, you don't play.

Player 2: I can't get here until 6 pm.

Coach: That's a bit late, the game starts at 6.15 pm. You [5]_____should_____ start warming up at 5.45, by 6 pm at the latest. You cycle here, don't you? If so, you [6]_____needn't / don't have to_____ do a big warm-up. But you [7]_____have to / must_____ be here by six, OK?

B Complete the TV interview with the present perfect simple or continuous form of the verbs in brackets.

Reporter: Hi, everyone. I'm with champion surfer Sally Gowen. Sally, [1]_____have_____ you _____been surfing_____ (surf) here all day?

Surfer: Hi, Maisie. Yes, I sure have. The water [2]_____has_____ _____been_____ (be) excellent all day. I love it here. I [3]_____have/'ve been coming_____ (come) here quite a lot recently.

Reporter: What [4]_____have_____ you _____been practising_____ (practise) today? Some new moves?

Surfer: No, no. Nothing too special. OK, I'm going back on the surf now.

Reporter: Ah, I [5]_____haven't finished_____ (finish) yet. Just one more … Sally? Sally! Oh, she [6]_____has/'s gone_____ (go).

C Complete the text with *had to*, *didn't have to*, *needed to* or *didn't need to*. Sometimes more than one answer is possible.

I remember my first year at university well. It was so different to being at school. Finally, we [1]_____didn't have to_____ wear a uniform every day, and I [2]_____didn't need to / didn't have to_____ tell my parents where I was all the time. I enjoyed that new freedom, and I [3]_____had to_____ grow up quickly, too. I [4]_____needed to / had to_____ take more responsibility for everyday things. I was lucky though because I lived in a student residence. I [5]_____didn't have to_____ live there, but I chose to because I wanted to meet other people easily. It was a good decision. We [6]_____had to_____ follow a few rules, but having a cleaner was great. I mean, we still [7]_____had to_____ wash the dishes and keep things clean, but a cleaner every week was good.

VOCABULARY

A Choose the best adjectives to complete the sentences.

1 Don't delay any more. Make your mind up. It's time to be *decisive* / *aggressive*.

2 Stop shouting! You're being very *effective* / *aggressive*.

3 He's very *creative* / *competitive*. He hates losing.

4 eSports are already *massive* / *expensive*. They'll definitely be in the Olympics soon.

5 You won 7–2? That's *impressive* / *aggressive*!

6 Running with the ball is not very *effective* / *competitive*. It's better to pass it quickly.

B Complete the text about sports with the missing words.

I loved my time as a football player. I only played for one club in the national [1]l e a g u e, but what a club! I had great [2]c o a c h e s who really improved my game, and our [3]s u p p o r t e r s were amazing, always singing and cheering us on. It was a great feeling walking into the [4]s t a d i u m, to hear that noise at the beginning of the game. And, of course, I played for the national team at three World Cup [5]t o u r n a m e n t s, and the 2018 one was the highlight of my career. How can anything be better than winning the [6]f i n a l and lifting the [7]t r o p h y, knowing you are the [8]c h a m p i o n s of the world? I bet all the [9]s p e c t a t o r s watching in the stadium and on TV were jealous! I think I can safely say I was a [10]t o p p l a y e r. After all, I won the 'Player of the Year' award twice! I certainly miss those days. I don't get the same feeling from running a restaurant.

C Complete the radio vox-pop with the words in the box.

| am | been | collect | get | joined | lost | took |

Yes, I [1]_____collect_____ stamps. I've [2]_____been_____ into stamp collecting for ages. I [3]_____took_____ it up when I was just a kid. Some people think it is boring, but I have never [4]_____lost_____ interest in it, and I'm 45 now. Of course, I [5]_____am_____ a member of my local stamp collecting society. I [6]_____joined_____ that ten years ago. The weekly meetings [7]_____get_____ me out of the house.

FUNCTIONAL LANGUAGE

Complete the TV discussion with the correct phrases to express opinions.

Mario: Let's ask our panel of experts. You first, Tim, what do you think?

Tim: Well, in my [1]_____opinion_____, they should be banned.

Asif: If you [2]_____ask_____ me, we shouldn't ban them.

Ana: As far as I'm [3]_____concerned_____, a ban is the answer.

Sue: I think we should do more research. Don't you [4]_____agree_____?

Tim: To be [5]_____honest_____, I disagree completely. We already know enough. To [6]_____give_____ you an example, there were five different stories about them in the newspapers last week.

FOOD

Food (n) the things that people or animals eat.
Synonyms: meal, cooking

So long as you have food in your mouth, you have solved all questions for the time being.

Franz Kafka

Lunch in Marrakesh: Rainbow salad bowl, falafel and mint tea.

The quote for this unit highlights the importance of food and suggests that as long as this basic need is met any other concerns are secondary.

Franz Kafka (1883–1924) was a German-speaking Jewish writer. His novels and short stories are concerned with the themes of social alienation, isolation and the harmful effects of bureaucracy on society.

OBJECTIVES

- talk about eating out
- make speculations and deductions about food
- compare different types of food
- compare a range of solutions and choose the best one
- make suggestions
- write a reply in an online discussion forum

Work with a partner. Discuss the questions.

1 Look at the photo. How many types of food can you name?
2 Read the quote. What do you think it means?
3 Do you think it is important to eat with your family or friends? Why/Why not?

FOOD   73

OBJECTIVES

Read the unit objectives to the class.

UNIT OPENER QUESTIONS

With books closed, put students into pairs. Ask what they think the best way to make a new friend or show what friendship is. Elicit an example, then tell students to think of more ideas with their partner. Elicit any new or interesting vocabulary on the board.

1 Tell students to open their books and look at the photo. Put students into pairs and give them two minutes to name as many foods as they can in the photo. Elicit and write any new vocabulary on the board at the end of the activity.

2 Tell students to read the quote. Put students into pairs to discuss what they think it means. Elicit ideas together as a whole class.

3 Ask students to discuss whether they think it is important to eat with their family or friends and why or why not. Ask them if they eat together with their family. You could also ask if they think this tradition varies at different ages, in different countries, etc. Another idea would be to ask them to talk about an occasion when they shared a special meal with their friends and/or family.

WORKSHEETS

Lesson 7.1 Eating out

Grammar: Modals of speculation and deduction (W25)

Vocabulary: Phrasal verbs (W26)

Lesson 7.2 Food fads

Grammar: Comparatives and superlatives; the … , the … (W27)

Vocabulary: Waste (W28)

7.1 Eating out

○— Talk about eating out
○— Make speculations and deductions about food

P— diphthongs; word stress with modals
G— modals of speculation and deduction

V— phrasal verbs; adjectives to describe food
S— hidden contrasts

READING

A SPEAK Work in groups and discuss the questions.

1 Do you often eat out in a restaurant? Why/Why not?

2 Do you usually leave a tip to thank the waiter for good service?

B READ FOR MAIN IDEA Read *Super supper clubs*. What are supper clubs? Why do many customers prefer supper clubs to traditional restaurants?

C Complete the notes on the differences between supper clubs and traditional restaurants. Use the strategies in the box to help you.

Paragraph	Supper clubs	Traditional restaurants
Choosing a dish (2)	*the chef chooses*	*you choose from a menu*
Where customers sit (2)	together with other customers	quietly at separate tables
Choosing when to go (2)	join a waiting list; wait for an invitation	turn up when you're feeling hungry
What to cook (4)	the chef has control	the chef cooks the same food again and again
The food (4)	amazing, but they might not like it	boring
The experience (5)	for all the senses; having fun	just food

Hidden contrasts

In articles about new or unusual things, writers often use words like *instead*, *just* and *even* to show contrasts with more normal things. These contrasts are often hidden, so it's difficult to notice them. But they help you to understand the points that the writer wants to make.

SUPER
SUPPER CLUBS

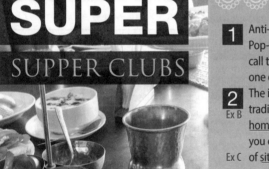

1 Anti-restaurants. Underground restaurants. Pop-up restaurants. Guestaurants. Whatever you call them, there's no <u>doubt</u> that supper clubs are one of the hottest trends in eating out today.

2 The idea is simple: instead of going to a traditional restaurant, <u>you eat in the chef's home</u>. Instead of choosing a dish from a menu, you eat what the chef gives you. And instead
Ex C of <u>sitting quietly at separate tables</u>, all the
Ex C <u>customers eat together</u>, chatting and making friends. But if that sounds like your perfect evening, there's some bad news. You can't just
Ex C <u>turn up when you're feeling hungry</u>; you'll
Ex C need to <u>join a waiting list and then wait for an invitation from the chef.</u>

3 The modern idea of supper clubs took off in Cuba in the 1990s. Cuba now has a huge amount of supper clubs, or *paladares*. Most of them started off as simply a room in the chef's
Ex B home. <u>They're popular with tourists, as well as people who want a simple home-cooked meal at a fair price.</u> One of Cuba's best *paladares* is Castas y Tal, on the 11th floor of a large apartment building in central Havana. The main restaurant area has only eight seats, but there are wonderful views of the city below.

4 For chefs, supper clubs <u>clearly</u> seem like a great idea. They're quite cheap and easy to set up because the chef can do everything at home. Instead of <u>having to cook the same food</u> Ex C <u>again and again</u>, supper clubs <u>give chefs control</u> over what Ex C to cook. <u>Customers don't mind</u> Ex B <u>giving up some choice because they know they'll eat amazing</u> Ex C <u>food that they've never eaten before. They might not like it,</u> but at least it won't be <u>boring</u>. Ex C

5 At the St Jude Project in Mumbai, India, Chef Gresham Fernandes tries out ideas while he's cooking ... and even while he's dishing up! He cooks in front of the guests, explaining what he's doing as he works.

6 So next time you're feeling adventurous, why not visit a supper club? It's <u>sure</u> to be an experience you won't forget!

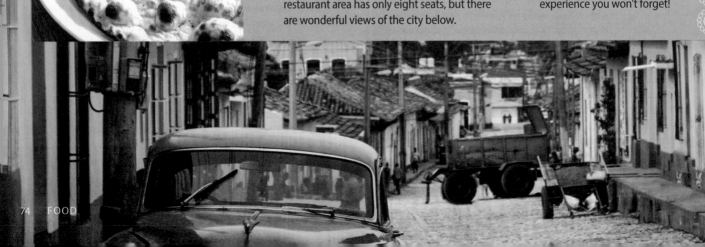

LEAD-IN

With books closed, write on the board: *food, price, service, atmosphere, location*. Tell students that these are things people think about when choosing or rating a restaurant. Ask students if they can add any other categories and add them to the list. Put students into pairs to rank them in order of which is the most important to them in a restaurant. Get feedback and encourage students to expand on and explain their answers.

READING

A Check students understand *leave a tip* by asking them if it is normal practice to do this in their country and who you might leave a tip for apart from a waiter. Tell them to open their books and to discuss the questions in small groups. Encourage students to ask follow-up questions. If your students are from different countries, explore different attitudes to tipping here.

B Tell students to look at the pictures and elicit what they think about the places shown. Tell them they're going to read an article about supper clubs. Ask if any students have any idea what a supper club is. Check understanding of *supper* but point out that it is not very common in modern usage. Tell students to read the questions and to predict the answers based on what they can see in the pictures. Students can then read the article to check their answers.

Possible answer: *They're restaurants in the chef's home. Many customers prefer supper clubs because they're a fair price, a simple home-cooked meal, the experience isn't boring and will be one they won't forget.*

C Point out the information in the box about hidden contrasts and ask students if they noticed the words *instead, just* and *even* in the text. Tell students to read the article again and to complete the table, paying special attention to how the writer uses those words to contrast supper clubs with traditional restaurants.

TEACHING IDEA
by David Seymour and Maria Popova

Topic: Food survey

Use this activity to extend the topic.

I'm going to dictate one question to each person. Mingle and ask all the other students your question. Make a note of their answers. (Dictate each question quickly, but go through them two or three times so that students get another chance to take down their question. After the survey, elicit the results and write them on the board.)

How much tea or coffee do you drink every day?

Do you eat healthy food?

Have you ever tried Indian/Japanese/Greek food?

How often do you eat out?

What is your biggest meal of the day?

Do you like fish and chips?

How much do you spend on food every week?

Do you prefer pizza or pasta?

What do you eat for breakfast?

Where do you buy your food?

Do you eat free-range eggs?

Do you eat a lot of chocolate?

TEACHING IDEA
by David Seymour and Maria Popova

Topic: Restaurants

Use this activity to extend the topic.

Work in small groups. I'll give each group a different type of restaurant. Create a menu and include starters, main courses, side dishes, desserts and drinks. Don't forget the prices.

> a steak house, a vegetarian café, an expensive French eatery, a motorway service station restaurant, a seafood restaurant

In pairs, describe your last visit to a restaurant in detail.

- when and where
- the food and drink
- who you were with
- the décor
- the waiter
- the music
- what you talked about
- the other people there

If anyone has experience of working in a restaurant, answer questions about the job from the class.

METHODOLOGY HUB
by Jim Scrivener

Lead-in Preparation

This may be to help raise motivation or interest (e.g. discussion of a picture related to the topic), or perhaps to focus on language items (e.g. items of vocabulary) that might be useful in the activity.

Typical lead-ins are:

- Show / draw a picture connected to the topic. Ask questions.
- Write up / read out a sentence stating a viewpoint. Elicit reactions.

- Tell a short personal anecdote related to the subject.
- Ask students if they have ever been / seen / done, etc.
- Hand out a short text on the topic. Students read the text and comment.
- Play 'devil's advocate' and make a strong / controversial statement (e.g. *I think relaxing is better than exercise for your health*) that students will be motivated to challenge / argue about.
- Write a key word (maybe the topic name) in the centre of a word-cloud on the board and elicit vocabulary from students which is added to the board.

7.1 Eating out

PRONUNCIATION

🔊 **A** Tell students to look at the underlined words in the *Super supper clubs* article and to match them with the correct pronunciation. If students are unfamiliar with phonemic script, point out that most of the symbols for consonant sounds are the same as the letters. When students have done this, play the audio for students to listen and check.

B Tell students that all the words contain diphthongs. Demonstrate the diphthong sound in the first word. Tell students to look at the words and to complete the rules. In feedback, highlight and drill pronunciation of all eight diphthongs again.

C Put students into pairs and tell them to make sentences using at least three of the words from Exercise A in each. Give an example, e.g. *I might wait at home.* Monitor to check students are using the words appropriately. When all pairs have a few sentences, tell them to practise saying them. Monitor to check they're pronouncing the diphthong sounds correctly. You could then change partners and tell students to model and drill their sentences with their new partner.

VOCABULARY

A Tell students to look at the sentences, then to look at the article again and to find sentences with the same meaning. Tell them to replace the underlined words with the words used in the article.

B Elicit that all the answers to Exercise A were phrasal verbs. Tell students to read the rules and to complete the examples with some of the phrasal verbs from Exercise A. Make sure students realise that it's not possible to work out the meaning of most phrasal verbs just from looking at the verb and the particle.

C Direct students to the **Vocabulary Hub** on page 145 for further practice of phrasal verbs.

D Tell students to cover the phrasal verbs in Exercise A and to complete the phrasal verbs in the questions. Let students uncover Exercise A to check. Ask students to discuss the questions in pairs. Encourage students to ask each other follow-up questions and to expand on their answers. Use the **Vocabulary Worksheet** on W26 for extra practice.

SPEAKING

A Put students into pairs and tell them that they're going to plan their own supper club. Tell them to think about the points and to make notes to help them present their ideas later. Monitor to help with language input. Check students are just making notes and not scripting every word that they're going to say.

B Put students into larger groups and ask them to take turns to present their supper clubs. Encourage students to ask each other questions after each presentation.

C Ask each group to decide which supper club they would most like to attend and why. Ask one student from each group to explain to the class which supper club was the favourite and why. Finish with some feedback on students' use of language during their presentations and discussions.

> **Extra activity**
> You can extend the activity by making groups write a short menu or advert for their supper clubs. As well as listening to presentations, students can walk around and read the menus or adverts before voting on their favourite supper club.

METHODOLOGY HUB by Jim Scrivener

Phrasal verbs

A phrasal verb expresses a complete meaning. The main verb on its own would not express the whole meaning. The meaning will often not be guessable from the sum of its parts. For example, a learner might understand the separate meanings of gave and up – but still not be able to work out the meaning of 'He gave up his job'.

Phrasal verbs are normal everyday language. Generally speaking, they are not slang, colloquial or lazy English.

In many cases, an equivalent single-word verb may sound over-formal when compared to the normal phrasal verb.

They put out the fire.

They extinguished the fire.

Watch out for these problems:

Students choose the wrong participle: *I turned ~~out~~ down his invitation.*

Students put a pronoun after a particle: *They looked ~~up it~~ it up in the library.*

Students use a transitive verb without an object: *We were excited about the party, but they decided to ~~put off~~ put it off till next week.*

TEACHING IDEA by David Seymour and Maria Popova

Call my bluff

Make small groups. Hand out four or five sentences with a phrasal verb (*The milk has gone off.*) to each group and ask them to keep them secret from other groups. For each phrasal verb, the groups should prepare three definitions – two of which are untrue and one which is true ('gone off' = (1) been spilled, (2) become bad, (3) been stolen). When students are ready, groups read out their sentences and each of their definitions. Students vote for which one they think is the correct definition / the group wins one point for every student who votes for one of the wrong definitions.

TEACHING IDEA by David Seymour and Maria Popova

Verb chain

Work in groups of four to six. Take turns to give a phrasal verb, alternately changing the particle and the verb, e.g. A – *Take off.* B – *Take up.* C – *Let up.* D – *Let down.* E – *Put down.* F – *Put on.*

If you can't think of one, you are out of the game. If you doubt another student's phrasal verb, challenge him/her to define it and give an example. If the student can't, he/she is out of the game. (Don't let students write during the activity, but make a note of the most useful phrasal verbs to revise at the end.)

PRONUNCIATION
Diphthongs

A Look at the underlined words in *Super supper clubs*. Match the words with their correct pronunciation (1–8). Then listen and check your answers.

1 weɪt
   _____wait_____

2 ˈklɪəli
   _____clearly_____

3 dʒɔɪn
   _____join_____

4 maɪt
   _____might_____

5 həʊm
   _____home_____

6 daʊt
   _____doubt_____

7 feə
   _____fair_____

8 ʃʊə
   _____sure_____

B WORK IT OUT The words in Exercise A all contain diphthongs. Choose the best word or phrase to complete the rules.

> ### Diphthongs
>
> 1 Diphthongs are long ***vowel*** / *consonant* sounds made from ***two*** / *three* short sounds.
>
> 2 We pronounce diphthongs by **moving quickly from one sound to the next** / *saying the two sounds separately*.
>
> 3 British English has ***eight*** / *ten* diphthongs: /eɪ/, /ɪə/, /ɔɪ/, /aɪ/, /əʊ/, /aʊ/, /eə/ and /ʊə/.

C SPEAK Work in pairs. Make sentences using at least three of the words from Exercises A and B. Then practise saying your sentences.

VOCABULARY
Phrasal verbs

A Look at *Super supper clubs* again. Find sentences that have the same meaning as the ones below. Which words are used instead of the underlined words?

1 You can't just arrive without making an appointment when you're feeling hungry. *turn up*

2 The modern idea of supper clubs really became popular in Cuba in the 1990s. *took off*

3 Most of them began their lives as simply a room in the chef's home. *started off*

4 They're quite cheap and easy to get ready to start. *set up*

5 Customers don't mind losing some choice. *giving up*

6 Chef Gresham Fernandes experiments with ideas while he's cooking … and even while he's putting the food on plates. *tries out* / *dishing up*

B WORK IT OUT Read the rules about phrasal verbs. Then complete the examples with phrasal verbs from Exercise A.

> ### Phrasal verbs
>
> 1 Phrasal verbs are usually made of two parts: a verb (e.g. *work, try*) and a particle (e.g. *out, up*).
>
> 2 Sometimes it's possible to guess the meaning from the two words, but often you just need to learn the meaning of the whole phrasal verb:
>
> • *You can't just* ᵃ___turn up_____ *at their house! Always phone first to check it's OK.*
>
> 3 Some phrasal verbs can have an object. When the object is short (e.g. a pronoun or one or two words), it usually comes in the middle:
>
> • *I have lots of ideas and I like to* ᵇ_____try_____ *them ____out____ while I'm cooking.*
>
> But when the object is a longer phrase, it usually comes at the end:
>
> • *I like to* ᶜ____try out_____ *lots of new ideas while I'm cooking.*

C Go to the Vocabulary Hub on page 145.

D SPEAK Complete the questions with the correct phrasal verbs. Then work in pairs and ask and answer the questions.

1 Do you think supper clubs will take ____off____ in your country?

2 Do you ever try ____out____ new meals while you're cooking or do you always plan carefully before you start?

3 Have your cooking skills ever let you ____down____? What went wrong?

SPEAKING

A Work in pairs. You are going to plan your own supper club. Make notes about:

- name
- location
- type of food
- cost
- number of guests
- what makes your supper club unique

B PRESENT Work in groups. Take turns to present your supper club to the group.

C REFLECT Decide which supper club you would like to attend and why.

VOCABULARY
Adjectives to describe food

A Work in groups. Look at the pictures and discuss the questions.

1 Where do you think each dish is from?

2 What do you think it contains?

B Go to the Vocabulary Hub on page 145.

C Many food adjectives end in -y (e.g. *spicy*). Complete the sentences with the missing adjectives. Use the words in bold to help you.

1 I didn't think this soup would **taste** very nice, but in fact it's really _____*tasty*_____!

2 Honey is very _____sticky_____. It **sticks** to the bread like glue!

3 I really love _____cheesy_____ pizza, so I always ask for extra **cheese** on the top.

4 This _____creamy_____ sauce is too rich for me. How much **cream** did you put into it?

D SPEAK Work in pairs. Think of some types of food and drinks that these adjectives might describe. Use the glossary to help you.

buttery chocolatey fatty fruity oily meaty
milky nutty peppery runny salty watery

E SPEAK Work in pairs. Use adjectives to describe:

1 your favourite soft drink.

2 your favourite flavour of ice cream.

3 your perfect breakfast.

4 your least favourite types of food.

LISTENING

A SPEAK Work in pairs. If you are invited to eat dinner at somebody's house, do you bring:

• flowers

• a gift

• something to drink

• dessert

• nothing

B Complete the description with the words in the box.

course dessert ~~dinner party~~
dishes host starter surprise

A¹ ___*dinner party*___ is an event where one person (the ²_____host_____) invites a group of friends to eat a meal at his or her house. At a traditional dinner party, the host cooks the food: a ³_____starter_____ and a main ⁴_____course_____. But the guests often bring something to drink, and perhaps also a ⁵_____dessert_____. In a pot luck dinner party, everybody (the host and guests) prepares one or two ⁶_____dishes_____. It's called pot luck because it's always a ⁷_____surprise_____: nobody knows what the others will bring.

C LISTEN FOR SPECIFIC INFORMATION Listen to a conversation at a pot luck dinner party. Match the people (1–5) with the dishes (a–e).

7.2

1 Vicky (the host)   a cheesy chicken pasta surprise

2 Charlie   b cream of chicken soup

3 Tina   c spicy buffalo wings

4 Felipe   d cheese and chilli salad

5 Markus   e chicken curry in creamy sauce

Glossary

allergic (adj) affected by an allergy (= a medical condition in which you become sick or your skin becomes covered with red marks as a reaction to something you eat, breathe or touch)

buffalo (n) a large African animal similar to a cow, with curved horns

dairy products (n) foods that are made from milk (e.g. cheese, butter, ice cream)

spicy (adj) food that has a strong hot flavour

7.1 Eating out

VOCABULARY

A Tell students to look at the pictures and elicit their reaction to the dishes shown. Put students into groups to discuss the questions. Share answers as a whole class and write any useful food vocabulary on the board. If any students are from a country where one of the dishes is from, ask them to tell the class more about it.

Picture a:
1 Thai chicken green curry from Thailand
2 It contains chicken, red chilli peppers, curry paste, cooking oil, coconut milk, Thai fish sauce, sugar, etc.

Picture b:
1 Chilli con carne from Texas
2 It contains minced beef, red kidney beans, chilli peppers, tomatoes, sweet corn, onions, etc; it's served here with rice, lettuce and tomatoes.

Picture c:
1 Olivieh potato salad from Iran
2 It contains potatoes, eggs, chicken, mayonnaise, lemon juice, oil; it's decorated with cherry tomatoes, carrot, egg and peas.

B Direct students to the **Vocabulary Hub** on page 145 to focus on adjectives to describe food. Check the meaning of *savoury* (not sweet). Point out that it is not a synonym of *salty*. Elicit example of foods for each adjective to consolidate understanding (e.g. *bread is savoury but not salty*).

C Elicit the noun *spice* and the adjective *spicy* and how by removing the *e* and adding a *y* we make the adjective from the noun. Tell students to look at the sentences and complete the gaps with an adjective formed from the words in bold.

D Write *buttery* on the board and elicit examples from the class of foods that are *buttery*. Put students into pairs to think of more examples of food that could be described with the other adjectives in the box.

Possible answers:
buttery: biscuits, pastry
chocolatey: cakes, biscuits
fatty: meat, chips
fruity: tea, ice cream
oily: fish, salad
meaty: soup, pasta sauce
milky: coffee, white chocolate
nutty: biscuits, chocolate bars
peppery: soup, omelettes
runny: soft cheese, eggs
salty: olives, crisps
watery: soup, pasta sauce

E Put students into pairs to describe the different items. To make this more engaging, tell them not to tell their partner what it is they are describing. Students have to listen to their partner's description and guess what it is.

LISTENING

A Put them into pairs to discuss the question.

B Tell students they're going to read about an unusual type of dinner party. Tell them to read the description and to complete the gaps with the words from the box.

🔊 **C** Tell them first to listen and to match the people with the dishes they bring.
7.2

GRAMMAR HUB

7.1 Modals of speculation and deduction

• We use *could*, *might* or *may* when we think something is possible, but we are not sure.

This dish is very hot – it could contain a lot of chillies.
Carla might be allergic to nuts – don't add any walnuts.
Paul may want sugar in his coffee.

• In the negative, we use *might not* and *may not* but NOT *could not*.

This restaurant may/might not be very good.
NOT ~~This restaurant could not be very good.~~

• We use *must* when we are sure something is true because we have strong evidence for our belief.

This cake is burnt – it must taste horrible!

• We use *can't* when we are sure something is not true because we have strong evidence for our belief.

These biscuits are white – they can't be chocolate biscuits.

• We don't use *must* and *can't* for facts we are 100% sure about.

7.1 Modals of speculation and deduction

A Decide if the statements are true or false.

1 'Kitty may serve fruit salad for dessert tonight.'
Dessert will definitely be fruit salad.   True /(False)

2 'I've been invited to three pot-luck dinners. They must be popular.'
Pot-luck dinners are popular.   (True)/ False

3 'This can't be tomato soup – it isn't red!'
It almost certainly isn't tomato soup.   (True)/ False

4 'Bitter chocolate could be nice in a cake.'
The speaker really doesn't like bitter chocolate.   True /(False)

5 'If you left the milk out all night, it could be sour.'
It's possible that the milk is sour.   (True)/ False

B Choose the correct option.

1 **A:** 'Are you going to order soup?'
  B: 'No, I'm very hungry and it *mustn't* /(*might not*) be very filling.'

2 **A:** 'Lara said she wants chicken.'
  B: 'But she doesn't eat meat. She (*can't*)/ *mustn't* want chicken.'

3 **A:** 'What's 'scampi'?'
  B: 'I don't know really. It (*could*)/ *can* be some kind of fish.'

4 **A:** 'Dinner is at seven tonight.'
  B: 'I *could* /(*may*) not get there in time as I have to work late.'

5 **A:** 'Look at that man! He's ordered three pizzas!'
  B: 'He *can* /(*must*) really like pizza!'

6 **A:** 'I've ordered sushi for lunch.'
  B: 'Hector (*might*)/ *could* not eat that but we'll see.'

➤ Go back to page 77.

D Tell students to try to complete the table from what they remember. Play the audio again for students to check.

E Put students into groups to discuss the questions. Encourage students to expand on their answers.

1 *The guests are either allergic to or don't like the food the other guests have brought.*

GRAMMAR

A Tell students to choose the correct meaning of each sentence.

B Tell students to look at the sentences in Exercise A to help them complete the rules.

C Direct students to the **Grammar Hub** on pages 134 and 135 (see TB76). Use the **Grammar Worksheet** on W25 for extra practice.

PRONUNCIATION

A–D Monitor as students complete the exercises and model pronunciation where necessary.

SPEAKING HUB

A Monitor to help as students write their descriptions.

B Put students into groups to follow the stages and monitor to help.

C Ask one or two students from each group to tell the class about their party.

AUDIOSCRIPT

🔊 **7.2**

Listening, Exercise C
V = Vicky   C = Charlie   T = Tina   M = Markus

V: Charlie! You're here at last!

Ex D Q1 **C:** Hi, Vicky. Sorry I'm a bit late.

V: No problem. You're only … 20 minutes late. Welcome to pot luck night.

C: Thanks. Am I the last person here?

V: No, actually, there's only one other person so far. He arrived half an hour early!

Ex D Q1 **C:** Ah, that must be Felipe, right? He's always early.

V: True. But it was good because he helped me make my dish: a cheese and chilli salad.

Ex D Q3 **C:** Ach … I'm allergic to dairy products. Oh, well. Never mind.

V: Hmm. Wow … those look delicious, Charlie. What are they?

C: Spicy buffalo wings. They're a traditional dish from New York state made with a hot sticky sauce.

V: Wow. That's … different.

Ex D Q2 **C:** Yes, that's what I thought. Er … can I heat them up in the oven? They just need 15 minutes.

Ex D Q2 **V:** Sure, but you'll have to wait ten minutes. I'm heating up Felipe's dish at the moment.

C: OK, no problem.

V: Great. Let me take your dish. Go and join Felipe – he's waiting in the garden.

C: OK, thanks.

V: Aha … Tina. Welcome to pot luck night!

T: Thanks. Is everyone else here already?

V: No, not yet. But Felipe's here, and Charlie.

T: Those look nice. What are they?

V: Buffalo wings. Charlie brought them. Hmm … I've never eaten buffalo meat before. I wonder what it tastes like.

T: Hang on … that can't be right. They can't be buffalo wings. Buffaloes don't have wings!

V: No, you're right. But they're definitely wings. They could be chicken or something like that.

T: Aha … yes. Isn't there a city called Buffalo in New York state? The name must come from the city, not the animal.

V: Good thinking. Anyway, what have you brought?

T: It's my own recipe. It's called cheesy chicken pasta surprise.

V: Oh, right. What's the surprise?

Ex D Q2 **T:** Aha … you'll have to wait and see. Can I just heat it up in the oven?

V: Well, er … you'll have to wait for Charlie's dish … and Felipe's dish. It's chicken curry in a creamy sauce.

T: Ah, yes, so that's what smells so good. I love hot, spicy food.

V: Great. So let me take your dish to the kitchen. Go and join the others out in the garden.

V: Markus! Great to see you. Come on in.

M: Thanks. I'm so sorry I'm late … again! You must think I'm so disorganised!

V: No, don't worry. Most of the others have just arrived, too. So … what have you brought?

M: Cream of chicken soup. I hope that's OK.

V: Er … yeah, I hope so, too. But I haven't got any soup bowls, so it might be a bit difficult. I suppose we could drink it from cups. Er … do I need to heat it up?

M: No, don't worry. I heated it up before I left. That looks lovely. What is it?

V: It's Tina's cheesy chicken pasta surprise.

M: Aha. It smells great, but … what are those red things?

V: They look like they might be chillies.

Ex D Q4 **M:** Oh, I hope not! I hate spicy food.

V: Well, they might not be chillies. They may be red peppers or something.

M: No, they're definitely chillies. Oh, well – hopefully there are some other dishes that I can eat.

V: Er … you may have a problem there. We've also got Felipe's spicy chicken curry and Charlie's spicy chicken wings.

M: Oh, no! Well, at least I've got my chicken soup. And it means there'll be more food for you.

Ex D Q5 **V:** Er … not really. I don't like chicken.

D Listen again. Tick (✓) the correct name(s).

	Vicky	Charlie	Felipe	Tina	Markus
1 Who arrived late?		✓		✓	✓
2 Whose dish needs to be heated up?		✓	✓	✓	
3 Who is allergic to dairy products?		✓			
4 Who doesn't like spicy food?					✓
5 Who doesn't eat chicken?	✓				

E SPEAK Work in groups and discuss the questions.

1 What went wrong with the pot luck dinner party?

2 Does it matter if some things go wrong at a party like this?

GRAMMAR
Modals of speculation and deduction

A WORK IT OUT Choose the correct meaning for the sentences from the conversation at the pot luck dinner party.

1 They **can't be** buffalo wings. Buffaloes don't have wings!
  a Maybe they aren't buffalo wings.
  (b) I'm sure they aren't buffalo wings.

2 They **could be** chicken or something like that.
  (a) It's possible that they're chicken.
  b It was possible that they were chicken.

3 You **must think** I'm so disorganised!
  (a) I'm sure you think this.
  b It's necessary for you to think this.

4 Well, they **might not be** chillies.
  a It isn't possible that they're chillies.
  (b) Perhaps they aren't chillies.

5 Er … you **may have** a problem there.
  (a) Maybe you have a problem.
  b I'm sure you have a problem.

B Look again at the sentences in Exercise A. Complete the rules (1–4) with the words in the box.

Modals of speculation and deduction

can't   could   may   may not   might   might not   must

1 We use _____**must**_____ when we are sure something is true.

2 We use _____**may**_____ , _____**might**_____ or _____**could**_____ when we think something is possibly true, but we are not sure.

3 We use _____**may not**_____ or _____**might not**_____ when we think something possibly isn't true, but we are not sure.

4 We use _____**can't**_____ when we are sure something is not true.

C Go to the Grammar Hub on page 134.

PRONUNCIATION
Word stress with modals

A Listen to the sentences (1–4) from the conversation at the pot luck dinner party. Then match the sentences with the rules (a–d). *7.3*

1 Ah, that <u>must</u> be Felipe, right?
2 Hang on … that <u>can't</u> be right.
3 The name <u>must</u> <u>come</u> from the city, not the animal.
4 They might <u>not</u> be chillies.

a We usually place <u>extra stress</u> on the word *not* or a negative modal verb.   **2** , **4**
b Modal verb + *be*: We usually <u>stress</u> the modal verb, not *be*.   **1** , **2**
c Modal verb + main verb: We usually <u>stress</u> both verbs about the same.   **3**
d When we're speaking quickly, we often don't pronounce the *t* in *must*.   **1** , **3**

B Look at the highlighted words in the sentences below and underline the stressed words. Then listen and check your answers. *7.4*

1 You're such a great host. You <u>must</u> have a lot of dinner parties!
2 'What's wrong with the oven?' 'I don't know. It might <u>not</u> be switched on, perhaps.'
3 I've made lots of soup because some people <u>may</u> want two or three bowls.
4 Oh, no! Felipe <u>can't</u> be here already! The party doesn't start for another 20 minutes!

C Listen again and repeat the sentences. Then work in pairs and practise saying the sentences. Listen and check your partner's pronunciation. *7.4*

D SPEAK Work in pairs. Make deductions and speculations about the people at the dinner party. Think about these questions.

1 How do they know each other?
2 What is the surprise in Tina's cheesy chicken pasta surprise?

⦿ SPEAKING HUB

A You have been invited to a pot luck dinner party. Write a short description of the dish you would like to bring.

B SPEAK Work in groups. Choose one person to be the host and give him/her your description. In your groups, decide:
• who brought which dish.
• which dishes you want to try.

C REFLECT Tell the class about your pot luck dinner party. Which dishes were the most popular?

◯– Talk about eating out
◯– Make speculations and deductions about food

READING

A SPEAK Read the definition of *fad*. Then work in pairs and discuss the questions.

fad – definition and synonyms

NOUN 🔊 Pronunciation /fæd/

1 something that is popular or fashionable for only a short time

1 Can you think of any current food fads? Which foods are fashionable now?

2 Are there any food fads connected with different ways of cooking? Or different ways of eating?

3 Which older food fads have gone out of fashion?

B READ FOR GIST Read *Food fads* quickly. What is the writer's opinion about superfoods?

a They're just a fad – they aren't really very good for you.

b Expensive superfoods are much healthier than cheaper food.

c You don't need to spend a lot of money to buy some superfoods.

d Most superfoods are actually bad for your health.

FOOD FADS

Hi again! This week, I've decided to look at one of the biggest food fads of the 21st century: superfoods. Let's try to sort the facts from the fiction!

Quinoa has a long history as a superfood: it was known to the ancient Incas as 'the mother of all grains' because it was so healthy. Even today it's recommended by NASA as the perfect food for long space flights. Ex C Q1 Like all whole grains, it can help your body fight a variety of diseases, and it contains lots of vitamins, minerals and fibre. It's also one of the best sources of protein, so it's perfect for vegetarians and vegans, too. Amazing!

Goji berries are another great source of plant-based protein. These sweet berries have been used in China for centuries as a way to protect against illness. They contain less sugar than other fruits, so they're one of the healthiest snacks around. Unfortunately, they can be dangerous for some people, Ex C Q5 so always check with your doctor before eating them.

Ex C Q3

Açaí berries are perhaps the most successful superfoods of all: not long ago, they were unknown outside of Brazil. Now, açaí products are big business. Ex C Q6 Why are they so popular? Well, some people believe these berries will help them to grow old more slowly ... or even to live longer. Like goji berries, they're full of chemicals which seem to protect our hearts and our brains. Sounds good, right?

Chia seeds are known as the healthiest food on the planet. The name 'chia' comes from the ancient Mayan word for 'strength'. Out of all the foods in the world, chia seeds contain some of the most nutrients for the fewest calories. They're also one of the best sources of fibre, which is great for your digestive system. Ex C Even better, they make you feel full ... so you'll eat fewer snacks! Ex C

7.2 Food fads

LEAD-IN

With books closed, write on the board *one year ago, five years ago* and *ten years ago*. Tell them to think of something that used to be very popular at that time but isn't any more. Elicit a couple of examples to get them started. Put students into pairs to compare ideas. Share ideas as a whole class to see how similar everyone's answers are.

READING

A Point out the definition of a *fad* and use students' answers from the *Lead-In* to check understanding. Put students into pairs

to discuss the questions. Get feedback and write any useful language that comes up on the board.

Possible answers:
1 non-dairy milk, e.g. almond milk; salted caramel
2 raw diets
3 low-fat diets

B Tell students they're going to read a blog post about food fads. Set a time limit and tell students to read the post and to choose which sentence best describes the writer's opinion. Point out the glossary but tell students they don't need to understand every word to do this task.

GRAMMAR HUB

7.2 Comparatives and superlatives; *the …, the …*
Comparatives and superlatives

	Comparative	Superlative
Short adjectives (one syllable)	adj + -er (+ *than*) cheap → cheap**er**	*the* + adj + -*est* cheap → **the** cheap**est**
Longer adjectives	*more* + adj (+ *than*) popular → **more** popular	*the most* + adj popular → **the most** popular
Irregular adjectives	good → **better** (+ *than*) bad → **worse** (+ *than*)	good → **the best** bad → **the worst**
Adverbs	*more* + adv (+ *than*) quickly → **more** quickly	*the most* + adv quickly → **the most** quickly
Irregular adverbs	badly → **worse** far → **farther/further** fast → fast**er** hard → hard**er** well → **better**	badly → **the worst** far → **the farthest / the furthest** fast → **the** fast**est** hard → **the** hard**est** well → **the best**
Countable nouns	many nutrients → **more** nutrients few nutrients → few**er** nutrients	many nutrients → **the most** nutrients few nutrients → **the** few**est** nutrients
Uncountable nouns	much protein → **more** protein little fibre → **less** fibre	much protein → **the most** protein little fibre → **the least** fibre

- We use comparative adjectives and adverbs to say how two or more things or actions are different.
- We use superlative adjectives and adverbs to say that something is the top or bottom of a group.
- For adjectives ending in *-e* or *-y* the rules differ a little.

  Your meal is larger than mine, but Harry's is the largest.
  Carrot soup is tastier than pea soup, but chicken soup is the tastiest of all.

- For adjectives which end with one vowel and one consonant, we double the final consonant before adding *-er* or *-est*.

  These melons are bigger than those ones.

- To make negative comparatives and superlatives, we use *less* instead of *more* and *the least* instead of *the most*.
- We never use *more* or *the most* together with *-er* or *-est*.

  I think juice is healthier than coffee. NOT ~~I think juice is more healthier than coffee.~~

- We only use *than* when it is followed by the thing we are comparing.

  This dish is good but this one is better. NOT ~~This dish is good but this one is better than.~~

the …, the …

the + comparative adjective + noun, *the* + comparative adjective + noun	**The fresher** the ingredients, **the better** the dish.
the + comparative adjective + clause, *the* + comparative adjective + clause	**The more tasty** it is, **the more satisfied** they will be.
the + comparative adverb + clause, *the* + comparative adverb + clause	**The faster** it boils, **the more quickly** it will be ready.
the + *more/less* + noun + clause, *the* + *more/less* + noun + clause	**The more recipes** you learn, **the more food** you can cook.
the + *more/less* + clause, *the* + *more/less* + clause	**The more I practised, the less I needed** a cookbook.

- We use *the …, the* to show that two changes are closely connected. As one thing changes, the other thing changes too.
- Sometimes we use the very simplest form of this structure, using comparative adjectives only, and no verb.

  The more, the merrier.

- We don't have to use only the forms shown in the table above. We can also combine different parts of the structures.

  The more complicated the recipe, the longer it takes.
  The less we spend on food, the more money we have.

C Tell students to read the post again and to match the foods to the questions. Tell students to underline the sections of the text which helped them find the answer. Check answers as a whole.

D Put students into groups to discuss the questions. Encourage students to expand on their answers and talk about their own experiences with superfoods or healthy food.

GRAMMAR

A Tell students to cover the blog post and to look at the sentences. Tell them to try to complete the sentences with one word in each space, either from what they remember or by guessing. When all students have tried this, tell them to uncover the post and check.

B Direct students to the Grammar Hub on pages 134 and 135 (see TB78 and below).

C Put students into pairs to compare the ideas. Point out the example and elicit another from the class. If students have strong opinions about any of the topics, offer them up for debate with the class. Encourage students to use as many comparatives as they can when comparing or contrasting the ideas.

SPEAKING

Point out the example and elicit one or two more to make sure students are confident at forming questions with the superlative. Tell students to ask and answer more questions in pairs. Ask students to share the most interesting answers to their questions with the class. Finish with feedback on how well students used superlatives during the task praising good usage and working through any errors you noticed.

GRAMMAR HUB

7.2 Comparatives and superlatives; the …, the …

A Complete the sentences with the correct form of the adjectives and adverbs in brackets.

1 The ____fastest____ (fast) the pizza delivery man can get here is 15 minutes.

2 You can buy cheese __more cheaply__ (cheaply) in the street market than in the shops.

3 The food in the airport was bad, but the meal on the plane was ____worse____ (bad).

4 I made the soup with ____fewer____ (few) ingredients than it says in the recipe.

5 The ____best____ (good) way to serve this dessert is with a little cream.

6 I would prefer to try a ____milder____ (mild) curry than the one you're eating.

B Complete the sentences with the words and phrases in the box.

> less meat   more often   more quickly   the better
>   the more money   the sweeter   you disagree

1 The ____less meat____ you eat, the healthier it is for your heart.

2 The more sugar you add, ____the sweeter____ the sauce will be.

3 The ____more quickly____ you eat your salad, the sooner you'll have dessert!

4 The more ____you disagree____ with me, the less likely I am to change my mind!

5 The ____more often____ you reheat food, the more unsafe it becomes.

6 The less food we throw away, __the more money__ we'll save.

C Correct the mistakes in each sentence.

1 The peas will cook ~~more fast~~ than the potatoes. *faster*

2 I think the ~~most~~ sourest taste of any food is vinegar.

3 Salad is the ~~least~~ filling than pasta. *less*

4 First prize in the competition will go to the person who cooks the ~~more~~ creatively. *most*

5 I put very little sugar in Jim's coffee, but he wanted even more ~~little~~! *less*

6 Chia seeds have ~~much~~ protein than some foods, but quinoa has the most. *more*

D Write one word in each gap to complete the sentences.

1 Is fast food ____more____ popular than home-cooking in your country?

2 My old mixer worked quite well, but this one works much ____better____.

3 Water is the ____least____ fattening drink you can have because it has zero calories!

4 Raw food is generally healthier ____than____ cooked food.

5 All these curries are spicy, but this one is the hottest ____of____ all!

6 The older the wine is, ____the____ better it gets.

7 The salad plates are quite large, but the dinner plates are __larger/bigger__.

8 Mmm! This is ____the____ most delicious meal I've ever had!

➤ Go back to page 80.

C READ FOR SPECIFIC INFORMATION   Read again. Write *A* (açaí berries), *B* (broccoli), *C* (chia seeds), *G* (goji berries) or *Q* (quinoa).

According to the blog post, which superfood …

1   isn't only eaten on our planet?   Q
2   is much cheaper than other superfoods?   B
3   might help you stay younger for longer?   A
4   can help you digest your food more effectively?   C
5   might not be safe for everybody?   G
6   has become popular very quickly?   A
7   helps you to eat less food between meals?   C

D SPEAK   Work in groups and discuss the questions.

1   Do you think it's worth paying more money for superfoods? Why/Why not?
2   Do you think it is more important for you to eat healthy food or tasty food? Why?
3   What are some simple ways that we can eat more healthily?

But before you all rush out to buy superfoods from your local health food shop, remember that superfoods are usually super expensive, too! And do you know what? Strawberries are probably just as good for you as goji berries and açaí berries. Similarly, quinoa and chia seeds are great because they're whole grains. But you can get all that fibre far more cheaply by eating plenty of brown bread, brown rice and whole grain pasta. And what's the best superfood of all? Broccoli! It's cheap, tasty and incredibly good   Ex C Q2 for you. It isn't quite as exciting as quinoa, but it's a lot less expensive!

Glossary

fibre (n) the parts of fruit, vegetables and grains that your body cannot digest (= turn into substances it can use); it helps food to pass through your body

nutrient (n) a substance in food that plants, animals and people need to live and grow

protein (n) a substance in food, such as meat, eggs read milk, that people need in order to grow and be healthy

GRAMMAR
Comparatives and superlatives

A Cover the *Food fads* article. Complete the sentences with one word in each space. Then check your answers in the blog post.

1   This week, I've decided to look at one of _____the_____ biggest food fads of the 21st century: superfoods.

2   They contain _____less_____ sugar _____than_____ other fruits, so they're one of _____the_____ healthiest snacks around.

3   Chia seeds contain some of the _____most_____ nutrients for the _____fewest_____ calories.

4   Even better, they make you feel full … so you'll eat _____fewer_____ snacks!

5   Some people believe these berries will help them to grow old _____more_____ slowly … or even to live _____longer____.

6   It isn't quite _____as_____ exciting _____as_____ quinoa, but it's a lot _____less_____ expensive!

B Go to the Grammar Hub on page 134.

C SPEAK   Work in pairs. Compare each set of ideas.

1   quinoa vs white rice
2   broccoli vs ice cream
3   supermarkets vs health food shops
4   fast food vs superfoods
5   cooking vs eating out
6   eating alone vs eating in a large group

A: *Quinoa is much tastier than white rice.*
B: *Yes, but it's a lot more expensive.*

SPEAKING

Work in pairs. Use the superlative form of the words and phrases in the box to ask and answer questions.

> bad   expensive   far (to travel for a meal)
> few ingredients   little money (to spend on food)
> much time (to spend preparing a meal)   spicy

A: *What's the furthest you've ever travelled for a meal?*
B: *Not very far. I usually buy all my food in the local shop. But once I spent an hour cycling to the 'best ice cream shop in town'. But it wasn't as good as I expected.*

7.2

LISTENING

A Work in pairs. Do the **Reduce Your Waste** quiz. Then go to the Communication Hub on page 153 to check your answers.

B You are going to listen to part of a radio show about a family who are trying to waste less food. Look at the pictures (1–6) and guess the answers to the questions. Then listen and check your answers.

7.5

REDUCE YOUR WASTE ♻ 🚚

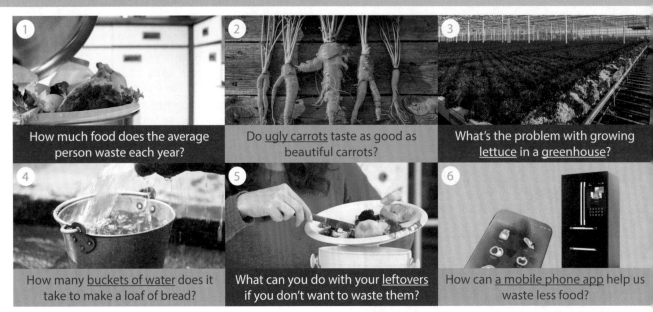

1 How long can you store these things before they go bad?
a fresh milk in a fridge
b frozen vegetables in a freezer
c fresh bananas
d dry food (e.g. pasta)
e an opened bottle of apple juice in a fridge
f a plate of leftovers in a fridge

2 True or false?
a You can safely reheat food as many times as you like.
b Most food is still safe to eat after it has passed its best-before date.
c You must eat rice within 24 hours of cooking it.

1 How much food does the average person waste each year?

2 Do <u>ugly carrots</u> taste as good as beautiful carrots?

3 What's the problem with growing <u>lettuce</u> in a <u>greenhouse</u>?

4 How many <u>buckets of water</u> does it take to make a loaf of bread?

5 What can you do with your <u>leftovers</u> if you don't want to waste them?

6 How can <u>a mobile phone app</u> help us waste less food?

C Who expressed each of these opinions: *Mrs Taylor, Mr Taylor, Alison* or *Philip*? Use the strategies in the box to help you.

Identifying people's opinions

When you're listening, pay attention to whether people are just <u>describing a situation</u> or <u>expressing an opinion</u> about it.

Adjectives like *great* and *awful* usually show that the person is expressing an opinion.

1 Food doesn't need to be beautiful.   *Mrs Taylor*

2 I like collecting and studying detailed information about our experiment.   Philip

3 Food waste is bad for our planet.   Mr Taylor

4 I didn't like eating the same food the next day.   Alison

5 I enjoy cooking meals to use up the food in the fridge.   Philip

6 Money isn't the most important reason for reducing waste.   Mr Taylor

D SPEAK Work in pairs. How much food do you think you waste in your family?

GRAMMAR
the ..., the ...

A WORK IT OUT Look at the sentences from the radio show. Match the beginnings of the sentences (1–5) with the endings (a–e).

1 The more I researched the topic,

2 The less food we throw away,

3 The less we cook,

4 The longer we do it,

5 The more carefully you count things,

a the more normal it feels.

b the better.

c the more I realised that we aren't just throwing away food.

d the more accurate your results will be.

e the less we waste.

B Read the rule and complete the example. Use the words in brackets to help you.

the ..., the ...

To show that two changes are closely connected, we use *the* + comparative, *the* + comparative. As one thing changes, it makes the other thing change.

As far as I'm concerned, the ____uglier____ *(ugly), the* ____better____ *(good)!*

C Go to the Grammar Hub on page 134.

7.2 Food fads

LISTENING

A Put students into pairs to do the quiz. Check understanding of *leftovers*, *reheat* and *passed its best-before date*. Share some ideas as a whole class and encourage debate if they have very different answers. Don't confirm or deny any answers yet. Direct students to the **Communication Hub** on page 153 to check their answers. Ask students if they found anything surprising.

B Tell students they're going to listen to a radio show about a family who are trying to waste less food. Tell students to look at the questions and the pictures and to guess the answers. Use the

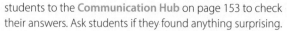

AUDIOSCRIPT

🔊 **7.5**

Listening, Exercise B
H = Host   MT = Mrs Taylor   MrT = Mr Taylor
P = Philip   A = Alison

H: Hello and welcome to The Food Fad Show. Today, we're talking about food waste. Did you know that globally, we waste a huge amount of the food we produce. The average person, just one person, wastes £200 of food every year. Can you believe that? £200!
In the studio today, we have the Taylor family. A year ago, they decided to reduce the amount of food they waste every year by 50 per cent. Tell us more, Mrs Taylor.

MT: Well, I've been interested in food waste for a long time. But the more I researched the topic, the more I realised that we aren't just throwing away food; we're also throwing away hundreds of pounds per year – enough to pay for a nice family holiday. That's when I decided we needed to cut our own waste dramatically.

H: OK, so what have you done to save money?

Ex C Q1 MT: Let me give you an example. Ugly carrots taste just as good as beautiful carrots, but in our local supermarket, they cost less than half as much. As far as I'm concerned, the uglier, the better! Also, my supermarket always lowers the price of meat or dairy products that are getting close to their best-before date. So it's usually possible to buy food a lot more cheaply by checking those dates carefully. As long as you eat the food soon after buying it, it's completely safe.

H: Right. So it's all about money, then, Mr Taylor?

Ex C Q6 MrT: No, not really. Food production has a massive impact on the environment: first to produce the food and distribute it, and then to get rid of any waste. I always thought the best way to save the planet was to reduce the amount of rubbish we throw away and to reuse and recycle as much

Ex C Q3 as possible. But in fact, the food itself has a much greater impact than the packaging it comes in. For example, throwing away a lettuce harms our planet 100 times more than throwing away the plastic bag.

H: Really? That's amazing. Why?

MrT: Well, just think of all the water needed to grow it, the electricity to keep the greenhouse at just the right temperature, and then the environmental cost of keeping it fresh all the way from the farm to your fridge. It all adds up!

H: Wow! I'd never thought of that!

MrT: Here's another example. It takes 100 buckets of water to bake one loaf of bread. A hundred! Think about that next time you throw away some one-day-old bread. If we could end all food waste

around the world, it would be like taking one quarter of the world's cars off the roads. As far as I'm concerned, the less food we throw away, the better.

H: OK, so what have you done to cut down on food waste? Alison?

A: Yes, well, before our experiment, Mum or Dad always dished up a large plate of food for each of us, but it was usually too much for me. So half of it always went in the bin. These days, we all help ourselves to food from a serving dish in the middle of the table. It's great because now we only take what we want – and we eat everything on our plates. It's much better because the less we cook, the less we waste.

H: OK, great. And what about leftovers?

A: When we started off, we had a rule that we had to eat yesterday's leftovers before any fresh food.

Ex C Q4 But it was awful, so we stopped it. I mean, yesterday's leftovers are disgusting! Who wants to eat those? But now we use those leftovers to make soup or a stew. It's still a bit strange, but the longer we do it, the more normal it feels.

H: Yes, I'm sure. OK, and what about Philip? Can I ask you a question or are you too busy playing on your phone?

P: Don't worry – I'm not playing. I wanted to show you a cool mobile phone app. It helps us keep track of exactly what food we've got in the house – and when that food will go bad.

H: Oh, right. Sorry. So … how does it work?

P: Well, you need to type in all the numbers whenever you buy – or eat – anything. Some people might find that a bit of a waste of time, but I like that sort of thing. Of course, you don't need to count every single potato, for example,

Ex C Q2 but the more carefully you count things, the more accurate your results will be. It's really fascinating when you study the numbers. Now, whenever we're in the supermarket, we can check what we need and what we don't. The app also sends us a notification when something is getting close to its best-before date. That's really useful.

H: Yes, I'm sure.

Ex C Q5 P: And it even suggests delicious meal ideas to use up the ingredients we've got, instead of buying new ones all the time. I never enjoyed cooking before, but thanks to the app, it's a lot more fun. And best of all, the app tells us exactly how much money we're saving every day.

H: Ah, yes. Tell us about the money, Mr Taylor.

MrT: Well, so far, it's been a great success. According to Philip's app, we've managed to save £730 in food bills alone over the past year. And guess what? We're off on holiday next week to celebrate our fantastic achievement.

H: Wow! Congratulations!

pictures to make sure students understand all the vocabulary in the questions. Elicit some ideas from the class but don't provide the answers yet. Ask students to listen to the radio show and check their answers. When checking answers, highlight the word *stew* (a dish made by cooking vegetables, and usually meat or fish, slowly in liquid), which is used in the answer to 5.

1 *7.2 million tonnes*
2 *yes*
3 *It has a high cost to the environment because you need to keep the temperature just right.*
4 *100*
5 *You can make them into soup or a stew.*
6 *by helping us to check the best-before dates of the food in our fridge; by suggesting ways of using the food we already have*

C Point out the information in the box about *identifying people's opinions*. Tell students to look at the opinions and try to remember who expressed each one. Tell students to listen again and to check using the strategies in the box to help them.

D Put students into pairs to discuss how much food they think they waste in their family. Elicit some ideas as a whole class and find out the most common causes of food waste in the class.

GRAMMAR

A Elicit that all the sentences are from the radio show. Tell them to match the beginnings of the sentences with the endings.

B Tell students to look at the rule, and at the sentences from Exercise A, then to complete the example. Check students remember the rules for how to form comparatives here as well.

C Direct students to the **Grammar Hub** on pages 134 and 135 (see TB78 and 79). Use the **Grammar Worksheet** on W27 for extra practice.

PRONUNCIATION

A Put students into pairs to pronounce the words above the box, using the information in the box. Play the audio for them to listen and repeat.

chew /tʃuː/
cow /kaʊ/
own /əʊn/
raw /rɔː/
stew /stjuː/

B Tell students to look at the words in bold in the sentences and to put them in the gaps in the box from Exercise A. Play the audio for students to check.

C Tell students to practise saying the sentences in Exercise B with a partner. Encourage them to say the sentences several times, getting a bit faster each time. Tell them to make sure their partners are still pronouncing the words properly.

VOCABULARY

A Elicit that the words in the box are all connected to waste. Tell them to match the words to their definitions.

B Tell students to complete the gaps in the questions with a word from Exercise A. Check answers as a whole class. Tell students to discuss the questions with a partner. Use the **Vocabulary Worksheet** on W28 for extra practice.

SPEAKING HUB

A Tell students they're going to think of ways to reduce food waste in their home by 50 per cent. Elicit examples of how this could be done, then put students into pairs. Tell them to look at the suggestions and to make notes about each one.

B Tell each pair to prepare their presentation, using the notes they made in Exercise A. When they are ready, tell each pair to make their presentation. Tell the other students to listen carefully and to think about how similar or different the other pairs' ideas are.

C Put students into groups to discuss the questions, using their notes to help them. When the groups have discussed all the questions, tell them to use those questions as criteria to choose the best two or three ideas.

D Put students into new groups to discuss the questions. Get whole-class feedback and find out which students are going to make the biggest changes to their lifestyle.

Simple variations on well-known games are helpful in familiarising students with phonemic symbols:

- **Phoneme bingo:** Hand out bingo cards with phonemes instead of numbers; call out sounds rather than numbers (see the *Phoneme bingo cards* resource on the DVD).

- **Anagrams:** Get students to work out anagrams of words using phonemes rather than normal alphabetic letters, e.g. /kbʊ/ (= book).

- **Category words:** Choose five or six categories – such as 'Food', 'Sports', 'Animals', 'Household objects', 'Clothing', etc – which students should copy down. Students work in small teams. When you call out (and write up) a phoneme, the teams must attempt to find a word containing that phoneme for each category. So, for example, if the phoneme is /iː/, a team could choose *cheese, skiing, sheep, teapot* and *jeans*. The teams then compare words and points are awarded.

PRONUNCIATION
Vowel + w

A How do you pronounce these words? Use the strategies in the box to help you. Then listen and repeat the words.

> chew   cow   own   raw   stew

Vowel + w

Three vowels, *a*, *e* and *o*, often combine with *w* to make a new sound. There are two possible sounds for *e + w* and *o + w*.

a + w /ɔ:/ for, draw, awful, ____awesome____, ____law____

e + w /ju:/ you, knew, view, ____few____

e + w /u:/ too, jewellery, threw, ____flew____, ____grew____

o + w /əʊ/ go, low, owe, ____flown____, ____throw____, ____know____, ____slowly____, ____grown____

o + w /aʊ/ out, how, wow, ____allowed____, ____flowers____, ____now____

B Look at the bold words in these sentences. Write them in the correct place in the box in Exercise A. Then listen and check your answers.

1 'Have you ever **flown** in a helicopter?' 'Yes, I **flew** in one a **few** weeks ago. It was **awesome**.'

2 You aren't **allowed** to **throw** away your rubbish here! Don't you **know** it's against the **law**!

3 The **flowers grew** quite **slowly** at first, but **now** they're **grown** really big.

C SPEAK Work in pairs. Practise saying the sentences in Exercise B. Listen and check your partner's pronunciation.

VOCABULARY
Waste

A Match the definitions (1–8) with the words and phrases in the box.

> bin   cut down   get rid of   recycle   reduce
> reuse   rubbish   throw away   use up   ~~waste~~

1 to not use something that you could use — ____waste____

2 a container for putting rubbish in — ____bin____

3 things that you throw away because they are no longer useful — ____rubbish____

4 to use all of something, so there's no waste — ____use up____

5 to change waste materials such as newspapers and bottles so that they can be used again — ____recycle____

6 to use something again — ____reuse____

7 to use less of something — ____cut down____, ____reduce____

8 to get rid of something that you no longer want — ____get rid of____, ____throw away____

B SPEAK Complete the questions with one word in each space. Then work in pairs and discuss the questions.

1 Do you ____recycle____ plastic and glass containers so they can be turned into new products, or do you just get ____rid____ of them?

2 Do you ____reuse____ plastic bags again and again, or throw them in the ____bin____?

3 How could restaurants cut ____down____ the amount of ____waste/rubbish____ they throw ____away____ each week?

SPEAKING HUB

A Work in pairs. How could you reduce food waste in your home by fifty per cent? Write notes about:

- shopping habits (how often? how much?)
- meal planning (weekly menus)
- leftovers
- food storage (fridge? cupboard? special containers?)
- apps and gadgets

B PRESENT Use your notes to prepare a short presentation on how you can help people reduce their food waste. Present your ideas to the class.

C DISCUSS Work in groups. Use these questions to compare your ideas from Exercise B. Then choose the best two or three ideas.

- Which ideas will be easiest for people to understand and follow?
- Which ideas will make the biggest difference?
- Which ideas might cost people more money? Which ideas might save them money?

D REFLECT Work in groups and discuss the questions.

1 Are you going to try to reduce your own food waste? How?

2 Will you try to persuade others to cut their food waste? How?

○ Compare different types of food
○ Compare a range of solutions and choose the best one

COMPREHENSION

A Work in pairs and discuss the questions.

What do you do when you're feeling upset or worried?

Do you cook, go for a run, phone a friend, watch a good film or something else?

B ▶ 00:00–01:30 **Watch the first part of the video and answer the questions.**

1 What is Gaby's big news? She really likes Sam.

2 What does Milly think about her news? She thinks it's great.

3 What is Gaby upset about? She left Sam a letter expressing her feelings for him and he hasn't mentioned it.

C ▶ 00:56–01:21 **Find and correct five mistakes in the story that Gaby told Milly. What advice do you think Milly will give? Watch to check your answers.**

It was about a week ago. ~~Last Wednesday,~~ Monday Sam had to leave work early and so he asked me to ~~took after~~ lock up the café. I had decided to tell him how I felt, and so before I locked up, I wrote a ~~poem~~ letter expressing my true feelings for him. ... And I left it on the ~~doormat~~ counter for him to find. He ~~can't~~ must have seen it.

FUNCTIONAL LANGUAGE
Making suggestions

A Match the two halves of the extracts from the video.

Making a suggestion

1	Have you tried		a	cook something delicious.
2	What about		b	take some time to think about it.
3	The best thing might be		c	talking to him about it?
4	If I were you, I'd		d	put on some whipped cream and sprinkles?
5	Why don't we		e	sending a text or an email or something?
6	We could		f	to just ask him if he got the letter.

B Complete the phrases in the table.

Saying no to a suggestion	Saying yes to a suggestion
No, I _____can't_____. I don't know what to say.	That's a good _____idea_____.
No, that wouldn't _____work_____. To say what?	It's worth a _____try_____.
That's a _____terrible_____ idea. I'm already really embarrassed.	Good _____plan_____.

C ▶ 01:21–04:13 **Watch the second part of the video and check your answers to Exercises A and B.**

MILLY   SAM   NEENA   ZAC   GABY

USEFUL PHRASES

A Match the useful phrases (1–4) with the screenshots (a–d).

1 What's up?   a   3 It'll help take your mind off Sam.   c

2 Great timing!   d   4 He's been acting like nothing happened!   b

B How do you say these useful phrases in your language?

PRONUNCIATION
Suggestions

A Listen to the extracts from the video and underline the stressed/key words. Does the intonation rise or fall at the end of each phrase?

Milly: Have you tried talking to him about it? (↑)

Gaby: No, I can't. I don't know what to say. (↓)

Milly: Or, what about sending him a text (↑) or an email or something? (↓)

Gaby: No, that wouldn't work. (↓) To say what? (↑)

Milly: I don't know exactly. The best thing might be to just ask him if he got the letter? (↓)

Gaby: No, no, no, no, no, no, no, no! That's a terrible idea. I'm already really embarrassed. (↓)

Milly: If I were you, I'd take some time to think about it. (↓)

B In pairs, practise the conversation. Copy the stress and intonation.

SPEAKING

A Work in pairs. Think about possible solutions to the problems below.

1 I'm having a dinner party, but I hate cooking.

2 I want to eat more healthily, but superfoods are too expensive.

3 I want to save some money, but I love going out to restaurants!

4 I often have leftover food, but I don't want to waste it.

5 I want to grow vegetables, but I live in an apartment.

B DISCUSS Take it in turns to read out a problem and make suggestions using the phrases in Functional Language Exercise A.

A: I'm having a dinner party, but I hate cooking.
B: What about getting a takeaway?

◯– Make suggestions

➤ Turn to page 162 to learn how to write a reply in an online discussion forum.

7.3 Comfort eating

LEAD-IN

Put students into two teams. Give students cards with different emotions on them (i.e. *worried, sad, happy, stressed, embarrassed*). The student with the card has to act the emotion out for their team to guess.

COMPREHENSION

A Check the meaning of *upset* and then elicit one or two ideas of things students do to make them feel better.

B ▶ 00:00–01:30 Elicit what they can remember about Gaby, Milly and Sam. Tell them to read the questions, then watch and answer them.

C ▶ 00:56–01:21 Tell students to find and correct the five factual mistakes in Gaby's story. Ask them to discuss with a partner what advice they think Milly will give. Play the video again for students to check.

FUNCTIONAL LANGUAGE

A Tell students to match the two halves to complete the sentences.

B Tell students to complete the spaces in the phrases in the table. Point out that the phrases are all related to saying yes or no to suggestions.

C ▶ 01:21–04:13 Play the video once again for students to check their answers to Exercises A and B.

USEFUL PHRASES

A Tell students to match the useful phrases from the video with the screenshots.

B Tell students to think about how they would say these phrases in their language.

PRONUNCIATION

7.8

A Tell students to listen to the extracts from the video and underline the stressed/keywords. Tell them to listen carefully to decide if the intonation rises or falls at the end of each phrase.

B Put students into pairs to practise reading the conversation, paying careful attention to the stress and intonation.

SPEAKING

A Elicit some solutions to the first problem as an example with the class. Next, put students into pairs to think of possible solutions to the other problems. Share ideas as a whole class.

B Tell students to work in pairs and to take it in turns to read out a problem. After one student has read out a problem, the other has to make a suggestion. The first student can either accept or reject the suggestion. If they reject it, their partner has to make another suggestion. Continue until the first student is happy with the suggested solution.

▶ VIDEOSCRIPT

M = Milly   G = Gabby   Z = Zac

M: So … I got your text. What's up?

G: Oh, Milly! It's big news.

M: Woah. You're starting to sound like Zac. What's going on?

G: Please – sit down.

M: So?

G: So … I like Sam.

M: So do I!

G: No, I mean, I really like Sam …

M: Oh … that's … great!

G: No. It's not great …

M: Why?

G: Well … It was about a week ago …
Last Monday, Sam had to leave work early and so he asked me to close up the café. I had decided to tell him how I felt, and so before I locked up, I wrote a letter expressing my true feelings for him.
… And I left it on the counter for him to find. He must have seen it.

M: So … What did he say?

G: Nothing. Nada. Zero. And all week, he's been acting like nothing happened!

M: Oh … Have you tried talking to him about it?

G: No … I can't, I … I don't know what to say … Anyway, he clearly doesn't feel the same, so … There's nothing to say …

M: Or … what about sending him a text or an email or something?

G: No, that wouldn't work … to say what?

M: I don't know exactly. The best thing might be to just ask him if he got the letter?

G: No no no no no! That's a terrible idea. I'm already really embarrassed. I'm not going to embarrass myself anymore.

M: Well … if that's how you feel …

G: I don't know Milly … I'm thinking about moving back to my parent's house in Madrid. You know, save up some money …

M: Well … If I were you, I'd take some time to think about it … Hey, I have an idea.

G: What?

M: You hungry?

G: A little.

M: Why don't we cook something delicious! It'll help take your mind off Sam!

G: OK. That's a good idea. It's worth a try.

M: OK … the recipe says it should be cooked by now.

G: Oh. It looks a bit sad. It looks like me.

M: We could put on some whipped cream and sprinkles?

G: And maybe some fruit on top?

M: Good plan.

G, Z, M (together): Oooooooooo!

Z: Great timing.

M: Ready?

G: GO!

Unit 7 Writing

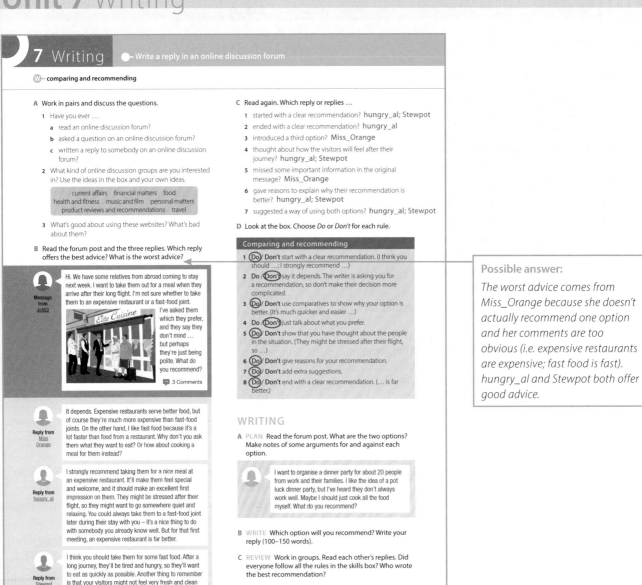

7 Writing ● Write a reply in an online discussion forum

W— comparing and recommending

A Work in pairs and discuss the questions.

1 Have you ever …
  a read an online discussion forum?
  b asked a question on an online discussion forum?
  c written a reply to somebody on an online discussion forum?

2 What kind of online discussion groups are you interested in? Use the ideas in the box and your own ideas.

> current affairs financial matters food
> health and fitness music and film personal matters
> product reviews and recommendations travel

3 What's good about using these websites? What's bad about them?

B Read the forum post and the three replies. Which reply offers the best advice? What is the worst advice?

Message from Jo493
Hi. We have some relatives from abroad coming to stay next week. I want to take them out for a meal when they arrive after their long journey. I'm not sure whether to take them to an expensive restaurant or a fast-food joint. I've asked them which they prefer, and they say they don't mind … but perhaps they're just being polite. What do you recommend?

💬 3 Comments

Reply from Miss Orange
It depends. Expensive restaurants serve better food, but of course they're much more expensive than fast-food joints. On the other hand, I like fast food because it's a lot faster than food from a restaurant. Why don't you ask them what they want to eat instead? Or how about cooking a meal for them instead?

Reply from hungry_al
I strongly recommend taking them for a nice meal at an expensive restaurant. It'll make them feel special and welcome, and it should make an excellent first impression on them. They might be stressed after their flight, so they might want to go somewhere quiet and relaxing. You could always take them to a fast-food joint later during their stay with you – it's a nice thing to do with somebody you already know well. But for that first meeting, an expensive restaurant is far better.

Reply from Stewpot
I think you should take them for some fast food. After a long journey, they'll be tired and hungry, so they'll want to eat as quickly as possible. Another thing to remember is that your visitors might not feel very fresh and clean after their journey, and they may not have suitable clothes for a nice restaurant. So you'll have to take them home first so they can change their clothes … and that could take hours. It's much quicker and easier if you take them for some simple food at a fast-food joint. After all, you can always take them to your favourite restaurant the next day. Good luck!

C Read again. Which reply or replies …

1 started with a clear recommendation? hungry_al; Stewpot
2 ended with a clear recommendation? hungry_al
3 introduced a third option? Miss_Orange
4 thought about how the visitors will feel after their journey? hungry_al; Stewpot
5 missed some important information in the original message? Miss_Orange
6 gave reasons to explain why their recommendation is better? hungry_al; Stewpot
7 suggested a way of using both options? hungry_al; Stewpot

D Look at the box. Choose *Do* or *Don't* for each rule.

Comparing and recommending

1 **Do** / Don't start with a clear recommendation. (I think you should …; I strongly recommend …)
2 Do / **Don't** say it depends. The writer is asking you for a recommendation, so don't make their decision more complicated.
3 **Do** / Don't use comparatives to show why your option is better. (It's much quicker and easier …)
4 Do / **Don't** just talk about what you prefer.
5 **Do** / Don't show that you have thought about the people in the situation. (They might be stressed after their flight, so …)
6 **Do** / Don't give reasons for your recommendation.
7 **Do** / Don't add extra suggestions.
8 **Do** / Don't end with a clear recommendation. (… is far better.)

WRITING

A PLAN Read the forum post. What are the two options? Make notes of some arguments for and against each option.

> I want to organise a dinner party for about 20 people from work and their families. I like the idea of a pot luck dinner party, but I've heard they don't always work well. Maybe I should just cook all the food myself. What do you recommend?

B WRITE Which option will you recommend? Write your reply (100–150 words).

C REVIEW Work in groups. Read each other's replies. Did everyone follow all the rules in the skills box? Who wrote the best recommendation?

Possible answer:
The worst advice comes from Miss_Orange because she doesn't actually recommend one option and her comments are too obvious (i.e. expensive restaurants are expensive; fast food is fast). hungry_al and Stewpot both offer good advice.

Refer students to these forum posts as a model for the writing task.

WRITING

Write *expensive restaurant* and *fast-food restaurant* on the board. Tell students to think of advantages and disadvantages of eating in each. Elicit an example, then put students into pairs to think of more.

A Put students into pairs to discuss the questions. Get answers from the class as a whole and encourage students to expand on their answers. If students have written on an online discussion forum, ask them to describe what they wrote about.

B Tell students to look at the picture and elicit what it shows. Tell them to read the forum post and replies and decide which advice they think is the best and the worst. Explain that *fast-food joint* is a more informal way of saying *fast-food restaurant*.

C Tell students to read the posts again and to match the replies to the questions.

D Tell students to use the replies to help them complete the dos and don'ts in the box. Elicit the first answer as an example, showing students that examples of this can be found in the posts that are more successfully written.

WRITING TASK

A Tell students to read the forum post and to find the two options. Establish that the two options are a pot luck dinner party or cooking all the food yourself for a dinner party. Put students into pairs to think of arguments for and against each option. Elicit ideas from the class as a whole to ensure everyone has a good number of ideas for the writing task.

B Tell students to choose which option they will recommend and write their reply. Tell them to refer to the dos and don'ts in Exercise D as they do this.

C Put students into groups to read each other's replies. Tell them to think about whether they agree with the suggestions and how well the writer has followed the dos and don'ts. Get some whole-class feedback on what are the best replies.

GRAMMAR

A Choose the best words to complete the conversation.

A: Do you want some of this pot luck stew? I made it from all of last week's leftovers: fish curry, cheesy chicken pasta, spicy vegetables …

B: Yuck! That ¹*can't / might not / **must*** taste disgusting!

A: Well, no, it actually tastes quite nice. Try it – you ²*can / might / must* like it.

B: Really? OK. I guess it ³*couldn't / **might not** / mustn't* be so bad. But don't forget I'm allergic to peanuts.

A: Don't worry, it ⁴***can't** / may not / might* contain any peanuts. I never cook with them. But it ⁵ *couldn't / **may** / must* contain some other types of nuts – I'm not sure. Is that OK?

B: Yes, that's fine. Hmm … this ⁶*can't / **could** / must* be a big mistake, but … OK, I'll try it.

B Complete the sentences with the correct form of the words in brackets.

1 I want to cook the most food for the _____least_____ (little) money. Any ideas?

2 Açaí berries are really good for you – they're much _____healthier_____ (healthy) than I thought.

3 If you want to lose weight, you need to eat _____fewer_____ (few) sweets.

4 You should come to the restaurant on a Tuesday lunchtime – that's the _____least crowded_____ (crowded) time.

5 You cooked this cake too fast! Next time, try cooking it _____more slowly_____ (slowly).

6 Cooking for ten people is far _____more stressful_____ (stressful) than cooking for one!

7 There's too much cream in this sauce. Can you make it a bit _____less creamy_____ (creamy) next time?

C Match the beginnings of the sentences (1–6) with the endings (a–f).

1 Bring all your friends to our dinner party – the more people who come,
2 The earlier you arrive at the restaurant,
3 The older I get,
4 The more sugar you add,
5 Natural food is much better for you; the fewer chemicals it contains,
6 Don't boil vegetables for too long; the longer you cook them,

a the more I prefer to stay in and cook at home.
b the less flavour they'll have.
c the more fun we'll have.
d the more likely you are to get a table.
e the sweeter it will be.
f the healthier it is.

VOCABULARY

A Complete the sentences with the correct form of the phrasal verbs in the box.

carry on   clear up   end up   put off   work out

1 I can't _____work out_____ how to turn on the microwave. Can you help me?
2 Sorry to interrupt your meal, but I need to go out for a minute. Please _____carry on_____ eating while I'm away.
3 I'm happy to cook dinner, but could you _____clear up_____ the dirty plates afterwards?
4 If you want to learn to cook, don't _____put_____ it _____off_____! Join our cookery classes today!
5 I was planning to cook a big meal, but then the oven broke so I _____ended up_____ buying takeaway pizzas for everybody.

B Choose the best adjectives to complete the sentences.

1 I think we need to cook this meat a little longer – it's still *delicious / mild / **raw*** in the middle.
2 I don't really like sweet snacks. Have you got anything *bitter / rich / **savoury***, like a sandwich?
3 Don't worry. This curry is very *buttery / **mild** / spicy* – there are no chillies or strong flavours in it.
4 The food was lovely, but it wasn't very *chewy / **filling** / spicy*. We were still hungry at the end of the meal!
5 I don't like dark chocolate – it's too *fatty / **bitter** / creamy* for me. I prefer something sweeter.
6 If you want a cheap and *disgusting / sour / **tasty*** lunch, Kate's café is the best place to go.

C Complete the advice about food waste with words in the box. There is one extra word.

bins   get   recycle   reduce   reuse   throw   use

Try these tips:
- Don't ¹ _____get_____ rid of yesterday's bread just because it isn't fresh. Make toast to ² _____use_____ up the last few pieces.
- Don't ³ _____throw_____ old plastic away. You can ⁴ _____reuse_____ the same shopping bags again and again.
- Use two (or more) ⁵ _____bins_____: one for food waste and one for containers that you can ⁶ _____recycle_____.

FUNCTIONAL LANGUAGE

Find and correct the mistakes in the sentences.

1 I don't feel like cooking tonight. Why we don't ^we eat out tonight
2 Yes, why not? What about go to The Food Zone?
   _____What about going to The Food Zone?_____
3 Again? We went there last week. Could we going to that new supper club, The Spicy Kitchen, instead?
   _____Could we go to that new supper club, The Spicy Kitchen, in_____
4 Good idea! The best thing might be phone them. They might have a free table tonight.
   _____The best thing might be to phone them._____
5 Yes, that's worth to try. Can you phone them and ask?
   _____Yes that's worth a try._____

8 Innovation

8 INNOVATION

Innovation (n) a new idea, method, piece of equipment. Synonym: breakthrough (n)

To invent, you need a good imagination and a pile of junk.

Thomas Edison

A helicopter mechanic double checks some wiring, Germany.

The quote suggests that you don't need anything very special in order to be an inventor except a good imagination. Check students understand the meaning of *junk* (old, broken or useless things).

Thomas Edison (1847–1931) was an American inventor and businessman. Edison created over 1000 inventions but one of his most famous was the light bulb. His inventions changed life all around the world.

OBJECTIVES

- explain how an invention works
- suggest and evaluate creative ideas
- use positive language to promote a new product
- give a friend advice about choosing a gadget
- give and follow instructions
- write a biography

Work with a partner. Discuss the questions.

1. Look at the picture. What characteristics would be helpful to have as a mechanic?
2. Look at the quote. Do you think you have to be imaginative to be an inventor?
3. Talk about a situation where you have been imaginative or innovative in your life.

INNOVATION   85

OBJECTIVES

Read the unit objectives to the class.

UNIT OPENER QUESTIONS

With books closed, write the word *innovation* on the board. Tell students they have one minute to make as many words as they can using only those letters. In feedback, find out who has made the most words, and who has made the longest. One of the longest possibilities is *ovation* with seven letters.

1. Tell students to open their books and to look at the picture. Elicit an example of how it could be considered creative or innovative. Drill pronunciation of both these words. Put students into pairs to think of more ways. Share any interesting answers as a whole class.

2. Tell students to read the quote and to discuss the questions. Elicit answers from the class and write any interesting vocabulary on the board.

3. Give a personal example of a situation where you have been imaginative or innovative. Encourage students to ask you follow-up questions. Put students into pairs to do the same. Share any interesting answers as a whole class.

WORKSHEETS

Lesson 8.1 Making a difference

Grammar: Relative clauses (W29)

Vocabulary: Word families; 'creative thinking' phrases (W30)

Lesson 8.2 Must-have gadgets

Grammar: Zero and first conditionals (W31)

Vocabulary: Positive adjectives (W32)

INNOVATION   TB85

- Explain how an invention works
- Suggest and evaluate creative ideas

V — word families; creative thinking   **G** — relative clauses   **P** — relative clauses
S — listening for problems and solutions

Eden Full Goh:

the inventor who is making a big difference

Eden Full Goh is perhaps not a name that you immediately recognise, but she is one of the most exciting and creative inventors of the 21st century.

Eden, who was born in Calgary, Canada, started to show talent at the age of nine, when she built a solar-powered toy car. That is where her interest in solar power began but certainly not where it stopped. She had not yet graduated from university when she came up with a very simple, but highly efficient, solar panel system that produces energy at low cost.

Eden's invention, which has won many prizes, is now used in 19 countries, where it makes a real difference to thousands of people's lives. Here is how to use it.

1. The SunSaluter is like a table. The top of the table is a solar panel, which can face in different directions.

2. Get up early in the morning when it's still dark. Fill one plastic bottle with sand and two more bottles with dirty water.

3. Attach the water bottles to the filter. At the bottom of the filter is a tube that takes clean water to a large container. At the top there's a hook that attaches the filter to the SunSaluter.

4. Hang the filter on one end of the SunSaluter, which will then go down. Hang the bottle that you filled with sand on the other end of the solar panel. Make sure the solar panel is facing the east, where the sun will rise.

5. At sunrise, when the sun comes up, the solar panel will start catching sunlight from the east.

6. During the day, the water will flow very slowly through the filter to the container, where it is stored. As the water bottles become lighter, the heavy sand bottle slowly pulls the other end of the SunSaluter down. At midday, when the sun is high in the sky, the solar panel will face upwards.

7. In the evening, when the water bottles are empty, the solar panel will face west. You can now drink the clean water that you collected during the day.

Glossary

solar panel (n) a piece of equipment that uses energy from the sun to create power

---

READING

A SPEAK **Work in pairs and discuss the questions.**

1. What famous inventors do you know? What did they invent?

2. What skills do inventors need?

B READ FOR GIST **Read** *Eden Full Goh: the inventor who is making a big difference.* **What is special about Eden and her invention?**

C READ FOR DETAIL **Read again. Match the explanations (1–7) in the text with the pictures (a–g).**

D SPEAK **Make a list of your own life goals. Use the ideas in the box to help you. Then work in pairs and compare your lists.**

> awards and prizes   career experiences   family helping other people qualifications

VOCABULARY

Word families

A **Read the box. Then complete the word families. Use** *Eden Full Goh: the inventor who is making a big difference* **to help you.**

Word families

Word families can help you learn many words together, not just one at a time. Here's an example:

innovation (n) = a new idea or product

innovator (n) = someone who thinks of new ideas or products

innovate (v) = to invent or begin using new ideas or products

innovative (adj) = an adjective to describe an innovator or an innovation

Noun (thing/idea)	Noun (person)	Verb	Adjective
a success	a success	to succeed (in something)	[1] *successful*
an [2] **invention**	an [3] **inventor**	to invent something	inventive
a design	a designer	to [4] **design** something	–
a product	a producer	to [5] **produce** something	productive
[6] **science**	a scientist	–	scientific
engineering	an [7] **engineer**	to engineer something	–

8.1 Making a difference

LEAD-IN

Put students into pairs to discuss which recent invention has made the biggest difference to their lives and what future invention would make a big difference to their lives. Ask students to discuss the ideas with their partner.

READING

A Put students into pairs to discuss the questions.

B Tell students to look at the pictures and to predict the answers to the question then tell them to read the article and check their predictions.

Possible answer: *Eden is a successful inventor although she's young. Her invention is very simple but it has made a big difference to many people's lives.*

C Tell students to read the text again and match the explanations (1–7) to the pictures (a–g).

D Tell students to look at the ideas in the box and to make a list of their own life goals connected to them. Then put students into pairs to compare and explain their lists.

VOCABULARY

A Tell students to read the information in the box about word families. Tell them to look at the word families in the table and to complete the gaps. Tell students all the words they need for this appear in the article about Eden Full Goh.

B Ask students to complete the sentences with words from the same family as the words in bold. Look at the example together and elicit that *successful* is the adjective and *succeed* is the verb. Use the **Vocabulary Worksheet** on W30 for extra practice.

METHODOLOGY HUB by Jim Scrivener

Model new words in context

When you teach lexical items, give students a chance to hear you saying the item naturally spoken in the context of a typical short phrase or sentence. Take care to stress naturally (rather than as a 'perfect' sentence). Allow students to repeat the phrase and give them honest feedback if there seem to be problems. If necessary, remodel it and let students work out what they are doing differently.

Modelling intonation

When you teach grammar, allow students to hear some typical examples of natural uses of the language. So, for example, when teaching the present perfect continuous, don't just teach it as dry examples, but model a typical real-life sentence or two yourself with real feeling, such as 'I've been waiting here for two hours!'. A loud, angry sentence like this will be much more memorable than a written example. Get students to repeat it to each other – and don't let them get away with flat, dull intonation. Encourage them to say it with real feeling.

GRAMMAR HUB

8.1 Relative clauses
Defining relative clauses

	Relative pronoun	
Person	who/that	The person **who/that** first had the idea was called Smith.
Thing	which/that	The thing **which/that** stops it being a success is the price.
Possession	whose	The man **whose** design won first prize was from China.
Place	where	The company **where** I work makes a difference to people's lives.
Time	when	Early in the morning is the time **when** I have my best ideas.

- We use a defining relative clause to give information about and identify a noun (person or thing).
- We use *who* or *that* for people, and *which* or *that* for things.
- With *who*, *which* and *that*, we can leave out the relative pronoun if it's followed by a subject + verb rather than just a verb.

  The design (that) he suggested was very good.

- When the relative pronoun is the subject of the relative clause, we don't add another pronoun.

  Do you know the name of the man **who invented** *this? NOT* ~~Do you know the name of the man who he invented this?~~

Non-defining relative clauses

	Relative pronoun	
Person	who	Carol Taylor, **who** presents science programmes, is a university professor.
Thing	which	The idea, **which** I first read about in the newspaper, is really very simple.
Possession	whose	Miriam, **whose** dad is a designer, would like to become an inventor.
Place	where	London, **where** her grandparents live, is where Sophie would like to find work.
Time	when	On Sundays, **when** Andrew isn't working, he likes to catch up with his reading.

- We use a non-defining relative clause when we want to include two pieces of information in the same sentence. The relative clause is usually an additional piece of information and is always separated by commas.

- We do not use *that* with non-defining relative clauses.
- When we remove a non-defining relative clause, the sentence still makes sense.

GRAMMAR

A Tell students to look at the article again and to decide what the highlighted words refer to. Go through the example with the students, demonstrating how *who* refers back to Eden.

B Tell students to read the rules about defining and non-defining relative clauses and to complete the examples with relative clauses from the article. Check students understand the difference between the essential information, without which the sentence isn't complete, in the defining relative clause, and the extra information, which could be removed, in the non-defining relative clause.

C Direct students to the **Grammar Hub** on pages 136 and 137 (see TB86 and below). Use the **Grammar Worksheet** on W29 for extra practice.

PRONUNCIATION

A Play the audio and tell students to listen carefully to the different pronunciation of the two sentences. Ask students what they noticed. Play again if they are unsure.

*We pause before and after **non-defining** relative clauses. Before each pause, our voice usually goes **down**.*

B Tell students to listen and repeat the sentences, paying special attention to the pauses and falling intonation.

C Put students into pairs for further pronunciation practice.

SPEAKING

A Ask students to work with a partner and write down three sentences using relative clauses describing a famous person, a place and an object. Monitor, to help with vocabulary.

B Put pairs of students together so they are working in groups of four. The pairs should take turns reading out their sentences with the other pair guessing the missing information.

GRAMMAR HUB

8.1 Relative clauses

A Choose the correct option.

1 There are lots of students *which* / *who* have great ideas.
2 The last century was the time *when* / *where* technology really progressed.
3 The magazine *who* / *that* I like best is called *New Scientist*.
4 Liverpool is the place *where* / *which* I studied for my degree.
5 I want to find a job *that* / *who* helps others.
6 John is the boy *who* / *whose* father is a doctor.
7 I don't know anyone *who* / *which* works in technology.
8 He was born at a time *when* / *where* computers didn't exist.

B Match to make sentences.

1 California is where _____ *b*
2 The computer is an invention _____ *d*
3 Steve Jobs was the person who _____ *a*
4 The experiences _____ *e*
5 Myra is the woman _____ *g*
6 My phone is the one thing _____ *c*
7 I really enjoyed the time _____ *f*

a   started Apple Computers.
b   most software industries started.
c   which I would hate to lose.
d   which has changed many people's lives.
e   that I had were more important than the money I made.
f   when I was studying at university.
g   who helped me choose my career.

C Join the two sentences to make one. Use non-defining relative clauses.

1 My aunt is a scientist. She lives in Boston.
   My aunt, who lives in Boston, is a scientist. / My aunt, who is a scientist, lives in Boston.

2 The invention is very simple. It has made a big difference to people's lives.
   The invention, which is very simple, has made a big difference to people's lives.

3 Justin is 23. He has just won a prize.
   Justin, who is 23, has just won a prize. / Justin, who has just won a prize, is 23.

4 Carl spoke to us from Lisbon. He lives there.
   Carl spoke to us from Lisbon, where he lives.

5 The invention won first prize. It is sold in many countries.
   The invention, which won first is sold in many countries. / The invention, whi sold in many countries, won first prize.

6 Marie loves inventing things. Her husband is also an engineer.
   Marie, whose husband is also an engineer, loves inventing things.

7 Next week the results come out. We'll see if you win anything.
   Next week, when the results come out, we'll see if you win anything.

➤ Go back to page 87.

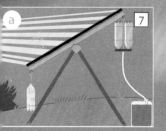
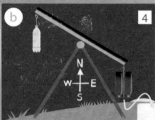
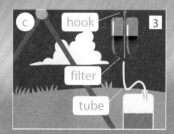

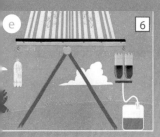

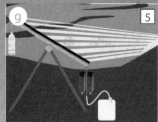

B Complete the sentences with words from the same family as the words in bold.

1 You don't need to be **successful** every time. You just need to ___*succeed*___ in the most important things.

2 I could never **invent** something – I'm not a very ___*inventive*___ person.

3 You can only call yourself an ___*engineer*___ after studying **engineering** at university.

4 A ___*designer*___ should concentrate on **designing** things that work well. That's more important than making them look beautiful.

5 I always think like a **scientist**. Being ___*scientific*___ means checking the facts before making a decision, and not focusing on opinions and feelings.

C SPEAK Work in pairs. Which sentences in Exercise B do you agree or disagree with? Tell your partner. Then make the sentences true for you.

GRAMMAR
Relative clauses

A WORK IT OUT Look at *Eden Full Goh: the inventor who is making a big difference*. What do the highlighted words in the article refer to?

1 who = ___*Eden*___ 4 which = ___*Eden's invention*___
2 when = ___early in the morning___ 5 that = ___the solar panel system___
3 where = ___the east___

B Read the rules and complete the examples with relative clauses from the article.

> **Relative clauses**
>
> Defining relative clauses tell us which person, thing, place or time we are talking about. Without the relative clause, the sentence isn't complete.
>
> Eden Full Goh: the inventor [1] ___who is making a big difference___.
>
> Non-defining relative clauses give extra information about a person, thing, place or time. We can cut the relative clause and the sentence is still complete. We use commas to separate the relative clause from the rest of the sentence.
>
> Eden's invention, [2] ___which has won many prizes___, is now used in 19 countries.

C Go to the Grammar Hub on page 136.

PRONUNCIATION
Relative clauses

A Listen to the two sentences. What do you notice about the pronunciation of defining and non-defining relative clauses?
8.1

1 The person who invented the SunSaluter has made a big difference to people's lives.

2 Eden Full Goh, who invented the SunSaluter, has made a big difference to people's lives.

B Listen and repeat the sentences.
8.2

1 Solar panels, which turn sunlight into electricity, are becoming cheaper all the time.

2 I've hidden my plans in a place where they'll be safe.

3 My favourite inventor is Mária Telkes, who created the first 100 per cent solar-powered house in 1947.

C SPEAK Work in pairs. Practise saying the sentences in Exercise B. Listen and check your partner's pronunciation.

SPEAKING

A Work in pairs. Write down three sentences using relative clauses. They should describe:

- a famous person
- a place
- an object

B Join another pair and take turns reading out your sentences, saying 'Beep' in place of the subject. The other pair must guess who, where or what you are talking about.

A: *Beep, who is American, invented the light bulb.*

B: *Is it Thomas Edison?*

Thinking outside THE BOX

Ex C Q1 Thinking outside the box means <u>looking at a problem in a new way.</u>
Ex C Q2 It means <u>forgetting about 'the way we normally do things'</u>, taking away unimportant rules and experimenting with new ideas. So for example, in the 'nine dots' problem, we see 'rules' that don't actually exist. Who said your lines have to stay inside the red box? In fact, do the lines ever need to go through the middle of each dot?

It's the same with the light bulb problem. We can't stop ourselves from thinking of a light bulb as something that we see with our eyes, as
Ex C Q3 something that can only be in two states, off or on. <u>But what if we think of it as something we can touch with our hands? Are there still only two states?</u>

Thinking outside the box also helps with brainstorming tasks, like the 'uses for old tickets' exercise. The key to successful brainstorming is
Ex C Q4 to break it into two stages: <u>generating ideas in the first place, and then</u>
Ex C Q5 <u>evaluating those ideas to see if they're useful or not. We need to keep those stages separate</u>; if we try to do both at the same time, we only generate boring, sensible ideas. But often it's the silly ideas that help us to find excellent ideas. For example, a single bus ticket wouldn't make a great poster for your wall, but what about a poster made from 100 bus tickets from around the world?

READING

A SPEAK Work in pairs. How creative are you? Follow the instructions to find out.

1 Take an object from your pocket/bag (e.g. a used bus ticket). Try to think of as many different uses as possible for this object. Your ideas can be sensible or silly. What's your best idea?

   A: We could cut it up to make a tiny jigsaw puzzle.

   B: Why don't we write a short shopping list on the back?

2 Draw four straight lines to connect all the dots without taking your pen off the page. Now try again with only three straight lines.

3 You're inside a room with three light switches on the wall. One of these switches turns on a light in a room on the other side of the house, but you don't know which switch. How can you find out? You can go to the other room to check only once.

B READ FOR GIST Read *Thinking outside the box.* How does it help with the questions in Exercise A?

C READ FOR DETAIL Choose *Do* or *Don't* for each piece of advice.

1 *Do* / *Don't* look at a problem in a new way.

2 *Do* / *Don't* do things the way you normally do them.

3 *Do* / *Don't* experiment with new ideas.

4 *Do* / *Don't* guess the rules and follow those rules.

5 *Do* / *Don't* evaluate ideas while you're generating them.

D SPEAK Work in groups. When do you need to brainstorm ideas? How could brainstorming silly ideas help you to think of useful ideas?

LISTENING

A SPEAK Work in pairs. The pictures show some techniques for becoming more creative. What do you think the techniques are?

a 3

b 5

c 1

d 2

e 6

f 4

B LISTEN FOR GIST Listen to a conversation between two friends, Caroline and Toby, to check your answers to Exercise A. Number the pictures in the order they are mentioned.

8.3

Glossary

wander (v) if your mind or thoughts wander, you stop concentrating and start thinking about other things

READING

A–D Ask students to discuss ideas and check answers in pairs before whole-class feedback.

The first paragraph reminds us that our lines don't need to stay inside the red box or go through the middle of each dot.

The second paragraph reminds us we can touch the light bulb. Therefore, we can turn on the first two switches for a few seconds and then turn off the middle switch. Then the temperature of the bulbs when we go in the room will tell us if it is the first, middle or third switch.

The third paragraph shows us how silly ideas can lead to sensible ideas.

AUDIOSCRIPT

 8.3

Listening, Exercise B
C = Caroline   T = Toby

C: Hey, Toby. Do you want a coffee?

T: No, thanks. I'm in a hurry. I need to go to the library to work on my project for university.

C: Really? What's the project?

T: We've got to invent 'something that will make a difference to people's lives'. But I'm terrible at coming up with ideas. They didn't teach us how to be creative when I was at school! But you, you're so creative. I mean, you write amazing stories; you design beautiful clothes. How do you do it?

C: Well, you can actually learn to use your imagination better. I've read a lot of books about creativity, and I've learnt some great techniques from them. *[Ex C Q1]*

T: Really? Can you give me an example?

C: Well, whenever I feel like I have too much work, I always stop working for an hour or so.

T: But I don't have time to stop. I'm really busy!

C: I always thought the same. But when I tried it, I found that a break actually boosted my creativity. When I'm relaxed, I have lots more creative ideas, and I'm much more productive after a break – I get more work done in less time. Tell me, how do you fill your time in the evenings? *[Ex C Q2]*

T: Er, I usually just watch TV or play games on my phone. I'm too tired to do anything else.

C: Aha. So that's what's blocking your creativity: you're filling your brain with information all the time. You need to switch off completely. Instead of watching TV, go for a run. You need to let your mind wander freely. *[Ex C Q3]*

T: OK, I guess I can watch less TV. But I hate running!

C: Well, it doesn't have to be running. You could go dancing or swimming, or get some other type of physical exercise. They're all good for generating new ideas. *[Ex C Q3]*

T: OK. I love swimming, so I guess I could go to the swimming pool once a week.

C: Great. Swimming's actually perfect because the water is blue.

T: Er, sorry? What does that have to do with creativity?

C: Well, I read recently that the colour blue makes us more creative. Whenever I need to think outside the box, I go to the beach and look at the sky and the sea. It always helps. *[Ex C Q4]*

T: OK, but it doesn't really help me with my project. I need to start work on it right now. I'm actually getting stressed about it.

C: Well, maybe that's the problem: you're letting your emotions block your creativity. You should look at a problem from the outside, to take away the emotions. Then it's much easier to find a solution. That's why it's easier to solve other people's problems than your own – because you can focus on the problems, not the emotions.

T: OK, but …

C: So another good technique is to discuss your ideas with other people – and listen to what they say. The best solutions often come from group discussions and brainstorming sessions. And if there's nobody you can talk to, you can imagine having a conversation with a friend. Look at the problem through someone else's eyes.

T: OK, yes, I know what you mean. But what about my project? I need to come up with an invention right now. But I haven't got any ideas at all. My mind's gone blank!

C: Well, there's one last trick I often use when I really have no ideas. I call it the alphabet technique. OK, so tell me three letters of the alphabet. *[Ex C Q5]*

T: Er, W, G and P.

C: Perfect. So your invention needs to solve a problem, and that problem needs to start with your first letter, W.

T: Water? It isn't really a problem, is it?

C: Well, let's use your second letter to help us. What was it?

T: G – for grass. Hmm, water, grass. Aha, maybe the invention could be a better way of watering the grass in people's gardens when they're away on holiday. I mean, just pouring water onto the grass all day and all night is really wasteful. But what's the solution?

C: I don't know. But it needs to start with your third letter, which was …?

T: P – for plastic bottles. Aha, I could use old plastic bottles, filled with water. Then I could make tiny holes in the bottles, so the water comes out really slowly, over a week or two.

C: Sounds good!

T: Hmm. I need to think about this carefully. Right, I'm going for a long walk along the beach to work out the details. See you later.

C: OK. Call me if you need any help! Good luck!

LISTENING

A Tell students to look at the pictures and tell them that they show techniques for becoming more creative. Put students into pairs to discuss what they think the techniques are. Elicit some ideas from the students but don't confirm or deny anything yet.

B Tell students to listen to the conversation to check their ideas. Tell students the speakers don't talk about the pictures in the same order as they appear in the book, so they need to number them in the order they are mentioned.

8.1 Making a difference

♪ 8.3

C Tell students to read the information in the box about *Listening for problems and solutions*. Tell them to use the strategies in the box to answer the questions as they listen again.

D Put students into pairs to discuss which, if any, of Caroline's techniques they have used or might like to use in the future. Ask students who have used the strategies before to share their experiences. How successful were they? Would they recommend them to others?

VOCABULARY

A Elicit that all the sentences were used in the conversation between Caroline and Toby and ask if they remember hearing any of them. Tell students to match the beginnings of the sentences with the endings, either from memory or according to what they think makes sense.

B Put students into pairs to discuss what they think the words in bold from the sentences in Exercise A mean. As students do this, write the definitions on the board. Then ask students to look at the definitions and to match them with the words. This will make feedback clearer and more focused. Ask students if the definitions they thought of at first were similar to the ones on the board.

1 *coming up with new ideas = think of new ideas*
2 *use your imagination = be creative*
3 *boost your creativity = enhance your creativity*
4 *switch off completely = to completely relax, not to think about anything*
5 *let your mind wander freely = not to concentrate on one thing*
6 *generating new ideas = think of new ideas*
7 *think outside the box = think in a new way*
8 *block your creativity = stop yourself from being able to think of new ideas*
9 *look at a problem from the outside = think about a problem from a different perspective*
10 *my mind's gone blank = unable to remember or think anything*

METHODOLOGY HUB by Jim Scrivener

Scaffolding

During a fluency activity, there may be a way to offer spontaneous correction that:

- does not interfere too much with the flow of conversation;
- offers useful language feedback;
- actually helps the speaker to construct his conversation.

'Scaffolding' refers to the way a competent language speaker helps a less competent one to communicate by both encouraging and providing possible elements of the conversation. It is the way a primary-school teacher might help a young child to communicate, or the way a chat-show host might draw out a guest. The listener offers support – like scaffolding round a building – to help the speaker create his own spoken structure.

Scaffolding in class isn't a normal conversation in the sense that the teacher/listener is not aiming to contribute any personal stories or opinions of her own; the aim of her own speaking is solely to help the speaker tell his story.

C Tell students to choose the best words to complete the questions. Check answers, then put students into groups to discuss the questions. Share any interesting answers with the class.

SPEAKING HUB

A Put students into groups and tell them that they are going to create a website that will make a big difference to people's lives. Remind students about Caroline's alphabet technique from the Listening and tell them to discuss the questions in their groups.

B Tell students to brainstorm five ideas for each of the questions. Remind them to think outside the box. Monitor to help with language input.

C Tell groups to look at their ideas from Exercise B and the details about their website from Exercise A. Tell them they now have everything they need for an excellent idea. Tell students to choose the best ideas and to prepare to present them to the class. Again, monitor to help with language if needed.

D Tell each group to present their website to the class. Tell students to listen carefully and to ask questions at the end of each presentation. After all the presentations have been made, ask students which of the websites they would visit and which they think could be successful. Finish with feedback on students' use of language during the presentations.

> **Extra activity**
>
> For homework, students can write the *About us* page for their websites. You can give students the following points to help structure their writing:
>
> - a summary or mission statement
> - the story behind the website
> - more detail on the problem you are trying to solve
> - how you will solve it
> - some personal details about your group

Scaffolding techniques

- Showing interest and agreeing: nodding, 'uh-huh', eye contact, 'yes', etc;
- Concisely asking for clarification of unclear information, e.g. repeating an unclear word;
- Encouragement echo: repeating the last word (perhaps with questioning intonation) in order to encourage the speaker to continue;
- Echoing meaning: picking on a key element of meaning and saying it back to the speaker, e.g. 'a foreign holiday';
- Asking conversation-oiling questions (ones that mainly recap already stated information), e.g. *Is it? Do you? Where was it?* etc;
- Asking brief questions (or using sentence heads) that encourage the speaker to extend the story, e.g. *And then … He went … She wanted …* etc;
- Unobtrusively saying the correct form of an incorrect word (but only if having the correct word makes a significant positive contribution to the communication);
- Giving the correct pronunciation of words in replies without drawing any particular attention to it;
- Unobtrusively giving a word or phrase that the speaker is looking for.

C Listen again. What was the solution to each problem? Use the strategies in the box to help you.

> **Listening for problems and solutions**
>
> When you're listening, it's useful to organise information into a set of problems and solutions. This usually makes it easier to understand a lot of information and to remember it better later.
>
> Listen carefully when you hear people talking about problems because they'll probably present a solution next.

1 You don't learn how to be creative at school.
  a Write stories and design clothes.
  b Go to creativity classes.
  (c) Read books about creativity.

2 You're too busy to stop working.
  (a) Take a break to make yourself more productive.
  b Work in the evenings so you can have a break during the day.
  c Relax – your work isn't as important as you think.

3 Your brain is filled with too much information.
  (a) Get some physical exercise.
  b Watch TV and play games on your phone.
  c Switch off your computer.

4 You need to think outside the box.
  a Go to the library to get some ideas.
  (b) Look at blue things.
  c Listen to some music.

5 You have no ideas at all.
  a Discuss your ideas with a group of friends.
  b Close your eyes for a few minutes.
  (c) Use letters of the alphabet to generate ideas.

D SPEAK Work in pairs. Which of Caroline's techniques have you used? Which might you use in the future? Tell your partner.

VOCABULARY
Creative thinking

A Match the beginnings of the sentences (1–10) with the endings (a–j).

g 1 I'm terrible at **coming up**
c 2 You can actually learn to **use your**
f 3 A break actually **boosted my**
i 4 You need to **switch off**
b 5 You need to **let your mind**
j 6 They're all good for **generating**
a 7 Whenever I need to **think outside**
d 8 You're letting your emotions **block**
h 9 You should **look at a problem**
e 10 My mind's

a the box, I go to the beach.
b wander freely.
c imagination better.
d your creativity.
e gone blank.
f creativity.
g with new ideas.
h from the outside.
i completely.
j new ideas.

B Look at the sentences in Exercise A. What do the phrases in bold mean?

C SPEAK Choose the best words to complete the questions. Then work in groups and ask and answer the questions.

1 Does your mind ever *boost* / *generate* / *wander* during boring activities? Think of some examples.

2 Is it possible to *come up* / *switch off* / *block* completely from the things that make you stressed? How can you do it?

3 What can you do when your *mind* / *creativity* / *imagination* goes blank in a stressful situation (e.g. when you're in an exam, giving a presentation or speaking English)?

SPEAKING HUB

A Work in groups. You have decided to create a website that will make a big difference to people's lives. Use the alphabet technique to generate some ideas – silly or serious!

Write down three letters of the alphabet.
- 1st letter: Who is your website for?
- 2nd letter: What problem do those people have?
- 3rd letter: How will you solve that problem?

B PLAN Think of five ideas for each of the questions below. Remember to think outside the box!

1 What will you call your website?
2 How can you make money from your website?
3 How will you tell the world about your website?

C ORGANISE Look at your ideas from Exercise B. Turn your silly ideas into excellent ideas. Choose your best idea.

D PRESENT Present your idea to the class. Which teams' websites would you visit?

○- **Explain how an invention works**
○- **Suggest and evaluate creative ideas**

LISTENING

A SPEAK   Work in pairs. Look at the pictures of inventions (a–d) and discuss the questions.

1 What do you think the gadgets in the pictures do?

2 How useful are they?

3 Do you like gadgets? What gadgets do you own?

B LISTEN FOR MAIN IDEA   Listen to a podcast about new gadgets and answer the questions.

8.4

1 Which gadgets from the pictures do the people discuss?

2 What is special about them?

C Listen again. Which gadgets do these sentences describe? Write O (Oombrella), C (CleverPet) or B (both).

8.4

1 It looks beautiful.   O

2 It's connected to the internet.   B

3 It sends messages to your phone.   O

4 It's useful for many years.   B

5 It gets more difficult to use over time.   C

6 It can lead to a longer life.   C

D SPEAK   Work in groups and discuss the questions.

1 What is good about the two gadgets? Which one is more useful?

2 Who do you think will buy the gadgets? Why?

VOCABULARY
Positive adjectives

> **Using positive adjectives**
>
> As your English improves, try to avoid using words like *good* or *nice* too often. There are many other positive words that you can use like *amazing*, *excellent* and *fantastic*.

A Match the positive adjectives (1–10) with the meanings (a–j).

h	1 gorgeous	**a**	you admire it because it is very good, large or shows great skill
e	2 sensible	**b**	making you very interested or attracted
j	3 practical	**c**	right for a particular purpose, person or situation
f	4 unforgettable	**d**	not the same as anything or anyone else
a	5 impressive	**e**	reasonable and practical
d	6 unique	**f**	will be remembered for a very long time
i	7 sophisticated	**g**	surprising, or difficult to believe
g	8 incredible	**h**	very beautiful
c	9 suitable	**i**	complicated and advanced in design
b	10 fascinating	**j**	intended to be useful

B Go to the Vocabulary Hub on page 145.

C SPEAK   Work in pairs. Write down the names of your favourite three possessions. Use positive adjectives to tell your partner why you like each one. Ask questions about your partner's possessions.

LEAD-IN

With books closed, write *Must-have_____* on the board. Elicit ideas about how to complete the phrase (e.g. *must-have books*).

LISTENING

A–D Give students time to compare answers before whole-class feedback.

    1 They discuss the umbrella (Oombrella) and the dog bowl

    2 The Oombrella is connected to the internet. CleverPet entertains dogs and cats with puzzles – they have to press buttons to win food.

VOCABULARY

A Tell students to match the positive adjectives with their meanings. Do the first one together as a whole class and drill pronunciation.

B Direct students to the **Vocabulary Hub** on page 145 for further practice of positive adjectives.

C Encourage students to ask their partner follow-up questions. Finish by commenting on how well students used the positive adjectives. Correct any inappropriate uses. Use the **Vocabulary Worksheet** on W32 for extra practice.

AUDIOSCRIPT

 8.4

Listening, Exercises B and C
L = Leo   T = Teresa

L: Hello, and welcome to this week's Must-have Gadgets podcast. I'm Leo Kovalski.

T: And I'm Teresa Martinez. Now, earlier this week, I went to the International Gadget Show, where I saw some really amazing gadgets. And I've brought two along today to show you, Leo.

L: Sounds great. So what have you got for us?

T: Well, let's start with a very sensible invention: the Oombrella. What do you think, Leo?

L: Er … it just looks like a normal umbrella. I mean, the design is gorgeous, really lovely, but … it isn't exactly innovative, is it?

T: Aha! But this Oombrella is unique. It's the world's first umbrella that's connected to the internet.

L: What? Why on earth do I need an umbrella that connects to the internet?

T: Well, did you bring an umbrella to work today?

L: No, unfortunately. I forgot to check the weather forecast, so I didn't know it was going to rain.

T: Aha. Well, you can borrow my Oombrella today. It'll check the weather forecast for you. If the forecast says it's going to rain later, Oombrella will send a message to your mobile phone.

L: OK, but why do I need a special umbrella just to send weather forecasts to my phone?

T: Well, the Oombrella is especially suitable for forgetful people, like you, who forget to check the weather forecast on their phones.

L: Yes, well, I am quite a forgetful person. But what do forgetful people do all the time? They leave their umbrellas behind in cafés, or on the bus! What if I lose your Oombrella tonight?

T: Well, if you leave it behind, you'll get a message on your phone. They call it the unforgettable umbrella because you can't forget it.

L: OK, yes, that is quite practical, I suppose.

T: Yes. And the Oombrella also has lots of sophisticated electronics: if you go for a long walk in the rain tonight, the app will send you a weather report when you get home. So you can read all about the weather during your walk.

L: Hmm … I'm not sure I need an Oombrella. I never go for a walk unless the sun's shining. The big question for me is: will it keep me dry if there's a storm tomorrow morning when I'm coming to work?

T: Absolutely! It's made of super-strong materials, so it won't break. You'll be able to use it for years.

L: Really? Well, that is impressive. My umbrellas always break after five minutes in a storm. So if this Oombrella lasts for years, I'll be very happy.

T: Well, I only said you could borrow mine. I'd like to have it back tomorrow.

L: Ah, yes, of course. So … what else have you got?

T: Well, the second gadget is called CleverPet. It's a food bowl for dogs and cats.

L: Fantastic. And don't tell me … it's connected to the internet, right?

T: Yes! How did you guess? Do you have any pets, Leo?

L: Yes, I have a dog called Henry.

T: And what does Henry do all day, while you're at work?

L: Er … not much. He sleeps most of the day, but sometimes he chews the furniture in my flat.

T: Well, that's because he's bored. Of course, he chews your furniture if he's got nothing else to do all day.

L: OK. And what has this got to do with your incredible internet-connected dog food bowl?

T: Well, it isn't just a bowl. It's a puzzle.

L: A puzzle? For dogs?

T: Yes. There are three buttons with lights. When a light flashes, the dog has to press a button. If he presses the right button, the light goes on again and he wins something to eat.

L: OK.

T: Then, over the next few days, weeks, even years, the puzzles get more and more difficult. The dog has to remember lots of information and press the buttons in the right order.

L: Oh, right. And, er, do dogs enjoy puzzles?

T: Absolutely! They love them. It keeps them busy for hours, which means they never get bored. And if they don't get bored, they don't chew the furniture.

L: Well, I must admit, it sounds fascinating.

T: It is. And it really helps pets stay active. Scientists have shown that pets stay healthier and they live longer if they keep busy. You should definitely get one for Henry.

L: Yes, I think I might!

T: Great.

L: OK, so that's all from today's podcast. We'll be back next time with more must-have gadgets. Thanks for listening.

GRAMMAR

🔊 **A** Tell students to match the beginnings of the sentences with
8.5   the endings. Play the audio for students to check their answers.

B Tell students to look at the sentences from Exercise A to help
them complete the rules. When checking answers, ensure
students understand that sentences 1 and 4 from Exercise A are
zero conditionals and sentences 2 and 3 are first conditionals.

C Direct students to the **Grammar Hub** on pages 136 and 137
(see below and TB92). Use the **Grammar Worksheet** on W31 for
extra practice.

PRONUNCIATION

🔊 **A** Point out the information in the box about *'ll* and *won't*. Tell
8.6   students to listen to the sentences and to circle the words
they hear.

🔊 **B** Play the audio again for students to listen and repeat the
8.6   sentences. Focus on the contractions, drilling pronunciation
of the contractions in isolation before building back up to
the whole sentence. Tell students that they don't necessarily
have to speak exactly like this but that an awareness of the
pronunciation will help them understand natural speech
more easily.

C Tell students either to show their partner a gadget they have
on them or to invent one that they think their partner would
be interested in. Choose an example as a whole class and elicit
some examples of zero and first conditionals to describe the
functions of your gadget and offer to lend it to someone in the
class but with certain conditions. Put students into pairs to do
the same. Ask the class to tell you about the most interesting
gadgets and offers. Comment on any successful use of
conditionals or any situations where students could have used
them but didn't.

SPEAKING

A Tell students that they are going to invent a new gadget and
then promote it to the class. Tell them to use the ideas in the
table, ideas from the previous activity or new ideas of their own.
Give students some time to work alone to think and make notes.
Monitor and help them with any new vocabulary they need.

B Put students into groups to share ideas and to agree on which
is the best gadget. When they have decided, tell each group to
prepare to promote their gadget. Tell them to think about the
questions and to make notes. Monitor to help with language
input. When students have finished, tell them to practise
making their presentation.

C Tell each group to promote their gadget to the class. Tell the
other students to listen carefully and to think of questions to
ask. At the end of each presentation, get the students to ask
their questions.

D Tell each group to decide which gadget they think is the best.
Tell them they can't vote for their own! Tell each group to vote,
then congratulate the winner. Ask students which gadgets
they would really buy, and which they think could become real
products. Finish with feedback on students' use of language
during the presentations and feedback.

GRAMMAR HUB

8.2 Zero and first conditionals; Conditionals with modals and imperatives

Zero conditional

Condition	Result
If **you listen**,	**you learn**.
If **you like** science,	**it helps**.

Question	Positive short answer	Negative short answer
If **I win**, **do I get** a prize?	Yes, **you do**.	No, **you don't**.
Does it help if you like science?	Yes, **it does**.	No, **it doesn't**.

- We use the zero conditional to talk about things that are always true.
- We can put the *if*-clause or the result clause first. The only difference is we do not use a comma if we begin with the result clause.
- We can use negatives and *unless* (which means *if not* or *except if*) in the zero conditional.

  If you don't pay attention, you make mistakes.
  = Unless you pay attention, you make mistakes.

First conditional

Condition	Result
If **you try** hard,	**you'll succeed**.
If **it doesn't work**,	**we'll start** again.

Question	Positive short answer	Negative short answer
If **we win** the award, **will we be** famous?	Yes, **we/you will**.	No, **we/you won't**.
Will we be famous if **we win** the award?		

- We use the first conditional to talk about possible situations in the future.
- We can put the *if*-clause or the result clause first. The only difference is we do not use a comma if we begin with the result clause.
- We can use negatives and *unless* (meaning *if not* or *except if*) in the first conditional.

  If you don't listen, you won't understand.
  = Unless you listen, you won't understand.

- We never put *will* in an *if*-clause.

Conditionals with modals and imperatives

- We can use other modal verbs (e.g. *can, could, might, should*) instead of *will*.

  If you work hard enough, you can do it!
  I might visit the science museum if it's open tomorrow.

- We can use an imperative instead of a result clause.

  If you see smoke, call for help.
  Phone me if you have any questions.

GRAMMAR
Zero and first conditionals

A Look at the extracts from the podcast about new gadgets. Match the beginnings of the sentences (1–4) with the endings (a–d). Then listen and check your answers.

1 I never go for a walk   **a** if there's a storm tomorrow morning?
2 Will it keep me dry   **b** if they keep busy.
3 If this Oombrella lasts for years,   **c** I'll be very happy.
4 Pets stay healthier and they live longer   **d** unless the sun's shining.

B **WORK IT OUT** Choose the correct words to complete the rules.

Zero and first conditional

1 Conditional sentences usually have **two** / four clauses: the *if*-clause and the result clause.
2 When the *if*-clause comes first, we **always** / never need a comma between the clauses.
3 We can use *unless* instead of *if*. It means **if not** / because.
4 We use the zero conditional to talk about things that are always true. We use past / **present** tenses in both clauses.
5 We use the first conditional to talk about possible situations in the **future** / past. We usually use **will** in the result clause.

C Go to the Grammar Hub on page 136.

PRONUNCIATION
'll and *won't*

'll and *won't*

It's often hard to hear the difference between words such as *you* and *you'll*, or *I* and *I'll*. It's also sometimes hard to hear the difference between *won't* and *want*. The rules for conditionals will help you work out what you hear.

 A Listen and circle the words you hear.
8.6

1 If you **want to go** / won't go to the supermarket, *you* / **you'll** need to bring a bag.
2 *I lend* / **I'll lend** you my raincoat if you **want to borrow** / won't borrow it.
3 If **you** / you'll like gadgets, *you* / **you'll** love this.
4 **You learn** / You'll earn a lot more if **you** / you'll listen carefully.

B Listen again and repeat the sentences.
8.6

C **SPEAK** Work in pairs. Imagine you are going to lend your partner a gadget tonight. Follow the instructions.

1 If you have a gadget with you (e.g. a phone, a smartwatch), show your partner what to do. Ask questions about your partner's gadget.
2 If you don't have a gadget, use an everyday object (e.g. a pen, your car keys) and pretend it's a gadget. Invent some cool functions for it.

SPEAKING

A You are going to invent a new gadget and then promote it to the class. Use the ideas below and your own ideas to invent a gadget.

What is it?	What's innovative about it?
a book, a chair, a food bowl, a hat, swimming goggles, a mirror, a light bulb, a plastic bottle, a puzzle, shoes, a toy, a TV, an umbrella	It can fly/talk/move by itself.
	It's connected to the internet.
	It contains a GPS device / a camera.
	It's for pets/birds/fish.
	It's very big/small.

B **PLAN** Work in groups. Choose the best idea for your group's gadget and answer the questions:

- What is special about your gadget?
- What problem does it solve?
- What else can you use to help you promote your gadget (e.g. pictures, stories)?
- What questions might people ask about your gadget?

C **PRESENT** Promote your gadget to the class. At the end of each presentation, ask questions about other groups' gadgets.

D **REFLECT** Have a class vote to find out the most popular gadget. Would you like to buy the other groups' gadgets? Why/Why not? Do you think your gadgets could become real products?

READING

A SPEAK Work in pairs. Look at the picture and answer the questions.

1 What do you think the people are doing? Why?

2 Have you ever done something similar? Why/Why not?

B PREDICT Work in pairs. Before you read *If you really can't wait …*, look at the five topic sentences (a–e) and discuss the questions. Use the strategies in the box to help you.

> ### Topic sentences
>
> The topic sentence is usually the first or second sentence in a paragraph. It tells you what the whole paragraph will be about.
>
> You can often understand a lot about a text just by reading and thinking about the topic sentences.
>
> You can also use them to make predictions before reading the whole text to check.

a Marketers have a name for people who buy new gadgets before everyone else: innovators.

Why do you think marketers have a special name for these people? Why are marketers interested in them?

b A little further back in the queue, I meet some fans who aren't just there to buy a phone.

Why do you think these fans are in the queue?

c Near the back of the queue, some people are feeling less positive.

Why do you think they're feeling less positive?

d It's five o'clock in the morning, and there are already over 200 people in the queue outside the phone shop.

Why do you think they're there so early in the morning?

e I decided to speak to some people in the queue outside the phone shop to find out … and I got a few surprises.

What surprises do you think the writer got?

If you really
can't wait ...

1 d It's cold and dark, but the people seem happy. In a few hours, the doors will open and they'll finally get their hands on the gadget of their dreams: a gorgeous new mobile phone. Of course, if you don't want to queue all night, you can come to the shop this afternoon when the queues will be gone. Even better, if you can wait six months or so, the same phone will cost half the price. But if you really need that phone right now, come and join the back of the queue.

2 a I've always thought that was a terrible name – innovation normally means doing something extremely clever, like inventing a new machine. But what's innovative about buying expensive gadgets just because they're new? Of course, marketers love 'innovators' for two reasons: innovators are happy to spend a lot of money and they persuade the rest of us to buy those gadgets a few months later.

So why do they do it? **3 e** The biggest surprise was that the people at the front of the queue were actually being paid to be there. 'I work for a gadget shop, Gary's Gadgets. My boss, Gary, is paying me,' said Bob, who is right at the front of the queue. 'It's good for business because when the doors open, I'll be on TV around the

world – wearing a T-shirt with the Gary's Gadgets logo.'

Ex D Q5 Janice and Damian, who are second and third in the queue, are also there for the money. 'We came here ten days ago, just to make sure we were first,' says Janice.

Ex D Q2 'But then Bob offered us $2500 to move ahead of us.'

Ex D Q6 **4 b** 'For me, it's a social event,' says a man called Mo. 'It's a great way to meet people who share my love of gadgets

Ex D Q1 I've had some amazing conversations in this queue. Many of us come every year, so it feels like meeting old friends.'

Ex D Q4 A woman called Ruby agrees, 'It's like going to a pop concert or a live sports game. I love the feeling of being at an important place at an important time.'

Ex D Q7 **5 c** 'I'm only here because of the special offer: 25 per cent off for the first 200 customers,' explains a stressed-looking young woman called Lucy, 'so I'll be really annoyed if

Ex D Q3 I'm number 201!' Her best friend, Fiona, looks annoyed already. 'I'm only here to keep Lucy company,' she says. 'I actually think it's a waste of time and money. I've been here all night and I'm really cold. I mean, this new phone looks exactly the same as last year's!' But Lucy looks shocked. 'There's only one difference that counts: the difference between the best … and second best.'

8.2 Must-have gadgets

READING

A Check understanding and pronunciation of *queue*, then put students into pairs to discuss the longest they've ever queued for something. Give a personal example, explaining what you were queuing for and why. Tell students to do the same with their partner. Get some feedback on the most interesting answers, then put them back into pairs to discuss the questions.

They're queuing to buy a new gadget (e.g. a phone).

B Do not give them the answers below yet.

a *spend a lot of money, persuade us to buy gadgets*

b *social event, big occasion, special offer, gone with a friend, promoting a business*

c *miss out on the offer, waste a long time in the queue*

d *to be the first to get the goods*

e *some people were paid to be there*

TEACHING IDEA by David Seymour and Maria Popova

Grammar: Functions

Use this activity to extend the grammar.

Here is a list of six functions. (Write them on the board.)
prediction, offer, warning, threat, advice, suggestions
I'm going to dictate six sentences. Write them down and decide which function they have. (Read out the sentences in a different order; they appear in the same order as the functions.)

1 If we don't leave now, we'll miss the train.
2 If you want, I'll do the dishes.
3 If you touch that wire, you'll get an electric shock.
4 If you don't stop doing that, I'll get angry.
5 If you explain why you did it, he'll understand.
6 If you turn it round the other way, it'll fit.

In pairs, compare your answers. Then write another conditional sentence for each function.

In groups, think of some situations where people make bargains with each other. Write an appropriate *If …* sentence for each. Read out your sentences for other groups to guess who is speaking to whom, e.g. If you're good, I'll buy you an ice cream (parent to child).

TEACHING IDEA by David Seymour and Maria Popova

Grammar: Anxiety roleplays

Use this activity to extend the grammar.

Work in pairs, A and B. Student A is very adventurous; student B is very anxious. In your pairs, roleplay a discussion between two good friends about the situation I give you, e.g.

A: I'm going to tour the Amazon.
B: What will you do if you catch malaria?
A: Don't worry. If I catch malaria, I'll go to see a local doctor.
B: But what if you're in the middle of the jungle?
A: If I'm in the jungle, I'll see an Amazonian Indian doctor.
B: What will happen if you get lost?
A: If I get lost …

1 You are going on holiday to South America, where you will spend six months taking photographs of the wildlife and landscapes, including the jungles, mountains, sea and desert.
2 You are giving up a well-paid job to become an art student in Paris.
3 You are getting married to a singer in a rock and roll band that has a reputation for very bad behaviour.

GRAMMAR HUB

8.2 Zero and first conditionals; Conditionals with modals and imperatives

A Find and correct the mistakes with the zero conditional.

1 If you ~~will~~ read a lot, you understand things better.
2 It's better if you ~~called~~ call me in the evenings.
3 Unless you ~~don't~~ try, you don't learn. If you don't try, you don't learn.
4 The roads ~~will~~ are more dangerous if it rains.
5 It doesn't work if you ~~won't~~ don't turn it on. It works if you turn it on.
6 ~~I'll~~ never go out if it's cold.

B Complete the first conditional sentences using the information in brackets.

1 The machine will not work *if you don't press this button.*
   (you / not / press this button)
2 If you find it at the right price, *will you buy it?*
   (you / buy it?)
3 What will we do *if it doesn't / does not work?*
   (it / not work?)
4 How will you get home *if you miss the bus?*
   (you / miss the bus?)
5 If it rains tomorrow, *will you still play football?*
   (you / still / play football?)
6 If you take an umbrella with you, *it'll / it will keep you dry.*
   (it / keep you dry)
7 I won't help him *unless he asks. if he doesn't / does not ask. /*
   (he / not ask)

C Choose the correct option.

1 If you see Jimmy, _____
   a will give him this note.
   b give him this note.
2 You will save money if _____
   a you can wait a few months.
   b you will wait a few months.
3 If you don't like it, _____
   a you can go home.
   b will you go home.
4 If you have any problems, _____
   a will call me.
   b call me.
5 If I feel like it, _____
   a I might go to the pop concert.
   b I can go to the pop concert.
6 Ask me if there's anything _____
   a you don't understand.
   b you won't understand.
7 If you want to have a good time, _____
   a you will come and join us on Saturday night!
   b come and join us on Saturday night!

➤ Go back to page 93.

C Tell students to read the article and to match the topic sentences from Exercise B with each paragraph. Set a time limit and tell students not to worry if they don't understand everything.

D Tell students to look at the questions and to try to remember which person each question is about. Then tell students to read the article again to check. Tell them to underline the parts of the text where they find the answers. Elicit which part of the text provided the answers when providing feedback to the class.

E Put students into groups to discuss the question. Share answers as a whole class and encourage students to expand on their answers. If students don't agree that people who buy new gadgets are innovators, ask what kind of people they do think innovators are.

GRAMMAR

A Tell students to cover the article and to read the rules in the box. Tell them that the examples all come from the first paragraph of the article. Tell students to try to complete the sentences without looking back at the text. Encourage students to work in pairs or groups on this, then tell them to uncover the text to check. Remind students about the zero and first conditional structures they saw previously, and check they understand that these are used in the same situations and for the same reasons.

B Direct students to the Grammar Hub on pages 136 and 137 (see TB91 and 92).

C As a way to make a multiple-choice controlled-practice activity more varied and fun, you could play Runaround. Divide the class into as many areas as there are possible answers (in this case, just two) and label these areas A, B, C, etc. Read out the first half of the sentence, then the two possible ways to complete it. Students have to run to the area of the class which matches the letter which they think is the correct answer. Give a time limit for this, then give the correct answer. Students in the wrong area are out and can act as judges for the next questions.

SPEAKING HUB

A Put students into pairs and tell them to think of a gadget they both know well. Do an example together as a whole class to demonstrate the task. Elicit advice about the price, features and risks. Elicit some conditionals as you do this (e.g. *If you buy the most expensive one, you'll be able to …*) to model how students could do the same. Tell students to choose a gadget and make notes about their advice. Monitor as they do this to help with language input.

B Put students into new pairs to roleplay the conversations, with first one student giving advice to their partner, then changing roles. Next, put students together with a new partner to repeat the task.

C Move students back to their original partner and tell them to tell each other about the gadgets their other partners told them about. Ask them to report what the best advice they heard was. Tell them to decide which gadget they would be most likely to buy. Decide as a whole class on the most popular gadgets and the best advice given. Finish with feedback on students' use of language.

METHODOLOGY HUB by Jim Scrivener

Classifying conditionals

There are two different ways of analysing conditional sentences.

Real/unreal

Grammar books tend to distinguish between real conditionals and unreal conditionals.

Real conditionals are made using exactly the verb tenses you would expect for the time they refer to.

If the children are playing in the garden, tell them to come in.

If you are going to fly to Paris, you'll need a new passport.

Unreal conditionals refer to unreal situations, i.e. when you are imagining impossible or unlikely futures or alternative possibilities for the past. These are made using special verb forms to indicate they are unreal:

Past simple = unlikely or impossible present or future

If human lived on Mars, do you think they'd get bored with the colour red?

The sentence is about a possible but unlikely present or future. *Lived* is a past form. The speaker uses a past form to indicate (in his / her view) the unlikeliness or the remoteness of this idea ever becoming true.

Past perfect = an alternative past

If I hadn't gone to university, my life would be very different now.

The sentence is about something that didn't happen in the past. The speaker is imagining an alternative reality. The past perfect form is used to indicate that the event never happened.

First, Second, Third, Zero

Coursebooks, teachers and students often prefer a classification into *First conditional, Second conditional, Third conditional* and *Zero conditional* (also known as *Conditional Type 1, Type 2, Type 3* and *Type 0*).

These are two different ways of dividing up and looking at the same cake. You'll have to decide which one is most suitable for you and your students. The first way is arguably more accurate and encompasses the wide variety of conditionals used in the real world. The other way is favoured by many teachers because it allows for a more sequenced way of presenting and practising a number of common types of conditional sentences.

C READ FOR GIST Read the article. Match the topic sentences (a–e) with the paragraphs (1–5).

D READ FOR DETAIL Read again. Write *B* (Bob), *J* (Janice), *M* (Mo), *R* (Ruby), *L* (Lucy) or *F* (Fiona).

Which person …

1 has met people from the queue at events like this before?   _M_

2 paid to be at the front of the queue?   _B_

3 doesn't want to buy a phone at all?   _F_

4 compares the experience to other exciting events?   _R_

5 arrived before anyone else?   _J_

6 enjoys talking to other people about gadgets?   _M_

7 is hoping to save some money?   _L_

E SPEAK Work in groups. Do you think it is right to call people who buy the latest gadgets *innovators*? Why/Why not?

Glossary

gadget (n) a small tool or piece of equipment that does something useful or impressive, sometimes using new technology

innovative (adj) new, original and advanced

innovator (n) a person who invents or begins using new ideas, methods, equipment, etc

GRAMMAR
Conditionals with modals and imperatives

A WORK IT OUT Read the rules. Then look at paragraph 1 of *If you really can't wait …* again and complete the examples.

Conditionals with modals and imperatives

Zero conditionals and first conditionals are very common. They can be very varied. Many patterns are possible.

For example, we can use imperatives in the result clause:

If you really need that phone right now, [1] ___come and join___ *the back of the queue.*

We can use modal verbs (e.g. *should, might, can, must*) in the *if*-clause or the result clause:

If you don't want to queue all night, you [2] ___can come___ *to the shop this afternoon.*

If you [3] ___can wait___ *six months or so, the same phone will cost half the price.*

B Go to the Grammar Hub on page 136.

C SPEAK Work in pairs. Write five pieces of advice for people who are thinking of queuing for the latest smartphone. Use these ideas and your own ideas:

- If you want to be at the front of the queue, you should …
- If you can't afford a new phone right now, …
- If somebody offers you $2500 for your place in the queue, …

SPEAKING HUB

A Work in pairs. Choose a gadget you both know well (e.g. phone, camera, laptop, webcam). You are going to give some advice to a friend who wants to buy one of these gadgets. Make notes on:

- price (simple version / best version?)
- features (what must/should it have?)
- risks (what might go wrong with it?)

B SPEAK Work in new pairs. Take turns to roleplay the conversation. Student A is the friend who needs advice. Student B gives advice.

A: I don't know anything about photography. Do you have any recommendations for a new camera?

B: Well, it does really depend on how much you want to spend …

C DISCUSS What was the best advice you received? Would you buy the gadget your partner recommended?

○– Use positive language to promote a new product

○– Give a friend advice about choosing a gadget

COMPREHENSION

A Work in pairs and discuss the questions.

- Have you ever tried to build a piece of furniture or put up a shelf?
- How would you describe the experience – successful, frustrating, etc?
- Are you good at giving and following instructions?

B Match the words in the box with the tools in the pictures (a–d). Which tools do you think Sam and Zac will need to build a shelf?

> allen key   drill   hammer   helmet
> pliers   screwdriver   spanner   tape measure

C ▶00:00–02:53 Watch the first part of the video. How many tools do they use?

one - the screwdriver

D ▶00:00–02:53 Put the instructions in the correct order (1–5). Watch the first part again and check your answers.

2 Lay out all the pieces in a row.

5 Insert the screws on both sides.

4 Put the screws into the correct holes.

3 Take the packet of screws.

1 Organise all of the pieces into the correct order.

E ▶02:54–04:13 How is Sam feeling and why? Watch the second part of the video to check your ideas.

FUNCTIONAL LANGUAGE
Giving and following instructions

A ▶02:54–04:13 Complete the phrases with the words in the box. Then watch the second part of the video again to check your answers.

> after   again   correct   do   how   let   sure   that   thing

Sequencing

1 The first ____thing____ to do is …

2 When you've done ____that____ …

3 ____After____ that, you …

Explaining

4 Make ____sure____ you …

5 ____Let____ me show you …

6 This is how you ____do____ it.

Checking

7 Sorry, can you say that ____again____.

8 Is this ____how____ you do it?

9 Are you sure this is ____correct____?

| MILLY | SAM | NEENA | ZAC | GABY |

B Work in pairs. Cover the functional language in Exercise A, and add sequencing phrases to the instructions in Comprehension Exercise D.

1 *The first thing to do is to organise all of the pieces into the correct order.*

2 _____ After that, you lay out all the pieces in a row. _____

3 _____ When you've done that, take the packet of screws. _____

4 _____ After that, you put the screws in the correct holes. _____

5 _____ Make sure you insert the screws on both sides. _____

USEFUL PHRASES

A Who says it? *Sam, Zac* or *Gaby*?

1 I know when something's wrong with you.
concerned   Zac

2 It's complicated. confused   Sam

3 She's been acting strangely around me.
puzzled   Sam

4 A bit cold and unfriendly. upset   Sam

5 Whatever! uninterested   Gaby

B How would you describe how each person feels in Exercise A? Choose the most appropriate adjective for each phrase.

> concerned   confused   puzzled   uninterested   upset

C How do you say these useful phrases in your language?

PRONUNCIATION
Sentence stress

 A Underline the stressed words in the sentences (1–7).
8.7   Then listen and check.

1 The first thing to do is to organise all of the pieces into the correct order.

2 Sorry, can you say that again.

3 What did you say?

4 When you've done that, take the packet of screws.

5 After that, you put the screws into the correct holes.

6 Is this how you do it?

7 Are you sure this is correct?

B Work in pairs. Practise saying the instructions in Exercise A, paying attention to the sentence stress.

SPEAKING

Work in pairs. Student A – go to the Communication Hub on page 155. Student B – go to the Communication Hub on page 151. Follow the instructions.

○– **Give and follow instructions**

➤ Turn to page 163 to learn how to write a biography.

8.3 Flat-packed

LEAD-IN

Put the students into pairs. Give one person a picture (of a house, for example) and the other person another picture (of an animal, for example). Tell the students not to show their picture to their partner but give them instructions on how to draw it. Their partner draws and they compare at the end.

COMPREHENSION

A Put students into pairs to discuss the questions.

B Put them into pairs to look at the picture and match the tools shown with the words in the box, and to discuss which tools Sam and Zac will need to build a shelf.
  a allen key, drill, helmet, screwdriver
  b tape measure
  c spanner, pliers
  d screwdriver, hammer

C Tell students to watch the extract from the video to check.

D ▶ 00:00-02:53 Tell students to look at the instructions and put them in order. Play the video for students to check.

E ▶ 00:00-02:53 Put students into pairs to discuss how they think Sam is feeling and why. Play the video for students to check.

He's feeling down/miserable/in a bad mood. You can tell because he's grumpy with Zac and tells him off for saying 'Right'. The problem is that he's in love with Gaby and she's acting cold.

FUNCTIONAL LANGUAGE

A ▶ 02:54-04:13 Elicit that all the phrases in the table were used in the video. Tell students to complete the phrases with the words in the box, then play the video again for them to check.

B Tell students to cover the Functional Language phrases from Exercise A and to look back at Comprehension Exercise D. Elicit the example, then tell students to put an appropriate sequencing phrase before the four remaining instructions.

USEFUL PHRASES

A Tell students to look at the useful phrases and to try to remember if each one was said by Sam, Zac or Gaby.

B Tell students to choose the adjectives that describe how each person was feeling when they said each of the phrases in Exercise C. Elicit that *puzzled* means confused.

C Tell students to think about how they would say the useful phrases in their language.

PRONUNCIATION

A 8.6 Tell students to look at the sentences (1–7) and underline what they think are the stressed words. Play the audio for students to check. Let students compare in pairs before feedback.

B Drill pronunciation of the sentences with the class. Then tell students to practise further in pairs, paying special attention to sentence stress.

SPEAKING

A Put students in pairs and make one student A and one student B. Direct student A to the **Communication Hub** on page 155 and student B to the **Communication Hub** on page 151.

▶ VIDEOSCRIPT

S = Sam   Z = Zac   G = Gaby

S: So … Let's do this.
Z: WAIT!
S: Why?
Z: We need to prepare.
S: Prepare for what?
Z: Ready! You?
S: Ready. OK. The first thing to do is organise all of the pieces into the correct order.
Z: Sorry, can you say that again?
S: If you take your helmet off, you'll be able to hear better.
Z: Oh, sure. What did you say?
S: Just lay out all the pieces in a row.
Z: OK, right!
S: When you've done that, take the packet of screws.
Z: OK, right!
S: Are you going to keep doing that?
Z: OK, right!
S: Can you stop saying that?
Z: OK … wrong …?
S: Yeah. Let's just get this done.
Z: OK … then.
S: Right … after that you … put the screws into the correct holes which are …
Z: You what?
S: You just put it all together I guess?
Z: Let's follow the pictures.
S: Make sure you … insert the screws on both sides … before letting go.

Z: There must be some pieces missing.
S: I think if you put the screws in on the other side, it will hold together.
Z: What screws?
S: These screws.
Z: Is this how you do it?
S: No! Let me show you … This is how you do it. There you go. Perfect?
Z: Are you sure this is correct?
S: Probably. Oh, I don't know.
Z: Are you OK?
S: Yeah, I'm fine.
Z: I know when something's wrong with you man. What's up?
S: It's … complicated.
Z: What is?
S: Look. I really like someone and I thought that maybe she felt the same, but recently she's been acting strangely around me …
Z: Strangely?
S: Yeah, a bit cold and unfriendly and I don't know why. The big problem is that I'm in love with …
Z: GABY!
S: How did you know?
G: Know what?
S: Umm, er, I was just asking Zac how he knew … which screw to use.
Z: We're building some shelves.
G: Oh … cool. Whatever.

TB94–95 **INNOVATION**

8 Writing — Write a biography

W— using linking words to show contrast

A SPEAK Work in pairs. Read the short biography *Sal Khan, founder of the Khan Academy*.

1 Who is Sal Khan?
2 What are the main events in his life?
3 How innovative is he? Why?

Sal Khan, founder of the Khan Academy

1 Sal Khan is one of the most innovative people in education today. The Khan Academy, which he started in 2006, makes free online videos to teach people around the world about maths, science and many other things.

2 Sal was born near New Orleans, USA, in 1976. After university, he found a well-paid job in finance. However, he soon realised there was more to life than money.

3 Sal's life changed in 2004, when he started giving maths lessons to members of his family. To save time, he decided to record his lessons and post them on YouTube. Despite the simple quality of the videos, they soon became popular around the world. Suddenly, he was teaching millions of people and making a real difference to their lives.

4 Although Sal didn't invent video-based learning, he helped make it popular and successful. His main innovation was to give everything away for free. As a result, he can really help those people who need it.

5 Sal's story teaches us that we don't need to be an inventor to be innovative, and we don't need to be powerful to change the world. In fact, we just need to do something we love. Hopefully, we can help other people along the way.

B Read again. Are the sentences true (T) or false (F)? Correct the false sentences.

1 You can only watch the videos in the USA. ___
2 Sal's first job was as a teacher. ___
3 He made videos because he wanted to be famous. ___
4 Sal was the first person to teach using YouTube videos. ___
5 The writer thinks that Sal loves his work. ___

C A good biography often has five sections. Match the sections (1–5) with the explanations (a-e). Use the biography of Sal Khan to help you.

1 introduction — a the story of the person's early life: family, education, first jobs, etc
2 backstory
3 turning point — b why the person is special; how they changed the world
4 impact
5 conclusion — c lessons for our own lives
   d who you are writing about and that person's biggest achievements
   e something happened that changed the person's life

D Look at the box. Add an example of each linking word from Sal Khan's biography.

Using linking words to show contrast

We use linking words (*although, despite, however*) to link two different or contrasting ideas, one of which is unexpected, surprising or seems to be contradictory.

although + subject + verb

• *Although* Sal Khan isn't an inventor, he's very innovative.
• Sal Khan is very innovative, *although* he isn't an inventor.

1 Although Sal didn't invent...

despite + noun

2 Despite the simple quality...

despite + (not) + verb + -ing

• *Despite* not being an inventor, Sal Khan is very innovative.

despite the fact that + subject + verb

• *Despite the fact that* he isn't an inventor, Sal Khan is very innovative.

however

• Sal Khan isn't an inventor. *However*, he's very innovative.
• Sal Khan is very innovative; *however*, he isn't an inventor.

3 However, he soon realised...

E Complete the sentences with the correct linking words.

1 __Despite__ the fact that he had no experience as an engineer, he solved an extremely difficult engineering problem.
2 Nobody was interested in her ideas at first, __although__ they became a lot more popular later.
3 Her invention was gorgeous and extremely innovative. __However__, it was far too expensive at first.
4 She ended up changing the world __despite having__ some very serious challenges at the beginning.
5 __Although__ he was only 14 at the time, he managed to win the design competition.

WRITING

A PREPARE You are going to write a short biography of a famous innovator or an innovative friend or family member.

B PLAN Use the five-section plan in Exercise C to help you.

C WRITE Write your biography (about 200 words). Try to use linking words to show contrasting ideas. Use the skills box to help you. Check your grammar and spelling.

D REVIEW Work in groups. Read the other students' biographies. Which biography is about the most innovative person?

WRITING   163

Answers

1 He's the founder of the Khan Academy, which uses videos to teach people.

2 He was born in 1976; he found a job after university; he started teaching in 2004; later, his videos became popular around the world.

3 Although he didn't invent anything, he is innovative because he decided to give away his lessons for free and this made a big difference to many people's lives.

Answers

1 F (You can watch the videos around the world.)

2 F (He first worked in finance.)

3 F (He made videos because he wanted to save time.)

4 F (He wasn't the first person to do this, but he helped make it popular and successful.)

5 T

WRITING

Ask students to discuss in pairs if they have ever read biographies. If they do, tell them to tell their partner about an interesting biography they have read.

A Tell students they're going to read a short biography. Tell them to read the biography and answer the questions.

B Tell the students to read the biography and decide if the sentences are true or false. Tell them to correct the false sentences.

C Explain that a good biography often has five sections. Tell students to look back at the biography once again to help them match the sections with the explanations.

D Tell students to look at the information in the box about *using linking words to show contrast*. Tell them to complete each gap with an example of how each linking word is used.

E Tell students to practise the linking words by completing the sentences with a linking word from Exercise D.

WRITING TASK

A Tell students to think of either a famous innovator or someone they know who is innovative in some way. Tell them they're going to write a biography of this person.

B Tell students to look back at the five sections of a good biography in Exercise C to help them structure their biography. Give them time to make notes about what they could write for each stage.

C Tell students to write their biography. Encourage them to use some of the linking words to show contrasting ideas from the box in Exercise D. Advise them not to overuse them as this would result in a very unnatural piece of writing. Monitor to help and highlight issues with grammar and spelling for students to correct.

D Put students into groups and tell them to read each other's biographies. When they have read them all, ask them who they think the most innovative person in the biographies is, and why. Discuss as a whole class with one member of each group explaining their choice. Finish with feedback on the biographies, commenting on the organisation and use of language.

Unit 8 Review

GRAMMAR

A Complete the dialogue with the relative clauses in the box.

> when   which   who

A: Hey, I like your watch. Is it new?

B: Yeah, I bought it last week ¹____when____ I was in London. It's got a built-in phone and a button ²____which____ you press to connect to the internet.

A: Cool. So what's the time?

B: Er … I don't know. It worked for the man ³____who____ sold it to me, but when I took it home, it didn't work at all.

B Choose the correct words to complete the article.

The litre of light

If ¹*you want* / *you'll want* to make a difference to people's lives, a good, simple idea is often enough. Brazilian engineer Alfredo Moser noticed that many people in his country live in houses with no electricity. Of course, if ²*there'll be* / *there's* no electricity, the houses are often very dark. It's hard for people to read or study at home ³*if* / *unless* they have enough light.
Alfredo's solution? Cut a hole in your roof and put a plastic water bottle through the hole. If ⁴*you do* / *you'll do* it properly, the water will bend the light from the sun, and your house will fill with light.

C Match the beginnings of the sentences (1–5) with the endings (a–e).

1 If you can't think of any good ideas,
2 If you must have the new phone today,
3 If you wear your smartwatch in the bath,
4 You shouldn't watch TV all the time
5 Don't worry

a if you're late – I'll wait for you.
b it might stop working properly.
c if you want to be more creative.
d join the queue outside the shop.
e go for a long walk.

VOCABULARY

A Complete the sentences with the correct form of the words in brackets.

1 My old website looked horrible, so I asked my sister to ____design____ (designer) a new one for me.
2 A great ____product____ (produce) is one that makes a difference.
3 This machine's broken again! Can you call an ____engineer____ (engineering) to come and fix it?
4 We've tried really hard, but we haven't had much ____success____ (succeed) yet.
5 You just copied all my ideas! That isn't very ____innovative____ (innovate), is it?

B Complete the advice with one word in each space.

Do you find it hard to come up ¹____with____ **new ideas? Try these techniques to boost your creativity!**

- If your mind goes ²____blank____, you probably need to take a break.
- Too much TV can block your creativity. Try to switch ³____off____ completely.
- Try to relax and ⁴____let____ your mind wander freely.
- Don't follow rules that don't exist! Learn to think outside the ⁵____box____!
- Talk to a friend. This will help you to look at your problems ⁶____from____ the outside.

C Complete the sentences with the best adjectives from the box.

> gorgeous   impressive   sensible
> sophisticated   suitable   unique

1 Each user has a ____unique____ username and password – it can't be the same as anybody else's.
2 **A:** 'I built a laptop computer in my garage when I was ten years old.'
   B: 'Wow! That's ____impressive____!'
3 This camera isn't really ____suitable____ for taking underwater pictures. If water gets into the electronics, it might break.
4 The best thing about my watch is that it looks ____gorgeous____. Isn't it beautiful!
5 You can buy a simple microphone in the supermarket, but if you need something more ____sophisticated____, with lots more options, you need to go to a specialist store.
6 It's fine to use another person's computer, but you need to be ____sensible____. For example, don't use it to check your bank account.

FUNCTIONAL LANGUAGE

Correct the mistake in each part of the dialogue.

1 **A:** OK, here are the instructions for the table. Let's build this! The first thing to do is take everything out of the box.
2 **B:** After that, put the legs on. Careful not to lose those screws.
3 **A:** Is this how you do it?
4 **B:** No, no, no! Those are the wrong screws. Let me show you how to do it.
5 **A:** Are you sure this is correct? It looks rubbish! Give me the instructions.

96   INNOVATION

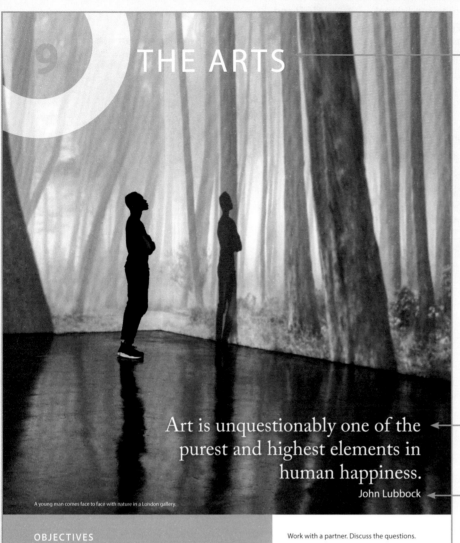

THE ARTS

The arts (n) activities such as art, music, film, theatre and dance considered together.

Art is unquestionably one of the purest and highest elements in human happiness.

John Lubbock

A young man comes face to face with nature in a London gallery.

This is part of a longer quote where the author suggests art 'trains the mind through the eye, and the eye through the mind'. It suggests that art is more than entertainment but a means of achieving happiness by connecting and training both body and mind.

John Lubbock (1834–1913) was an English banker, politician and scientist. He was influential in establishing archaeology as a science discipline and a law protecting archeological heritage.

OBJECTIVES

- suggest improvements to a proposal
- plan an arts event
- report a conversation
- create a collaborative story
- talk about films and books
- write a review

Work with a partner. Discuss the questions.

1 Look at the picture. Do you think this is art?
2 Look at the quote. Do you agree? Why/Why not?
3 Which of the arts do you like? What do you not like? Why? Are the arts important? Why/Why not?

THE ARTS   97

OBJECTIVES

Read the unit objectives to the class.

UNIT OPENER QUESTIONS

With books closed, write *Picasso* on the board. Elicit the names of other artists and their famous works of art and write these on the board, too. Ask students if they have ever seen any of the famous works of art and what they thought of them. Monitor and write any useful vocabulary on the board at the end of the activity.

Put students into pairs to discuss the questions. Discuss as a whole class and encourage students to expand on their answers and share experiences. Write further useful vocabulary that comes up on the board.

WORKSHEETS

Lesson 9.1 Art for everybody
Grammar: Second conditional (W33)
Vocabulary: The arts; verbal idioms (W34)

Lesson 9.2 Tell me a story
Grammar: Reported speech (W35)
Vocabulary: Reporting verbs (W36)

9.1 Art for everybody

● Suggest improvements to a proposal
● Plan an arts event

V — the arts; verbal idioms   G — second conditional   P — /tʃ/, /ʃ/ and /k/
S — using linking words to understand the writer's opinion

A NEW ARTS VENUE FOR THE CITY CENTRE

After the recent closure of a furniture factory in the city centre, the city council has become the owner of a large warehouse. Council members voted last week to turn the warehouse into a major public arts venue. There will be a competition to choose the best use of the space. Please visit the council website for information on how to submit a proposal.
The warehouse consists of a large empty hall (120 m x 150 m), with offices upstairs.

LISTENING

A Look at the picture and read the article above. What would you like to use the warehouse for?

◄)) B **LISTEN FOR GIST** Listen to the three finalists from the competition speaking at a council meeting. Match the finalists
9.1 (1–3) with the pictures (a–c).

1 Leon MacGregor   c   3 Florian Quirk   a
2 Violet Spring   b

◄)) C **LISTEN FOR DETAIL** Listen again. Choose the correct answers.
9.1
1 Who does Leon mostly want to help?
   a people who don't work now
   b professional musicians
   c people who go out very often

2 What exactly is Leon's dream?
   a to teach people to play musical instruments
   b to bring people together to learn new skills
   c to make money by selling tickets to concerts

3 Why do people travel to other cities to visit the theatre?
   a because they are open every day
   b because there's no theatre in their own city
   c because they don't want to spend their money at the Grand Theatre

4 What is special about immersive theatre?
   a The audience is on the stage with the actors.
   b Tickets are a lot more expensive than for other plays.
   c The audience doesn't just watch the play.

5 Why does Florian think art is important?
   a It makes money that can be spent on roads and schools.
   b It helps you to understand new ideas.
   c It helps you to relax when you're stressed.

6 How will Florian's idea help the people of the city?
   a It will give them a place to perform.
   b It will help the city's artists to sell their paintings.
   c It will make them think in a different way.

D **SPEAK** Work in pairs. Which proposal sounds the most interesting? Explain why.

LEAD-IN

With books closed, elicit some ideas from the class about what kind of services a community needs and write them on the board. If students don't suggest anything related to culture and the arts, add that to the list. Put students into pairs and tell them to rank the services on the board in order of their importance to a community. Discuss as a whole class and encourage students to explain their answers.

LISTENING

A Tell students to open their books and to look at the picture. Check understanding of *warehouse* (a big building where large amounts of goods are stored), then put students into pairs to read the article and discuss the question. Discuss as a whole class and compare students' opinions.

B Tell students they're going to listen to the three finalists from the competition speaking at a council meeting. Tell students to look at the pictures and elicit what they show. Then tell students to listen and to match the finalists with the pictures.

C Tell students to read the questions and to try to answer them from what they remember. Play the audio again for students to listen and check. Ask students to explain their answers with reference to exactly what the speakers said.

D Put students into pairs to discuss which proposal they think sounds most interesting and why. Discuss as a whole class and encourage students to give reasons for their answers.

AUDIOSCRIPT

 9.1

Listening, Exercise B
C = Chair   L = Leon   V = Violet   F = Florian

C: Welcome to the final of the Warehouse Project competition. Now, we received hundreds of excellent ideas, but there can only be one winner. Today, the three finalists are here to present their proposals before the public vote later this evening. But for now, let's hear from the first finalist, Leon MacGregor.

L: Thank you. I'd like to present my proposal to turn the warehouse into a community music centre, with modern recording studios, rehearsal rooms and a performance area for live concerts. If the proposal is successful, people will be able to use the centre free of charge. I believe music can make a big

Ex C Q1   difference to our community, especially for older people who have retired from work. If we open a community music centre, it will change thousands of people's lives, by giving them opportunities to go out, meet new people and learn new skills. Won't

Ex C Q2   that be wonderful for our city? My dream is for the people of this city to join music classes with professional musicians, to learn how to sing or to play a musical instrument. They'll work together to form bands, orchestras and choirs. They'll have the space and equipment they need to rehearse and create new music. And they'll be able to perform live in front of an audience. If you share my dream, vote for my proposal to help it come true. Music … for the community.

C: Thank you, Leon. Our next finalist is Violet Spring.

V: Thank you. As an actor, I love the theatre. And I'm not alone – tens of thousands of people all over the country visit the theatre every day. But not in this

Ex C Q3   city. Since the Grand Theatre closed down ten years ago, theatre-lovers have had nowhere to go. They have to travel to theatres in other cities – and spend their money there instead of here. But I'm convinced that if we had a good, modern theatre in this city, it would be extremely popular. What do I mean by a modern theatre? Well, I firmly believe that

Ex C Q4   the future is immersive theatre. Immersive theatre is where the audience becomes part of the performance. There's no stage – just one shared space for actors and spectators alike. You don't just watch a play – you experience it. Immersive theatre works best in a large open area, where groups of audience members can move around to watch different scenes of the play in different parts of the theatre. And I think the city's warehouse would make a wonderful immersive theatre. But it isn't just about art. Immersive theatre is also a great business. The best shows attract rich international tourists who are prepared to pay premium prices. If we turned the warehouse into a theatre, it would make a lot of money. This money could be spent on schools, roads and other important things for the city. If you like the sound of that, please support my proposal.

C: Thank you, Violet. Very interesting. Our final finalist is Florian Quirk.

F: Thank you. Let me ask you a question. What … is the purpose … of art? To keep bored people busy? To make money from rich tourists? No, I don't think

Ex C Q5   so. Art is about opening your mind to new experiences, new emotions. It's about losing yourself … and finding yourself. Great art makes you laugh; it

Ex C Q6   makes you cry; it makes you think. It helps you see things you've never seen, feel things you've never felt, understand things you've never understood. In short, the purpose of art … is to give a purpose … to life. That's why I'd like to turn the warehouse into a gallery of modern art. A place where audiences can view the works of today's best artists, including exhibitions by some of the talented artists from this city. And if we make it free of charge, all the people of this city can enjoy the exhibitions, displays and live performances. So if you really want to use this space for the arts, then forget about business plans and community projects. Let's create a gallery that will change the way the people of this city think … forever. Thank you.

C: OK, thank you. Well, I must say, all three proposals sound excellent! If the city council had three warehouses, maybe we could do all of those wonderful things. But we only have one warehouse, unfortunately, so we need to make a choice. I'd like to call a 15-minute break now so we can …

VOCABULARY

A Point out that some words can go in more than one box. Monitor to help explain meaning.

Theatre: an audience, a performance, to rehearse, a scene, a spectator, a stage

Art: a display, an exhibition, a gallery

Music: an audience, a choir, an instrument, a live concert, a musician, an orchestra, to perform live, a performance, a recording studio, to rehearse, a rehearsal room, a spectator, a stage

B Check answers by eliciting ideas from the class.

C Put students into pairs to discuss the questions.

GRAMMAR

A Put students into pairs to complete activities.

B Tell students to use the sentences to help them complete the rules.

C Direct students to the **Grammar Hub** on pages 138 and 139 (see below).

D Put students into pairs to discuss the questions. Use the **Grammar Worksheet** on W33 for extra practice.

SPEAKING

A Put students into groups. Student A should look at the box on the page. Direct student B to the **Communication Hub** on page 152 and student C to page 154.

B Pair student As and students Bs together and ask them to tell each other about the proposal they read about.

C Tell groups to decide which proposal should win and why. Share ideas as a class and ask students to justify opinions.

GRAMMAR HUB

9.1 Second conditional

Condition	Result
If **you submitted** a proposal,	**they would accept** it.
If **she didn't teach** music,	**she'd be** a full-time musician.
If **the show were** expensive,	**I wouldn't go** to it.
If **we didn't have** an art venue,	**we wouldn't see** much art.

Question	Positive short answer	Negative short answer
If **you had** more free time, **would you spend** it creatively?	Yes, **I would**.	No, **I wouldn't**.
Would you spend your free time creatively if **you had** more of it?		

- We use the second conditional to talk about present situations that aren't real and future events that are unlikely but possible.
- Although it uses the past simple, the second conditional is NOT about the past.
- We use *if* + past simple in the *if*-clause and *would* + infinitive in the result clause.
- We can use *might* or *could* in the result clause if we are not sure of the result.

  If she rehearsed every day, she might improve her skills.

  We could display community art if we had a local arts venue.

- With the verb *be*, we generally use *were* instead of *was* with all subjects, including *I*.

9.1 Second conditional

A Choose the correct option.

1 If I (*knew*) / *know* the words to the song, I would sing it.
2 If she had a better idea for the story, she *uses* / (*would use*) it.
3 If we *would hold* / (*held*) an art competition, many people would take part.
4 The public *liked* / (*might like*) his proposal if he presented it to them.
5 If you *invite* / (*invited*) Monique to the play, would she come?
6 If they allowed the public behind the stage, the actors *weren't* / (*wouldn't be*) pleased.
7 I'd study art at Kingston University if I (*were*) / *am* you.

B Correct the mistakes in these second conditional sentences.

1 If you ~~get~~ *got* rid of your guitar, you would miss it later.
2 If we bought cheaper tickets, we would ~~saved~~ save a lot of money.
3 If they ~~interact~~ *interacted* with the audience, the play would be more exciting.
4 I ~~won't~~ *wouldn't* be terribly upset if my bandmates and I didn't make up.
5 ~~Will~~ *Would* Chanda enjoy it more if she spent more time in her studio?
6 If the show took place outdoors, more people ~~can~~ *could* come.
7 Everyone would be very unhappy if it ~~rains~~ *rained* the day of the concert.
8 If he ~~doesn't~~ *didn't* make fun of his classmates, would they like him more?

C Write the correct form of the verbs in brackets. Use *would* if necessary.

1 If the city ___*built*___ (build) a new theatre, many people would attend it.
2 If we rehearsed every day, we ___*would become*___ (become) the best!
3 If my favourite musician ___*performed*___ (perform) for free, thousands would go to see it.
4 Jean-Philippe ___*would sell*___ (sell) millions of copies if he recorded his songs.
5 The public would be disappointed if the gallery ___*closed*___ (close) its doors.
6 If I ___*were*___ (be) a famous artist, could I sell my paintings for £1 million?
7 If you ___*told*___ (tell) your story, I think people would show an interest in it.
8 Most people ___*wouldn't like*___ (not like) it if I sang in public!

➤ Go back to page 99.

VOCABULARY
The arts

A Complete the table with the words in the box. Some words can go in more than one place.

> an audience   a choir   a display   an exhibition
> a gallery   an instrument   a live concert   a musician
> an orchestra   to perform live   a performance
> a recording studio   a rehearsal room   to rehearse
> a scene   a spectator   a stage

Theatre	Art (e.g. paintings)	Music
an audience		an audience

B What other words can you add to each group? Think about people and places connected with each topic.

C SPEAK Work in pairs and ask and answer the questions.

1 Do you ever rehearse what you are going to say before you say it? Think of examples.

2 Do you prefer to be a performer on a stage or a member of the audience? Why?

3 Can you play any musical instruments? Would you like to?

GRAMMAR
Second conditional

A WORK IT OUT Work in pairs. Look at the sentences (a–d) from the council meeting and discuss the questions (1–3).

a If we open a community music centre, it will change thousands of people's lives.

b If we turned the warehouse into a theatre, it would make a lot of money.

c If we had a good, modern theatre in this city, it would be extremely popular.

d If the city council had three warehouses, maybe we could do all of those wonderful things.

1 Sentences **a** and **b** are both about the future. Which speaker is more certain that their plans will really happen? **a** uses *will* not *would*

2 In sentence **c**, does the city have a theatre at the moment? *no*

3 In sentence **d**, does the city council have three warehouses? Can they do all three things? *no*

B Complete the rules with the words in the box.

> could   infinitive   past   unreal   were

Second conditional

1 Conditional sentences usually have two clauses: the *if-*clause and the result clause. To make second conditional sentences, we use *If* + _____past_____ simple and *would* + _____infinitive_____ without *to*.

2 With the verb *be*, we use _____were_____ instead of *was*.
   If I were you, I'd vote for the first proposal.

3 We use the second conditional to talk about _____unreal_____ or impossible situations in the present or future.

4 If we are not sure of the result, we can use **might** or _____could_____ instead of **would** in the result clause.

C Go to the Grammar Hub on page 138.

D SPEAK Work in pairs and discuss the questions.

1 How would you feel if somebody asked you to sing in public?

2 If you were a successful musician, what sort of music would you play?

SPEAKING

A Work in pairs. Student A – read the box below. Student B – go to the Communication Hub on page 152. Student C – go to the Communication Hub on page 154. Read about one of the proposals for the Warehouse Project. Make notes on the advantages and disadvantages.

Proposal 1: Community music centre

Costs (= money going out)		Income (= money coming in)
Building work: £450,000	Staff: £50,000/year	None – everything will be free for community groups
Equipment: £350,000	Other costs (e.g. electricity): £100,000/ year	

* The community music centre will save money by only opening for a few hours each day.
* Rehearsals/Workshops: Mondays, Wednesdays and Fridays, 10 am to 3 pm
* Concerts: Tuesdays and Thursdays, 12 pm to 2 pm
* Evenings and weekends: closed

B Tell your partner about your proposal. Then discuss what you like about each one. Suggest some improvements.

C Decide which proposal should win the competition. Why? Then share your ideas with the class.

READING

A SPEAK Work in pairs. Imagine you are watching a traditional play. What would you do if a character on the stage spoke to you? Would you be happy or would you feel uncomfortable?

B READ FOR MAIN IDEA Read the first paragraph of *The best (and the worst) of immersive theatre*. Why has the writer written the article?

C READ FOR GIST Read the rest of the article. Match the recommendations (a–g) with the sections (1–6). There is one extra recommendation.

a Keep it simple. 3
b Tell a story. 5
c Make the audience feel special. 2
d Make it an experience for all the senses. 6
e Keep ticket prices as low as possible.
f Keep the rest of the audience out of sight. 4
g Make good use of the space. 1

The best (and the worst) of **immersive theatre**

For most people, going to the theatre is a chance to relax and let the actors do all the work. But in recent years, a new type of theatre has appeared where the audience takes part in the play! When it works well, immersive theatre can be breathtaking. But when it goes wrong, it can be awful. Here are my six recommendations based on my favourite (and least favourite!) immersive plays.

¹ g
Sometimes the building itself is part of the Ex D Q1 experience. A good example is *Hotel Impossible*, which took place in a real hotel building. Similarly, *The Dark Tunnels* took place inside real tunnels, which created a very scary atmosphere. However, a great location isn't everything. *Dangerous Heart* was in a beautiful palace, but the play didn't really take advantage of the space.

² c
In *Step by Step*, the audience was limited to 15, so we could interact one-to-one with the characters. During the play, the audience had to solve a crime, so we really had to pay attention to what we saw and heard. By the end, I was terrified and exhausted, but it was an unforgettable experience.

³ a
Some immersive plays feel far too complicated, with too many characters and storylines. For example, *Yellow and Blue* had amazing special effects, but I couldn't keep track of who was who. In *The Quiet* Ex D Q2 *Visitors*, however, there were only six characters in a large empty room. We had to use our imaginations, Ex D Q3 and the effect was incredibly powerful.

⁴ f
The worst thing about immersive theatre? Other members of the audience! The play *Life with the Lions* got rid of this problem by making the audience wear animal costumes. I felt silly in my zebra costume, but at least we couldn't tell the difference between actors and spectators. In *The Dark Tunnels*, we all wore black clothes and masks so the members of the audience were almost invisible to each other.

⁵ b
Without a strong story, immersive theatre can easily fall flat – it feels like something's missing. In *Hotel Impossible*, for example, lots of interesting things happened, but the whole play didn't really go Ex D Q4 anywhere. In *The Quiet Visitors*, however, there was a clear beginning, a middle … and a shocking surprise at the end.

⁶ d
It isn't just about what the audience sees and hears. The best immersive plays make use of the senses of taste, smell and touch, too. In *Dangerous Heart*, we enjoyed a delicious meal as part of the experience. Similarly, in *The Dark Tunnels*, the unpleasant Ex D Q5 underground smell added to the sense of danger. And in *The Quiet Visitors*, when the room suddenly went as cold as ice, the effect was terrifying. Ex D Q6

9.1 Art for everybody

READING

A Check understanding of *a play* and elicit some examples. Ask students if they enjoy watching plays and why or why not. Put students into pairs to discuss the questions. Share answers as a whole class and ask students to explain their responses.

B Point out the pictures and elicit what they show and how they could be connected to theatre. Tell the students they are going to read an article about *immersive theatre*. Elicit ideas for what they think *immersive theatre* is. Tell students to read the first paragraph to check their ideas and to answer the question. Tell students not to worry about the highlighted and underlined words at this stage, as you're going to focus on them later.

Possible answer: *To make recommendations for people who want to make immersive theatre plays*

C Tell students to read the rest of the article and to match the recommendations with the sections. Point out that there is one recommendation that they don't need to use.

D Point out the information in the box about *using linking words to understand the writer's opinion* and tell students to look at the highlighted words in the article. Go through the first one as an example to show how *similarly* links one positive opinion to another. Tell students to use the same strategies to decide if the writer has positive or negative opinions about the other things. When checking answers, ask students to explain their answers with reference to how the linking words are used.

E Put students into pairs to discuss which of the plays from the article they would most and least like to see and why. Discuss as a whole class, encouraging students to explain their answers and express opposing opinions.

TEACHING IDEA by David Seymour and Maria Popova
Grammar: What if . . .

Use this activity to practise the grammar.

Supposing you could meet anyone you wanted, alive or dead, who would it be? Why? What would you say to him/her?

If you could live in another place and time in history, what would it be?

In small groups, brainstorm some endings for these sentences. Choose the best from your group and write the whole sentence down. (Ask the groups to read out their ideas and invite the class to choose their favourites.)

If the world was flat . . . If animals could speak . . . If we were all clones . . . If cows could fly . . . If you had two heads . . . If money grew on trees . . . If time travel was possible . . . If there was no money . . . If nobody knew how to read . . . If everyone was telepathic . . .

If I gave you one million euros, what would you do with it? Write a list of five things. Read out your list. Who does the class think should get the money?

METHODOLOGY HUB by David Seymour and Maria Popova
Reading skills and exams

Reading texts do not necessarily need to be exam texts to practise key skills for exams such as IELTS and TOEFL. Here are two examples of reading skills which are crucial to exams, which can be practised on many different types of texts, like the *The best (and the worst) of immersive theatre*.

Reading for main information

On exams such as IELTS, candidates are sometimes required to extract the main information from a long text in order to complete a summary or notes on the text.

Students need to practice identifying the broad meaning of the text and the main points it contains, using, for example, the titles, introduction and conclusion, and topic sentences within the original article.

Reading for arguments

Reading texts on exams such as IELTS and TOEFL often contain more than just facts and information. Arguments and opinions are presented and the reader needs to be able to recognise these. Looking for keywords and phrases is an effective and efficient way to identify arguments and follow the logical connections the writer is making. Highlighting these words and phrases helps the reader to understand what is fact and what is argument or opinion.

METHODOLOGY HUB by David Seymour and Maria Popova
Lexical practice activities and games

Lexical practice activities and games

After students have seen and heard a new lexical item for the first time, they will need opportunities to become more familiar with it, to practise recognising, manipulating and using it. Many simple lexical practice activities are based around the following ideas:

- discussions, communicative activities and role play requiring use of the lexical items;
- making use of the lexis in written tasks.

There are many published exercises on lexis. These include:

- matching pictures to lexical items;
- matching parts of lexical items to other parts, eg beginnings and endings;
- matching lexical items to others, eg collocations, synonyms, opposites, sets of related words, etc;
- using prefixes and suffixes to build new lexical items from given words;
- classifying items into lists;
- using given lexical items to complete a specific task;
- filling in crosswords, grids or diagrams;
- filling in gaps in sentences;
- memory games.

Many such tasks seem to be designed for students working on their own, but can easily be used in class.

VOCABULARY

A Point out the information in the box about verbal idioms, then direct students to the **Vocabulary Hub** on page 146. Tell students that the answers to Exercise A are all verbal idioms used in the article *The best (and the worst) of immersive theatre*. Tell them to try to complete the gaps without looking back at the text. When they have done this, tell students to look back at the text to check. Check answers as a whole class and check understanding of the idioms by eliciting personalised examples that will be relevant and memorable to the students. Students can then do Exercise B to focus on more verbal idioms.

B Tell students to work alone to complete the sentences so they are true for them. Then put them into pairs to compare and explain their sentences. To demonstrate, elicit an example from one student and ask the others to ask follow-up questions and react appropriately. Share the most interesting answers as a whole class. Use the **Vocabulary Worksheet** on W34 for extra practice.

PRONUNCIATION

🔊 **9.2** A Point out the information in the box about the pronunciation of *ch*. Put students into pairs to discuss how they think the words are pronounced. Then play the audio for students to listen and check. Tell them to repeat each word as they hear it.

In charge and choice, ch is pronounced the usual way, /tʃ/.
In chef, it sounds like /ʃ/.
In character, choir and orchestra, it sounds like /k/.

B Tell students to find and underline *ch* in the sentences and decide on the pronunciation of *ch* in each case.

🔊 **9.3** C Play the audio for students to listen and check. Then play it again for them to repeat the sentences. Repeat if necessary, or model and drill the sentences yourself if students need extra help with any words.

D Put students into pairs to practise saying the sentences. Encourage them to listen carefully to their partner to check their pronunciation. Monitor and help if any students are still having difficulty.

SPEAKING HUB

A Put students into groups and tell them they're going to devise their own immersive theatre performance. Tell them to discuss the questions to help them brainstorm ideas for the story, the location and the interactive element. Tell them to think of as many ideas as they can at this stage. Monitor and help or prompt if necessary.

B Tell the groups to choose their best idea to make into an immersive theatre performance. Tell them to look back at the article *The best (and the worst) of immersive theatre* on page 100 for advice as they add details to their idea. Tell students they're going to present their idea to the class when they've finished preparing. Monitor to help with language if needed. When students have finished, tell them to practise making their presentation in their group.

C Tell each group to present their idea to the class. Tell the other groups to listen carefully and to ask questions at the end.

D Make new groups and tell students to discuss which of the immersive plays they would most like to watch, and why. Tell students it's not a competitive activity, so they can give their honest opinion and don't have to argue for their idea. Discuss as a whole class and find out which is the most popular idea. Ask students to explain their opinions. Finish with feedback on students' use of language during the presentation and reflection stages.

> **Extra activity**
> For homework, students can write a short advertisement for an immersive play. Without giving away the full plot, students should provide information about:
> - the story
> - the location
> - how it is interactive or immersive
> - why people should see it

TEACHING IDEA by David Seymour and Maria Popova

Topic: High culture

Use this activity to extend the topic.

What cultural activities do you take part in?

In pairs, tell each other about what you do and the places you go, e.g. cinemas, theatres, galleries, museums, etc. (Ask students to specify films, plays and exhibitions.)

Mingle with the rest of the class and find out everyone's favourite painting, building and piece of music. Note down the name of anyone who shares your opinion. Did anyone find someone with the same three favourites?

TEACHING IDEA by David Seymour and Maria Popova

Grammar: Chain story

Use this activity to practise the grammar.

Tell a chain story about a boy called Tom who dreams of being an astronaut. (*If I were a grown-up, I'd become an astronaut. If I were an astronaut, I'd go to Mars. If I went to Mars, I think I'd meet some aliens. If I met them, we'd become good friends.*)

D Look at the highlighted words in the article. What is the writer's opinion? Use the strategies in the box to help you. Choose + (positive) or – (negative).

Using linking words to understand the writer's opinion

When you're trying to work out the writer's opinion, don't just look for positive words (e.g. *amazing*, *interesting*) and negative words (e.g. *unpleasant*, *terrifying*).

Writers often use words like *for example*, *similarly* and *however* to link their opinions to earlier sentences.

1 the location for *The Dark Tunnels* ⊕/ –
2 the characters and story in *Yellow and Blue* + /⊝
3 the characters and story in *The Quiet Visitors* ⊕/ –
4 the story in *Hotel Impossible* + /⊝
5 the experience for the senses in *The Dark Tunnels* ⊕/ –
6 the experience for the senses in *The Quiet Visitors* ⊕/ –

E SPEAK Work in pairs. Which of the plays from the article would you most like to see? Which would you least like to see? Why? Tell your partner.

VOCABULARY
Verbal idioms

Verbal idioms

Verbal idioms are fixed phrases that work as verbs with a single meaning.

A Go to the Vocabulary Hub on page 146.

B SPEAK Complete the sentences so they are true for you. Then work in pairs and tell your partner what happened.

1 I had an opportunity to … but I didn't take advantage of it, because …
2 Everything went wrong when I …
3 I'm planning to get rid of …
4 I once tried to (tell a joke/story, etc), but it fell flat, because …

PRONUNCIATION
/tʃ/, /ʃ/ and /k/

 A How do you pronounce *ch* in these words? Listen and repeat.
9.2

character   charge   chef   choice   choir   orchestra

ch

ch is usually pronounced /tʃ/ (as in *cheese*). But there are also a few words where *ch* is pronounced /ʃ/ (as in *moustache*) or /k/ (as in *chemist*).

B Find and underline *ch* in these sentences. Then write /tʃ/, /ʃ/ or /k/ above each example.

/tʃ/
1 My children didn't go to school today – they both had bad stomach aches. /k/ /k/ /k/
2 If I were a mechanic, I might be able to fix this machine, but I don't know anything about technology. /k/ /ʃ/ /k/
3 My sister is a chemist; she's doing some research into new techniques for recycling harmful chemicals. /k/ /tʃ/ /k/ /k/

C Listen and check.
9.3

D SPEAK Work in pairs. Practise saying the sentences. Listen and check your partner's pronunciation.

SPEAKING HUB

A Work in groups. Discuss ideas for an immersive theatre performance. Think about:
- story: Will you use an existing story or create your own?
- location: Where will it take place? How could you make use of the location?
- interactivity: How will the actors interact with the audience?

B PLAN Choose your best idea and add more details. Follow the advice in *The best (and the worst) of immersive theatre* on page 100.

C PRESENT Present your idea to the class.

D REFLECT Which immersive play would you most like to watch? Why?

○– Suggest improvements to a proposal
○– Plan an arts event

- Report a conversation
- Create a collaborative story

G— reported speech   V— reporting verbs   P— using your voice to make a story more interesting

S— listening for definitions of new words

Francis Scott Key Fitzgerald (1896–1940) was one of the most important American writers of the 20th century. His best-known novel, *The Great Gatsby* (1925), is an American classic. It paints a powerful portrait of life in 1920s America, a period known as the Jazz Age. For many young people in America, this was a time for partying and having fun, with new types of music, new ways of dancing and new fashions.

READING

A Work in pairs. Read about F Scott Fitzgerald and look at the pictures. Have you read *The Great Gatsby*? Why do you think it is 'an American classic'?

I haven't read the book but I have seen the film starring Leonardo DiCaprio.

 B Listen to a conversation between two friends, José and Nadia. Answer the questions.

9.4

1 Who is Jay Gatsby?

2 Why doesn't José want to borrow the book? Why does he change his mind?

3 Why does Nadia like the book?

CHAPTER 3: I MEET GATSBY

PART 1

One day, I was invited to one of Gatsby's parties. As soon as I arrived, I began to look for Gatsby to thank him for his Ex C Q1 invitation. But no one knew where he was.

As I went to get a drink, I saw Jordan Baker. I walked Ex C Q2 towards her, glad to see someone I knew.

'I thought you might be here,' Jordan said. Ex C Q3

We took our drinks and sat down at a small table under a tree. Jordan began to talk to a girl in a yellow dress.

'Do you come to these parties often?' Jordan asked her.

'I come when I can,' the girl said. 'No one cares what I do, so I always have a good time. Last time I was here, I tore my dress. Do you know, Gatsby sent me a new one! It cost him Ex C Q4 265 dollars!'

PART 2

Supper was now being served. Jordan and I left our table and went to look for Gatsby.

People were dancing now. The voices and the laughter were very loud. The moon was high in the sky.

Jordan and I sat down at a table with a well-dressed man of Ex D Q1 my own age. I was enjoying myself, now. The music stopped for a moment. The man at our table looked at me and smiled.

'I think I know your face,' the man said. 'Weren't you in Ex D Q3 France during the War?'

'Yes, I was.'

'Me, too,' he said. We talked about the War for a few minutes. Then the man told me that **he had a new motorboat.**

'Want to go out with me in the morning, old sport?' he asked.

'Sure, what time?'

'Let's say nine o'clock.'

I looked at the garden and smiled.

'This is an unusual party,' I told the man. 'I haven't seen my host yet. Gatsby sent me an invitation this morning. I ought to thank him.'

The man stared at me in surprise.

'I'm Gatsby,' he said. 'I thought you knew, old sport. I'm Ex not a very good host, am I?'

Gatsby smiled. He had a pleasant smile. His smile made me feel important. I looked at Gatsby with interest. He Ex was a tough-looking young man, but he had beautiful clothes and beautiful manners.

PART 3

A few guests were standing near Gatsby. I went up to him to say goodbye.

'Don't forget we're going out in the boat, old sport,' he said. 'At nine o'clock.'

Gatsby smiled at me.

'Goodnight, old sport, goodnight.'

I walked across the lawn in the moonlight. The cars drove away. The gardens were quiet and empty.

All alone, Gatsby stood on the white steps, waving goodbye.

> **Glossary**
>
> **old sport (phrase)** a popular way of saying 'my friend' in the 1920s

LEAD-IN

Ask students to think of a classic book or film from their country. Put students into pairs to discuss their choices.

READING

A–B Students work in pairs then individually to complete the exercises.

Joe: Hey, Nadia, what are you reading?

Nadia: Oh, hi, Joe. It's The Great Gatsby – one of my favourite novels. Have you read it?

Joe: No. I've heard of it, but I don't know much about it. It's American, isn't it?

Nadia: Yeah. It's one of the classics of American literature. It was written in the 1920s.

Joe: So, what's it about?

Nadia: Well, it's about a man called Jay Gatsby. He's rich and he has lots of amazing parties, but he has a hidden secret.

Joe: Really? What's the secret?

Nadia: I can't tell you. You'll have to read the book. Borrow mine when I finish.

Joe: Erm … How long is it? Classics tend to be quite long don't they?

Nadia: No, not at all, it's 180 pages.

Joe: Oh that's not too bad. So … why should I read it?

Nadia: Well, it's a great story – it's told by a man called Nick Carraway, who meets Gatsby at one of his parties, and then makes friends with him.

Joe: OK.

Nadia: But I think the best thing about the book is that it really paints a picture of America in the 1920s. I really feel as if I'm there, inside the story. It's very well written.

Joe: Cool. I might read it. Can I have a look?

GRAMMAR HUB

9.2 Reported speech

Direct speech	Reported speech
present simple	past simple
'**We enjoy** live concerts the best.'	They said (that) **they enjoyed** live concerts the best.
present continuous	past continuous
'**We are learning** how to write a short story.'	They said (that) **they were learning** how to write a short story.
will	would
'**I will** read my book later.'	She said (that) **she would** read her book later.
may	might
'**Elle may** sing in the play.'	He said (that) **Elle might** sing in the play.
can	could
'**We can** film our daily lives.'	They said (that) **they could** film their daily lives.
should	should (no change)
'**He should try out** for that role.'	She said (that) he **should try out** for that role.
For commands and instructions	tell + object (+ not) + to + infinitive
'**Rehearse** the scene again.'	He told them **to rehearse** the scene again.
'**Don't look** at the camera.'	She told me **not to look** at the camera.

- We use reported speech to report what people say. We use a reporting verb in the past simple (e.g. said, asked, told).
- When we report what someone says, the reported verb usually goes back one tense.
- When we report questions, the subject comes before the verb (the same as in sentences).

  Alain: 'Where **is he acting**?' → Alain asked where **he was acting**.

- With yes/no questions, we start the reported question with if or whether.

  Chloe: 'Will Tom attend the show?' → Chloe asked **if/whether** Tom would attend the show.

- We change some pronouns from direct speech to reported speech depending on the speaker (I to he/she, you to me, my to his/her, etc).

  Kieran: 'I've given **you my** ticket already.' → He said he had given **me his** ticket already.

- We sometimes also need to change words which refer to time and place.

Direct speech	Reported speech
tomorrow	the next day / the following day
today	that day
here	there
this	that/the

- We often don't change the verb tenses if we are reporting facts that are still true in the present.

  Our coach said that acting **requires** a great deal of time and effort.

C Tell students they're going to read an extract from the novel. Tell them to read part 1 first and to decide if the sentences are true or false and to correct the false ones. Let students compare with their partner before feedback.

D Tell students to read part 2 and to make notes on what we find out about Gatsby.

E Tell students to read part 3 and then discuss the question with a partner.

GRAMMAR

A Tell students to look at the phrase in bold in part 2. Ask if this is direct or reported speech. Tell students to complete the sentence for what they think Gatsby's exact words were. Elicit how the verb changes from direct speech to reported speech.

B Tell the students to read and complete the examples. Do the first one together as a whole class as an example.

C Direct students to the **Grammar Hub** on pages 138 and 139 (see TB102 and below).

D Tell students to report the sentences from *The Great Gatsby*. Elicit that they are all in direct speech. Tell students to change them into reported speech.

E Put students into pairs to imagine how the story continues. Tell them to write a conversation between Jay and Nick the following morning, using reported speech. Use the **Grammar Worksheet** on W35 for extra practice.

SPEAKING

A Tell students to think about the questions and make notes. Monitor and provide students with language they request.

B Put students into pairs to ask and answer the questions. Tell them to ask each other follow-up questions to find out as much information about each other as possible. To demonstrate this, start by eliciting some answers as a whole class.

C Put students with a new partner and tell them to tell each other as much as they can remember about their previous partner. Discuss as a whole class and find out who remembered the most and who was most accurate.

GRAMMAR HUB

9.2 Reported speech

A Choose the correct option.

1 Maya: 'I'm going to an outdoor concert tonight.'
She said she *is* / (*was*) going to an outdoor concert that night.

2 Dan and Tracy: 'We're rehearsing all day tomorrow.'
They said they **were rehearsing** / **will rehearse** all day the following day.

3 Joe to Lyn: 'I can give you my proposal.'
He said he **can** / **could** give her his proposal.

4 Nadia to me: 'I will ask the doorman to let you in for free.'
She said she **asked** / **would ask** the doorman to let me in for free.

5 The teachers: 'We've chosen a local warehouse.'
They said they **will choose** / **had chosen** a local warehouse.

6 Me: 'I'm not writing a review of the play this evening.'
You said you weren't writing the review **this** / **that** evening.

7 John to Isabel: 'Come to the concert hall at 7 pm.'
John **said** / **told** Isabel to come to the concert hall at 7 pm.

B Report the statements.

1 Hanna: 'I'm performing at the theatre tomorrow.'
She said *(that) she was performing at the theatre the next/following day.*

2 Alexis: 'I've never written a novel before.'
He said (that) he had never written a novel before.

3 Marcia: 'I'll buy my tickets online.'
She said (that) she would buy her tickets online.

4 Davide and Maria: 'We're meeting a famous actor today.'
They said (that) they were meeting a famous actor that day.

5 Anastasiya: 'I can't hear from the back row.'
She said (that) she couldn't / could not hear from the back r

6 Hussein: 'I gave Sonia my seat.'
He said (that) he had given Sonia his seat.

C Choose the correct option.

1 Sara: 'When is the concert?'
She asked _____.
a if the concert was today   (b) when the concert was
c when is the concert

2 Elena to Jim: 'You'll love Paulina's performance.'
She promised that Jim _____ Paulina's performanc
a loves   b will love
(c) would love

3 Soraya to me: 'Have you read *The Great Gatsby*?'
She asked me _____ *The Great Gatsby*.
a whether I read   (b) if I had read
c why I had read

4 Georgia and Hans: 'Are our seats in front?'
They asked _____.
a if our seats are in front   b if our seats were in fro
(c) if their seats were in front

5 Mary to me: 'How did you end up working in film?'
She asked me _____ working in film.
(a) how I had ended up   b how I would end up
c if I ended up

➤ Go back to page 103.

C READ FOR DETAIL Read *The Great Gatsby*, Chapter 3, Part 1. Are the sentences true (T) or false (F)? Correct the false sentences.

1 Gatsby invited Nick Carraway (the storyteller) to his party. Nick did not know people at the party, and was glad to see Jordan.   T

2 ~~Nick already knew most of the people at the party.~~   F
   Jordan expected to see Nick.

3 ~~Jordan was surprised to see Nick.~~   F
Gatsby spends a lot of money, and is generous with his money.

4 ~~Gatsby is very careful with his money.~~   F

D Read Part 2. What do we learn about Gatsby? Make notes on:

1 his appearance (= his clothes and the way he looks).

2 his manners (= the way he treats other people).

3 his background (= what he has done in the past).

E Read Part 3. Why do you think Gatsby has so many parties?

GRAMMAR
Reported speech

A WORK IT OUT Look at the phrase in bold from *The Great Gatsby*, Chapter 3, Part 2. What do you think Gatsby actually said?

Direct speech: 'I _____ have _____ a new motorboat.'

B Complete the examples in the correct tense.

Direct speech	Reported speech
Present simple	Past simple
'My name's Jay Gatsby.'	He told me his name ¹ _____ was _____ Jay Gatsby.
Present continuous	Past continuous
'I'm really enjoying the party.'	I told him I ² _____ was _____ really enjoying the party.
Present perfect	Past perfect
'I've never met Gatsby.'	He said he ³ _____ had _____ never met Gatsby.
Past simple	Past perfect
'Gatsby sent me a new dress.'	She said Gatsby ⁴ _____ had _____ sent her a new dress.
can	*could*
'I can't see the host.'	I told him I ⁵ _____ couldn't _____ see the host.
will	*would*
'We'll have a great time on my boat.'	He said we ⁶ _____ would _____ have a great time on his boat.

C Go to the Grammar Hub on page 138.

D Report the sentences (1–5) from *The Great Gatsby*.

1 'Do you come to these parties often?' Jordan asked her.
   Jordan asked the girl if she came to these parties often.

2 'I come when I can,' the girl said.
   The girl/She said she came when she could.
   _____

3 'I think I know your face,' the man said.
   The man/He said he thought he knew Nick's/his face.
   _____

4 'This is an unusual party,' I told the man. 'I haven't seen my host yet.'
   Nick/He told the man that it was an unusual party. He said he hadn't seen his host yet.

5 'Gatsby sent me an invitation this morning.'
   Nick/He said that Gatsby had sent him an invitation that morning.

E SPEAK Work in pairs. Use your imagination to tell the next part of the story. Report the conversation between Jay and Nick the next morning.

SPEAKING

A Think about the questions below. Make notes.

1 Do you read a lot of novels? What sort of books do you enjoy? Which books would you recommend? Why?

2 Do you ever read books in English? What have you read? Did you find it easy or difficult? Do you need to understand every word or can you simply relax and enjoy the story?

B Work in pairs. Ask and answer the questions from Exercise A. Ask follow-up questions and give examples.

C Work with a new partner. Tell your new partner about your conversation.

LISTENING

A **SPEAK** Work in groups and discuss the questions.

1 What are some situations where people tell each other stories?

2 Are stories just a bit of fun, or do they have a serious purpose?

3 Do you like telling stories? What kind of stories?

4 What skills do you need to tell great stories? When was the last time you told a story?

- Where were you?
- Who did you tell it to?
- Why did you tell it?
- What was the story about?

B **LISTEN FOR GIST** Listen to the conversation between two friends, Zoe and Jacob. They are talking about storytelling. Put the pictures (a–c) in the order that they discuss them (1–3).

9.5

1 b   2 a   3 c

Glossary

dice (n) a small block of wood or plastic with six sides marked with spots that you roll or throw to play a game

end up (with) (phrasal verb) to be in a particular place or state after doing something or because of doing it

a

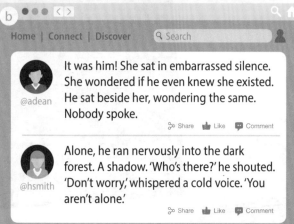
b

Home | Connect | Discover   🔍 Search

@adean — It was him! She sat in embarrassed silence. She wondered if he even knew she existed. He sat beside her, wondering the same. Nobody spoke.
⤴ Share 👍 Like 💬 Comment

@hsmith — Alone, he ran nervously into the dark forest. A shadow. 'Who's there?' he shouted. 'Don't worry,' whispered a cold voice. 'You aren't alone.'
⤴ Share 👍 Like 💬 Comment

C **LISTEN FOR KEY WORDS** Listen again and complete the definitions of the new words. Use the strategies in the box to help you.

9.5

Listening for definitions of new words

Speakers often pause before and after an important new word. They usually place extra stress on the word itself.

When you hear an important new word, listen carefully for a definition or explanation.

1 Flash fiction: A story with a word limit, usually _____1000_____ words.

2 Micro-stories: These are stories on social _____media_____ sites (e.g. Twitter). A whole story told in a _____140_____-character message.

3 A twist: When something happens in the story that you didn't _____expect_____.

4 Collaborative stories: Stories that are created by a large group of people working _____together_____.

5 Pass the paper: You write one line of a _____story_____ on a sheet of paper, fold it down and pass it to the next player, who writes the next _____line_____, and so on.

6 Add a word: You sit in a _____circle_____. The first person says the first _____word_____ from a sentence, and then the next person says the next word.

7 Story dice: A set of _____12_____ dice, and each one has six _____pictures_____, one on each side.

D **SPEAK** Work in groups. Play *Add a word*.

E **DISCUSS** Work in groups and discuss the questions.

1 Have you ever played any of the games or tried any of the story techniques mentioned in the conversation? Would you like to?

2 Do you think word limits make it easier or harder to write a good story?

3 Do you prefer working collaboratively or by yourself?

c

9.2 Tell me a story

LISTENING

A Put students into groups to discuss the questions.

B Tell students to look at the pictures. Elicit what each one shows. Tell them to number the pictures in the order the friends discuss them.

C Ask students to explain what helped them work out the answers. Ask how useful they found the strategies in the box.

D Tell students they're going to play *Add a word*, one of the games described in the conversation. Choose a stronger student and do a quick example to model the task. Put students into pairs to do the same. Share stories as a whole class.

E Put students into groups to discuss the questions.

9.2 Tell me a story

VOCABULARY

A Tell students to look back at the examples of micro-stories in Listening Exercise B, picture b. Ask students what they notice about the verbs used. Elicit an example of a verb used instead of *say* or *think*, then put students into pairs to find more and to answer the question.

wonder (instead of think) and shout and whisper (instead of say) These verbs are more interesting and they allow you to communicate more information with a single word.

B Tell students to look at the information in the box about reporting verbs. Tell them to check the meaning of any verbs with a dictionary. Put students into pairs or threes to explain the meaning of some of the words together. Monitor and help with examples yourself as they do this. If the students speak the same language, and you speak the language as well, encourage translation of the verbs. Ask students if the verbs are used in the same pattern when translated into their language.

C Tell students to look at the sentences from the conversation between Zoe and Jacob. Tell them to choose the best reporting verb to complete each one. Do the first together as a whole class to demonstrate how students have to consider both the meaning of the verb and the pattern which follows it. When checking answers, use the context created by the sentences to further check and consolidate understanding of the meaning of the verbs. Use the **Vocabulary Worksheet** on W36 for extra practice.

PRONUNCIATION

9.6

A Tell students to listen to Jacob reading two micro-stories and to think about how he uses his voice to make them sound more interesting. Point out the ideas for students to think about as they listen.

Possible answers: *In the first micro-story, he speaks quite slowly and quietly, and his voice becomes very quiet at the end. He sounds excited at the beginning. He pauses a lot in the middle of sentences (e.g. after some verbs).*
In the second story, he speaks much faster and louder, but he becomes much slower and quieter at the end. His voice mostly expresses fear. He mostly pauses between sentences.

B Tell students to turn to the **Audioscript** on page 176. Tell them to work in pairs and to take turns to read the stories aloud. Remind them of how Jacob used his voice to make the stories sound more interesting and encourage them to do the same.

C Tell students to look back at the story they wrote earlier. Tell them to practise reading it together, trying to use some of the same techniques to make it sound interesting. Monitor to help if necessary. When students have had time to practise, tell each pair to read their story to the class. Tell the others to listen carefully and to think about how well the stories are told.

D Put students into new groups to discuss which story they thought was the best. Tell them to think about the content, how well the reporting verbs were used and how well the storyteller used their voice. Get feedback from the class on which stories the students liked best and why. Give your own feedback on what you liked about the stories and any way they could have been improved.

SPEAKING HUB

A Put the students into pairs. Direct student A to the **Communication Hub** on page 147 and student B to page 154. Tell them to look at the pictures and to spend one minute thinking about the story the pictures tell.

B Tell students to take it in turns to tell their story to their partner. Tell them to listen carefully to their partner and to help if they run out of ideas.

C Tell students to work together to improve and develop their stories. Tell them to try and combine them into one story if possible. Point out the suggested ideas to help with this. Monitor to help with language or ideas if needed. When students have finished, tell them to practise reading them aloud. Remind them of the strategies for using their voice to make it sound more interesting.

D Tell students to share their stories with the class, remembering to use their voice to try and make them sound as interesting as possible. Tell the others to listen carefully and to think about which is their favourite.

E Put students into new groups to discuss which story they liked best and why. As a whole class, decide who was the best storyteller. Finish with feedback on students' use of language in the stories.

Extra activity
As homework, this speaking activity can be extended into writing practice. Students can write up their stories. If the class were able to combine their stories into one version during the class, then students can compare their stories in the next class by asking:

How are they similar? How are they different?

METHODOLOGY HUB by Jim Scrivener

Speaking: Recognise the feeling

Write up four or five short spoken phrases on the left of the board (e.g. *Where are you going?, Yes, please.*). Write up a number of 'moods' on the right (e.g. *angry, delighted, sarcastic*). Read out one of the phrases in one of the moods (adapting your intonation and stress to transmit a clear feeling). Ask students to compare ideas with each other and decide which was used. Later, learners can continue playing the game in small groups.

TEACHING IDEA by David Seymour and Maria Popova

Picture story

In four groups, choose one person to draw four pictures on separate pieces of paper: 1) an animate object, 2) an inanimate object, 3) a place, 4) an action. (Collect them all together and shuffle them.) Join another group so that there are two groups. Take half the pictures each and use all the pictures your group receives to compose a story.

VOCABULARY
Reporting verbs

A Look at the examples of micro-stories in Listening Exercise B, picture b. Which verbs are used instead of *say* and *think*? Why?

B Look at the information in the box. Use a dictionary to check any new verbs.

Reporting verbs

Instead of using *say* and *tell*, we can use more interesting and descriptive reporting verbs.

verb (+ *that*) + reported speech: *add, admit, agree, argue, explain, insist, mention, predict, promise, repeat, reply, say, shout, warn, whisper*

verb + somebody (+ *that*) + reported speech: *advise, persuade, promise, remind, tell, warn*

verb + reported question: *ask, explain, wonder*

verb + *to* + infinitive: *agree, ask, promise, refuse*

verb + somebody + *to* + infinitive: *advise, ask, persuade, promise, remind, tell, warn*

C Choose the best reporting verbs to complete the sentences from the conversation between Zoe and Jacob.

1 Zoe asked how Jacob's creative writing class was going, and he *added / reminded / replied* that it was going really well.

2 Zoe *agreed / mentioned / wondered* whether Jacob was joking about micro-stories.

3 Jacob *persuaded / warned / whispered* Zoe that it's often better if the writer provides less information.

4 Zoe *agreed / insisted / predicted* that the second story was quite powerful.

5 Zoe *added / explained / persuaded* how 'Pass the paper' works.

6 Zoe *agreed / promised / shouted* that Jacob would enjoy playing 'Pass the paper', but Jacob *admitted / insisted / refused* to play.

7 Jacob *admitted / predicted / shouted* that most of the stories are rubbish.

8 Zoe *argued / explained / mentioned* that she had been a student in Ireland.

9 Jacob *argued / predicted / reminded* Zoe that the story could have up to 1,000 words.

10 Jacob *insisted / warned / whispered* Zoe that it wouldn't be easy to write the story.

PRONUNCIATION
Using your voice to make a story more interesting

9.6

A Listen again to Jacob reading the two micro-stories. How does he use his voice to make the stories sound more interesting? Think about:

- speaking quickly, slowly, loudly or quietly.
- showing emotions.
- pausing.

B SPEAK Work in pairs. Look at the audioscript on page 176. Take turns to read the two stories aloud. Try to use your voice to make the stories sound more interesting.

C SPEAK Look at the story you wrote in Listening Exercise D. How can you use your voice to make it sound more interesting? Read your story to the class.

D REFLECT Work in groups. Which is the best story? Which storyteller used his/her voice most effectively?

SPEAKING HUB

A You are going to tell a story based on four pictures. Student A – go to the Communication Hub on page 147. Student B – go to the Communication Hub on page 154. Look at the pictures and spend one minute thinking about your story. Do not worry if your story is not very good yet!

B SPEAK Work in pairs. Take turns to tell your story. While your partner is talking, listen carefully to his/her story. You can help if your partner runs out of ideas.

C PLAN Work together to improve your stories and make them longer. Can you join your two stories together into a single story? Use these ideas to help you:

- Who exactly were the people?
- What were the characters trying to do?
- How did they feel?
- What did they say?
- What happened next?

D PRESENT Share your stories with the class. Use your voice to make them as interesting as possible.

E REFLECT Work in groups. Which story did you like best? Why? Who was the best storyteller?

○ Report a conversation
○ Create a collaborative story

Café Hub

9.3 Leaving London

F – talk about films and books   **P** – words connected to films

COMPREHENSION

A Work in pairs and discuss the questions.

- What kind of films do you like and dislike?
- Do you ever cry at films? When was the last time?
- Do you prefer reading a book or watching the film based on the book?

B Think of a film you have seen recently and answer the questions.

1 What kind of film was it? Romantic comedy, horror, etc?
2 Who was in it?
3 What kind of ending did it have?

C ▶ 00:00–03:36 Watch the first part of the video and answer the questions in Exercise B. Why is Gaby so emotional?

1. a sad, romantic film, a tale of romance 2. Jessica Brune 3. A sad one.

D ▶ 03:36–05:03 Watch the second part of the video with the volume turned off. What do you think is happening? Discuss with a partner and then watch with the volume turned up and check your ideas.

FUNCTIONAL LANGUAGE
Talking about films

▶ Match the two halves of phrases you can use to talk about films. Watch the video again and check your ideas.

Talking about films	
1 If you like sad and romantic films,	a sad ending.
2 It's got Jessica Brune in it.	b tearjerker.
3 It's a real	c where he writes the letter to her.
4 That was a really	d reading.
5 It's really worth	e amazing performance.
6 I thought the plot was good	f Oh really, she's a brilliant actor.
7 What an	g then this is the one for you.
8 I loved the scene	h and it felt like real life.

USEFUL PHRASES

A Match the useful phrases (1–6) with the phrases that have a similar meaning (a–f).

1 Yeah, right!
2 Things don't always work out perfectly.
3 There's something I've been meaning to tell you.
4 We're going to miss you.
5 Do you want a hand?
6 Just finishing up here.

a There isn't always a happy ending.
b I've nearly done all my work.
c We don't believe you.
d I've been waiting for the right time to say this.
e We don't want you to leave.
f Can I help you?

B How do you say these useful phrases in your language?

MILLY

SAM

NEENA

ZAC

GABY

PRONUNCIATION
Words connected to films

A These are some of the words connected to films that appear in the video. Put them in the correct column according to the word stress. Listen and check your answers.

> actor amazing brilliant comedy ending
> horror movie performance review
> romantic tearjerker terrible

●●	●●	●●●	●●●
review	movie	romantic	terrible
	horror	amazing	tearjerker
	brilliant	performance	comedy
	actor		
	ending		

B Work in pairs. Complete the sentences so that they are true for you. Compare with your partner.

1 The most terrible film I've ever seen was …
2 My favourite comedy is …
3 The most brilliant actor in my country is …
4 I'd give the Oscar for the most amazing performance to …
5 The best place to read film reviews is …

SPEAKING

A Think of your favourite film of all time and make notes.

1 What's the title of the film?
2 What kind of film is it?
3 Who stars in the film?
4 What happens and how does it end?
5 What do you particularly like about the plot and characters?
6 How did the film make you feel?

B DISCUSS Work in pairs. Take turns to describe your favourite film.

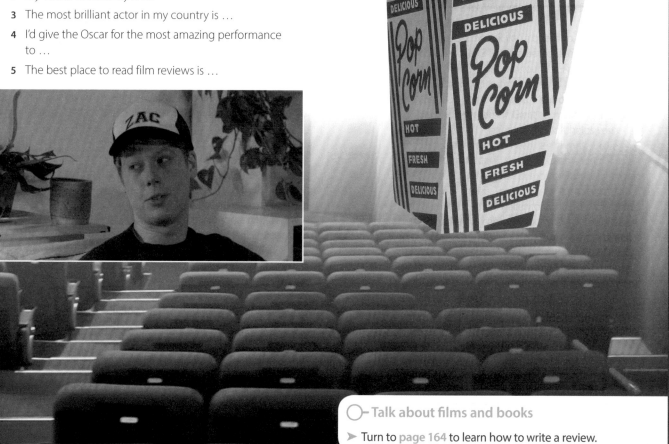

○ Talk about films and books

➤ Turn to page 164 to learn how to write a review.

LEAD-IN

Play a game of *Pictionary* with your students. Put them into two teams and give each team five films to guess. Students take it in turns to draw the film for their team until they guess.

COMPREHENSION

A Put students into pairs to discuss the questions. Discuss as a whole class and ask students to expand on their answers.

B Elicit the name of a film some of the students have seen recently (maybe one that is currently out at the cinema) and elicit some details about it. Then put students into pairs to tell their partner about a film they've seen recently.

C ▶ 00:00-03:36 Tell students to watch an extract from the video series. Tell them to answer the questions from Exercise B and to find out why Gaby is so emotional.

D ▶ 03:36-05:03 Tell students to watch the next extract from the video series without sound. Put them into pairs to discuss what they thought was happening. Play the extract with the volume turned up for students to check.

Gaby says she's moving out. Neena and Zac are shocked. Zac calls Sam. Sam writes a letter and goes to post it but then goes to their shared house and puts it through the letterbox.

FUNCTIONAL LANGUAGE

▶ Tell them to match the halves to complete the phrases, then play the video again for students to check. Check understanding of *tearjerker*.

USEFUL PHRASES

A Tell students to look at the useful phrases used in the video and to match them with their meanings.

B Ask students to think about how they would say these phrases in their language.

PRONUNCIATION

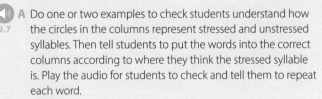
9.7

A Do one or two examples to check students understand how the circles in the columns represent stressed and unstressed syllables. Then tell students to put the words into the correct columns according to where they think the stressed syllable is. Play the audio for students to check and tell them to repeat each word.

B Tell students to complete the sentences so that they're true for them. Then put students into pairs to compare and explain their answers.

SPEAKING

A Tell students they're going to tell each other about their favourite film of all time. Tell them to look at the questions and to make notes. Monitor to help with language if needed.

B Put students into pairs to tell each other about their favourite film. Encourage them to ask each other follow-up questions. If they've both seen the film, tell them to say if they agree or disagree with their partner's opinion.

▶ VIDEOSCRIPT

Z = Zac   N = Neena   G = Gaby   S = Sam

Z: Big news. It's film night. So what are we watching tonight?

N: A film called 'Come Home' – I read the book a few years ago. The review in the paper says: 'If you like sad and romantic films, then this is the one for you. It's a modern tale of romance – two friends work together in London, they're both in love with each other, but they don't realise it.' Zac! Sit down!

Z: I think I have some work to do.

G: Zac! You made us watch that terrible horror movie for the last film night, so you have to watch this one now.

Z: OK …

N: Plus it's got Jessica Brune in it.

Z: Oh really! She's a brilliant actor.

N: Apparently it's a real tearjerker.

Z: Not for me! I never cry during movies.

G: Yeah right!

N: Here we go. Wow. What an amazing performance … I loved the scene when he writes the letter to her.

Z: Yeah … But she never got the letter. And so she never knew that he was also in love with her… And then she just left! Oh man, that was a really sad ending …
Neena – I have to admit, that was a really good movie.

N: See! I knew you'd like it! You should definitely check out the book. It's really worth reading.

Z: Sounds good. What do you think, Gaby?

G: I thought the plot was good and it felt like real life … because … that's what happens in real life. Things don't always work out perfectly and not everyone falls in love … it's sad. It's tragic. But it's true.

N: Maybe we should watch a romantic comedy next time?

Z: No, please no.

G: Oh … about next time. There's something I've been meaning to tell you.

Z: Oh, you won't be here for the next film night? Oh, that's OK, we can just …

G: No … I mean … I won't be here at all.

Z: Oh.

G: I'm moving back to Madrid. I love it here and I love living with you, but work isn't good and … and other things.

N: When are you thinking of leaving?

G: I've already booked my flight. I leave on Friday evening.

N: That's so soon!

G: I know. I'm sorry. I just want to go home now.

Z: We're gonna miss you, Gaby.

N: Yeah, we will.

G: I'm … going to do some packing.

N: Do you want a hand?

G: Yeah.

Z: Sam!

S: Hey buddy, just finishing up. What's going on?

Z: Sam … I have some … some big news.

S: What is it?

Z: It's Gaby – she's leaving London and going back to live with her parents in Madrid.

S: Oh … when?

Z: … Friday …

S: Look, I gotta go. I'll see you soon, OK?

Z: OK. Take care. Call me.

S: OK sure. Bye.

9 Writing ● Write a review

Ⓦ– using colons to introduce explanations

A Look at the pictures and read the reviews. Which event was better, the exhibition or the concert? **the exhibition**

Robert Gonsalves exhibition at the TACA

One of my favourite artists is Robert Gonsalves (1959–2017). I fell in love with his incredible paintings years ago, so I was delighted to visit an exhibition of his work last month at the Toronto Academy of Contemporary Art. **Ex E**
His paintings show beautiful scenes with a twist: they all show two different worlds coming together. This means you can enjoy the paintings on two levels: first as objects of beauty, and then as amazing ideas to help you see the world differently.
However, I visited the exhibition on a Saturday afternoon, when it was extremely crowded. At times, it was difficult to get close to the paintings. Also, the space felt too small for so many paintings. If there were only one painting on each wall, it would create a much more powerful impression.
Overall, I would strongly recommend the exhibition, but you should go when it is less crowded.

1H

Mel Montuno in concert at the City Arena

Last night I attended a concert by Mel Montuno, one of today's most exciting young musicians. I became a fan of Mel's music two years ago, when I saw her performing live for an audience of 30. Now she is an international star – she usually has audiences of 10,000!
Although Mel is still an incredible songwriter with a beautiful voice, I definitely preferred her before she was famous. Last night's concert felt 'too big': she looked uncomfortable with such a large audience and hardly interacted with her fans at all.
More seriously, the music was too loud and the lights were painfully bright. After half an hour, I had to leave, to give my ears and eyes a break!
Mel Montuno is currently on an eight-city tour of the country. If you like huge concerts, you might want to buy a ticket. But if, like me, you prefer calm, beautiful music, I recommend buying Mel's new CD, *My Jazz Age*, instead.

164 WRITING

B Read again and answer the questions.

1 Why did the writer decide to go to the exhibition/concert?
2 What did the writer like?
3 What wasn't so good?
4 What does the writer recommend? Why?

C What is the purpose of the paragraphs in each review? How are the two reviews similar? How are they different? **includes bad things; they don't both recommend**

D Read the advice about writing reviews. Find examples of each piece of advice in the reviews.

1 Add a personal touch to describe how you felt.
2 Include practical information.
3 Don't be too negative – write about how you would do things differently or why people might not mind the problems.
4 Avoid repeating words like *beautiful* or *amazing*. Try to include a range of words instead.
5 Always end with a clear recommendation for your readers.

E Look at the box. Find three colons in the reviews. Underline the explanations after each colon. Circle the key phrase before each colon.

Using colons to introduce explanations

We can use colons (:) to join two sentences together and show how they are connected. The information after the colon provides an explanation for the key phrase before the colon.

F Match the beginnings of the review writers' sentences (1–3) with the endings (a–c).

1 There were three problems with the restaurant:
2 My recommendation couldn't be clearer:
3 When I arrived at the festival, I got an unpleasant surprise:

a go and buy tickets for this concert immediately.
b the food was bad, the service was slow and the prices were too high.
c half of the musicians had cancelled their live shows because of the bad weather.

WRITING

A PREPARE You are going to write a review of an arts event. Write about a real event that you attended or invent one.

B PLAN Make notes. Think about:
1 What was good about the event?
2 What would you improve? How?
3 Would you recommend the event to other people?

C WRITE Write your review (150–200 words).

D REVIEW Work in groups. Read some of your classmates' reviews. Which events would you like to attend?

WRITING

A Tell students to look at the pictures and elicit what they show. Then tell to read and to decide which was better.

B Tell students to read the reviews again and to answer the questions.

C Elicit the purpose of the first paragraph of the first review to help students get started.

Paragraph 1: background (who, where, why, etc)
Paragraph 2 (the exhibition): good things/information about paintings
Paragraph 2 (the concert): good and bad things/information about the concert
Paragraph 3: bad things/information about the events
Paragraph 4: recommendation

D Do the first one together as a whole class to clarify the task.

E Again, elicit an example before students underline and circle.

F Tell students to practise by matching the beginnings of the sentences with the endings.

WRITING TASK

A Tell students they're going to write a review of a real arts event they have been to. Tell them to choose a play, a concert, a music festival or an exhibition they'd like to write about.

B Tell students to make notes about the three questions. Monitor to help with language if needed.

C Tell students to look back at the advice about writing reviews in Exercise D and to follow it as they write their own review.

D Put students into groups to read each other's reviews. Encourage them to ask each other questions about the events they reviewed. As a whole class discuss which events students would most like to attend. Finish with feedback on students' use of language in the reviews.

A Correct the four mistakes in the sentences.

1 I'd feel really strange if one of the actors ~~start~~ talking to me.
   I'd feel really strange if one of the actors started talking to me.

2 If I had a bit more time, ~~I'll~~ come and watch the film with you, but I'm much too busy.
   If I had a bit more time, I'd come and watch the film with you, but I'm much too busy.

3 If ~~I'd know~~ the answer, I'd tell you, but I don't so I can't.
   If I knew the answer, I'd tell you, but I don't so I can't.

4 You'd be a better actor if you ~~can~~ remember your lines!
   You'd be a better actor if you could remember your lines!

B Change the direct speech into reported speech.

1 'My daughter is a talented artist.'
   He said that ___his daughter was___ a talented artist.

2 'Immersive theatre is becoming a lot more popular all the time.'
   She said that immersive theatre ___was becoming___ a lot more popular all the time.

3 'Do you prefer reading books or watching films?'
   He asked me ___if/whether I preferred___ reading books or watching films.

4 'I can't paint, but I can draw quite well.'
   She told me she ___couldn't paint, but she___ quite well.
   could draw

5 'How much will the tickets cost?'
   She asked me ___how much the tickets would cost___

6 'Be quiet! We're trying to rehearse!'
   They told me ___to be quiet___ because they ___were trying___ to rehearse.

7 'Have you ever seen a famous band live in concert?'
   He asked me ___if/whether I had/I'd ever___ a famous band live in concert. seen

VOCABULARY

A Complete the sentences with the words in the box.

choir   display   gallery   orchestra   scene   spectators

Reviews

1 We went to an amazing classical music concert last week. The ___orchestra___ had over 50 musicians!

2 The play was very clever. There was an unexpected twist in the final ___scene___.

3 The Japanese Culture Week ended with a wonderful ___display___ by a group of traditional dancers.

4 I'm a member of a ___choir___. There are 30 of us, and we practise singing three times a week.

5 I'm really excited. There's going to be an exhibition of my paintings at the local ___gallery___!

6 It was such an amazing tennis game. The ___spectators___ clapped for ten minutes!

B Read the conversation and choose the correct verb to complete the idioms.

A: So? What did you think of my short story?

B: Well, I thought it was a bit too complicated. I couldn't [1]*stay* / *keep* track of who was who.

A: Really? So do you think I should [2]*get* / *go* rid of some of the main characters?

B: Yes, that would be much better. And some of your characters were too similar to each other. It needs to be much easier for the reader to [3]*tell* / *talk* the difference between them.

A: OK, that's a good point. I'll try to [4]*hold* / *pay* attention to things like that in future. Anything else?

B: The beginning was excellent, and I loved the fact that the whole story [5]*takes* / *starts* place on a train, but then you didn't really [6]*do* / *make* use of that idea later in the book. I think you should definitely try to [7]*take* / *make* advantage of the train journey more.

A: OK. What did you think of the ending?

B: I thought the ending was quite weak, so the story kind of [8]*falls* / *keeps* flat at the end. But … apart from that, it was fantastic.

C Match the beginnings of the sentences (1–7) with the endings (a–g).

1 'Shhh! Don't talk during the play,'   a she reminded him

2 'You must keep your promise and come to watch the show,'   b he admitted.

c she predicted.

3 'The gallery might be quite crowded tomorrow,'   d he insisted.

e she wondered.

4 'Don't forget to buy a ticket,'   f he agreed.

5 'Yes, you're absolutely right,'   g she whispered.

6 'I didn't write my story – I copied it from the internet,'

7 'Where is everybody?'

FUNCTIONAL LANGUAGE

Choose the correct words to complete the conversation.

A: I want to go to the cinema tonight, but all the new films look a bit boring.

B: Really? What about *Silly Story 2*? I thought the lead actor, Max Connor, was brilliant [1]*at* / *in* / *on* / *with* it. If you like funny films, it's definitely the film [2]*by* / *for* / *of* / *to* you.

A: Ah, yes, I saw the advert for it. But I didn't like *Silly Story 1*. The plot was really difficult to [3]*follow* / *mention* / *predict* / *record*, and it was quite sad at the end.

B: Yeah, I know what you mean. But this one's much better, and it really [4]*had* / *did* / *made* / *took* me laugh. And it's got a really happy [5]*ending* / *finishing* / *starting* / *stopping*.

A: Don't tell me how it finishes! You'll spoil it for me!

B: OK, sorry, but I think it's really [6]*worth* / *love* / *miss* / *recommend* seeing. Definitely watch this film.

10 PSYCHOLOGY

Psychology (n) the study of the mind and how it affects behaviour.

The purpose of psychology is to give us a completely different idea of the things we know best.

Paul Valéry

A hiker watches a storm approach in New South Wales, Australia.

The quote for this unit highlights the importance of psychology in giving us a fresh perspective on what we take for granted, for example, our own and other people's behaviour.

Paul Valéry (1871–1945) was a French poet and well-known intellectual and public speaker.

OBJECTIVES

- talk about different versions of past events
- talk about past mistakes
- talk about your wishes and regrets
- plan a to-do list
- make and accept apologies
- write a report

Work with a partner. Discuss the questions.

1 Look at the picture. Where do you go when you want to think?
2 Look at the quote. Do you agree?
3 Work in pairs. Tell your partner what you do when you need to reflect on a problem.

PSYCHOLOGY 109

OBJECTIVES

Read the unit objectives to the class.

UNIT OPENER QUESTIONS

With books closed, write on the board *The purpose of psychology is* _____. Put students into pairs to discuss how they would complete the sentence. Get some feedback and write the different suggested endings on the board, correcting students' language as appropriate.

1 Tell students to open their books and look at the picture. Elicit that the person has gone somewhere peaceful to think. Ask students to tell their partner where they go when they want to think.

2 Tell students to read the quote and ask them if they agree or disagree with it. Ask if they prefer any of their sentences that they created at the start of the class to Paul Valéry's quote and why.

3 Put students into pairs and ask them what they do when they have a problem and they want to reflect on it. Give students a couple of minutes to make some notes on their own about their ideas. Monitor and assist with language input. When they are ready, ask them to share their ideas with their partner.

WORKSHEETS

Lesson 10.1 Making up your mind

Grammar: Third conditional; *should have / shouldn't have done* (W37)

Vocabulary: Expressions with *mind* (W38)

Lesson 10.2 Wish lists

Grammar: Hopes and wishes (W39)

Vocabulary: Staying organised (W40)

10.1 Making up your mind

○— Talk about different versions of past event
○— Talk about past mistakes

V— psychology verbs; expressions with *mind*
P— third conditional

G— third conditional; *should have* + past participle
S— listening for phrases that support an argument

READING

A SPEAK Work in pairs. Go the Communication Hub on page 150.

B READ FOR MAIN IDEA Read *Do you think you think rationally? Think again!* What is the connection between the three sub-headings and pictures 1–3 above?

C READ FOR DETAIL Read again. Are the sentences true (T) or false (F)? Correct the false sentences.

1 New research has shown that we're ~~good~~ <u>much less</u> rational than we think. ~~at making rational decisions.~~ **F**

2 After we've thought about a hook number, it's ~~easy~~ <u>harder</u> to think of a number that's a long way from that hook. **F**

3 We would probably make better decisions if we ignored hook numbers. **T**

4 If we were more rational, we ~~would~~ <u>wouldn't</u> worry ~~more~~ about ∧deep costs. **F**

5 In the example about the weekend break, the money you've spent on the hotel and travel is a deep cost. **T**

6 Filtering involves presenting a situation in a way that makes it sound better (or worse) than it really is. **T**

D SPEAK Work in pairs. Can you think of any examples of hook numbers, deep costs or filtering from your own life? Tell your partner.

DO YOU THINK YOU THINK RATIONALLY? THINK AGAIN!

For centuries, psychologists assumed that people think rationally and make decisions based on facts But we're actually much less rational than we think

HOOK NUMBERS

Look again at the quiz. Question 1a is clearly nonsense: of course we have more than 70 thoughts per day! So it shouldn't affect our answers to question 1b. But <u>for most people, the number 70 acts as a hook. It encourages us to think of a number that isn't too far from 70.</u> But if the hook number had been much higher, say 70 million, it would have made us think of a number in the millions. And <u>if we hadn't seen a hook at all, we might have chosen a more likely answer:</u> around 70,000 thoughts per day.

Sales people use hook numbers to persuade us to spend much more than we should, for example, by tricking us into believing a watch must be worth thousands of pounds.

BURIED COSTS

A buried cost is time, money or effort that we've already spent and can't get back. <u>It would be rational to ignore buried costs when making decisions;</u> they're gone, so we should forget about them. But for most of us, waste feels like physical pain, and we often spend even more time, money and effort trying to avoid that pain.

Look back at question 2 in the quiz. <u>The money you've spent is gone.</u> Instead of regretting the past, we should forget it and focus on the future. When you're ill, you should stay home and get better.

LEAD-IN

Tell students to think of one moment in their life they would like to relive. Give a personal example, explaining why you would like to relive this moment. Then put students into pairs to tell each other about their chosen moments.

READING

A Direct students to the **Communication Hub** on page 150 and look at the psychology quiz. Tell them first to read the quiz and think about their own answers, then put them into pairs to compare and explain their answers.

B Ask students what they think the connection is between the pictures and the three subheadings in the psychology quiz. Tell them to read the article and find out.

Possible answers:

Picture 1 is connected to Hook Numbers. These are numbers that are there to draw us towards them like how a big piece of bait would attract a fish.

Picture 2 is connected to Deep Costs. Like the treasure chest buried beneath the ground, there is little chance of getting money spent back.

Picture 3 is connected to Filtering. Although the paintings are the same, different colour filters make the paintings look better/worse. In the same way, words like pass and fail make the schools in question 3 sound better/worse.

C Tell students to read the sentences about the article and to try to remember if they're true or false. Then tell them to read the article again and check.

D Put students into pairs to discuss the questions. Monitor and assist as required. Ask students to expand on their answers and share experiences with the whole class.

TEACHING IDEA
by David Seymour and Maria Popova

Grammar: If I hadn't done that …

1 Use pictures to build a situation of two friends, Jo and Tony, who can't decide what to do. There is a party tonight and a good programme on TV. Establish that Jo decided to go to the party, while Tony stays at home.

2 It is two hours later. Draw Jo looking miserable at the party – and Tony looking miserable watching TV. Check that the students are clear what they chose and that they regret their choices. Elicit what they are thinking and feeling (If I'd stayed at home, I could have watched …; If I'd gone to the party, I could have …).

3 You could extend the situation to make more sentences if you wish (If I hadn't been so tired, I would've had a better time).

GRAMMAR HUB

10.1 Third conditional; *should have* + past participle

Third conditional

Condition	Result
I would have made a better decision	if **Daniel had done** the research.
If **I had known** all the facts,	he **wouldn't have made** his discovery.

Question	Positive short answer	Negative short answer
If **you had thought** about it more, **would you have made** the same decision?	Yes, **I would (have)**.	No, **I wouldn't (have)**.
Would they have passed the exam if **they had answered** correctly?	Yes, **they would (have)**.	No, **they wouldn't (have)**.

- We use the third conditional to imagine a situation in the past that didn't actually happen.

  *If I had set my alarm clock, I wouldn't have been late for work. (= I **didn't** set my alarm clock and I **was** late for work.)*

- As with other conditionals, we only use a comma when the *if*-clause comes first.

- We can use *could have* or *might have* instead of *would have* to express possibility.

  I could have answered correctly if I'd had more time.

- In answer to a third conditional question, we can use either *I would* or *I would have*

  Would you have made the same decision if you'd known all the facts? Yes, I would. / Yes, I would have. / No, I wouldn't. / No, I wouldn't have.

should have + past participle

Positive	Negative	Question
She should have bought the first pair.	**You shouldn't have spent** so much money.	**Should I have changed** my mind?
They should have offered more choice.	**I shouldn't have bought** these shoes.	How much **should they have paid**?

- We use *should/shouldn't have* + the past participle of the main verb to talk about mistakes that we made in the past. We regret those actions and try to imagine how we could have acted differently.

  *She shouldn't have changed her mind. (= She **did** change her mind and this was a mistake.)*

- We always put the past participle of the main verb after *should/shouldn't have*.

  They should have thought about their decision more carefully. NOT ~~They should have think about their decision more carefully.~~

10.1 Making up your mind

VOCABULARY

A Tell students to find the verbs in the text and to think about what they mean. Then tell them to match the beginnings of the definitions to the endings.

B Tell students to choose the correct verb to complete the questions.

C Put students into pairs to discuss the questions in Exercise B.

GRAMMAR

A Tell students to look at the sentence and elicit that it's an example of the third conditional. Ask them to look at the sentence again in pairs and answer the questions in the box.

B Tell students to look back at the article to find and underline another example of the third conditional. Elicit that *might* is used instead of *would* because the writer is less sure about the result.

And if we hadn't seen a hook at all, we might have chosen a more likely answer: around 70,000 thoughts per day.

C Direct students to the **Grammar Hub** on pages 140 and 141 (TB110 and below).

D Write a personal example (e.g. *If I hadn't met …, I wouldn't have …*), then tell students to write three third conditional sentences that are true for themselves. Put students into pairs to compare and explain their sentences.

PRONUNCIATION

A Tell students to listen and repeat the sentence. Ask students what they noticed about the pronunciation of the auxiliary verbs *had*, *would* and *have*.

had and *would* in third conditionals are often contracted and pronounced /d/.

have is usually pronounced /əv/ after modal verbs *like would*, *could* and *might*. It sounds the same as *of*.

B Put students into pairs to practise saying the sentences they wrote in Grammar Exercise D. Monitor and help if needed.

SPEAKING

Tell students a brief anecdote and then elicit a third conditional sentence to summarise the situation. Put students into pairs to discuss the questions. Monitor and make notes.

Extra activity

You can add to the two discussion questions with the following question or use it as a model for your anecdote:

Think of a time in the past when something bad nearly happened (e.g. somebody tried to trick you). What stopped the bad thing from happening? What might have been the result if it had happened? What did you learn from the experience?

I got an email from my bank last week telling me to click on a link to change my password. Luckily, I noticed that the link was to a completely different site, so I didn't click on it. But if I hadn't noticed …

GRAMMAR HUB

10.1 Third conditional; *should have* + past participle

A Read the sentences and choose the option which is true.

1 He should have made a decision based on the facts.

   a He considered the facts.   **(b)** He didn't consider the facts.

2 She could have avoided the other car if she'd stopped in time.

   a She avoided the other car.   **(b)** She didn't avoid the other car.

3 If you had listened to me, you wouldn't have made a foolish decision.

   (a) You made a foolish decision.   b You didn't make a foolish decision.

4 If David had gone to a smaller shop, he would have felt less stressed.

   a David went to a small shop.   **(b)** David went to a big shop.

5 You shouldn't have encouraged her to spend all that money!

   (a) She spent a lot of money.   b She didn't spend a lot of money.

6 We wouldn't have bought this house if we'd known it was so noisy here.

   (a) We bought the house.   b We didn't buy the house.

B Correct the mistakes in each sentence.

1 I shouldn't ^*have* paid so much for this smartphone.

2 If our teacher ~~gave~~ *had given* us time to revise, we would all have got better marks.

3 ~~Will~~ *Would* the show have attracted more people if we had advertised it better?

4 I'm sorry – I ~~would~~ *should* have listened to your advice.

5 If you ~~have~~ *had* bought your shoes in the first shop, you would have saved time!

6 Should we have ~~count~~ *counted* the sunk costs?

7 Would you ~~had~~ *have* agreed to take part if you had known it was a trick?

8 I should ~~realise~~ *have realised* that the watch was made of plastic!

C Choose the correct option.

The trainers were fashionable, attractive and cheap, so I bought them. However, I [1] **shouldn't** / wouldn't have been so easily influenced by the saleswoman. A few days later, I searched for that brand online and discovered that they were made by child workers! If I [2] **had known** / would know that they were made by children, I would never [3] buy / **have bought** them. In fact, I [4] had avoided / **would have avoided** that shop completely! If I [5] would discover / **had discovered** the truth sooner, I would have complained to the shop. And of course I [6] hadn't encouraged / **wouldn't have encouraged** my friends to buy them either! It's really important that, as shoppers, we act responsibly. I've found an online group which persuades customers not to buy products like these. I joined it straight away. If I [7] **had heard** / heard about it sooner, I [8] **would** / will have joined months ago!

➤ Go back to page 111.

VOCABULARY
Psychology verbs

A Match the beginnings of the definitions (1–8) with the endings (a–h). Use *Do you think you think rationally? Think again!* to help you.

1 If something **affects** or **influences** you, g
2 If you **assume** that something is true, d
3 If something **attracts** you, h
4 If you **avoid** doing something, e
5 If you **encourage** or **persuade** somebody to do something, a
6 If you **regret** something, b
7 If something **tempts** you, f
8 If somebody **tricks** you into doing something, c

a you say something that makes him/her want to do it.
b you feel bad about something you did (or didn't do) in the past.
c they make you do it by lying or hiding the truth.
d you believe it although you haven't checked for sure.
e you are careful not to do it.
f you want it, even though it might be bad for you.
g it changes the way you think or behave.
h you like it and want to have it.

B Choose the correct verbs to complete the questions.

1 How do marketers and advertisers *avoid* / *tempt* us to buy things we don't really want or need?
2 When you go shopping, which things *attract* / *influence* your decision to buy something? Is it possible that the shops use psychological tricks to affect your choices?

C SPEAK Work in pairs. Ask and answer the questions in Exercise B.

FILTERING

In question 3 from the quiz, were you tempted by School A? That 75 per cent pass rate sounds great, doesn't it? What about School B, with all those failures? No, thanks! Of course, your rational side knows that School B is better – a 20 per cent failure rate means there's an 80 per cent pass rate. But we can't help being influenced by Ex C Q6 words like *pass* and *fail*.
We're strongly attracted to positive words like *success, save* and *free*. But negative words are even more powerful. We hate *losing, wasting* or *missing* things. So if you see an advert that warns, 'Don't miss your last chance to save,' remember that someone is trying to trick our irrational minds.

Glossary

bury (v) to put something in the ground and cover it with earth
filter (v) if you filter a photo, you change or improve the appearance of the image before posting it on social media
hook (n) a curved piece of metal or plastic fixed to a pole or with a handle at the other end, used for catching hold of something

GRAMMAR
Third conditional

A WORK IT OUT Work in pairs. Look at the sentence from *Do you think you think rationally? Think again!* Then choose the correct words to complete the rules.

If the hook number had been much higher, say 70 million, it would have made us think of a number in the millions.

Third conditional

1 We use the third conditional to talk about imaginary situations in **the past** / **the present**.
2 Conditional sentences usually have **two** / **three** clauses: the **if**-clause and the result clause. To make a third conditional sentence, we use:
   if + past perfect, **would** + **have** + past participle
3 We **can** / **can't** use **might** or **could** instead of **would** in the result clause.

B Find and underline another third conditional sentence in the article.

C Go to the Grammar Hub on page 140.

D SPEAK Work in pairs. Write three third conditional sentences that are true for you. Tell your partner about the situations in your sentences.

PRONUNCIATION
Third conditional

A Listen and repeat the third conditional sentence. What do you notice about the pronunciation of *had*, *would* and *have*?

10.1

If I'd thought about it more carefully, I'd have made a better decision.

B SPEAK Work in pairs. Practise saying the sentences you wrote in Grammar Exercise D. Listen and check your partner's pronunciation.

SPEAKING

Work in pairs and discuss the questions.

1 Think of a time in the past when you paid too much for something or bought something you didn't really want or need. What happened? Why? What would have happened if you'd thought more carefully?

When I bought my first car, I thought it was perfect. But I didn't check whether it actually worked properly! In the end, I spent loads of money fixing it and sold it again. If I'd …

2 Think of a time in the past when you made a bad decision because you didn't have enough information or experience. What would you have done differently if you'd known then what you know now?

I got an email from my bank last week telling me to click on a link to change my password. Luckily, I noticed that the link was to a completely different site. But if I hadn't noticed …

LISTENING

A **SPEAK** Work in groups and discuss the questions.

1 Do you find shopping relaxing or stressful? Why?

2 When you're shopping for clothes and shoes, do you find it easy to decide what to buy?

B **LISTEN FOR MAIN IDEA** Listen to a conversation between two friends, Robert and Vicky. What do they say about the items in the pictures (a–d)?
10.2

Glossary

common sense (n) the ability to use good judgment and make sensible decisions

paradox (n) a statement consisting of two parts that seem to mean the opposite of each other

perfectionist (n) someone who always wants things to be done perfectly

C **Listen again. How does Robert support his arguments?** Use the strategies in the box to help you.
10.2

Listening for phrases that support an argument

Sometimes when you listen, you need to decide how strong a person's arguments are. Pay attention to the techniques they use to support their argument.

Common sense:

• *Surely, Of course, Obviously, Clearly, As you can imagine, …*

Facts and statistics:

• *In fact, …; The researchers found that …*

Examples and details:

• *For example, …; For instance, …*

Expert opinions:

• *According to Professor Schwartz …; He's shown that …*

D **LISTEN FOR DETAIL** Listen again. Complete the notes about the conversations.
10.2

1 **The Paradox of Choice:** According to Professor Barry Schwartz (an ___American___ psychologist), too much ___choice___ makes us ___stressed___.

2 **Shampoo company:** Cut choices from ___26___ to ___15___. Sales went up by ___10___ per cent.

3 **Robert's experience of buying a laptop:** He went to a small shop with ___three___ laptops to choose from. Took ___five___ minutes to choose and buy a laptop.

4 **Perfectionists regret their choices:** Vicky bought ___two___ different pairs of shoes, but took each pair back to the shop.

5 **Quick deciders don't worry about perfection:** When Robert finds jeans that are ___good___ enough, he buys them and stops worrying. Only takes them back to shop if they're ___damaged___.

E **SPEAK** Work in groups and discuss the questions.

1 Have you ever experienced the Paradox of Choice? Think about the following situations:

• shopping

• choosing what to watch on TV or online

• making important life decisions

• cooking or eating

2 Are you a perfectionist or a quick decider? What about other people in your family?

3 How can shops, websites and other businesses help us deal with the Paradox of Choice?

LISTENING

A Put students into groups to discuss the questions. If any students have very strong opinions, encourage them to share and expand on them.

B Tell students to look at the pictures and elicit what they show. Tell students they're going to listen to a conversation between two friends. Ask them to listen for what they say about the items in the pictures. Point out the glossary but tell students not to worry if there are some words they don't understand at this stage.

Possible answers:

a Vicky tried to buy a laptop but there was too much choice and she couldn't decide which one to buy. Robert bought his laptop easily because he only had three choices.

b A shampoo company cut the number of shampoo choices and sales went up.

c Vicky bought some shoes but she kept changing her mind.

d When Robert is buying jeans, he makes a quick decision and sticks with it.

 C Point out the information in the box about *Listening for phrases that support an argument*. Tell students to listen again and to think about which of the strategies Robert uses.

10.2

Possible answers:

He used all four techniques.

He used common sense to explain why some choice is better than no choice.

He used facts and statistics to explain the examples with shampoo and jam.

He gave well-known examples (shampoo, jam) as well as examples from his own life (his laptop, jeans).

He gave the opinions of Professor Schwartz.

 D Tell students to look at the notes and to try to complete them with what they remember from the conversations. Play the audio again for students to listen and check.

10.2

E Put students into groups to discuss the questions. Briefly drill pronunciation of perfectionist /pə(r)ˈfekʃənɪst/. Ask students to expand on their answers and ask each other follow-up questions.

10.2

Listening, Exercise B
R = Robert   V = Vicky

R: Would you mind if I borrowed your laptop for a few minutes?

V: No, of course not. Go ahead. Just bear in mind that it's really slow and it keeps crashing all the time.

R: Sounds like you need a new one.

V: Yeah, I know. I'm trying to buy one, but … it's difficult.

R: What do you mean?

V: Well, I went to the electrical store last week. They had over 100 laptops to choose from. After about three hours in the shop, looking at every single laptop, I found two that I liked, but I was in two minds and I couldn't decide which one to buy. It was horrible. In the end, I gave up! But never mind. I've still got my old computer, so it isn't so bad.

R: Aha. Sounds like the Paradox of Choice.

V: What's that?

R: Well, the name comes from an American

Ex D Q1 psychologist, Professor Barry Schwartz. According to Professor Schwartz, most people assume that lots of choice is always a good thing. But he's shown that in fact too much choice is bad for us. It makes us stressed, so we can't make decisions.

V: Er … OK. So why do shops give us so many choices? Surely they'd sell more if they reduced the number of choices?

R: Exactly. The problem is, most companies still think more is better. But a few smart companies have realised that they'll sell more if they offer less

Ex D Q2 choice. I read recently that a shampoo company cut the number of shampoo choices from 26 to 15. Everyone thought they'd lose sales, but in fact, their sales went up by ten per cent.

V: Really? Wow! So less choice is better.

R: Yes, in general. But of course, it's better to have some choice than no choice at all – that's just common sense.

V: Right.

R: So with your laptop, you should have gone to a smaller shop. If you'd done that, you'd have had

less choice, but your decision would have been

Ex D Q3 much easier. The shop where I bought mine had just three laptops to choose from. One was too expensive; one was too basic; the third one was absolutely fine, so I bought it. It took me five minutes. And I'm very happy with it.

V: Wow! I could never do that. I'd be worried that I'd missed the chance to buy a better computer somewhere else.

R: That's because you're a perfectionist.

V: A perfectionist? What's that?

R: It's a person who always looks for the perfect thing to buy. You can't relax unless you're sure you've studied every option and chosen the best one. And even after you've made a decision, you still worry that you've made the wrong choice.

V: Yeah, that definitely sounds like me! For example, I went shopping for some new shoes last week. After about six hours, I finally bought a pair. But when I got them home, I regretted my decision

Ex D Q4 immediately. I realised that they weren't perfect and I shouldn't have bought them. So I took them back to the shop to get my money back. Then I bought a different pair of shoes, but I took them back to the shop a few days later. In the end, I bought the first pair again.

R: Yes, you're definitely a perfectionist. I, on the other hand, am what I call a 'quick decider'.

V: What's that?

R: It's a person who makes quick decisions without worrying about perfection. When I'm shopping for

Ex D Q5 new jeans, for instance, and I find some jeans that are good enough, I buy them and stop worrying about them. And I never take them back to the shop – unless they're damaged, of course. Once I've made up my mind, I stick with my decision.

V: Wow! You're so lucky. I could never do that!

R: Well, you think it's impossible, but maybe it's all in the mind. I think you can become a quick decider – you just need to put your mind to it! It'll make life much easier.

V: Yes, you're right. I'll definitely do that! From now on, I'm going to be a quick decider. But, er, what if I change my mind later?

GRAMMAR

A Tell students to look at the sentences to complete the rules. Check students' understanding of the meaning.

B Direct students to the **Grammar Hub** on pages 140 and 141 (see TB110 and TB111).

A good way to consolidate students' understanding of the meaning and form of a structure like this is through translation. After feedback, when students all have the correct sentences, tell them to choose three sentences and to translate them into their own language. When they have done this, tell them to cover the original English sentence so they can only see their translation. Then tell students to translate the sentences back into English. Students can then look back at the original sentences and see how similar they are to their English version.

C Put students into pairs to discuss what Angela and Kasia should or shouldn't have done in the two situations. Use the **Grammar Worksheet** on W37 for extra practice.

VOCABULARY

A Elicit that all the sentences are from the conversation between Vicky and Robert. Tell them to try to complete the gaps with the expressions in the box. Play the audio for students to check.

B Put students into pairs to discuss what they think the expressions from Exercise A mean. Tell them to look at the way the expressions are used in the sentences from the conversation to help them work out the meanings. Once students have discussed what they think, you could give them the definitions below on a handout or write them on the board and tell them to match the expressions to the definitions. Consolidate understanding of the meaning by eliciting personal examples that are meaningful to the students if necessary.

1 *Would you mind if (= Is it a problem if …)*

2 *bear in mind (= remember / be careful because …)*

3 *in two minds (= unable to make a decision)*

4 *never mind (= it doesn't matter)*

5 *made up my mind (= decided)*

6 *all in the mind (= something you imagine, not something in the real world)*

7 *put your mind to (= try hard / make an effort to achieve)*

8 *change my mind (= make a different decision later)*

C Put students into pairs to discuss the questions. Discuss answers as a class and find out how similar their ideas are. Use the **Vocabulary Worksheet** on W38 for extra practice.

SPEAKING HUB

A Tell students to read the sentences about regrets. Put students into pairs to discuss if they agree with the sentences.

B Tell students to think about two or three mistakes they've made in the past. Elicit an example as a whole class, then tell students to make notes about the questions. Monitor and help them correct their notes or provide requested vocabulary.

C Put students back into pairs and tell them to tell each other about their mistakes. Monitor and make notes to give as feedback at the end of the activity.

D Put students into different pairs to discuss the questions.

> **Extra activity**
>
> You can always extend a communicative activity like this one by asking pairs or groups to be ready to report back on their discussions to the whole class. Set a time limit to allow them to prepare. This actually provides further speaking practice, gives students time to structure responses and can often encourage more thoughtful contributions.

METHODOLOGY HUB by Jim Scrivener

If I hadn't done that …

The following activity can also be extended to introduce *should have*:

1. Use board pictures to build a situation of two friends, Jo and Tony, who can't decide what to do. There is party tonight and a good programme on TV. Establish that Jo decides to go to the party while Tony chooses to stay at home.

2. It is two hours later. Draw Jo looking miserable at the party – and Tony looking miserable watching TV. Check that students are clear what they chose and that they regret their choices. Elicit what the students are feeling and thinking (*If I'd stayed at home, I could have watched Spacecops. If I'd gone to the party, I could have met some nice people.*).

3. You could extend the situation to make more sentences if you wish (*If I hadn't been so tired, I would have had a better time*).

TEACHING IDEA by David Seymour and Maria Popova

The unreal past

In pairs, look at the following sentences and decide whether the people in each situation feel happy about what happened, unhappy about it or just neutral, e.g.

Ray went to the party. – *If Ray hadn't gone to the party, he wouldn't have met Maggie* (happy, because he met her). – *If he hadn't gone to the party, he would have felt better the next morning* (unhappy, because he went to the party and now he is tired). – *If Ray hadn't gone to the party, he'd have gone clubbing instead* (neutral, because he'd have spent the night dancing anyway).

> Terry moved to New York. He didn't know she was coming. James crashed his car. Vera lost her lottery ticket. Sonya went to Japan. Irene didn't have a spare key. Roger didn't pass the exam. Tracy couldn't sell her house.

Imagine you were the person in some of the situations. Work with a partner and write some sentences to express regret. Use *should (not) have done*, e.g. *I shouldn't have stayed up so late.*

GRAMMAR

should have + past participle

A WORK IT OUT Look at the sentences from the conversation between Vicky and Robert. Then choose the correct words to complete the rules.

So with your laptop, you **should have gone** to a smaller shop.

I realised that they weren't perfect and I **shouldn't have bought** them.

should have + past participle

1 We write **should** (*not*) + **have** + <u>past participle</u> / infinitive.
2 We use **should have done** to talk about mistakes that we make / <u>made</u> in the past and imagine how we could have avoided those mistakes.

B Go to the Grammar Hub on page 140.

C SPEAK Work in pairs. Use *should/shouldn't have done* to talk about these situations.

1 Angela went shopping for a new coat. She found a great coat in the first shop, but she went to ten more shops to make sure it was the best one. When she went back to buy it, somebody else had bought it.

2 Kasia bought a second-hand computer five years ago, but it didn't work properly. Although she had enough money to buy a new one, she kept using the old one for years.

VOCABULARY

Expressions with *mind*

A Complete the sentences (1–8) from the conversation with the expressions in the box. Then listen again and check your answers.

> all in the mind   bear in mind   change my mind
> in two minds   made up my mind   never mind
> put your mind to   would you mind if

1 _____ Would you mind if _____ I borrowed your laptop for a few minutes? (= Is it a problem if …)

2 Just _____ bear in mind _____ that it's really slow. (= remember / be careful because …)

3 I found two that I liked, but I was _____ in two minds _____ and I couldn't decide which one to buy. (= unable to make a decision)

4 But _____ never mind _____. I've still got my old computer, so it isn't so bad. (= it doesn't matter)

5 Once I've _____ made up my mind _____, I stick with my decision. (= decided)

6 You think it's impossible, but maybe it's _____ all in the mind _____. (= something you imagine, not something in the real world)

7 I think you can become a quick decider – you just need to _____ put your mind to _____ it! (= try hard / make an effort to achieve)

8 But what if I _____ change my mind _____ later? (= make a different decision later)

B SPEAK Work in pairs. What do you think the expressions in Exercise A mean?

C SPEAK Work in pairs and discuss the questions.

1 Quick deciders are generally less stressed, but there are some dangers connected with making quick decisions. What should they **bear in mind** before making a decision?

2 How long does it usually take you to **make up your mind** about whether you can trust somebody? What might make you **change your mind** about them?

○ SPEAKING HUB

A Read the sentences about regrets. Do you agree or disagree with them? Why?

1 You should never regret anything. Your mistakes are part of who you are.

2 You should regret the things you haven't done more than the things you have done.

B Think about two or three mistakes you have made in the past. What did you do? What did you not do? What should or should you not have done?

C Work in pairs. Tell your partner about some of the mistakes you have made. While your partner is talking, listen carefully, and then ask questions to find out more information.

Finding out more information

Really? So what did you do? Why did you do that?

What do you think you should have done?

But if you hadn't done that, what do you think would have happened?

D Work in pairs and discuss the questions.

1 What can you learn from the mistakes you have made in the past?

2 What would you do differently if you were in the same situation in the future?

3 Is it good to talk about past mistakes?

○– Talk about different versions of past events
○– Talk about past mistakes

V — reflexive verbs; staying organised   P — emphasis and reflexive pronouns   G — hopes and wishes
S — bridge sentences

LISTENING

A SPEAK **Work in pairs and discuss the questions.**

1 Do you have any habits that you'd like to stop?

2 Are there any good habits that you'd like to start?

3 How easy is it to change your habits?

4 Look at the diagram. What do you think it shows?

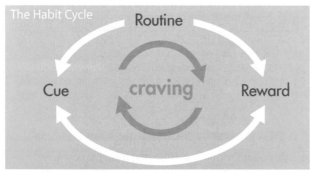

The Habit Cycle — Routine — Cue — craving — Reward

B LISTEN FOR GIST **Listen to a radio show about habits.**
10.3 **Which habits in the pictures do the speakers talk about?**
eating fast food, drinking coffee, drinking water

C LISTEN FOR DETAIL **Listen again and choose the correct**
10.3 **answers.**

1 What is David's main cue for eating fast food?

   a He sees a sign while he's driving.

   ⓑ He smells food in a shopping centre.

2 What happens when a routine is part of a true habit?

   ⓐ You can follow the steps without thinking.

   b You do it although you don't want to.

3 Why are cravings dangerous?

   a Because you don't want the reward any more.

   ⓑ Because you feel that you need the reward.

4 What's the only way to change a habit?

   ⓐ Change the routine.

   b Change the reward.

5 Why does Leo make coffee when he arrives at work?

   a Because he loves the taste of coffee.

   ⓑ Because he's tired and he needs a break.

D SPEAK **Work in pairs and discuss the questions.**

1 What are some cues for bad habits? What routines and rewards can we use to change those bad habits?

2 What cues and rewards can we use to start good habits?

VOCABULARY
Reflexive verbs

A **Complete the sentences from the conversation (1–8) with**
10.4 **the words in the box. Then listen and check your answers.**

| blame   control   get   help   make   reward   set   treat |

1 When I drive past a sign for a fast-food restaurant, I _____ **treat** _____ myself to a snack from the packet.

2 'Can I try one of those?'
   'Sure! _____ **Help** _____ yourself.'

3 I wish I could stop, but I can't _____ **control** _____ myself.

4 I always _____ **make** _____ myself a cup of coffee before I check my emails.

5 I suppose I could _____ **get** _____ myself a glass of water.

6 I always _____ **set** _____ myself goals, but nothing seems to work.

7 First of all, Alice, don't _____ **blame** _____ yourself.

8 How will you _____ **reward** _____ yourself for being good?

Reflexive verbs

A reflexive verb is a verb + a reflexive pronoun (*myself, yourself, himself, herself, itself, ourselves, yourselves, themselves*).

Some reflexive verbs have a special meaning:

Help yourself! = Please take as much as you want; there's no need to ask.

LEAD-IN

Draw two columns on the board and write *Good habits* at the top of one and *Bad habits* at the top of the other. Students face the board in two lines by each column, and either write good or bad habits under the columns. The line that writes the most words wins. Give a time limit.

LISTENING

A–D Check answers and feedback as a whole class after students complete the exercises.

AUDIOSCRIPT

 10.3

Listening, Exercise B
D = David   B = Barbara   A = Alice   L = Leo

D: Hello, and welcome back to All in the Mind. In today's show, we're talking about habits. I'm joined by Professor Barbara Janovich, an expert in habits. Welcome to the show, Professor.

B: Thanks, David.

D: So, Barbara, why do we develop bad habits? And why are they so hard to break?

B: Well, the best way to understand habits is to break them into four parts. First, there's a cue, which might be something that you see or hear or feel. So in your example with fast food, the cue might be that you're driving in your car and you see a sign for a fast-food restaurant. Or perhaps you're walking through a shopping centre and suddenly you smell the fast food.

Ex C Q1 **D:** Ah, yes. That smell always makes me want to eat fast food, even when I'm not hungry! I wish it didn't, but it does!

B: Exactly. So the next stage is the routine – the actions you always take. So this is where you go into the fast-food restaurant, order your food and eat it. In a true Ex C Q2 habit, you can do all of this without really thinking – it kind of happens to you, and your brain almost switches off.

D: OK.

B: And then the third part is the reward: something nice happens. In this case, the sugar and salt in the food cause your brain to produce feel-good chemicals.

D: OK, so the cycle is cue, routine, reward. But you said there are four parts. What's the fourth part?

B: Well, this is the dangerous part: the craving. Let me explain. If you repeat the cycle a few times, your brain produces those feel-good chemicals earlier and earlier in the process. So instead of being part of the reward, you get that nice feeling at the cue stage – when you see the restaurant sign, for example, or you smell the food and you know the reward is coming soon. And now you've got a Ex C Q3 problem: you've had the good feeling, but you haven't had the reward yet. This creates the craving – a powerful need to get your reward. Now you can't relax until you've got your reward.

D: Aha. I wish I'd known about all this a few years ago! But I guess it's too late for me now. Is there anything I can do to break the cycle?

VOCABULARY

 A Tell students to complete the sentences with the correct verb from the box. Play the audio again for them to check. Check understanding of the meaning of the verbs with reference to how they are used in the sentences and with further personal examples. Then point out the information in the box about reflexive verbs.

Ex C Q4 **B:** Yes, but it isn't easy. You can't stop the cues, and you still need the reward. So the trick is to change the routine. So, for example, I always keep a packet of low-fat salty snacks in my bag. That means that when I drive past a sign for a fast-food restaurant, I treat myself to a snack from the packet.

D: Er, can I try one of those?

B: Sure! Help yourself. So the cue is the same, and the reward is similar – salty food – but I've changed the routine. Of course, salty snacks aren't perfect, but they're a lot cheaper and healthier than a burger and fries.

D: Sounds good. OK, so earlier we asked our listeners to phone in to tell us about their bad habits. Our first caller is Leo. Leo, what's your habit?

L: Hello. Well, it's coffee. I drink about eight cups a day, but I don't even like it very much! I wish I could stop, but I can't control myself.

B: OK. Well, let's start with the first cup of coffee each day, Leo. What's your cue for drinking it?

L: It's when I arrive at work. I always make myself a cup of coffee before I check my emails.

B: How long does it take to get to work?

L: About an hour. Why?

Ex C Q5 **B:** Well, it sounds like the reward isn't really the coffee, but a five-minute break after your long, tiring journey.

L: Er, yes, maybe.

B: So now we know the cue and the reward, the question is: is there a different routine that would give you the same reward after your journey to work?

L: I suppose I could get myself a glass of water and go for a quick walk around the office.

B: Sounds good.

D: OK, great. I hope your new routine works for you, Leo. I wish we had time to talk about your other seven cups of coffee, but we need to go to our next caller, Alice. What's your bad habit, Alice?

A: Well, actually, I'd like some help creating a new habit. You see, I wish I could run a marathon next year. I go running from time to time, but I want to get into the habit of running every day. I always set myself goals, but nothing seems to work. I really wish I were better organised.

D: Thanks for that, Alice. Professor?

B: Well, first of all, Alice, don't blame yourself. This is a very common problem. If you want to create a new habit, again you need to think about cues and rewards: what will make you remember to go running at the same time every day? How will you reward yourself for being good? So let's start by creating your cue, Alice. When would be a good time of day to go running?

B Direct students to the **Vocabulary Hub** on page 146 for further practice of reflexive verbs.

C Put students into pairs to discuss the questions. Monitor and give feedback on any really good or any incorrect use of reflexive verbs.

PRONUNCIATION

A Tell students to listen carefully to the sentences from the radio show and to decide if the reflexive pronouns are stressed or unstressed. Do the first one together as a whole class to demonstrate the task.

B Tell students to look back at the sentences from Exercise A to help them complete the rules about emphasis and reflexive pronouns. Check students understand how sentence 3 is an example of emphasis. Model the pronunciation of sentence 3 again, exaggerating the stress at first, then more naturally.

C Put students into pairs to practise saying the sentences from Exercise A. Encourage them to listen carefully and check their partner's pronunciation. Monitor to check and help if necessary.

GRAMMAR

A Elicit that the sentences are also all from the radio show. Tell them to match the sentences with the explanations. Check answers and then point out the information in the box about hopes and wishes and the grammar box. Check students understand the difference between *likely* and *unlikely*, and clarify that *hope* is only used for a likely situation and *wish* only for an unlikely or unreal situation. You could emphasise this by writing some negative examples (e.g. *I wish I'll pass the exam*) on the board and explicitly correcting them.

B Direct students to the **Grammar Hub** on pages 140 and 141 (see below and TB116).

C Tell students to practise by completing the gaps with *hope* or *wish* and choosing the correct form of the verbs in bold. Use the **Grammar Worksheet** on W39 for extra practice.

SPEAKING

Put students into pairs to discuss the questions. If time allows, put students with a new partner to interview a different classmate. You could organise this with students arranged in an inner and an outer circle. After five minutes, tell all the students in the inner circle to move clockwise one place and speak to a new partner.

Finish with feedback on students' use of language during the conversations, especially how well they expressed their hopes and wishes.

GRAMMAR HUB

10.2 Hopes and wishes

wish + past simple	imagining a different present situation (unreal present)	**I wish she were** more organised. **I wish I weren't** so hungry! **He wishes he knew** the answer.
wish + past perfect	imagining a different past situation (unreal past)	**We wish our son had won** the race. **They wish they hadn't eaten** so much.
wish + *could*	imagining an unlikely future possibility (unlikely future)	**I wish I could stop** drinking coffee.
hope (that) + present simple/continuous	imagining a likely future possibility (likely future)	**I hope that you enjoy** yourself tomorrow. **I hope that you are enjoying** yourself on holiday! **We hope that she doesn't make** the wrong decision.

- We can use *wish* to talk about ourselves or other people.

  I wish I had more friends. / I wish Sarah had more friends. / Sarah wishes her brother had more friends.
- We usually use *were* instead of *was* after *I wish* or *He/She wishes*.

  I wish I were better organised.
- We use *wish* + *could* to talk about something that we want to be different in the future. However, by using *could*, we express a belief that our wish probably won't come true.

  I wish I could treat myself to a holiday. (= I know that I won't be able to do this because I don't have the money, time, etc.)

- Although *hope* refers to the future, it is followed by a verb in the present tense. You can include the word *that*, but it is usually omitted.

  I hope (that) the snacks aren't too salty.
  We hope (that) the fast food restaurant is open tomorrow.
- We use the negative for the verb which **follows** *wish* or *hope*.

  I hope it doesn't rain tomorrow.
  NOT I don't hope it rains.
  I wish I hadn't spent so much money.
  NOT I don't wish I had spent so much money.

B Go to the Vocabulary Hub on page 146.

C SPEAK Work in pairs and discuss the questions.

1 Where do you see yourself in ten years?

2 How do you amuse yourself when you're on a long journey?

3 Can you think of any situations where you can't trust yourself?

PRONUNCIATION
Emphasis and reflexive pronouns

A Listen to the sentences from the radio show. For each sentence, decide if the reflexive pronouns are stressed or unstressed.

1 I treat myself to a snack from the packet. unstressed

2 I always make myself a cup of coffee before I check my emails. unstressed

3 Don't blame yourself. stressed

4 How will you reward yourself for being good? unstressed

B Now choose the best word or phrase to complete the rules.

Emphasis and reflexive pronouns

1 When a reflexive pronoun follows a verb, the pronoun is / ~~is not~~ usually stressed.

2 But when we want to emphasise the subject at the end of a clause, we ~~can~~ / can't stress the pronoun.

C SPEAK Work in pairs. Practise saying the sentences in Exercise A. Listen and check your partner's pronunciation.

GRAMMAR
Hopes and wishes

A WORK IT OUT Match the sentences from the conversation (1–5) with the explanations (a–d).

1 I wish I'd known about all this a few years ago! But I guess it's too late for me now.

2 I hope your new routine works for you, Leo.

3 I wish we had time to talk about your other seven cups of coffee, but we need to go to our next caller.

4 I wish I could run a marathon next year.

5 I really wish I were better organised.

a The speaker is talking about something that's likely to happen in the future.

b The speaker is talking about something that's unlikely to happen in the future.

c The speaker is imagining a different present situation.

d The speaker is imagining a different past situation.

Hopes and wishes

When we talk about hopes and wishes, we use very similar structures to the first, second and third conditionals.

	Conditional sentences	Hopes and wishes
Likely future	It'll be good if your idea works.	I hope your idea works.
Unlikely future	I'd be happy if I could find a new job. (or: … if I found a new job.)	I wish I could find a new job. (NOT: I wish I found a new job.)
Unreal present	It would be nice if I were taller.	I wish I were taller.
Unreal past	It would have been better if you'd told me.	I wish you'd told me.

B Go to the Grammar Hub on page 140.

C Complete the sentences with *hope* or *wish*. Then choose the correct words to complete the hopes and wishes.

1 I _____hope_____ you *have* / *had* / *could have* a lovely time on holiday next week.

2 I started playing tennis last year and I love it, but I'm too old to become a top player. I _____wish_____ I *start* / *started* / *'d started* playing when I was younger.

3 It's great that you're coming to my city next week. I _____wish_____ I *met* / *could meet* / *'d met* you while you're here, but unfortunately I'll be away all week.

4 I'm a bit worried about Frank and Donna. They should have arrived an hour ago. I _____hope_____ they *arrive* / *'d arrived* / *arrived* soon.

5 I never have time to do all the things I need to do each week. Sometimes I _____wish_____ there *were* / *are* / *had been* eight days in a week!

6 My main regret is that I didn't spend enough time with my children when they were younger. I _____wish_____ I *don't spend* / *didn't spend* / *hadn't spent* so much time working in those days!

7 My dream is to be the first person to travel to Mars! I really _____wish_____ I *went* / *could go* / *'d gone* there one day, but I know it's never going to happen.

SPEAKING

Work in pairs and discuss the questions.

1 Do you have any regrets about your habits? What do you wish you'd started earlier? What do you wish you'd never started?

2 What do you wish you could change about yourself?

3 What are your hopes for the future? Think about next week, next month and next year.

4 What are your dreams for the future? What do you wish you could do one day?

READING

A SPEAK Work in pairs and discuss the questions.

1 What is a to-do list? What information does it contain?

2 Why do you think psychologists are interested in to-do lists?

3 Do you keep a to-do list? Why/Why not?

B READ FOR GIST Read *The psychology of to-do lists*. Match the headings (a–g) with the paragraphs (1–7).

a Organisation, motivation and satisfaction

b The benefits of forgetting

c Not as difficult as it sounds

d An experiment over dinner

e Keeping tasks small and simple

f Using to-do lists to cut stress

g The stress of not finishing things

The psychology of **to-do lists**

1 d

One day in the 1920s, a large group of psychologists were having a meal at their favourite restaurant. They were discussing the waiter's amazing memory: he always remembered everybody's orders perfectly, but he never wrote anything down. One of the psychologists, Bluma Zeigarnik, decided to try an experiment. She told everyone to cover their plates. Then she asked the waiter to come back to the table, and to try to remember what was on each plate. Amazingly, he couldn't remember anything, even though he himself had put the plates on the table only a few minutes earlier. How was it possible that a man with such an amazing memory had forgotten everything a few minutes later?

2 b

Ex D Zeigarnik realised that there was in fact nothing special about the waiter. In fact, we're all good at remembering current tasks – things that we still need to do. But as soon as they're finished, we forget all about them. The 'Zeigarnik effect', as it's now called, is our brains' way of tidying up and sorting information. If we had to remember everything forever, our brains would soon run out of space.

3 g

Ex D But there's a dark side to the Zeigarnik effect. Studies have shown that people perform badly in tests when they're worrying about other unfinished tasks. It seems that we can't stop thinking about what we still need to do. This makes us stressed and prevents us from focusing on new tasks.

4 f

Is there anything we can do about this problem? Recent research suggests that we can reduce our stress levels by keeping a record of all our current tasks in a to-do list. This simple action tells our brains to stop worrying about the task, which means we can give our full attention to other tasks.

5 a

To-do lists have three additional benefits. First, they help us to stay organised. Secondly, they are a useful record of what we've achieved and when. It can be highly motivating to look back at our past achievements – especially because the Zeigarnik effect usually makes us forget them. However, the best thing about to-do lists is the satisfying feeling you get when you cross each item off the list.

6 e

The key to successful to-do lists is to break large objectives into smaller action points. Instead of writing 'Learn to drive' on your list, focus on small and practical jobs that you can achieve very quickly, such as 'Find a list of driving schools in my city' and 'Read a website with reviews of different schools'. The smaller the tasks, the better. Dave Allen, a time-management expert, also recommends an archive to store all the things you might need and a system of 43 folders to schedule when to do each task.

7 c

If that sounds like too much hard work, think again. With a good system, life is much easier. You can relax and enjoy the rest of the day, happy in the knowledge that everything is under control.

> **Glossary**
>
> **archive (n)** a place where you store documents and records

10.2 Wish lists

READING

A Put students into pairs to discuss the questions. Monitor and check students have understood the concept of a *to-do* list (a list of things you have to do).

B Tell students to look at the pictures and ask what they think they have to do with the psychology of to-do lists. Tell students to read the text to check and to match the headings with the paragraphs. Point out the glossary but tell students not to worry if there are some words in the article that they don't understand. Tell students not to focus on the underlined words yet.

TEACHING IDEA by David Seymour and Maria Popova

Grammar: I wish and If only

Use this activity to practise the grammar.

In pairs, rewrite these sentences with *I wish / If only* in two ways, one with a past tense and the other with *would*, e.g. *It's raining.* – (1) *I wish / If only it wasn't raining.* (2) *I wish / If only it would stop raining.*

> She's singing that awful song again. I've had a nasty cold all week. You're unemployed. He's late for the meeting again. It's cold outside. They never write to us. The lift is still not working. The streets here are filthy.

TEACHING IDEA by David Seymour and Maria Popova

Grammar: A better place to live

Use this activity to practise the grammar.

In pairs, write five sentences beginning *I wish . . .* about the town or city where you live in order to make it a better place to live, e.g. *I wish the buses ran all through the night so I didn't have to take a taxi home.*

Join with another pair. Discuss your sentences and decide which are the best five of your ideas from your combined lists. Then join with another group of four students and choose the best five ideas again. Choose someone from your group to write your ideas up on the board. As a class, decide on the best five sentences.

(Variation: This activity also works well with ideas for improving the school.)

GRAMMAR HUB

10.2 Hopes and wishes

A Match the situations to the people's comments.

1 Brett's too short for the basketball team. — d
2 Dad is always losing his keys. — g
3 I don't know any of the answers. — b
4 Josh's journey to work takes 90 minutes. — a
5 I want to stop eating sugar completely. — f
6 Phoebe feels lonely. — c
7 Anna is really tired. — e

a 'I wish I didn't have to drive so far.'
b 'I wish I had studied more.'
c 'I wish I had more friends.'
d 'I wish I were taller.'
e 'I wish I hadn't stayed up all night.'
f 'I hope you achieve your goal.'
g 'I wish I wasn't so disorganised.'

B Choose the correct option.

1 I *wish* / (*hope*) to achieve everything on my to-do list.
2 Do you wish you *don't give* / (*hadn't given*) in to your cravings?
3 The children wish they (*could stay*) / *stayed* up late to watch the film.
4 I wish I *have* / (*had*) more money to spend on clothes.
5 Kate wishes her husband *is* / (*were*) more focused on his career.
6 They wish they (*didn't live*) / *couldn't live* near a noisy shopping centre.
7 Jared (*wishes*) / *hopes* he could take a holiday.
8 I wish you *didn't persuade* / (*hadn't persuaded*) me to eat this burger – it's horrible!

C Complete the sentences with the correct form of the verb in brackets.

1 I never have enough time. I wish there _____ were _____ (be) more hours in the day!
2 I hope this snack _____ isn't _____ (not / be) high in salt.
3 The children are full of energy. I wish they __ hadn't eaten __ (not / eat) so many sugary snacks!
4 My children wish I ___ didn't work ___ (not / work) such long hours. doesn't change /
5 I hope Pam _ hasn't changed _ (not / change) her mind!
6 Alisha wants to buy a laptop but wishes she _____ knew _____ (know) more about them.
7 I wish my best friend _____ were/was _____ (be) here to help me make the right choice!
8 She _____ wishes _____ (wish) she could give up drinking sugary drinks but says it's very difficult.

➤ Go back to page 115.

C Tell students to read the information in the box about bridge sentences. Remind students about topic sentences, which they saw in Unit 8 in the article *If you really can't wait … about buying the latest gadgets.* Put students into pairs to answer the questions.

Possible answers: *The first sentence in a paragraph is often both the topic sentence and a bridge sentence. But not always: some paragraphs don't have a bridge sentence (including the first paragraph); the topic sentence isn't always the first sentence. Bridge sentences refer back to the previous paragraph. Topic sentences introduce the main points of the current paragraph.*

D Tell students to read the first sentence in each paragraph and answer the questions. Do the first one together as a whole class. Put students into pairs to discuss the rest.

Possible answers:

1 '*One day in the 1920s, a large group of psychologists were having a meal at their favourite restaurant.' This can't be a bridge sentence because it's the first paragraph.*

2 '*Zeigarnik realised that there was in fact nothing special about the waiter.' This is a bridge sentence. It isn't a topic sentence. In fact refers to a contrast between what the people first thought (paragraph 1) and what was actually true (paragraph 2). The words Zeigarnik, nothing special and the waiter also refer back to the previous paragraph.*

3 '*But there's a dark side to the Zeigarnik effect.' This is a bridge sentence. But refers to a contrast between the positive things in paragraph 2 and the negative things in paragraph 3. The phrase the Zeigarnik effect also forms a bridge to the previous paragraph.*

4 '*Is there anything we can do about this problem?' This is a bridge sentence. This problem refers back to the problem described in paragraph 3.*

5 '*To-do lists have three additional benefits.' This is a bridge sentence. Additional refers back to the first benefit of to-do lists, which was described in paragraph 4.*

6 '*The key to successful to-do lists is to break large objectives into smaller action points.' This isn't a bridge sentence because the whole article is about to-do lists. This paragraph introduces a completely separate point about them.*

7 '*If that sounds like too much hard work, think again.' This is a bridge sentence. That refers back to Dave Allen's system from paragraph 6.*

E Put students into pairs to discuss the questions.

VOCABULARY

A Tell students to look at the underlined words in the article and to match them with the definitions. Tell students to read the sentences carefully to help them work out the meanings of the words. Go through the example with the whole class to demonstrate how to do this, replacing the word in the text with different definitions until one makes sense. Consolidate students' understanding of the words by eliciting personal, more memorable examples.

B Put students into pairs to discuss the questions. If any students keep a record of tasks they need to do, encourage other students to ask further questions about how useful and effective they find it. Use the **Vocabulary Worksheet** on W40 for extra practice.

SPEAKING HUB

A Tell students to prepare a short wish list, either using the suggestions given or their own ideas. Elicit a few examples from the class for further guidance and inspiration.

B Put students into groups to share and explain their lists. When they have discussed all the lists, tell each group to choose the most interesting items and to create a to-do list. Tell them that they're going to present these lists to the class. Point out the tips and encourage students to follow them. Monitor to help with language if needed, and check students are following the suggested structure for their lists. When they've finished, tell them to practise presenting their list.

C Tell each group to stand up and present their list to the class. Tell the other students to listen carefully and make notes about any positive suggestions they could give to support and encourage their classmates with their plans.

D Put students into new groups to discuss the questions.

METHODOLOGY HUB by Jim Scrivener

Fluency and confidence

Fluency and confidence are important goals when considering speaking lessons. There is no point knowing a lot about language if you can't use it (which, sadly, has been the experience of many language learners in the past – able to conjugate a verb, but unable to respond to a simple question). To help achieve this aim, we often want to find ways of enabling as many students as possible to speak as much as possible. Sometimes an all-class speaking activity is useful, but if it takes up the whole lesson, it actually offers very little speaking time to each individual student. It's usually a good idea to organise speaking activities in pairs, threes and small groups, as well as with the class as a whole.

TEACHING IDEA by David Seymour and Maria Popova

Grammar: Mountain rescue

Use this activity to practise the grammar.

(Write up the sentences below in random order on the board.) These situations are all connected to the same adventure. Work in groups and put them in order. Imagine you were stuck on the mountain. Write two sentences for each situation, one using *If only / I wish . . .* and one using *should (not) have done.*

We didn't tell anyone at the hostel where we were going.

Leo forgot to pack a compass.

We left later than planned.

The cloud came down, but we decided to continue walking.

We lost the path.

Kathy fell and broke her leg.

No one had a mobile phone or torch.

Ben tried to go back down the mountain.

What order did your group decide on? Talk together and decide what happened next. Did everyone survive?

C Read the box about bridge sentences. What is the connection between bridge sentences and topic sentences (see Unit 8)? What's the difference between them?

Bridge sentences

The first sentence in a paragraph is often a bridge sentence, which shows how the paragraph is connected to the previous paragraph. For example, it might use words like *however* to introduce a contrast, or words like *another* to add extra information.

Not all paragraphs have a bridge sentence.

D **READ FOR KEY INFORMATION** Read the first sentence in each paragraph again. Which five are bridge sentences? Underline the words and phrases in the sentences that refer back to the previous paragraph. What exactly do they refer to?

E **SPEAK** Work in pairs and discuss the questions.

1 Have you ever experienced the Zeigarnik effect? Think about:
   • preparing for a test.
   • learning a speech, a song or a poem.
   • remembering people's names and faces.

2 Do you ever look back at your past achievements? Would you find it motivating?

VOCABULARY
Staying organised

A Look at the underlined words in *The psychology of to-do lists*. Find words or phrases that mean the following.

1 a job that you need to do
   a _t a s k_

2 to keep something in a safe place
   to _s t o r e_ something

3 to put things back in the right places
   to _t i d y_ up

4 to plan exactly when you will do something
   to _s c h e d u l e_ something

5 a small thing that you're going to do
   an _a c t i o n_ point

6 to put things in the right order
   to _s o r t_ things

7 a large thing that you want to achieve
   an _o b j e c t i v e_

8 to write something down
   to keep a _r e c o r d_ of something

B **SPEAK** Work in pairs and discuss the questions.

1 How many **tasks** are on your to-do list?

2 Do you **keep a record** of the tasks you need to do? Would you like to start?

⭕ SPEAKING HUB

A **PREPARE** Write a short wish list. Use the ideas below or your own ideas.
   • a problem that you would like to solve
   • a good habit that you hope you will start / wish you could start
   • a way to become less stressed or better organised
   • how you'll continue learning/using English after this course

B **PLAN** Work in groups. Discuss your wish lists. As a group, choose the most interesting items from your wish lists and create a to-do list. Try to:
   • plan cues, routines and rewards for any habits you want to change.
   • turn your objectives into tasks and action points.

C **PRESENT** Stand up and tell the class what you plan to do and when. When others are speaking, listen carefully and be positive about their plans.

D **REFLECT** Work in groups and discuss the questions.

1 How will you make sure you'll do the things on your list?

2 How will you motivate each other to do those things?

◯– **Talk about your wishes and regrets**
◯– **Plan a to-do list**

COMPREHENSION

A When was the last time you had to say goodbye to someone? How did you feel? How long was it before you saw that person again?

B Number the pictures in the order you think they happened. What do you think happened?

a 5

b 2

c 1

d 3

e 4

f 6

C ▶ 00:00–02:25 Watch the first part of the video and check your ideas. How do you think the video will end?

D ▶ 02:25–04:29 Complete the letter that Sam wrote to Gaby by choosing the correct words below. Watch the second part of the video and check your answers. Does the video end how you predicted?

1 leaving / in / over
2 words / time / pen
3 should / usually / never
4 city / life / home
5 business / Madrid / yourself

> Dear Gaby,
>
> I've just heard that you're ¹____leaving____ London and … I wish I had said this to you in person, but I just couldn't find the ²____words____. I'm so sorry, but I ³_____never_____ know the right thing to say. I know you've already made your mind up about leaving, and I'm going to miss you so much. The thought of not having you in my ⁴_____life_____ hurts because … I love you. I always have. I just didn't know how to say it before. Take good care of ⁵_____yourself_____.

| MILLY | SAM | NEENA | ZAC | GABY |

FUNCTIONAL LANGUAGE
Making and accepting apologies

A Put the words in the correct order. Then put each phrase under the correct heading in the table.

1 quickly / leave / sorry / to / so / I'm / really

I'm really sorry to leave so quickly.

2 you'll / worry / be / don't / fine

Don't worry; you'll be fine.

3 apologise / need / no / there's / to

There's no need to apologise.

4 worry / don't / it / about

Don't worry about it.

5 just / things / of / those / one / it's

It's just one of those things.

6 OK / all / to / be / it's / going

It's all going to be OK.

7 my / it's / fault

It's my fault.

8 not / fault / fault / it's / it's / my / your

It's not your fault; it's my fault.

9 nothing / about / worry / there's / to

There's nothing to worry about.

10 great / is / this / to / be / going

This is going to be great.

Making an apology	Accepting an apology	Giving reassurance
I'm really sorry to leave so quickly.	There's no need to apologise.	Don't worry; you'll be fine.
	Don't worry about it.	It's just one of those things.
It's my fault.	It's not your fault; it's my fault.	It's all going to be OK.
		There's nothing to worry about.
		This is going to be great.

B ▶ Watch the video again and tick (✓) each phrase as you hear it.

USEFUL PHRASES

A Match the useful phrases (1–5) with the phrases that come before or after them (a–e).

1 It's time to go. c
2 I wish I had said this to you in person. d
3 I'm such an idiot! b
4 I've changed my mind about leaving. a
5 I'm scared. e

a What about your plane? You're going to miss it.
b I can't believe that I missed her.
c You'll be fine; don't worry.
d But I just couldn't find the words.
e There's nothing to worry about.

B How do you say these useful phrases in your language?

PRONUNCIATION
Vowel sounds

A Match words with the same vowel sounds from boxes A, B and C.

| A | airport | housemate | <u>mind</u> | person | sorry | worry |

| B | apologise | <u>guys</u> | hurt | love | strangely | thought |

| C | gone | <u>my</u> | of course | paying | under | words |

🔊 **B** Listen, check and repeat the words. Copy the sounds.

10.6

SPEAKING

A Work in pairs. Write conversations about the following situations or your own ideas. Student A – apologise. Student B – accept the apology and reassure Student A.

arrive late / for meeting   break / chair
forget / to call   miss / party   spill / coffee

A: _I'm really sorry about breaking your chair._
B: _Oh, don't worry about it – it's not your fault._
   It's just one of those things.

B PRESENT Act out your conversations. Take turns to be Student A and Student B.

◯– Make and accept apologies

➤ Turn to page 165 to learn how to write a report.

10.3 Come home

LEAD-IN

Write the word *Goodbye* on the board. Put students into two teams. Give them a time limit of one minute to see how many different languages they know how to say *Hello* and *Goodbye* in.

COMPREHENSION

A Put students into pairs to discuss the questions.

B Elicit that the pictures are in the wrong order. Put students into pairs to put the pictures into the correct order. Tell them to discuss what they think happens.

C ▶ 00:00-02:25 Play the video and tell students to watch and check their answers. Encourage them to predict the ending.

D ▶ 02:25-04:29 Tell students to choose the correct words to complete the gaps in the letter. Play the video for students to check, and to check if their predictions about the ending were correct.

FUNCTIONAL LANGUAGE

A Tell students to put the words in the correct order, then to put the completed phrases in the correct column in the table. Check understanding of *it's my fault* (I'm responsible for the bad situation) / *it's not your fault* (you're not responsible for the bad situation).

B ▶ Tell the students to watch the video one more time and to tick each phrase as they hear it.

USEFUL PHRASES

A Tell students to match the useful phrases from the video with the phrases that come just before or just after them.

B Tell the students to think about how they say the useful phrases in their own language.

PRONUNCIATION

A Read out all the words from boxes A, B and C in random order and get students to tell you which box they are in (i.e. *hurt*, B, *housemate*, A). Go through the example together to ensure students fully understand the task. Put students into pairs to group the other words according to their pronunciation.

B Play the audio for students to listen, check and repeat the words.
🔊 10.6

> *airport, thought, of course*
> *housemate, strangely, paying*
> *person, hurt, words*
> *sorry, apologise, gone*
> *worry, love, under*

SPEAKING

A Put students into pairs and tell them they're going to write some conversations where people make and accept apologies. When students have prepared two or three conversations, tell them to practise acting them out. Tell them to change roles in each different conversation.

B Tell each pair to act out their conversations taking turns to be student A and student B. Tell the other students to listen and think about how appropriate the apologies and responses are. Ask students if they would have accepted the apologies, or if they would have been reassured by the replies.

▶ VIDEOSCRIPT

G = Gaby   Z = Zac   N = Neena   S = Sam

G: It's time to go … I think … Thanks. See you. Oh no.

Z: You'll be fine, don't worry.

G: Thanks, Zac. I'm really sorry to leave so quickly.

Z: There's no need to apologise!

G: I'll keep paying the rent until you get a new housemate. I'm sure you'll find someone soon.

N: Honestly, it's fine. Don't worry about it – it's just one of those things. I'm really going to miss you!

G: You have to come and visit me!

Z: Of course, we will!

N: Oh, this letter arrived for you.

G: Thanks … that's my taxi … well … goodbye.

S: Gaby?

Z: Whoa, you just missed her. What's going on?

S: It's from Gaby. I thought she'd been acting strangely.

N: What does it say?

S: That … that she's in love with me.

Z: But you're also …

S: Yeah, I know!

N: Oh, Sam!

S: And … she's gone.
Dear Gaby. I've just heard that you're leaving London and … I wish I had said this to you in person, but I just couldn't find the words. I'm so sorry but I never know the right thing to say. I know you've already made your mind up about

leaving and I'm going to miss you so much. The thought of not having you in my life hurts, because I love you. I always have. I just didn't know how to say it before. Take good care of yourself.

Z: … She's probably getting to the airport about now …

N: Zac! I'm not sure that's helpful. Listen, Sam. It's all going to be OK.

S: I'm such an idiot! I can't believe that I missed her.

G: You didn't.

S: Gaby!

G: Hi … sorry, I forgot to leave my key …

S: I just found your letter! It was under the counter. I wish I'd known. It's my fault …

G: I thought you'd read it! Oh, Sam. It's not your fault. It's my fault – I should've said something.

S: Me, too.

G: I know …

S: … What about your plane? You're going to miss it?

G: I've changed my mind about leaving.

Z: Well … it seems like you guys have totally got this all under control, so we might …

N: … Yeah …

S: I'm scared.

G: Me, too. But there's nothing to worry about. This is going to be great.

S: Come here. Zac!

Z: Sorry!

Unit 10 Writing

10 Writing ● Write a report

Ⓦ writing a report

A Work in pairs and discuss the questions.

1 Why do people write reports? What are some situations where non-business people write reports?

2 Why do people read reports? What information do they need?

B Read the *Report on charity auction* and answer the questions.

1 Why has the writer written the report?

2 What went well with the auction? What went wrong?

3 What did the writer learn from the experience?

REPORT ON CHARITY AUCTION

Summary:
On 15th December, we held a charity auction to raise money for the local hospital. The auction raised less money than expected. This report explores what we did wrong.

Background:
We asked 24 local celebrities (e.g. sportspeople, TV presenters) to donate gifts for our auction. We received 55 gifts, including many valuable items (e.g. a signed football, a beautiful painting). We expected to raise around £5,000. 720 people attended our auction event. The auction only raised £322. Many of the items were not sold.

Analysis:
1 **Paradox of choice:** There were too many items, so people could not decide. If we had limited the auction to around ten items, we would probably have made more money.
2 **Hook numbers:** We wanted to attract large numbers of people to the auction, so in our marketing materials, we showed pictures of the best items with low starting prices, e.g. £2 for the signed football. We shouldn't have done this because it encouraged people to make offers of a few pounds, not hundreds of pounds.

Ex D

Recommendations:
• For future auctions, limit the number of items to around ten.
• In marketing materials, show the value of the items (e.g. *Worth over £500*) rather than the starting price.

Glossary
auction (n) a public occasion when things are sold to the people who offer the most money for them
donate (v) to give something such as money or goods to an organisation, especially to a school, hospital, political party or charity

C Look at the box. Match the features of a report (1–8) with the explanations (a–h). Find examples in the report.

Writing a report

A report describes a past event or a present situation and ends with recommendations for the future.

1 title	d	5 numbered lists	e
2 summary	c	6 full forms	h
3 headings	f	7 facts and figures	b
4 bullet points	a	8 examples	g

a Use these small black circles to make it easier to read lists of items.

b Your report should include dates, names, numbers, etc.

c In the first paragraph, say briefly what happened and why you've written the report.

d The reader can see immediately what the report is about.

e You can use these to show that the order of items in a list is important.

f Use words like *Analysis* and *Recommendations* to show you're starting a new section.

g Include these to explain important points. You can put them in brackets: (e.g. …).

h Reports are usually quite formal, so it's best to write separate words (e.g. *do not*) instead of contractions (e.g. *don't*).

D Find examples of the third conditional and *should have done* in the report. Which section are they in? Why?
analysis – thinking about what went wrong

WRITING

A PREPARE You are going to write a short report about an event where some things could have been better. Think about:

● will you write about a real event or will you invent one?

● what event will you describe? Something from your work or studies? An accident that you had?

● who will read your report? Why?

B PLAN Make notes under these headings:

● Background: What happened?

● Analysis: What went wrong? Why?

● Recommendations: What should happen differently in future?

C WRITE Write your report. Remember to use headings, bullet points or numbered lists. When you finish writing the three main sections, write a short summary at the beginning.

D REVIEW Work in groups. Read some of your groups' reports. Do you agree with their recommendations?

Answers

1 explore what went wrong at a charity auction

2 well: received 55 gifts not well: only raised £322, too many items, showed best items with low starting prices

3 Limit number of items, show value of items not starting price

Refer students to this report as a model for the writing task.

Remind students to pay attention to whether they need to use the past, present or future tense in their writing.

WRITING

With books closed, tell students to imagine that they were asked to raise money for a local hospital. Put students into pairs to discuss how they would do this. Share the best ideas with the class.

A Tell students to open their books and to discuss the questions with their partner. Get some brief feedback as a whole class and ask students if they ever write or read reports and why.

B Tell students to read the report and answer the questions. Point out the glossary and check students understand the words. These words are very important to understand the content of the report.

C Point out the information in the box about writing a report, then tell students to match the features of a report with their explanations. Tell students to find an example of each feature in the report about the charity auction.

D Tell students to find an example of the third conditional and of *should have done* in the report. Tell students to think about which section these are in and why.

WRITING TASK

A Tell students they're going to write a short report about an event where some things could have been better. Tell them to think about the questions.

B Tell students to make notes under the headings.

C Tell students to write their report. Remind students about the features of a report to help them organise their writing appropriately. Tell them to go back and write a short summary at the start of the report when they have finished writing the three main sections.

D Put students into groups to read each other's reports. When they have read all the report, tell the groups to discuss if they agree with the recommendations and why, or why not.

GRAMMAR

A Complete the third conditional sentences. Use the correct form of the underlined verbs.

1 The waiter <u>forgot</u> our order because he didn't <u>write</u> it down.

   If the waiter _____*had written*_____ down our order, he _____*wouldn't have forgotten*_____ it.

2 You didn't <u>finish</u> anything on your to-do list. Maybe it's because all the items <u>were</u> too big.

   You might _____*have finished*_____ some things on your to-do list if they _____*'d/had been*_____ a bit smaller.

3 I <u>saw</u> a sign for a fast-food restaurant, so I <u>felt</u> a need to eat.

   If I _____*hadn't seen*_____ a sign for the fast-food restaurant, I _____*wouldn't have felt*_____ a need to eat!

4 I didn't have time to <u>try</u> on these jeans, but I <u>bought</u> them anyway.

   I _____*wouldn't have bought*_____ these jeans if I _____*'d/had tried*_____ them on first! They're much too small!

B Write sentences with *should/shouldn't have done*.

1 I wish you'd been more careful.

   You _____*should have been more careful*_____.

2 I regret buying these shoes.

   I _____*shouldn't have bought these shoes*_____.

3 Why didn't they listen to us?

   They _____*should have listened to us*_____.

4 It was a mistake to go out yesterday.

   We _____*shouldn't have gone out yesterday*_____.

C Complete the conversation with the correct form of the verbs in brackets.

A: Hey! I'm having a dinner party tomorrow night. I hope you [1]_____*can come*_____ (can come). It's going to be excellent.

B: Ah, I wish I [2]_____*could come*_____ (can come), but I can't. I've got tickets for a football match tomorrow, and it's the final.

A: Oh, I didn't know it's the final tomorrow! I wish I [3]_____*had/'d known*_____ (know)! I'd have arranged the party for a different night. Anyway, I hope your team [4]_____*wins/win*_____ (win)!

B: Well, my team isn't in the final. I wish we [5]_____*were*_____ (be)! But we lost in the semi-final last week. I wish I [6]_____*hadn't bought*_____ (not buy) a ticket – then I could come to your party!

VOCABULARY

A Choose the correct verbs to complete the sentences.

1 I got an email from somebody who tried to *persuade* / **tric** me into giving my bank account number.

2 I didn't want to buy a camera at all, but the saleswoman *affected* / **persuaded** me to buy one.

3 Whenever I walk past a fast-food restaurant, I'm *regretted* / **tempted** to go inside.

4 For a long time, businesses **assumed** / *influenced* that more choice meant more sales.

B Find and correct one mistake in each underlined phrase.

[1]<u>Would you mind ~~that~~ **if**</u> I asked you for some advice? You see, I want to go somewhere new this weekend, but I'm [2]<u>in ~~three~~ **two** minds</u> about where to go. This morning, I [3]<u>made up my mind</u> and decided to go cycling in the forest, but then I heard the weather is going to be horrible, so I [4]<u>changed ~~the~~ **my** mind</u> and decided to go to the new museum instead. But … I don't really like museums. What should I do? [5]<u>Bear **in** ~~to~~ mind</u>, I don't have a car, so it needs to be somewhere with good bus connections.

C Match the beginnings of the tips for staying organised (1–5) with the endings (a–e).

1 Don't do everything at once. Focus — d
2 Remember to schedule — c
3 Use a to-do list to keep — a
4 Break big objectives into smaller action — e
5 Use an archive to store — b

a a record of your tasks.
b important old documents.
c some time to relax!
d on one task at a time.
e points.

D Choose the correct reflexive verb to complete the sentence

1 You shouldn't **blame** / *control* yourself. It's not your fault.

2 *Help* / **get** yourself to anything you want.

3 I always go into fast food restaurants when I see them. I can't *make* / **control** myself.

4 He's trained so hard for the race. Why doesn't he *treat* / **se** himself to a night off and just relax?

FUNCTIONAL LANGUAGE

Complete the conversation with the words in the box. There are two extra words.

about   apologise   blame   fault   not   so   those   worry

Dimitri: Hey, Igor! Have you eaten my pizza?

Igor: Don't [1]_____*blame*_____ me! I've been out all day. I don't know anything about it.

Dimitri: Oh … I'm [2]_____*so*_____ sorry. I shouldn't have blamed you.

Igor: It's OK. Don't [3]_____*worry*_____ about it. So I wonde who ate your pizza …

Rob: Er, sorry, but it's my [4]_____*fault*_____. I was really hungry when I got home last night and I hadn't gone to the shops!

Dimitri: Oh, there's no need to [5]_____*apologise*_____. It's just on of [6]_____*those*_____ things.

Vocabulary and Communication Hub

Contents

Vocabulary Hub

1.1 Seeing and hearing

Match the beginnings of the sentences (1–5) with the endings (a–e).

1 If you **spot** somebody, b
2 If you **recognise** somebody, e
3 If you **notice** something, c
4 If you **observe** something, d
5 If you **stare at** something, a

a you look at it for a long time, maybe too long.
b you see him/her by chance.
c you see it for the first time.
d you watch it carefully over a long time.
e you see him/her and know who he/she is.

➤ Go back to page 5.

1.2 Languages

A Put the letters in bold in the correct order to make words about language learning.

1 Which is more important when you're speaking English? Speaking ~~uelcartyac~~ *accurately* or ~~tnulyife~~ *fluently*? Why?
2 Do you know any ~~midosi~~ *idioms* in English? What's your favourite?
3 Are most people in your country ~~nanoliomlgu~~ *monolingual* or ~~ialinglub~~ *bilingual*? What about in your family?
4 Can you tell where somebody is from just by listening to their ~~cectna~~ *accent*? In your language? In English?

B SPEAK Work in pairs. Ask and answer the questions in Exercise A.

➤ Go back to page 9.

2.2 Problems and solutions

Complete the advice with the correct form of the verbs in the box. Sometimes more than one answer is possible.

> agree on   analyse   come up with
>   deal with   solve   suggest

1 If you really want to <u>solve / deal with</u> a problem, you'll find a way. If you don't, you'll find an excuse.
2 If you are stuck and can't <u>agree on / come up</u> with a solution, go and do something different until you have some fresh ideas.
3 It is best to <u>analyse</u> a problem in as much detail as you can. This will make it easier to solve.
4 It is not always difficult to say what the problem is at work. The real challenge is to <u>suggest</u> a solution to your colleagues.
5 People often have different ideas about how to solve problems. In those situations, you should find a solution everyone <u>agrees on</u>.

➤ Go back to page 21.

3.1 Collocations: travel information

Complete the sentences with the correct travel collocations.

1 We are sorry to announce there are <u>severe delays</u> on line 1, of approximately 45 minutes.
2 Let's leave really early, before rush hour, to avoid the <u>heavy traffic</u>.
3 Don't go that way. It's closed due to <u>roadworks</u> – they're replacing the pavement.
4 It's always very crowded on the trains during <u>rush hour</u>, with lots of people standing for a long time.
5 Following the earlier delays, we now have a <u>good service</u> on all lines. All lines are running normally.
6 We're stuck in a <u>traffic jam</u> on the motorway; we'll be at least half an hour late.
7 Look, they've just <u>cancelled the train</u> We'll have to wait another hour now, for the next one.
8 The first <u>underground line</u> opened in 1863 and went from Paddington station to Farringdon Street station, in London.

➤ Go back to page 27.

3.1 Nouns ending in -ion

Complete the sentences with the nouns in the box.

> communication   connection   decisions
> expectation   expression   inspiration
> reaction   situations

I think _communication_ between the driver and the passengers is important when a train is delayed.

In my country, there has been a negative ____reaction____ to driverless cars.

Environmental issues don't change the ____decisions____ that I make about transport.

I think it is important to have a ____connection____ with the people you see every day.

There are some travel ____situations____ that make me annoyed or angry.

I generally have a blank ____expression____ when out in public. I never smile at others.

I find people that can talk to strangers an ____inspiration____. I wish I were so confident.

When I was on holiday, the transport system was better than my ____expectation____.

➤ Go back to page 29.

3.2 Gradable and ungradable adjectives

Complete the sentences with the adjectives in the box.

> enormous   excellent   filthy   furious
> good   hilarious   terrible   tiny

Your hands are absolutely ____filthy____. Wash them before dinner.

____Excellent____ work. You made no mistakes at all.

We had a really ____good____ time on holiday. We really didn't want to come back home!

Don't talk to him now. He's absolutely ____furious____ because you lost his bike. Let him calm down first.

Don't go to that restaurant. The food's really ____terrible____.

Charlie thought the show was absolutely ____hilarious____. He laughed from the beginning to the end.

The Gobi Desert is extremely large, but the Sahara Desert is ____enormous____; it's seven times bigger!

Compared to Russia, the UK is absolutely ____tiny____. Russia is 70 times bigger!

➤ Go back to page 33.

4.1 Collocations: goals and resolutions

Complete the sentences with the correct collocations.

1 He didn't stop drinking fizzy drinks completely but he ____cut down____ to two cans a week.

2 When I make a plan I stick to it. I've kept the resolution(s) I made last year.

3 She finally reached her target of running for thirty minutes every day.

4 He ____quit____ eating sugary food three months ago and he already feels healthier.

5 He made a resolution to quit eating chocolate last New Year.

➤ Go back to page 39.

4.2 Prefixes: dis-, mis-, over-, re-, under-

Choose the correct prefix to complete the word.

1 I (dis)/ mis like working late and try to make sure I finish on time each day.

2 I moved out of that city because it is re /(over) populated. There are just too many people.

3 I didn't mean that. You (mis)/ dis understood what I was trying to say!

4 Many people at the company feel they don't earn enough. Personally I agree that they are (under)/ mis paid.

5 I don't think this is the best strategy. We should under / (re) think this.

➤ Go back to page 45.

Vocabulary Hub

5.1 Verbs of influence

A Match the beginnings of the sentences (1–4) with the endings (a–d).

1 My boss persuaded me   <u>c</u>
2 My boss made me   <u>d</u>
3 I told him   <u>a</u>
4 My friend advised me not   <u>b</u>

a to work at the weekend, but he refused.
b to work at home because I might feel lonely.
c to work overtime by offering me some extra money.
d apologise to the customer for being rude.

B Match the beginnings of the sentences (1–4) with the endings (a–d).

1 Our company lets us   <u>d</u>
2 I want my boss   <u>c</u>
3 My colleague encouraged me   <u>b</u>
4 My company allows us   <u>a</u>

a to use our personal social media at work.
b to apply for the job, and now I'm her boss!
c to go on holiday forever. I can't stand him.
d leave early on Fridays.

➤ Go back to page 53.

5.2 Business collocations

Which noun cannot be used to complete each sentence?

1 Over the last few years, the company has built its …
very successfully.
    a brand   b reputation   (c) customers

2 Recently, we have done a lot of … overseas.
    (a) money   b deals   c business

3 The … was launched at the end of last year.
    (a) reputation   b product   c campaign

4 The sales team are very good at making …
    (a) business.   b money.   c a profit.

5 The media attention has helped us to attract new …
    a customers.   b investors.   (c) expenses.

➤ Go back to page 57.

6.2 Hobbies and free time activities

Complete the texts with the verb phrases in the box.

> collect   escape from daily stress   get you out of the house
> is a fan   is into   is relaxing   isn't my thing
> joined a society   keeps you fit   lost interest in   took up

My brother [1]_____ <u>is into</u> _____ football.
He [2]_____ <u>is a fan</u> _____ of Liverpool
Football Club and he goes to nearly all their games. To be
honest, football [3]_____ <u>isn't my thing</u> _____,
so I've only been to one game with him. I like to
[4]_____ <u>collect</u> _____ stamps. I've
recently [5]_____ <u>joined a society</u> _____ for
that, and I'm going to my first meeting with the other
members now. Who says stamp collecting doesn't
[6]_____ <u>get you out of the house</u> _____?!

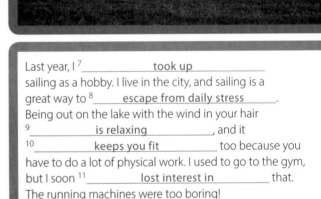

Last year, I [7]_____ <u>took up</u> _____
sailing as a hobby. I live in the city, and sailing is a
great way to [8]_____ <u>escape from daily stress</u> _____.
Being out on the lake with the wind in your hair
[9]_____ <u>is relaxing</u> _____, and it
[10]_____ <u>keeps you fit</u> _____ too because you
have to do a lot of physical work. I used to go to the gym,
but I soon [11]_____ <u>lost interest in</u> _____ that.
The running machines were too boring!

➤ Go back to page 66.

7.1 Phrasal verbs

Work in pairs. Match the underlined phrasal verbs (1–9) with the definitions (a–i).

1 I can't <u>work out</u> what ingredients you've used here. What are they?

2 A: 'Maybe I'll start studying for my exams next week …'
B: 'Don't <u>put it off</u>! Start today!'

3 We've eaten out every night this week. Let's <u>stay in</u> this evening and cook some food at home.

4 Sorry to <u>let</u> you <u>down</u>, but I can't come to your party.

5 I asked everybody to be quiet for a few minutes, but most people just <u>carried on</u> talking.

6 Can you <u>turn</u> the oven <u>down</u> to 150°C in ten minutes? If you leave it at 220°C for too long, the food will burn.

7 I don't mind cooking, but can you <u>clear up</u> afterwards?

8 Can you <u>put</u> your phone <u>away</u>, please! It's really rude to check your messages while we're eating dinner!

9 Great job! <u>Keep up</u> the good work!

a continue without stopping

b take something that's in the wrong place and put it in the right place

c continue at the same high level

d make everything clean and tidy again after making a mess

e not go out

f find the answer by thinking carefully

g decide to do something later, not now

h make something lower/colder/quieter

i make somebody feel sad because you don't do something that you promised to do

➤ Go back to page 75.

7.1 Adjectives to describe food

A Complete the sentences with the adjectives in the box.

delicious disgusting filling mild savoury sour

1 Our bakery sells a mix of sweet products, like cakes and fruit pies, and ____savoury____ products, like bread and meat pies.

2 Do you prefer strong flavours or ____mild____ flavours?

3 Mmm … I love this meal. It's absolutely ____delicious____!

4 I love ____sour____ food like lemons, grapefruit and pickled cabbage.

5 Ugh! How long has this milk been in the fridge? Two weeks? It tastes ____disgusting____!

6 This meal is lovely, but it's very ____filling____ – I feel completely full already.

B Label the pictures with the adjectives in the box.

bitter raw rich spicy

____bitter____   ____raw____

____spicy____   ____rich____

➤ Go back to page 76.

8.2 Positive adjectives

Choose the best adjectives to complete the sentences.

1 A: My dog pressed six buttons in the right order!
B: That's so unique / (impressive!)

2 I just want an umbrella that's incredible / (practical) – if it keeps me dry, I'm happy.

3 I read a (fascinating)/ gorgeous article about the dangers of technology.

4 The party was sensible / (unforgettable) – I'll remember it for the rest of my life.

5 It's unique / (incredible) that people waste so much money on stupid gadgets!

6 It looks like a normal umbrella, but it contains very (sophisticated) / gorgeous electronics.

7 The CleverPet is sophisticated / (suitable) for small pets, like cats and dogs, but not large animals, like horses.

8 A: I lost my Oombrella. I forgot to take my phone with me.
B: Well, that wasn't very (sensible) / unique, was it?

➤ Go back to page 90.

Vocabulary Hub

9.1 Verbal idioms

A Complete the sentences with the underlined verbal idioms in *The best (and the worst) of immersive theatre.*

① I can't really **tell** _____the_____ _____difference_____ _____between_____ immersive theatre and interactive theatre. Aren't they the same?

② I tried to tell a joke, but it **fell** _____flat_____. Nobody understood it.

③ If you agree to help people all the time, they might **take** _____advantage_____ _____of_____ your kindness. You need to say 'no' more often.

④ Do you still have your old guitar, or have you **got** _____rid_____ _____of_____ it?

⑤ Immersive plays often **take** _____place_____ in unusual locations.

⑥ They have a lovely big garden, but they don't really **make** _____use_____ _____of_____ it.

⑦ Six actors **took** _____part_____ _____in_____ the play: four adults and two children.

⑧ I always write down the money I spend to help me **keep** _____track_____ _____of_____ my finances.

⑨ Everything is **going** _____wrong_____ today! My computer's stopped working and my car's broken down!

⑩ If you don't **pay** _____attention_____ _____to_____ your teacher, you won't learn very much.

B Complete the verbal idioms with the words in the box.

attention   friends   fun   note   sure   true

1   I've always dreamed of being a chef, but I'm not sure my dream will ever **come** _____true_____.

2   You shouldn't **make** _____fun_____ **of** other people's mistakes. They aren't funny at all.

3   When someone gives you good advice, always **take** _____note_____ **of** what they say.

4   I **made** _____friends_____ **with** Alissa when we were at school, and we've liked each other ever since.

5   I didn't notice the sculpture in the corner. They should put it in the middle of the room to **draw** _____attention_____ **to** it!

6   I think I know the answer, but I need to check the internet to **make** _____sure_____ .

➤ Go back to page 101.

10.2 Reflexive verbs

Complete the sentences with the correct reflexive pronouns. What do you think the reflexive verbs mean?

1   Can you all please behave _____yourselves_____! You're making too much noise!

2   Daisy bought _____herself_____ a box of chocolates this morning and ate every single one!

3   Where do you see _____yourself_____ ten years from now, Hannah? Will you still be doing the same job?

4   Many people find it difficult to express _____themselves_____ when they're speaking a foreign language. They know what they want to say, but they can't say it.

5   Look at that dog! It's having a lovely time playing in the water! It's really enjoying _____itself_____!

6   I want to do some exercise every day, but I don't trust _____myself_____. I'll probably give up after a week!

7   I need to go out for half an hour. Can you all amuse _____yourselves_____ while I'm gone?

➤ Go back to page 115.

1   If you behave yourself, you're good and you follow the rules.

2   If you buy yourself something, it's a present for you and you don't share it with others.

3   If you see yourself somewhere / doing something, you believe that's where you'll be / what you'll be doing at a point in the future.

4   If you express yourself, you speak/write clearly, so that others understand exactly how you feel.

5   If you enjoy yourself, you have fun.

6   If you trust yourself, you know you won't be tempted to break your own rules.

7   If you amuse yourself, you choose something to do so you don't get bored.

Communication Hub

4.1 Students A and B

The top ten most common New Year's resolutions (in descending order):

1 change the food you eat
2 get organised
3 spend less, save more
4 enjoy life to the fullest

5 get fit and healthy
6 learn something exciting
7 quit unhealthy habits
8 help others achieve their dreams

9 fall in love
10 spend more time with family

➤ Go back to page 38.

5.1 Student B

A Do the quiz. Choose the answer that is most true for you.

1 **When you get a new piece of picture editing software or an app, do you**
   a just use the basic functions?
   b teach yourself how to use all of its functions?
   c ask a friend to show you how to use it?

2 **When your teacher suddenly tells you that you are going to do an important speaking test in the next lesson, do you**
   a get nervous and make extra mistakes?
   b enjoy the challenge and do your best?
   c say it is not fair and ask to do the test the next day?

3 **When you disagree with someone's suggestion, do you usually**
   a say nothing?
   b explain your opinion clearly, and listen carefully to their views?
   c tell them directly that it is a bad idea?

4 **If you are brainstorming ideas in a group, do you suggest**
   a similar ideas to other people?
   b many, and often different, ideas?
   c very little?

B Ask your partner the questions and make a note of his/her answers. Then answer his/her questions.

C Go to page 149 to find out your score and what it means!

➤ Go back to page 50.

9.2 Student A

➤ Go back to page 105.

Communication Hub

4.1 Student A

You can only see your side of the conversation. Read through your lines, and practise your intonation. Roleplay the conversation with your partner. You will start the conversation. Listen carefully in order to speak at the right time.

A: Hi, [name].

B: _____

A: Oh! Oops! I'll do it now. Hold on. There we go.

B: _____

A: And happy New Year to you!

B: _____

A: Great. We had a lovely time on New Year's Eve.

B: _____

A: That sounds amazing!

B: _____

A: Oh! I bet it was freezing, too. I'm glad I was at a party.

B: _____

A: Is that one of your New Year's resolutions?

B: _____

A: Haven't you? I've made quite a few.

B: _____

A: Well, I've decided to get fit this year, so I'm going to join a gym, and I'm going to study English more seriously.

B: _____

A: Well, not good enough. In fact, I'm meeting a new teacher on Thursday, for one-to-one lessons.

B: _____

A: Well, there's no point in putting things off. What about your chocolate habit?

B: _____

A: You eat some every day, don't you?

B: _____

➤ Go back to page 39.

2.1 Student A

Has your partner done these things? If he/she has, find out more details.

- go surfing
- climb a tree
- hold a snake
- relax in a natural hot spring
- have a cycling holiday
- bake some bread
- give blood
- see a lion in the wild
- stay in an ice hotel
- learn to fly a plane

➤ Go back to page 15.

2.2 Personality test scores

In general, the higher your score in this test, the better your attitude towards challenging situations and the better your problem-solving skills. The highest possible score is 30.

A low score for a question shows an area to consider improving in order to become a truly effective problem solver.

Questions ❶–❸ reveal your attitude towards problems.

Questions ❹–❻ reveal your problem-solving skills.

➤ Go back to page 21.

4.2 Students A and B

1 a I'll make a lot of money.
  b I make a lot of money.

2 a You have many friends at university.
  b You'll have many friends at university.

3 a She'll shut the window because she hates the cold.
  b She shut the window because she hates the cold.

4 a Everyone put solar panels on their roof.
  b Everyone'll put solar panels on their roof.

5 a They use mobile phones in school lessons.
  b They'll use mobile phones in school lessons.

➤ Go back to page 43.

3.1 Students A and B

SPEAK Work in pairs. Put the pictures in the correct order and use them to retell the two stories.

Junko's story

Alan's story

➤ Go back to page 27.

1.2 Student A

A SPEAK Work in pairs. Ask and answer questions to complete the information about the percentage of people with English as a first language in different countries around the world.

Percentage of people with English as a first language		
Ireland	93 per cent	
UK	92 per cent	
New Zealand	86	per cent
USA	79 per cent	
Canada	57 per cent	
Singapore	37 per cent	
Jamaica	17	per cent
South Africa	9.3 per cent	
Sierra Leone	8.5	per cent
Pakistan	8 per cent	

Where **do** 93 per cent of people **speak** English as a first language?

How many people in New Zealand **speak** English as a first language?

B SPEAK Work in pairs. Are you surprised by any of the information?

➤ Go back to page 7.

5.1 Student A and B

Score 2 points for every time you chose answer b. Score nothing for all other answers.

6–8: You have a very good set of general skills and qualities for employment. Reflect on which are stronger than others, and look for jobs that use your clear strengths. What other employability skills do you have? Can you improve them?

2–5: You have some key skills that are important to employers, but there is room for improvement. Identify those skills, and find out what employers are looking for in those areas. What improvements could you make?

0–1: Employers want people to use their skills in certain ways in the workplace. Learn more about employability skills, and find opportunities to practise, for example group projects or leadership roles. Which skills could you focus on first?

➤ Go back to page 50.

4.1 Student A

A Make a resolution for each of these topics:

- studying English
- food and diet
- money
- house and home

B Tell your partner about your resolutions and why you have made them.

C Ask your partner to make resolutions for these topics.

D Make resolutions for your partner's topics.

➤ Go back to page 39.

Communication Hub

1.2 Student B

A SPEAK Work in pairs. Ask and answer questions to complete the information about the percentage of people with English as a first language in different countries around the world.

Percentage of people with English as a first language	
Ireland	93 per cent
UK	_____92_____ per cent
New Zealand	86 per cent
_____USA_____	79 per cent
Canada	57 per cent
_____Singapore_____	37 per cent
Jamaica	17 per cent
South Africa	_____9.3_____ per cent
Sierra Leone	8.5 per cent
Pakistan	_____8_____ per cent

How many people in the UK **speak** *English as a first language?*
Where **do** *79 per cent of people* **speak** *English as a first language?*

B SPEAK Work in pairs. Are you surprised by any of the information?

➤ Go back to page 7.

4.1 Student B

A Make a resolution for each of these topics.

- work or study
- physical fitness
- family and friends
- the internet and digital media

B Tell your partner about your resolutions and why you have made them.

C Ask your partner to make resolutions for these topics.

D Make resolutions for your partner's topics.

➤ Go back to page 39.

6.2 Student A

Look at the table. Do you currently do these things? Complete the table so it is true for you. Then ask your partner questions and make a note of his/her answers.

	You		Your partner		
Activities	Yes/No?	How long?	Yes/No?	How long?	Other details
Use an app to study English					
Follow a celebrity on social media					
Regularly go to a favourite café					
Play a sport					
Collect something					
States					
Be a member of an online-only group					
Know someone from another country					
Have a desktop computer					
Have a car					

➤ Go back to page 67.

10.1 Students A and B

Do the quiz.

Psychology quiz

1 **a** Do we have more than 70 thoughts per day or fewer than 70?

b How many thoughts do we have each day?

2 You have paid for a weekend break in an expensive hotel. On the morning of your long journey, you feel ill and you just want to stay in bed. But it's too late to cancel your trip and get your money back. What do you do?

3 You're choosing a language school to help you pass an important exam. You know that 75 per cent of School A's students passed the exam last year. You also know that 20 per cent of School B's students failed the exam. Which school sounds better?

➤ Go back to page 110.

Possible answers:

1 a more; b Some experts suggest we have around 70,000 thoughts per day, but it's almost impossible to count accurately.

2 The best thing to do is to stay in bed, but most people would feel bad about wasting the money, and many would choose to go on the weekend break.

3 School B is better (because 80 per cent passed the exam), but School A probably sounds better (because of the words passed and failed).

8.3 Student B

Use the pictures and notes to write instructions for making a paper heart. Use sequencing phrases. Then read out your instructions so that Student A can make a paper heart.

How to make a heart

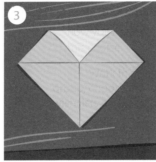
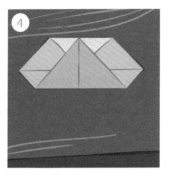

You will need a square piece of paper.

Fold the piece of paper in half both ways, and unfold it so that you see the fold marks.

Turn the piece of paper round so that the point is at the top, and fold the top corner down to the middle.

Fold the bottom corner to the top.

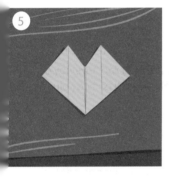
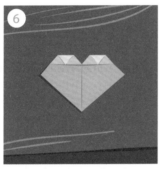
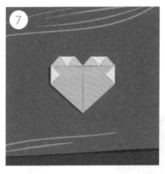
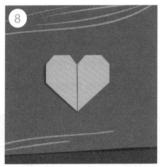

Fold the bottom edges to the middle.

Turn the paper over and fold the two top corners down.

Fold the corners down on both sides.

The heart is ready.

➤ Go back to page 95.

3.2 Students

The local mayor has decided to cancel the city's Car-Free Day. She wants a new project and campaign to reduce the traffic problems and pollution. Read the proposals.

TRANSPORT PROPOSALS

1 Reduce your car use!
Encourage people to leave their car at home. Run a media publicity campaign to promote:
- shopping locally, not using out-of-town supermarket.
- walking or cycling for short trips.
- working from home.
- setting up a city council app for car-sharing on common journeys.
- increasing city centre car parking fees.

2 Go electric!
Encourage the purchase and use of electric cars:
- Install car-charging points around the city.
- Provide cheap loans for the purchase of electric cars.
- Allow free parking for electric cars.

3 A wheely good future!
Encourage cycling:
- Run a media publicity campaign to promote riding your bike to work.
- Introduce a city bike hire scheme.
- Hold 'Cycle Fun Days' in local park.

➤ Go back to page 33.

Communication Hub

9.1 Student B

Proposal 2: Immersive theatre

Costs (= money going out)		Income (= money coming in)
Building work: £100,000	Marketing: £150,000/year	Ticket sales: £1,500,000/year
Equipment: £150,000	Other costs (e.g. electricity): £150,000/year	Sponsorship: £500,000/year
Staff: £500,000/year		

- Sponsorship: Companies pay for their names/logos to be in the theatre, on posters, etc.
- Ticket prices: £50–£100
- 80–100 tickets/performance; 400 performances/year (evenings and weekends only)
- No plans to help the community (e.g. free tickets for schools)

➤ Go back to page 99.

5.1 Student A

A Do the quiz. Choose the answer that is most true for you.

1 **When two friends are arguing about what to do at the weekend, do you**
   a ignore them until they finish?
   b calm them down and help them decide?
   c tell them to stop and make the decision for them?

2 **When you have many things to do next week, do you**
   a start doing them this week and see how many you can finish?
   b make a plan before starting?
   c do nothing at first and then rush to do them late next week?

3 **When you work on a group project, do you**
   a focus on your personal tasks?
   b do your tasks and support others with theirs?
   c do little, and let others do a lot?

4 **When you borrow a little money from someone and say you will return it the next day, do you**
   a pay it back a few days later?
   b pay it back the next day?
   c need reminding to pay it back.

B Ask your partner the questions and make a note of his/her answers. Then answer his/her questions.

C Go to page 149 to find out your score and what it means!

➤ Go back to page 50.

5.2 Students

Basic information

Country:	Finland
Business name:	Arctic Diamond
Slogan:	'Luxury chilling'
Founded by:	Mika Hakala
Products:	Ice cubes from the Arctic
Price:	€50 for 100 grams

Production process

collected by hand / packed in freezer boxes / delivered by air and courier

Sales

Online business: 15 orders in first two weeks / €20,000 in first year of business
Current customers: European restaurants and bars, hotels in Abu Dhabi and Dubai
Future markets: China, United States

Arctic Diamond

➤ Go back to page 55.

4.1 Student B

You can only see your side of the conversation. Read through your lines, and practise your intonation. Roleplay the conversation with your partner. Listen carefully in order to speak at the right time. Your partner will start the conversation.

A: _____

B: Hi, [name]. I can't see you – I don't think you've clicked the video button.

A: _____

B: That's better. Good to see you. Happy New Year!

A: _____

B: How's everything going in Spain?

A: _____

B: Well, lucky you! We went to see the fireworks.

A: _____

B: Yeah, it was fantastic! Mind you, it was a long wait. We got there at nine.

A: _____

B: Yeah! Lucky you. I didn't have a hat or anything. In fact, I'm going to look for one tomorrow.

A: _____

B: Actually, I've not made any resolutions yet.

A: _____

B: Really? What have you decided?

A: _____

B: That's a surprise! I always thought your English was really good.

A: _____

B: Really? That's quick!

A: _____

B: My chocolate habit? What do you mean?

A: _____

B: Well, just a little.

➤ Go back to page 39.

5.2 Student B

Company:	H&M stores, Sweden and worldwide
Retail sector:	Fashion clothing
Environmental idea:	Customers hand in their old clothes (even ones they didn't buy at H&M). The company either sells them as second-hand clothes, or turns them into other clothing items.
Reason:	To stop old clothes going to waste.
Result:	In a four-year period, the company received more than 40,000 tonnes of clothing items (enough material to make 150 million T-shirts).

➤ Go back to page 57.

2.1 Student B

Has your partner done these things? If he/she has, find out more details.

- go sailing
- climb a mountain
- hold a monkey
- relax on a beach all day
- have a camping holiday
- bake a cake
- give someone flowers
- see a tiger in the wild
- stay in an underwater hotel
- learn to drive

➤ Go back to page 15.

7.2 Students A and B

1 a about a week   e about 3 days
   b 8–10 months   f about 2 days
   c 4–5 days
   d 18–24 months

2 a False. You should only reheat food once.
   b True. After the best-before date, the food may lose some taste or colour, but it's probably still safe to eat for a little longer.
   c True. Rice sometimes contains very strong bacteria which aren't killed by cooking. So after cooking, put any leftover rice in the fridge and eat within 24 hours.

➤ Go back to page 80.

Communication Hub

9.1 Student C

Proposal 3: Modern art gallery

Costs (= money going out)	Income (= money coming in)
Building work and equipment: £150,000	Gift shop and snack bar: £150,000/year
Staff: £150,000/year	Sales of paintings, etc: £200,000–£500,000/year
Marketing: £50,000/year	
Other costs (e.g. electricity): £100,000/year	

- Two major exhibitions each year (international artists, etc)
- Smaller exhibitions each month (local artists, etc)
- Free entry for all people to all exhibitions
- The gallery will take 40 per cent of the sale price of any paintings (e.g. by local artists) that it sells.

➤ Go back to page 99.

3.1 Students

A Look at the list of annoying behaviour on public transport. Number them in order of how annoying they are (1 = most annoying, 10 = least annoying). Think about the reasons for your choices.

___ people talking loudly on the phone

___ people playing loud music and not using headphones

___ people walking too slowly

___ people eating takeaway food

___ people not queuing or not waiting their turn to board

___ people leaving litter behind

___ people not giving up their seats to people who need them

___ people coughing and sneezing because of a cold

___ people trying to talk to me

➤ Go back to page 29.

9.2 Student B

➤ Go back to page 105.

6.2 Student B

Look at the table. Do you currently do these things? Complete the table so it is true for you. Then ask your partner questions and make a note of his/her answers.

	You		Your partner		
Activities	Yes/No?	How long?	Yes/No?	How long?	Other details
Use an app to order food					
Write a blog					
Regularly go to a favourite cinema					
Play a musical instrument					
Work for a company					
States					
Be a member of a club or society					
Know someone famous					
Have a laptop computer					
Have a pet					

➤ Go back to page 67.

8.3 Student A

Use the pictures and notes to write instructions for making a paper airplane. Use sequencing phrases. Then read out your instructions so that Student B can make a paper airplane.

How to make a paper airplane

Put a piece of paper on the table.

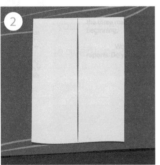

Fold the piece of paper in half lengthways, then unfold it.

Smooth it down.

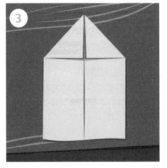

Form a point at the top of the paper.

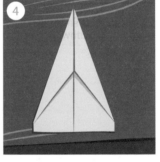

Fold the edges again.

Smooth down the edges with a ruler.

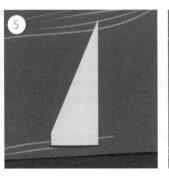

Fold the right side of the paper over the left side.

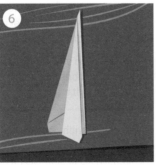

Create the wings.

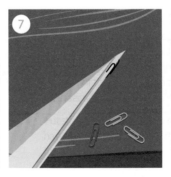

Attach a paperclip to the nose of the airplane – it will make it fly better.

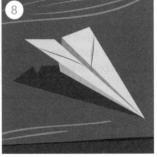

Unfold the wings and you're ready for takeoff.

➤ Go back to page 95.

Present simple and present continuous

A Read the blog post about Simon and complete the sentences with the present simple or the present continuous verb forms.

On Saturdays, I _____ (*play*) football with my brother in the park. I also try to do some exercise in the week because I'm _____ (*try*) to get fit. At the moment, I am _____ (*learn*) Italian because I'm _____ (*go*) on holiday to Rome in two weeks – I can't wait! Probably, I'm most excited about _____ (*eat*) the food there – pasta, pizza … I really _____ (*like*) Italian food because it's delicious!

B Which questions would you need to ask to get the information in Exercise A?

1 What _____ on Saturdays?

2 When _____ exercise?

3 What _____ today?

4 Where _____ on holiday?

5 What _____ excited about?

6 What _____ Italian food?

C Work in pairs. Ask and answer the questions (1–6) in Exercise B.

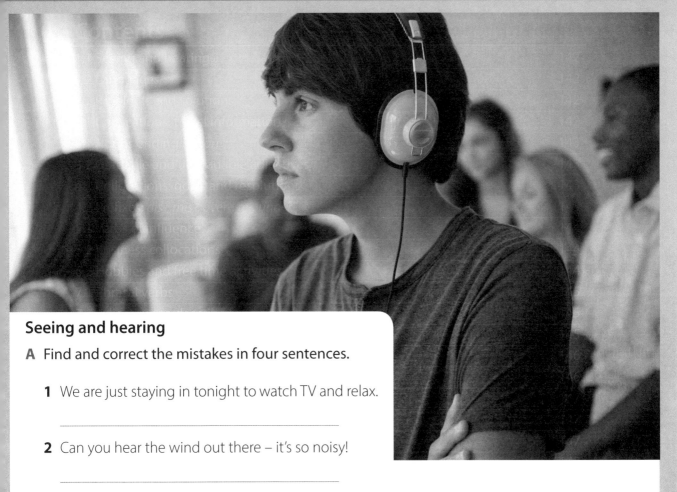

Seeing and hearing

A Find and correct the mistakes in four sentences.

1 We are just staying in tonight to watch TV and relax.

_____

2 Can you hear the wind out there – it's so noisy!

_____

3 Thanks for inviting me. That hears great.

_____

4 I'm going to watch the paintings at the exhibition on Tuesday.

_____

5 It looks like it will rain.

_____

6 His music listens fantastic!

_____

7 I don't think the food in that restaurant looks very good.

_____

8 Where is my watch? I can't look at it anywhere!

_____

B What would you expect to see, watch, listen to or hear:

- on a busy street
- on a plane
- at a party
- on the beach

Subject and object questions

Student A

A Complete the questions with the verb in brackets.

1 What _____ you happy? (*make*)

2 Where _____ your best friend? (*meet*)

3 Who _____ most time with? (*spend*)

4 Who _____ your name? (*choose*)

5 What _____ for your last birthday? (*get*)

6 What _____ you cry? (*make*)

7 Where _____ your shoes? (*get*)

8 Who _____ you to cook? (*teach*)

B What do you think your partner's answer for each question would be? Write it after the question, but don't ask your partner yet.

C Ask your questions to your partner. How many did you guess correctly?

Student B

A Complete the questions with the verb in brackets.

1 What _____ you angry? (*make*)

2 When _____ your best friend? (*meet*)

3 Who _____ most on the phone? (*speak to*)

4 Who _____ you the last present you received? (*give*)

5 Where _____ on your last holiday? (*go*)

6 What _____ you laugh? (*make*)

7 Why _____ those shoes? (*choose*)

8 Who _____ you to swim? (*teach*)

B What do you think your partner's answer for each question would be? Write it after the question, but don't ask your partner yet.

C Ask your questions to your partner. How many did you guess correctly?

Languages

A Read the information about the three different teachers and choose the correct words in bold.

Ana is from your country, but her parents are English so she's completely *bilingual / monolingual*. She understands the problems you have with English, and sometimes she translates things to help you understand. When she *speaks / talks* English, she has a very strong *idiom / accent,* which you find difficult to understand.

Chris is a native speaker. He loves teaching *idioms / bilingual* and modern, *phrases / informal* language, but he never gives you a very clear answer when you ask him questions about grammar. He doesn't speak your language and he doesn't like it when you try to *accent / translate* anything.

Diana has lived in lots of different countries and speaks lots of languages. She won't tell you exactly where she's from, but she speaks English very fluently with an American accent. She only lets you use a *phrases / monolingual* dictionary to look up words. Even though she says she *talks / speaks* your language, you've never heard her use it.

B Who would you prefer to be taught by? Why?

C Which of the following qualities of an English teacher are most important:

- being bilingual in your language
- having a native accent
- teaching informal language and idioms
- speaking many languages fluently

D What are the five most important qualities for you in a good teacher?

Present perfect simple and past simple

A Make questions from the prompts below, using the present perfect simple or past simple.

1 plant a tree? _Have you ever planted a tree?_

2 get into trouble when you were at school? _____

3 ride a horse? _____

4 watch (a famous sporting event)? _____

5 meet (name of a famous person who is not alive)? _____

6 do a parachute jump? _____

7 have a big party on your 18th birthday? _____

8 swim with dolphins? _____

9 celebrate (an important event or national holiday)? _____

10 meet (a famous person who is still alive)? _____

11 go out last night? _____

12 write a poem? _____

B Work in pairs. Ask and answer six of the questions. For every question, you must answer 'Yes'. Ask your partner further questions to decide if they are telling the truth.

2.1 Vocabulary

Collocations: making big decisions

A Read about an important career choice and complete the questions (1–6) with the correct form of the verb in brackets.

I work as a chef in a restaurant. The hours are long and the work is often quite tiring but being able to create my own recipes and to make food that I love helps me to stay motivated. One day, I dream of opening my own restaurant – I'd love to be able to turn that dream into reality. For now, my short-term goal is to finish my training and improve my skills as a chef, but in the future, I'd love to move to America. Leaving my old job to start a new career was the biggest decision I've made, but I think it's really important to try new things.

1 What _____ (*help*) you stay motivated when you're working?

2 What's one dream you'd love to _____ (*turn*) into reality?

3 What's one goal you're currently _____ (*work*) towards?

4 What's one long-term goal you've _____ (*set*) yourself?

5 What's the last important decision you _____ (*make*)?

6 What would make you lose heart if you were _____ (*try*) to do something difficult?

B Work in pairs. Ask each other the questions (1–6). Then ask other questions to find out more information.

> For example:
>
> *What else helps you stay motivated?*
>
> *I like that I'm creative when I'm meeting goals.*
>
> *Is that important for you?*
>
> *Yes, but work hours are more important. I lose heart if I need to work long hours.*

last year

today

Present and past ability

A Look at the pictures above. What couldn't the woman do last year that she can do today?

B Make sentences using phrases from the table and your own ideas.

Last year	I	could …
When I was ten	my parents	couldn't …
In the last century	my best friend	was / were able to …
Yesterday	my boss	wasn't / weren't able to …
Years ago	people	managed to …
Today	children	didn't manage to …
In my country	scientists	can …
	doctors	can't …
		am / are able to …

_____
_____
_____
_____
_____
_____
_____
_____
_____
_____
_____
_____

C Compare your sentences with a partner. Describe four things which you couldn't do in the past but you can do now.

Dependent prepositions (verb/adjective + *for/of*)

A Match the sentence halves, and add *for* or *of* between them to complete the sentences.

1	I'm looking	**a**	long hours?
2	I don't want to work	**b**	my qualifications.
3	Are you aware	**c**	a big company.
4	I'm quite proud	**d**	the kind of thing I normally do.
5	I don't think that would be suitable	**e**	a new job.
6	Have you asked her	**f**	how important contacts are?
7	Are you prepared	**g**	me at all.
8	My last job wasn't typical	**h**	a reference?

B The sentences are from a conversation between a careers adviser and someone looking for work. Work with a partner and write the conversation, including the sentences above in the correct order.

_____

_____

_____

_____

_____

_____

_____

_____

_____

_____

C Join with another pair and perform your conversations to each other. How similar are they?

Narrative tenses

Work in groups. One person tosses a coin and moves one place for heads or two places for tails. They talk for one minute about the topic they land on. The other players ask further questions. Then the next person tosses the coin and moves from the previous player's position.

Tell your group about …

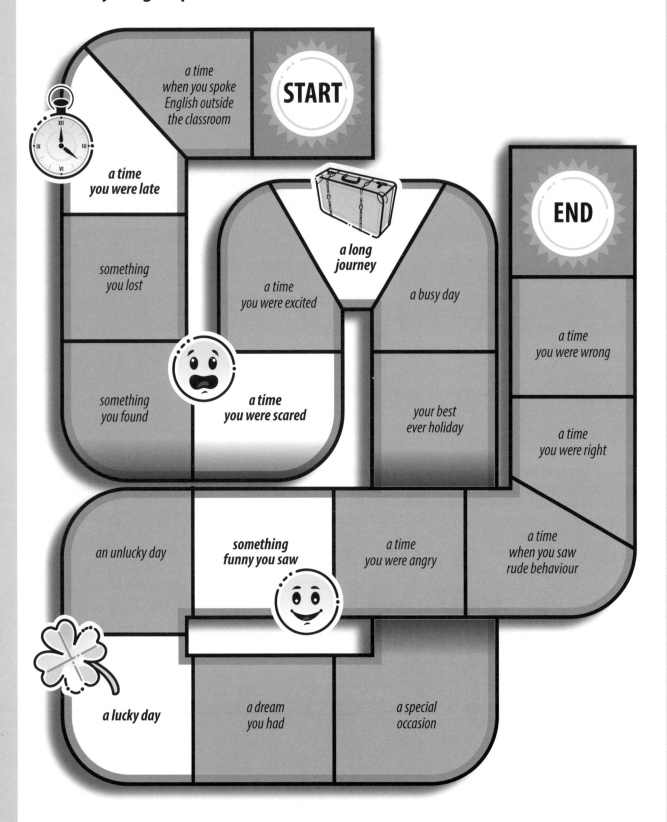

Collocations: travel information

A Correct any mistakes in the sentences.

1 There are often severe delays on the trains.

2 I never travel in the busy hour.

3 There's always heavy traffic in the city centre.

4 I spend a lot of time stuck in traffic lines.

5 I hate waiting at the road lights when they're red.

6 There's usually a good operation on the underground.

7 There are a lot of road works at the moment.

8 I don't like driving in heavy rain.

9 The buses are often overbusy.

B Work in pairs and discuss which sentences are true for you, or true about where you live.

Articles and quantifiers

A Read the article about Rio de Janeiro. Complete the gaps (1–10) with *a, an, the* or – (no article) and choose the correct quantifier for each sentence.

1 *A lot of / few* people visit Rio de Janeiro in _____ February and March to celebrate Carnival.

2 _____ costumes people wear are really fantastic and colourful.

3 I felt that I should have brought *more / less* clothes with me on holiday so that I could have dressed up a bit more.

4 *Some / few* people dance in _____ street parade as musicians play samba.

5 _____ atmosphere is amazing!

6 It's _____ incredible experience to be able to celebrate with so *many / a lot of* people.

7 Another fantastic thing about Rio is _____ food!

8 My favourite dish is *feijoada*, which is _____ stew made from _____ black beans and _____ beef or _____ pork.

9 *A lot of / few* Brazilian people love this. In fact it is so popular that it is often considered _____ national dish.

10 I wish I could stay in Brazil for longer – Rio is such _____ wonderful city!

B Work in pairs. Discuss a city you have visited that you thought was an amazing place. What did you like about it?

Gradable and ungradable adjectives

A Read the reviews and change the gradable adjectives in bold to make the meanings stronger.

1 Although people had said the film wasn't great, I didn't expect it to be so **bad**! The person behind me kept on kicking my seat and made me feel **angry**!

2 The new Japanese restaurant on Newport Street is **great**. I ordered sushi and it came with a lot of **good** side dishes. That was a **nice** surprise!

3 I'm not at all sure about her new album. I was a **big** fan of her earlier music, but then she got popular and her style changed. The new songs are just not the same. In fact, I'd say her new stuff is **bad**.

4 I didn't think I'd ever eat snails, but when I tried them I thought they were **good**.

5 I wasn't disappointed with this horror film. It was frightening! The twist in the end of the story was unexpected and I was **scared**.

6 The first time I watched the programme I thought it was boring. But after the third episode I was hooked. The main actor is **funny**.

B Work in pairs and talk about the following:

- a film you've seen recently
- a meal you had in a restaurant
- a book which you read but didn't like
- your favourite singer or band

Future forms

A Read the conversation between two people who are going to a pop concert. Use *will, going to* or the present perfect continuous to complete the sentences.

Sandra: Have you heard the new Tamara Lopez album? It's brilliant! I'm ¹_____ buy it today.

Henry: I know! Did you know she's ²_____ a concert at the Royal Albert Hall in July?

Sandra: No? Are you ³_____ go?

Henry: Yes, ⁴_____ get you a ticket, if you like?

Sandra: Great! Thanks … oh, wait … did you say she's ⁵_____ in July?

Henry: Yes.

Sandra: Oh. I actually don't think I'm ⁶_____ be able to go. I'll be ⁷_____ America in July.

Henry: Lucky you! That ⁸_____ be fantastic! You ⁹_____ have a great time!

B Choose one thing you want to achieve:

- learn a musical instrument
- learn a new language
- save money
- eat more healthily
- make more friends

C Now make a list of things you're going to do to achieve it.

Learn a musical instrument
- start lessons next week

Work in pairs. Tell a partner what you're going to do. Listen to their advice.

Collocations: goals and resolutions

A Complete the phrases in the table with the correct collocations below.

> quit   stick   keeps   reached   cut down   set   breaks

Find someone who:	Extra information:
1 has _____ a bad habit Name:	
2 has _____ on something unhealthy Name:	
3 always _____ resolutions Name:	
4 finds it difficult to _____ resolutions Name:	
5 has _____ himself/herself an unrealistic goal Name:	
6 has almost _____ a target Name:	
7 always _____ to a plan Name:	

B Interview your classmates and find one person that each of 1–7 is true for.

C Tell the class about someone you spoke to. Include any extra information they gave on their goals and resolutions.

Ask them extra questions to get more information.

Making predictions

A Complete the sentences using the super-forecaster's phrases.

Over the next ten years:

My country's economy _____ improve.

Unemployment in my country _____ fall.

The world's population _____ increase dramatically.

The world _____ be more peaceful.

Technology _____ make our lives better.

I _____ make a lot of progress in my career.

My national football team _____ win the World Cup.

People _____ do more to protect the environment.

People _____ eat more healthily.

The world _____ end.

B Compare your predictions with a partner. Who is more optimistic about the future?

Prefixes: *dis-, mis-, over-, re-, under-*

A Add the correct prefix *dis-, mis-, over-, re- or under-* to the words in bold. Then complete the sentences with the correct form of the new words.

1	I can't believe I _____ and missed my meeting.	**sleep**
2	There's no way that coffee cost £9! I must have been _____.	**charge**
3	The man at the train station was really _____! He was so rude.	**respect**
4	My keys can't have just _____. They must be somewhere.	**appear**
5	I thought that was what she was saying, but I may have _____.	**understand**
6	I just can't understand a word he says – he _____ everything!	**pronounce**
7	This chicken is still pink. I definitely _____ it.	**cook**
8	Are they planning _____ the old school?	**build**
9	Ever since he _____ his watch, he's late for everything!	**place**
10	There's always so much to do. We've been feeling a bit _____.	**work**

B Write five sentences about yourself using the words from Exercise A. Work in pairs. Tell each other your sentences. Ask questions to find out more information.

Past habits and states

A Read the article about the people below and complete the gaps in the sentences with *used to, would* or *didn't use to*.

We both studied Medicine at university and I remember how we _____ work in the library together to study for exams. We _____ sit there for hours and hours, reading over our notes. We _____ often go out with our friends after lectures to discuss what we had learned. Because we were students, we _____ have much money, so we cooked at home or went to our friends' houses. We _____ make pizzas for everyone and we _____ stay up quite late, chatting and socialising. When I wasn't working, I _____ get up very early. I always _____ dream of becoming a doctor, but I didn't think about how much hard work it is! It's definitely worth it though. I love helping people.

B Make sentences about your own past. Write two true sentences and one false sentence.

C Work in pairs. Tell each other your sentences and ask questions to guess the false sentence.

5.1 Vocabulary

Employment skills and qualities

A Match the sentence beginnings (1–7) and endings (a–g).

1 Is it more important for a boss to be ___

2 Do you work better or worse when you're under ___

3 Do all young people nowadays have good digital ___

4 In what jobs is it especially important to be good at team ___

5 In what jobs is it not important to be good at time ___

6 Did you learn creative ___

7 Is having good communication ___

a work?

b pressure?

c management?

d thinking skills at school?

e creative or reliable?

f technology skills?

g skills the most important quality nowadays?

B Discuss the questions with a partner.

The passive

A Choose the best option to complete the sentences. Then work with a partner to guess what the product is.

This product is usually *used in* / *made of* various materials like plastic, glass and metal. It is currently *bought by* / *sold in* people across the world. It is *made by* / *made of* the biggest technology companies in the world. It is *used for* / *known as* staying in contact, taking photographs and searching online. It is *found in* / *known as* technology shops and phone shops.

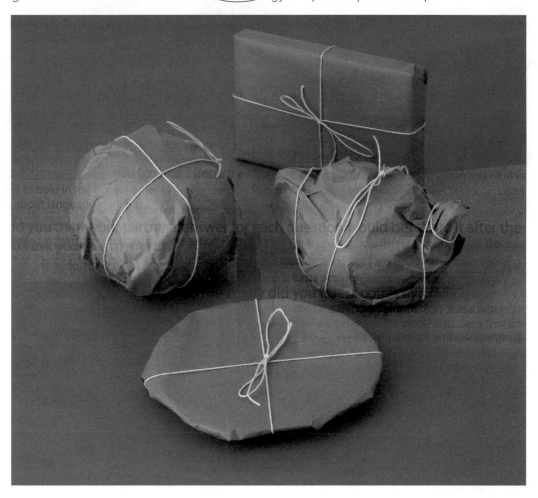

B Work in pairs. Choose a product and write five sentences to describe it. Use the phrases above and your own ideas. Write the first sentence so it is difficult to guess what the product is and make it easier with each sentence.

> made of   made in   made by   used in   used by   used for   found in
> known as   sold in   bought by   marketed as   loved by   watched by
> eaten by   eaten with   served with   considered to be

C Work in pairs. Read your sentences to each other. Try to guess what your partner's product is before they read their last sentence.

Business collocations

A Put the nouns into the correct column to complete the table.

campaign   investors   deals   money   reputation

launch	run	build	make	attract
a product	a company a business	a brand	a profit	customers

B Cover the table. Complete the sentences with the correct form of one of the verbs.

Think of:

1 a company that _____ a good reputation.

2 a business you'd like _____.

3 an easy way _____ money.

4 a product that _____ recently.

5 something your school could do _____ more students.

C Work in pairs. Discuss the sentences (1–5).

Modals of obligation

A Read the rules about playing basketball. Choose the best option to complete the sentences.

The rules of basketball

1 Players *mustn't / needn't* walk or run with the ball for more than one and a half steps.

2 The referee *has to / should* disqualify a player who fouls five times.

3 Players *should / needn't* wear appropriate footwear.

4 A player *must / shouldn't* pass the ball to another player within five seconds.

5 Players *mustn't / don't have to* kick the ball to pass.

6 New players *should / have to* set themselves goals to work towards so they can improve their skills.

7 Players *need to / needn't* think about controlling their feet as well as their hands to play well.

8 You *shouldn't / have to* practise regularly if you want to improve your skills.

B Work in small groups. Design a new sport. Make notes in the box below to help you with your ideas. Write ten rules for how to play your sport.

> NOTES:
> equipment:
> location:
> players:
> rules:
> how to win:

C Explain your sport to the other groups. Which sport do you like the most? Why?

Adjectives ending in -ive

A Complete the questions with the adjectives in the box.

> massive attractive decisive active competitive
> effective impressive creative inexpensive aggressive

1 When you are trying to choose what to have in a restaurant, are you _____?

2 Are you more _____ at work or when you're playing a sport or a game?

3 What's a quality you find _____ in a person?

4 What sports/song/band/film is _____ in your country at the moment?

5 Do you prefer to relax on holidays or stay busy and _____?

6 How do you have an _____ night out when you are saving?

7 What's your most _____ achievement?

8 What's the most _____ way to stop hiccupping?

9 Are you an _____ driver?

10 Are you a _____ person that likes writing, painting or playing music?

B Work in pairs. Ask and answer the questions. How similar are you?

C Write five new questions using the adjectives above. Ask your partner.

had to / needed to

A Complete the sentences in the paragraphs below with the correct form of *had to* or *needed to*.

1 After I decided to take up running, I knew that I _____ get fit. I was out of breath after just ten minutes – it was so embarrassing! I _____ buy new running shoes because my brother had bought me some for my birthday, but I decided that I _____ get a fitbit, to see how much my fitness improve.

2 I've always loved cycling, so when I saw my friend's new road bike, I knew I _____ get the same one. It was quite expensive, so for a couple of months, I _____ save money. I'm so glad that I did! It's the best thing that I've ever bought.

B Work in pairs. Student A, complete the sentences below about a sport you played. Student B, complete the sentences below about an event you went to. Don't say what the sport or event is.

Student A: a sport you played

I had to _____ and I needed to _____, but I didn't have to _____ and I didn't need to _____.

Student B: an event you went to

I had to _____ and I needed to _____, but I didn't have to _____ and I didn't need to _____.

C Read your sentences. Can you guess what sport or event your partner is describing?

Hobbies and free-time activities

A Read the two texts.
Complete each sentence with the
correct form of one of the verbs in the box.

> join   be   take   keep   escape   lose   get

1 Taking up cycling

OK, so I've never _____ a member of a sports club before and team sports really
_____ my thing. But last week, I _____ my university cycling society.
Best thing ever! It _____ you out of the house and _____ you fit. It
also helps you _____ weight. Win-win!

2 Taking up the guitar

I've always _____ a music fan. I think it helps you _____ reality
and your daily stress for a bit. That's why I wanted to _____ up guitar. I've never
_____ into piano and _____ interest with other instruments I tried to
learn. But playing guitar _____ so relaxing. I don't think I'll ever get bored.

B Work with a partner. Make questions using the collocations from Exercise A. Discuss the
questions with your partner.

1 Which club _____?

2 What hobbies _____?

3 Which instruments _____?

4 What do you do to _____?

C Work in groups of three. Each person chooses two hobbies from the list below. Tell your group
about your choices. Then as a group, choose the best hobby to do together.

- flower arranging
- judo
- history of art
- salsa dancing
- sewing
- rock climbing
- foreign language conversation

Modals of speculation and deduction

A Write a story. Write one sentence for each picture using the words below and describe what you think is happening.

> may   could   might   must   can   might not   mustn't

Example: *I think he might be waiting for someone.*

B Work in pairs. Compare stories. How are they similar? How are they different?

C Work in groups. Choose the best version of the story to present to the class.

Phrasal verbs

A Read the blog about a night market and replace each word in bold with a phrasal verb from the box.

turn up   work out   put off   keep up   stay up   stay in
start off   dish up   carry on   try out

Although I was tired from the long flight, I didn't want to **remain indoors**. I tried a tour of the night market in Chiang Mai. After we **found** the best route, we went straight there from our hostel. The great thing about the tour is you don't need to book, you can just **arrive without appointment**. A variety of hot food is **put on plates** so you can **experiment** with the local specialities.

B Work in pairs. Choose four phrasal verbs and discuss your own experience of visiting a new place.

C Discuss the questions with a partner.

1 Do you usually go out or stay in on Saturday night?

2 What new experiences would you like to try out?

3 Have you given anything up for your work or studies?

4 How do you feel if someone turns up late for an appointment?

5 What's something you often put off?

6 Can you think of anything that has really taken off recently?

7 Would you like to set up a business? If so, what kind?

8 Do you prefer cooking or clearing up?

Comparatives and superlatives; *the …, the …*

A Work in groups and find out who:

- has the biggest family.
- has the most pets.
- has the best phone.
- works the hardest.
- travels the furthest to get to work/school.
- has been to most countries.
- has known their best friend the longest.
- has the most pairs of shoes.
- is the best cook.
- can say the alphabet in English the fastest.

B Change groups. Tell your new group about your old group.

C Work in pairs. Find and correct the mistakes in five sentences.

1 The more friends you have, the happier you are.
2 The more expensive a restaurant, the more good it is.
3 The sooner you pay a bill, the better.
4 The slowlier you drive, the safer you are.
5 The more books you've read, the more interesting you are.
6 The more you sleep, the more tired you feel.
7 The more organised are you, the less time you waste.
8 The beautifuler someone is, the less interesting they are.
9 The unhealthier something is, the nicer it tastes.
10 The more early you get up, the more you achieve.

D Do you agree with the sentences? Why/Why not?

7.2 Vocabulary

Waste

A Read the article and form collocations about waste from the words in bold.

< >   ✕

Waste

Reduce

One way to **wnd ocut** on waste is to **deurce** amount of products you use. For example, you could use both sides of a piece of paper after you print something.

Reuse

Instead of **wringtho yawa** plastic shopping bags, why not **sreue** them? Then you don't have to buy another plastic bag when you go shopping. Cut down on the amount of packaging you **ret gio df** by reusing old jars and pots as storage containers.

Recycle

Rather than **gtering tid fo** all your rubbish in one **ibn**, make sure that you separate glass, plastics and paper ready for **rgcecyinl**. Try to think of new ways to recycle old items – this will also save you money.

B Work in pairs and discuss:

- something you need to cut down on
- something you threw away recently
- something that can't be recycled
- something you often reuse
- something that is often wasted
- something you often use up
- something you'd like to get rid of

Relative clauses

A Read the article. Choose the correct answers for the words in bold.

Leonardo da Vinci

 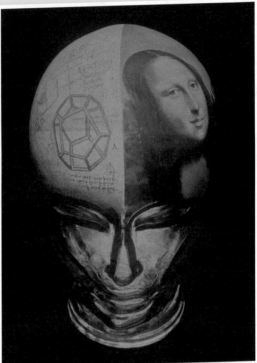

Leonardo da Vinci is probably most famous for his painting of the *Mona Lisa* **which/who** is a unique work of art. But he was also a man **who/which** had a variety of other interests. Da Vinci had many ideas for inventions **who/which** became a reality in the future. His drawings of flying machines **who/that** looked like a mixture of a bicycle and a helicopter are just one example. These machines, **where/which** were designed to flap with wings like those of a bat, were not flown in his lifetime. However, he did design a hang glider **who/that** could have worked. Da Vinci, **who/that** was born to a poor family, had never received an education. His achievements were truly amazing.

B Work in pairs. Make sentences to describe an important inventor or invention. Use the phrases below to help you.

a person who …

an invention which …

a place where …

an object that …

8.1 Vocabulary

Word families; Creative thinking

A Complete the questions (1–8) with phrases from the box. Use the correct verb form for each sentence.

> come up with ideas   use your imagination   boost your creativity   switch off completely
> let your mind wander freely   generate new ideas   think outside the box
> block your creativity   your mind goes blank   look at a problem from the outside

1 Where's the best place to _____?

2 What's the best way to _____?

3 What's something that _____?

4 Who's someone who _____?

5 Who's someone who helps you _____?

6 Think of a time when _____?

7 Do you find it easy to _____?

8 How often does _____?

B Work in pairs. Ask and answer your questions.

C Work in groups. Choose one of the problems below or use your own ideas. Tell the group your problem and give each other advice to solve them. Then decide which is the best solution to each problem.

- you are stressed about a presentation
- you can't finish an essay
- you are too busy at work
- you are stuck with some creative writing
- your mind goes blank in interviews
- your mind wanders in lectures

8.2 Grammar

Zero and first conditionals

A Match the sentences (1–8) with (a–h).

1 If I win some money,		**a**	I'll pass the exam.
2 If he has time,		**b**	it boils.
3 If they buy a puppy,		**c**	drink it!
4 If my boss asks me,		**d**	I'll work overtime.
5 If she doesn't bring an umbrella,		**e**	she will get wet.
6 If you heat water,		**f**	he will finish the project.
7 If she buys you a coffee,		**g**	they will walk it.
8 If I study,		**h**	I will give it to charity.

B Work in pairs. You are organising an event for work. Read the tasks below. Decide which four tasks you most want to do:

- give a speech
- find speakers
- write a web page for the event
- create a poster
- find a venue
- work out costs
- make a video for the event
- promote the event on social media

C Agree which four tasks you will do. Use the sentence below when agreeing tasks.

I'll … if you … .

8.2 Vocabulary

Positive adjectives

A Complete the reviews with the words from the box. More than one answer may be possible but use each word only once.

Fitness tracker

This _____ device has an _____ range of product features. It is _____ amongst trackers because as well as checking weight, heart rate and steps, you can actually pay in shops with it. It looks good too with a _____ design available in a wide range of colours. It is light but resistant so it is very _____ to use while doing exercise.

Wireless headphones

With so many features in one device, this product has a complex, _____ design. But it is very easy to use, making it _____ for anyone. It is not the most stylish option on the market, but its price and features make it a _____ choice. The sound quality is excellent so it provides an _____ listening experience.

> gorgeous   sensible   practical   unforgettable   impressive
> unique   sophisticated   incredible   suitable

B Work in pairs. Choose positive adjectives from the box and describe:

- a person
- a place
- a building
- an event
- an experience
- a holiday
- a gadget
- a meal
- a piece of art
- a story in the news

Second conditional

A Complete the sentences and use the correct form of the verb in brackets.

1 If I _____ (win) a new car …

2 If I _____ (see) my favourite actress in a café …

3 If I _____ (buy) someone a present they didn't like …

4 If I _____ (ask) for money by someone on the street …

5 If I _____ (be) late for work …

6 If I _____ (play) the guitar …

7 If I _____ (be) you …

8 If I _____ (speak) …

B Ask your classmates: *What would you do if …?* and write down their answers in the column next to each question. Write their name next to their responses.

What would you do if …?	Answer	Name
1		
2		
3		
4		
5		
6		
7		
8		

C Discuss as a class. Whose answer did you like the most? Why?

The arts; Verbal idioms

A Find words in the word search to complete the sentences.

N	C	O	N	C	E	R	T	I	B
O	D	I	R	G	N	T	A	X	E
I	X	Y	R	E	L	L	A	G	P
T	O	C	N	A	E	H	U	D	B
I	Y	A	L	P	S	I	D	O	R
B	E	I	O	U	A	V	I	G	X
I	N	S	T	R	U	M	E	N	T
H	Z	T	R	X	W	T	N	A	M
X	H	U	I	A	E	X	C	C	Z
E	F	D	B	O	E	R	E	H	W
B	L	I	V	E	A	H	C	O	R
C	G	O	N	D	I	C	E	I	S
G	N	I	D	R	O	C	E	R	T

1 I'd love to be able to play an _____ really well.

2 My dream would be to have a session in a _____.

3 There's an _____ on at the moment that I'd really like to see.

4 I only ever go to a _____ if it's free.

5 I prefer being at a _____ to listening to music at home.

6 I used to sing in a _____ when I was younger, but I haven't got time nowadays.

7 It's really exciting to be part of the _____ at the theatre.

8 I saw an amazing fireworks _____ once.

B Tell your partner if the sentences are true or false for you, and why.

Reported speech

Without looking, each student in the class should choose one of the cards.

What's the first film you ever saw at the cinema?	What's the last film you saw at the cinema?	What's the longest book you've ever read?
What's the oldest book you've ever read?	What's your favourite scene from a film?	Who's your favourite singer?
Who's your favourite actor?	Who's your favourite writer?	How much time do you spend watching TV?
Do you prefer watching a film at home or in the cinema?	How often do you go to the cinema?	Have you ever written a poem?

A Ask your question to every student in the class. Make a note of their answers.

B Work in pairs. Can you remember the questions that your classmates asked you?

C Tell your partner the answers your classmates gave to the question you asked. Which answers were the most interesting?

Reporting verbs

A Choose the correct answers for the sentences (1–10).

1 Julie *said / promised / argued* Ben that she had switched off the oven.

2 Ben *insisted / persuaded / wondered* that they should go home and check.

3 Ben *worried / argued / persuaded* that the front door was unlocked.

4 Julie *admitted / promised / insisted* that they would miss their flight if they went home to check.

5 Julie *refused / explained / persuaded* to go all the way back home.

6 Ben *explained / replied / agreed* that there could be a fire in the house.

7 When they went home, Julie *predicted / admitted / mentioned* that she had forgotten to lock the front door.

8 After that, Ben *warned / argued / mentioned* that he had forgotten to turn off the kitchen tap.

9 At the airport, they *argued / shouted / reminded* with their security officials.

10 Unfortunately, they *whispered / insisted / mentioned* that it was too late for Ben and Julie to get on their plane.

B Work in pairs and discuss:

- the last argument you had
- a time when you persuaded someone to do something
- the last prediction you made which came true
- a time when you warned someone about something

Third conditional; *should have* + past participle

A Work in pairs. Discuss two or three answers to the following questions.

What would have happened if ...

- you'd been born in a different country?

- you'd been born in a different era?

- you'd chosen a different English school?

- you'd decided to study something different?

- you hadn't started learning English?

- you'd got up earlier today?

- you'd worn a different pair of shoes today?

- you'd had a bigger breakfast?

- the internet had never been invented?

- your parents had never met?

B Compare your answers in a group. For each question, whose answer is the most realistic / the funniest / the most imaginative?

10.1 Vocabulary

Expressions with *mind*

Student A

A Read these situations to your partner. Your partner will answer from one of the phrases on their paper.

> **What do you say if:**
>
> **1** you're in a restaurant and you can't decide between the chicken or the fish?
>
> **2** someone is upset because they've missed the bus?
>
> **3** you've finally decided what to wear to a party?
>
> **4** you want to open the window on a train?

B Listen to your partner and choose which of the phrases below you would say in each situation.

> I can if I put my mind to it   I've changed my mind
> Bear in mind that you should …   It's all in the mind

C Act out each situation with a short conversation.

Student B

A Listen to your partner and choose which of the phrases below you would say in each situation.

> I've made up my mind   I'm in two minds   Would you mind if I …?   Never mind

B Read these situations to your partner. Your partner will answer from one of the phrases on their paper.

> **What do you say if:**
>
> **1** you were going to have chicken for dinner, but now you want fish?
>
> **2** you're trying to convince someone not to be afraid of the dark?
>
> **3** someone tells you something is impossible, but you don't believe them?
>
> **4** you're giving someone some advice about visiting your country?

C Act out each situation with a short conversation.

Hopes and wishes

1 _____

2 _____

3 _____

4 _____

5 _____

6 _____

A Match the pictures (1–6) to the words from the box below.

> your house/flat   friendships   family   hobbies   possessions   career

B Write sentences about these topics using the phrases below and discuss your ideas with a partner.

> I wish I'd …

> I wish I were …

> I hope I …

> I wish we had …

> I wish I could …

Staying organised

A Read the article and replace the underlined definitions with a word or phrase which means the same from the box below.

> tasks   record   plan   motivated   tidy up   objective   schedule   to-do list   file

Ways to stay organised

The best way to keep on track and get everything done without missing deadlines is firstly to ¹get rid of, or throw away, anything you don't need, so that there is no clutter on your desk or workspace. This will make you less anxious and better able to work. ²Put all documents away in folders, and then put these neatly away in drawers or cabinets.

Once you have done this, you can then write ³a list of the things that you need to work on. After you've got that down on paper, you can think about how to ⁴divide your time or think ahead so what you need to do is achieved on ⁵the date and time it is due. Keeping a ⁶written document each day of what you have been working on will help you to meet the ⁷main goal you are working towards. Dividing a large project into a series of smaller ⁸jobs is a helpful way to stay on track with the work you need to finish, and you should also allow yourself time to see what you have achieved as this makes you feel ⁹encouraged.

B Work in pairs. Do you agree with the advice in the article? What would you add to this?

Answer key

1.1 Grammar

A
1 play
2 trying
3 learning
4 going
5 eating
6 like

B
1 do you do
2 do you do / do you
3 are you doing
4 are you going
5 are you feeling / are you
6 do you like about

1.1 Vocabulary

A
1 –
2 –
3 Thanks for inviting me. That ~~hears~~ **sounds** great.
4 I'm going to ~~watch~~ **look** at the paintings at the exhibition on Tuesday.
5 –
6 His music ~~listens~~ **sounds** fantastic.
7 –
8 Where is my watch? I can't ~~look at~~ see it anywhere!

1.2 Grammar

A

STUDENT A

1 makes	5 did you get
2 did you meet	6 makes
3 do you spend	7 did you get
4 chose	8 taught

STUDENT B

1 makes	5 did you go
2 did you meet	6 makes
3 do you speak to	7 did you choose
4 gave	8 taught

1.2 Vocabulary

A
Ana – bilingual, speaks, accent
Chris – idioms, informal, translate
Diana – monolingual, speaks

2.1 Grammar

A
2 Did you ever get into trouble when you were at school?
3 Have you ever ridden a horse?
4 Have you ever watched …?
5 Did you ever meet …?
6 Have you ever done a parachute jump?
7 Did you have a big party on your 18th birthday?
8 Have you ever swum with dolphins?
9 Have you ever celebrated …?
10 Have you met …?
11 Did you go out last night?
12 Have you ever written a poem?

2.1 Vocabulary

A
1 helps
2 turn
3 working
4 set
5 made
6 trying

2.2 Grammar

A
Last year the woman couldn't drive, today she can.

2.2 Vocabulary

A
1 e, for 2 c, for 3 f, of 4 b, of 5 g, for 6 h, for
7 a, for 8 d, of

3.1 Vocabulary

A
1 –
2 ~~in the busy hour~~ during rush hour
3 –
4 ~~traffic lines~~ traffic jams
5 ~~road lights~~ traffic lights
6 ~~operation~~ service
7 –
8 –
9 ~~overbusy~~ overcrowded

3.2 Grammar

A
1 A lot of, –
2 The
3 more
4 Some, the
5 The
6 an, many
7 the
8 a, –, –, –
9 A lot of, the
10 a

3.2 Vocabulary

A
Possible answers:
1 **bad:** awful, terrible **angry:** furious
2 **great:** wonderful **good:** excellent **nice:** fantastic
3 **big:** huge **bad:** terrible
4 **good:** delicious
5 **scared:** terrified
6 **funny:** hilarious

4.1 Grammar

A
1 going to
2 going to
3 going to
4 I'll / I will
5 playing
6 going to
7 visiting / going to
8 will
9 will / 'll

4.1 Vocabulary

1 quit
2 cut down
3 breaks
4 keep
5 set
6 reached
7 sticks

4.2 Vocabulary

1 overslept
2 overcharged
3 disrespectful
4 disappeared
5 misunderstood
6 mispronounces
7 undercooked
8 to rebuild
9 misplaced
10 overworked

5.1 Grammar

A
used to, would, would, didn't use to, used to, would, used to, used to

5.1 Vocabulary

1 e   2 b   3 f   4 a   5 c   6 d   7 g

5.2 Grammar

A
1 made of
2 bought by
3 made by
4 used for
5 found in

5.2 Vocabulary

A
launch: a campaign
run: a campaign
build: a reputation
make: money, deals
attract: investors

B
1 has built
2 to run
3 to make
4 has built a good reputation / has attracted customers
5 to attract

6.1 Grammar

A
1 mustn't
2 has to
3 should
4 must
5 mustn't
6 should
7 need to
8 have to

6.1 Vocabulary

A
1 decisive
2 competitive
3 attractive
4 massive
5 active
6 inexpensive
7 impressive
8 effective
9 aggressive
10 creative

6.2 Grammar

A
1 had to / needed to, didn't need to / didn't have to, need to
2 had to / needed to, had to / needed to

6.2 Vocabulary

A
1 been, aren't, joined, keeps, gets, lose
2 been, escape, take, gotten, lost, is

B
1 have you joined
2 have you taken up
3 can you play
4 escape reality

7.1 Vocabulary

A
remain indoors: stay in
found: worked out
arrive without appointment: turn up
put on plates: dish up
experiment: try out

7.2 Grammar

C
1 –
2 the ~~more good~~ better it is
3 –
4 the ~~slowlier~~ slower you drive
5 –
6 –
7 – The more organised ~~are you~~ you are
8 the ~~beautifuler~~ more beautiful
9 –
10 the ~~more early~~ earlier you get up

7.2 Vocabulary

A
Reduce: cut down, reduce
Reuse: throwing away, reuse, get rid of
Recycle: getting rid of, bin, recycling

8.1 Grammar

which, who, which, that, which, that, who

8.2 Grammar

1 h 2 f 3 g 4 d 5 e 6 b 7 c 8 a

8.2 Vocabulary

Fitness tracker: incredible, impressive, unique, gorgeous, practical
Wireless headphones: sophisticated, suitable, sensible, unforgettable

9.1 Grammar

A

1 won
2 saw
3 bought
4 was asked
5 was / were
6 played
7 was / were
8 spoke

9.1 Vocabulary

A

1 instrument
2 recording studio
3 exhibition
4 gallery
5 concert
6 choir
7 audience
8 display

9.2 Vocabulary

1 promised
2 insisted
3 worried
4 insisted
5 refused
6 explained
7 admitted
8 mentioned
9 argued
10 insisted

10.1 Vocabulary

Student A

1 I'm in two minds.
2 Never mind.
3 I've made up my mind.
4 Would you mind if I …?

Student B

1 I've changed my mind.
2 It's all in the mind.
3 I can if I put my mind to it.
4 Bear in mind that you should …

10.2 Grammar

1 friendship
2 hobbies
3 family
4 your house/flat
5 possessions
6 career

10.2 Vocabulary

1 tidy up
2 file
3 to do list
4 motivated
5 schedule
6 record
7 objective
8 tasks
9 motivated